Leipzig Studies on International,
European and Foreign Public Law

Edited by
Prof. Dr. Markus Kotzur
Prof. Dr. Stephanie Schiedermair
Prof. Dr. Dominik Steiger
Prof. Dr. Mattias Wendel, Maître en droit

Institute for International Law, European Law and
Foreign Public Law at the University of Leipzig

Volume 24

Stephanie Schiedermair | Alexander Schwarz
Dominik Steiger (eds.)

Theory and Practice of the European Convention on Human Rights

HART

Nomos

Onlineversion
Nomos eLibrary

The Deutsche Nationalbibliothek lists this publication in the Deutsche Nationalbibliografie; detailed bibliographic data are available on the Internet at http://dnb.d-nb.de

ISBN: HB (Nomos) 978-3-8487-7966-6
ePDF (Nomos) 978-3-7489-2350-3

British Library Cataloguing-in-Publication Data
A catalogue record for this book is available from the British Library.

ISBN: HB (Hart) 978-1-5099-4597-9

Library of Congress Cataloging-in-Publication Data
Schiedermair, Stephanie | Schwarz, Alexander | Steiger, Dominik
Theory and Practice of the European Convention on Human Rights
Stephanie Schiedermair | Alexander Schwarz | Dominik Steiger (eds.)
310 pp.
Includes bibliographic references.

ISBN 978-1-5099-4597-9 (hardcover Hart)

1st Edition 2022

Contents

Preface

This book is the product of a collaborative international project of the Law Faculty of the University of Leipzig and the Center for International Studies (Zentrum für Internationale Studien) of Technische Universität Dresden, Germany. Two years ago, the two institutions decided to organize a summer school on human rights protection under the European Convention on Human Rights. Over 20 speakers and about 100 participants from 30 countries turned our first Human Rights Summer School in Leipzig into a space of lively discussion. The positive responses from the participants encouraged us to continue with the Summer School and have a second round in 2021 – this time taking place in Dresden.

One of the Summer School's special ingredients is that speakers include both academics as well as practitioners, offering the unique opportunity to gain insights into current theoretical discussions as well as the everyday challenges of practicing law. This approach also provides the basis for the collection of authors provided in this volume, for which internationally renowned practitioners as well as scholars were invited to contribute.

The book is divided into three overarching focal points. The first part deals with the important procedural aspects of human rights protection (A.). Human rights in general face the problem of a theoretically high level of protection on the one side and an often ineffective enforcement on the other. The question how to implement human rights best, is therefore a crucial one. The opening essay by *Jacopo Roberti di Sarsina* and *Katharina Braun* deals with that question by analyzing the ECtHR's increasing engagement with procedural obligations of the member states to criminalise, investigate, and prosecute, which has partly been criticized as an undue restriction on State's prerogatives. The second chapter deals with a problem from the present ECtHR's judicature as well: *Christiane Schmaltz* reflects on Article 18 ECHR, which limits restrictions on rights to only the reasons listed in the Convention, as an underestimated provision of the ECHR system, whose presence or absence in the jurisprudence of the ECtHR can be taken as an indicator for the state of democracy in the member states. In the third chapter, *Helga Molbæk-Steensig* takes a close look into the Interlaken Process supposed to deal with the overload of cases the ECtHR is confronted with.

The second part is dedicated to new challenges arising for fundamental human rights principles (B.). Here *Edith Wagner* deals with the ECtHR's quest to deal more efficiently with repetitive cases and the rise of strikeouts under article 37 para. 1 lit. c ECHR. The chapter also critically examines the ECtHR's largest-ever strikeout that led to the dismissal of 12,148 cases. The following two chapters turn to the protection of especially vulnerable groups. *Veronika Bílková* analyses the special needs of Human Rights Defenders and Whistleblowers, who are often victim of abuses by states and non-state actors due to their activities. The chapter is followed by *Hanaa Hakiki* looking critically at the ECtHR's recent application of the prohibition of collective expulsions at European borders. Two recently much-debated phenomena provide the basis for the reflections of *Dominik Steiger* who analyses the limits of legislation countering fake news and hate speech in the light of the ECHR´s guarantee to freedom of speech. A procedural-related challenge is the topic of *Alain Zysset's* contribution on the turn to procedural review and the normative function of proportionality at the ECtHR. The article is one of the rare accounts of the turn to procedural review dealing with its broader significance and the impacts for our understanding of the Court's nature, function and legitimacy.

The third part turns the gaze to the legal orders of the member states (C.). *Stefanie Lemke* explores how judges and prosecutors deal with politically sensitive cases and uphold European human rights standards, particularly with regard to the right to a fair trial, in three member states: Azerbaijan, Russia and Ukraine. A special relationship is examined by *Barbara Sonczyk* and *Beti Hohler* who explore the role and impact of the ECHR in Kosovo, thus investigating an example of the Convention's potential to influence human rights protection in non-state parties. The volume is concluded by *Robert Frau*, who takes in developments in Germany by reflecting on the various approaches of the German Federal Constitutional Court concerning the extraterritorial applicability of the ECHR.

The editors would like to thank everyone who made this book possible. First of all, the speakers of the Summer School for their live and written contributions and their time spent on preparation of the chapters of this volume. Secondly, the support from Gabriel Armas-Cardona (Esq., NYU) in proofreading and editing cannot be overestimated. Further thanks go to David Koppe, without whose support the first edition of the summer school would not have been possible.

Lastly, we would like to express special thanks to the Friends of the University of Leipzig (Förderverein der Juristenfakultät der Universität Leipzig) as well as to the Technische Universität Dresden, where one of the editors holds the Chair of Public International Law, European Union Law and Public Law, for their financial support of this volume.

Leipzig/Tunis/Dresden, July 2021 *Stephanie Schiedermair, Alexander Schwarz & Dominik Steiger*

A. Human Rights and Procedural Law

Protecting Human Rights Through Criminal Law: The Revival of the Procedural Obligations

Jacopo Roberti di Sarsina / Katharina Braun[1]

A. Introduction

Human rights protect from an overreach of criminal law, but they also require protection through criminal law. To borrow from Judge Françoise Tulkens, human rights have 'both a defensive and an offensive role, a role of both neutralizing and triggering the criminal law.'[2] This article is focused on the 'offensive role' of human rights, i.e., the triggering of criminal law in the jurisprudence of the European Court of Human Rights ('ECtHR' or 'the Court').

In order to ensure enjoyment of the rights recognised in the European Convention on Human Rights ('ECHR' or 'the Convention') infringements upon them – be it through State officials or private individuals – must be effectively deterred. How can the Court fight impunity without overstepping its mandate and becoming a criminal court? In its jurisprudence, the Court has to balance between an overly extensive approach to criminal law that could be perceived as interfering with State's sovereignty and an unduly restrictive approach allowing human rights violations to go unpunished. This article focuses on the dichotomy between calls for effective criminal prosecution of human rights violations and the risk of overreach of the Court into the area of domestic criminal law.

The jurisprudence of the ECtHR with regard to criminal law measures has already been analysed in depth.[3] Contributions have also focused on

---

1 Dr Jacopo Roberti di Sarsina, LL.M. (New York University), Member of the Legal Service (CFSP and External Relations Team), European Commission. Katharina Braun, LL.M. (University of Connecticut), doctoral candidate at Freie Universität Berlin. The views expressed in this article are those of the authors and may not in any circumstances be regarded as stating an official position of the European Commission.

2 Tulkens, 'The Paradoxical Relationship between Criminal Law and Human Rights' (2011), 9 *JICJ*, 577 (579).

3 Mallinder, 'Investigations, Prosecutions and Amnesties under Articles 2 & 3 of the European Convention on Human Rights' (2015) Transitional Justice Institute, Re-

the issue of amnesties, which will not be discussed at length here.[4] Instead, this article centres on the most recent cases and developments regarding the obligations to criminalise, investigate, and prosecute infringements of Article 2 ('right to life') and, to a lesser extent, Article 3 ('prohibition of torture') of the ECHR. Particular attention is paid to a category of cases that has so far received little attention, namely cases arising from unintentional infringements of the right to life. This issue was raised and problematised most recently in February 2020 by Judges Paulo Pinto de Albuquerque and María Elósegui in their joint concurring opinion in *Vovk and Bogdanov v. Russia*, where they questioned whether the Court's approach to criminal law measures in cases arising from the unintentional infliction of death or life-threatening injuries is consistent with international law and its long-established jurisprudence.[5] This article also addresses the criticism of the Court's involvement with criminal law and examines the rationales behind the Court's demand for criminal law measures. It concludes that a proactive approach by the Court with regard to criminal law measures is needed in order to ensure the protection of the rights recognised in the ECHR but this would require the Court to better define its role in the interplay between international human rights law and criminal law.

---

search Paper No. 15–05, https://papers.ssrn.com/sol3/papers.cfm?abstract_id=2668106; Schabas, *The European Convention on Human Rights: A Commentary* (2015), 134 ff.; Jackson, 'Amnesties in Strasbourg' (2018) 38:3 *Oxf. J. Leg. Stud.*, 451; Seibert-Fohr, *Prosecuting Serious Human Rights Violations* (2009), 111 ff.; Chevalier-Watts, 'Effective Investigations under Article 2 of the European Convention on Human Rights: Securing the Right to Life or an Onerous Burden on a State?' (2010) 21 *EJIL*, 701; Mavronicola, 'Taking Life and Liberty Seriously' (2017) 80(6) *MLR*, 1026; Roberti di Sarsina, *Transitional Justice and a State's Response to Mass Atrocity* (2019), 71 ff.

4 The debate on amnesties and the ECtHR is still ongoing. See e.g. Mallinder, 'Investigations, Prosecutions and Amnesties under Articles 2 & 3 of the European Convention on Human Rights' (2015) Transitional Justice Institute, Research Paper no. 15–05, available at: https://papers.ssrn.com/sol3/papers.cfm?abstract_id=2668106 (last accessed 23 September 2020); Schabas, *The European Convention on Human Rights: A Commentary* (2015), 128; Jackson, 'Amnesties in Strasbourg' (2018) 38:3, 451; see Roberti di Sarsina, *Transitional Justice and a State's Response to Mass Atrocity* (2019), 140 ff.

5 ECtHR, Judgment, 11 February 2020, *Vovk and Bogdanov v Russia*, Application No. 15613/10, Joint Concurring Opinion of Judges Pinto de Albuquerque and Elósegui.

B. *Protecting Human Rights through Criminal Law: The Jurisprudence of the ECtHR*

Treaties and conventions designed to prevent international crimes, such as genocide, torture, apartheid and enforced disappearances, contain clear obligations to investigate and prosecute the commission of the crimes enshrined therein.[6] Comprehensive human rights treaties, such as the International Covenant on Civil and Political Rights, the American Convention on Human Rights and the ECHR, confer substantive rights vis-à-vis the State upon individuals. Little can be inferred from these treaties regarding the means by which those rights are to be protected. It is thus the practice of international courts and bodies that has clarified the means by which such rights are to be enforced, mainly in the jurisprudence stemming from Article 2 ('right to life') and Article 3 ('prohibition of torture') of the ECHR.

The obligations to criminalise, investigate, and prosecute that arise from Article 2 and Article 3 of the ECHR are often read together with Article 1 ('obligation to respect and protect human rights'), and often discussed in context of Article 13 ('right to an effective remedy').[7] Article 2 and Article 3 of the Convention enshrine 'one of the basic values of the democratic so-

6 The Convention on the Prevention and Punishment of the Crime of Genocide (Articles 1, 4, 6), the Convention against Torture and Other Cruel, Inhumane or Degrading Treatment or Punishment (Articles 6 para. 2, 7, 12, 16), the International Convention on the Suppression and Punishment of the Crime of Apartheid (Article 4), and the International Convention for the Protection of All Persons from Enforced Disappearance (Articles 3, 10, para. 2, 12).

7 Article 8 ('right to respect for private and family life') is also highly relevant in this context. In *X and Y v The Netherlands*, the Court found that the State's failure to enact criminal law provisions breached its positive obligations to secure enjoyment of the right to private life as guaranteed under Article 8 ECHR (ECtHR, Judgment, 26 March 1985, *X and Y v The Netherlands*, Application No. 8978/80). While admitting that State parties do have a margin of appreciation in determining the means to secure the rights protected by the Convention (para. 24), the Court found that, given the case's specific circumstances of the rape of a handicapped minor, only criminal law measures were appropriate (para. 27). The Court rejected the view that civil damages could suffice on the grounds that they would not achieve effective deterrence. In *M.C. v Bulgaria*, the Court found that Article 8 and Article 3 of the Convention require 'the penalisation and effective prosecution of any non-consensual sexual act, including in the absence of physical resistance by the victim' (ECtHR, Judgment, 4 December 2003 *M.C. v Bulgaria*, Application No. 39272/98, para. 166). Other cases in which the Court found a violation of Article 8 or Article 8 and Article 3 based on the failure to enact effective criminal law provisions or prosecute individuals also concerned sexual abuse of minors and rape. See ECtHR,

cieties making up the Council of Europe.'[8] Their fundamental importance is reflected in their prominent position in the Convention and explains the expanding criminal law protection offered by the Court.

I. Positive Obligations and Criminal Law

Besides the negative obligation not to interfere with the right to life, a State is under a positive obligation to protect the right to life. The positive obligation consists of two aspects: (1) providing a 'regulatory framework', and (2) taking operational measures aimed at preventing human rights infringements.[9] As the Court most recently stated in *Makaratzis v. Greece*, a State must

> take appropriate steps within its internal legal order to safeguard the lives of those within its jurisdiction [...]. This involves a primary duty on the State to secure the right to life by putting in place an appropriate legal and administrative framework to deter the commission of offences against the person, backed up by law-enforcement machinery for the prevention, suppression and punishment of breaches of such provisions.[10]

The Court made clear that an effective legal system, as required under Article 2 ECHR, 'may, and under certain circumstances must, include recourse to the criminal law.'[11] In other cases, the Court stated that the State

---

Judgment (GC), 12 November 2013, *Söderman v. Sveden,* Application No. 5786/08; ECtHR, Judgment, 28 May 2020, *Z. v. Bulgaria,* Application No. 39257/17. ECtHR, Judgment, 28 May 2020, *Z. v. Bulgaria,* Application No. 39257/17 (request for referral to the Grand Chamber pending).

8 ECtHR, Judgment, 10 September 2020, *Shuriyya Zeynalov v. Azerbaijan*, Application No. 69460/12, para. 66; see also ECtHR, Judgment, 1 September 2020, *R.R. and R.D. v Slovakia*, Application No. 20649/8, para. 146.

9 ECtHR, 'Guide on Article 2 of the European Convention on Human Rights, Right to Life', updated 31 August 2020, https://www.echr.coe.int/Documents/Guide_Art_2_ENG.pdf, 8.

10 ECtHR, Judgment (GC), 20 December 2004, *Makaratzis v Greece*, No. 50385/99 para. 57; see also ECtHR, Judgment, 4 August 2020, *Tërshana v Albania*, Application No. 48756/14, para. 147.

11 ECtHR, Decision, 11 March 2014, *Cioban v Romania*, Application No. 18295/08, para. 25; see also ECtHR, Judgment, 5 January 2010, *Railean v Moldova,* Application No. 23401/04, para. 27; ECtHR, Judgment, 6 February 2020, *Sakvarelidze v Georgia*, Application No. 40394/10, para. 51.

must put in place 'effective criminal-law provisions.'[12] Furthermore, the State is under a duty to ensure 'the effective functioning' of the framework designed to protect the right to life.[13] In light of this, the obligation to put in place and to enforce criminal law norms prohibiting the taking of life can be described as the centre of the positive obligations of the State to secure the protection of the right to life and the freedom from torture.[14]

Positive obligations apply 'in the context of any activity, whether public or not, in which the right to life may be at stake.'[15] Thus, they apply in a variety of different contexts including a broad range of dangerous activities[16] but also in the sphere of public health[17] and road safety.[18] They also apply in the context of armed conflicts.[19]

In *Osman v. The United Kingdom*, the Court held that the positive obligations apply not only to violations of the right to life through agents of the State, but also to acts of non-State agents. In that regard, the Court stated that

> [i]t is thus accepted by those appearing before the Court that Article 2 of the Convention may also imply in certain well-defined circumstances a positive obligation on the authorities to take preventive oper-

---

12 ECtHR, Judgment, 2 June 2020, *A. and B. v Romania*, Application Nos. 48442/16 and 48831/16, para. 116; ECtHR, Judgment, 4 December 2012, *R.R. and Others v Hungary*, Application No. 19400/11, para 28; ECtHR, Judgment, 12 May 2020, *Danciu and Others v Romania*, Application No. 48395/16, para. 76.

13 ECtHR, Judgment, 17 September 2020, *Kotilainen and others v Finland*, Application No. 62439/12, para. 66; see also ECtHR, 2 February 2016, *Cavit Tınarlıoğlu v Turkey*, Application No. 3648/04, para. 86.

14 See Schabas, *The European Convention on Human Rights: A Commentary* (2015), 127.

15 ECtHR, Judgment (GC), 14 July 2014, *Centre for Legal Resources on behalf of Valentin Câmpeanu v Romania*, Application No. 47848/08, para. 130.

16 ECtHR, Judgment (GC), 30 November 2004, *Öneryildiz v Turkey*, Application No. 48939/99, para. 101; ECtHR, Judgment,.17 November 2015, *M. Özel and Others v Turkey*, Application Nos. 14350/05, 15245/05, 6051/05, paras. 198, 190.

17 ECtHR, Judgment (GC), 17 January 2002, *Calvelli and Ciglio v Italy*, Application No. 32967/96, para. 49.

18 ECtHR, Judgment, 24 May 2011, *Anna Todorova v Bulgaria*, Application No. 23302/03, para. 72.

19 Gioia, 'The Role of the European Court of Human Rights in Monitoring Compliance with Humanitarian Law in Armed Conflict' in Ben-Naftali (ed), *International Humanitarian Law and International Human Rights Law* (2011), 201 (234 ff.).

> ational measures to protect an individual whose life is at risk from the criminal acts of another individual.[20]

However, the Court was careful to limit this obligation when it acknowledged that,

> bearing in mind the difficulties involved in policing modern societies, the unpredictability of human conduct and the operational choices which must be made in terms of priorities and resources, such an obligation must be interpreted in a way which does not impose an impossible or disproportionate burden on the authorities. Accordingly, not every risk to life can entail for the authorities a Convention requirement to take operational measures to prevent that risk from materialising.[21]

In general, the conditions for finding a violation of the positive obligations are quite stringent. In this sense, the Court clarified that:

> it must be established that the authorities knew or ought to have known at the time, of the existence of a real and immediate risk to the life of an identified individual or individuals from the criminal acts of a third party and that they failed to take measures within the scope of their powers which, judged reasonably, might have been expected to avoid that risk.[22]

However, in a few cases, the Court also found the positive obligations to be violated when there was a risk not to identified individuals but to members of the public more generally. These arose from criminal acts

---

20 ECtHR, Judgment (GC), 28 October 1998, *Osman v The United Kingdom*, Application No. 87/1997/871/1083, para. 115; see also ECtHR, Judgment, 4 August 2020, *Tërshana v Albania*, Application No. 48756/14, para. 147; ECtHR, Judgment (GC), 31 January 2019, *Fernandes de Oliveira v Portugal*, Application No. 78103/14, para. 108.

21 ECtHR, Judgment (GC), 28 October 1998, *Osman v The United Kingdom*, Application No. 87/1997/871/1083, para. 116; see also ECtHR, Judgment, 4 August 2020, *Tërshana v Albania*, Application No. 48756/14, para. 147; ECtHR, Judgment (GC), 31 January 2019, *Fernandes de Oliveira v Portugal*, Application No. 78103/14, para. 108.

22 ECtHR, Judgment, 17 September 2020, *Kotilainen and others v Finland*, Application No. 62439/12, para. 69; see also ECtHR, Judgment (GC), 28 October 1998, *Osman v The United Kingdom*, Application No. 87/1997/871/1083, para. 105 f.

of individuals under the control of State authorities, for example, the criminal acts of dangerous prisoners.[23]

With regard to Article 3 ECHR, positive obligations have played a less prominent role. William Schabas notes that the ECtHR has applied Article 3 ECHR mainly where the risk to the individual emanates from intentional acts by State authorities.[24] This puts the negative obligation to refrain from such acts in the foreground. In that regard, the State is required to 'take measures designed to ensure that individuals within their jurisdiction are not subjected to ill-treatment, including ill-treatment administered by private individuals.'[25]

II. The Procedural Obligations to Investigate and Prosecute

Articles 2 and 3 read in conjunction with Article 1 of the Convention are interpreted to enshrine the procedural obligations to investigate and prosecute.[26] Initially, in the landmark case *McCann and Others v. The United Kingdom*, the Court derived procedural obligations in the context of the use of lethal force by State agents. The Court grounded these obligations in the finding that a prohibition of arbitrary killings would be ineffective if the lawfulness of killings through State agents were not subject to review.[27] Since then, the Court has expanded the procedural obligations to a number of other situations, including when the loss of life is not the result of the use of force.[28]

---

23 ECtHR, Judgment (GC), 24 October 2002, *Mastromatteo v Italy*, Application No. 37703/97, para. 69.

24 Schabas, *The European Convention on Human Rights: A Commentary* (2015), 191.

25 ECtHR, Judgment, 26 May 2020, *I.E. v The Republic of Moldova*, Application No. 45422/3, para. 38.

26 In *Nikolova and Velichkova v Bulgaria*, the Court even took issue with the length of a criminal sentence, see ECtHR, Judgment, 20 December 2007, *Nikolova and Velichkova v Bulgaria*, Application No. 7888/03, para. 60 ff.

27 ECtHR, Judgment (GC), 27 September 1995, *McCann and Others v The United Kingdom*, Application No. 18984/9, para. 61. See also ECtHR, Guide on Article 2 of the European Convention on Human Rights, Right to Life, Updated 31 August 2020, 31.

28 Chevalier-Watts illustrates how the obligation to conduct an investigation expanded since *McCann and others v The United Kingdom*. Chevalier-Watts. 'Effective investigations under Article 2 of the European Convention on Human Rights: Securing the Right to Life or an Onerous Burden on a State?' (2010) 21 *EJIL* 701 (705 ff.).

It is well established in the jurisprudence of the Court that the substantive Articles 2 and 3 of the Convention include procedural requirements.[29] From 1959 to 2019, the Court found a violation of Article 2 and Article 3 for lack of effective investigation in 816 (Article 2) and 893 (Article 3) cases, respectively.[30] As anticipated, this procedural dimension arises from the respective article read in conjunction with Article 1 of the Convention, according to which State Parties have a duty to 'secure to everyone within their jurisdiction the rights and freedoms defined in [...] [the] Convention.'[31] In recent cases, the Court often simply refers to the 'procedural obligation' or 'procedural limb' of Article 2 and Article 3 of the Convention, rather than explicitly deriving the obligation from the respective article read in conjunction with Article 1 of the Convention.[32] In *Šilih v. Slovenia*, elaborating on its prior jurisprudence, the Court concluded that 'the procedural obligation to carry out an effective investigation under Article 2 has evolved into a separate and autonomous duty.'[33]

The obligations to investigate and prosecute arising from Articles 2 and 3 should not be confused with the obligations arising from Article 13 of the Convention. Generally, State Parties enjoy a margin of appreciation regarding the adoption of effective remedies.[34] However, the Court significantly narrows down this margin of appreciation when the taking of life

---

29 See e.g. ECtHR, Judgment (GC), April 2009, *Šilih v Slovenia*, Application No. 71463/019, para 153; ECtHR, Judgment (GC), 27 September 1995, *McCann and Others v The United Kingdom*, Application No. 18984/9, paras. 157–164. See also Schabas, *The European Convention on Human Rights: A Commentary* (2015), 134 ff. (on Article 2), 191 ff. (on Article 3).

30 Overview ECHR 1959 – 2019, European Court of Human Rights 2020, https://www.echr.coe.int/Documents/Overview_19592019_ENG.pdf.

31 See e.g. ECtHR, Judgment (GC), 6 April 2000, *Labita v Italy*, Application No. 26772/95, para. 131; ECtHR, Judgment 22 October 2009, *Isayev v Russia*, Application No. 20756/04, para. 103.

32 ECtHR, Judgment, 4 August 2020, *Tërshana v Albania*, Application No. 48756/14, para. 153; ECtHR, Judgment, 9 July 2019, *Volodina v Russia*, Application No. 41261/17, para. 92 (on Article 3). But see ECtHR, Judgment, 12 November 2019, *A. v Russia*, Application No. 37735/09, para. 53; ECtHR, Judgment, 30 January 2020, *Saribekyan and Balyan v Azerbaijan*, Application No. 35746/11, para. 62; but see ECtHR, Judgment, 1 September 2020, *R.R. and R.D. v Slovakia*, Application No. 20649/18, para. 176 (where the Court derives the procedural obligation to conduct an effective investigation from Articles 2 and 3 in conjunction with Article 1).

33 ECtHR, Judgment (GC), 9 April 2009, *Šilih v Slovenia*, Application No. 71463/019, para. 159.

34 Seibert-Fohr, *Prosecuting Serious Human Rights Violations* (2009), 124; ECtHR, Judgment, 14 December 2000, *Gül v Turkey*, Application No. 22676/93, para. 100.

is concerned.[35] An effective remedy, according to the Court entails 'in addition to the payment of compensation where appropriate, a thorough and effective investigation capable of leading to the identification and punishment of those responsible.'[36]

The difference between the procedural obligations derived from substantive Articles 2 and 3 in conjunction with Article 1, and obligations derived from Article 13 of the Convention is however not entirely clear in the jurisprudence of the Court.[37] In that regard, Anja Seibert-Fohr observes that the Court uses the same terminology in the context of Article 13 ECHR as in the context of the substantive articles.[38] The difference seems to be related to the fact that Article 13 ECHR, as opposed to the substantive articles, confers an individual right upon the victim.[39] Schabas argues that the Court has considered the duties stemming from Article 13 to be broader than the procedural obligations stemming from either the substantive Article 2 or 3 of the Convention.[40]

1. *The Standard for an Effective Investigation*

In *Isayeva v. Russia*, the Court clarified the standards of the procedural obligations required for the protection of the right to life. From Article 2

35 Seibert-Fohr, *Prosecuting Serious Human Rights Violations* (2009), 124; ECtHR, Judgment, 14 December 2000, *Gül v Turkey*, Application No. 22676/93, para. 100; ECtHR, Judgment, 3 April 2000, *Keenan v The United Kingdom*, Application No. 27229/95, para. 123.

36 ECtHR, Judgment, 24 July 2014, *Husayn (Abu Zubaydah) v Poland*, Application No. 7511/13, para. 541; ECtHR, Judgment, 13 June 2002, *Anguelova v Bulgaria*, Application No. 38361/97, para. 161 f.; ECtHR, Judgment (GC), 13 December 2012, *El Masri v The former Yugoslav Republic of Macedonia*, Application No. 39630/09, para. 255.

37 See Seibert-Fohr, *Prosecuting Serious Human Rights Violations* (2009), 124 f.

38 *Id.*, 125.

39 *Ibid.*

40 Schabas, *The European Convention on Human Rights: A Commentary* (2015), 552; citing ECtHR, 24 July 2014, *Husayn (Abu Zubaydah) v Poland*, Application No. 7511/13, para. 542; ECtHR, Judgment (GC), 13 December 2012, *El Masri v The former Yugoslav Republic of Macedonia*, Application No. 39630/09, para. 255; ECtHR, Judgment, 24 February 2005, *Khashiyev and Akayeva v Russia*, Application Nos. 57942/00 and 57945/00, para. 183; ECtHR, Judgment, 25 May 1998, *Kurt v Turkey*, Application No. 15/1997/799/1002, para. 140; ECtHR, Judgment, 18 June 2002, *Orhan v Turkey*, Application No. 25656/94, para. 384; ECtHR, Judgment, 28 March 2002, *Kiliç v Turkey*, Application No 22492/93, para. 93.

in conjunction with Article 1 ECHR, the Court inferred that 'there should be some form of effective official investigation when individuals have been killed as a result of the use of force.'[41] The Court then clarified what the relevant criteria are. Most notably the investigation must be independent, *ex officio*, prompt, subject to public scrutiny and 'capable of leading to a determination of whether the force [...] was or was not justified in the circumstances [...] and to the identification and punishment of those responsible.'[42] With regard to the investigation being capable of leading to conclusions about justification of the use of force as well as the identification and punishment of those responsible, the Court was careful to state that this is 'not an obligation of result, but of means.'[43] However, the Court left open the question of the legal nature of the investigation. While stressing that '[t]he essential purpose of such investigation is to secure the effective implementation of the domestic laws which protect the right to life and, in those cases involving State agents or bodies, to ensure their accountability for deaths occurring under their responsibility', the Court stated that '[w]hat form of investigation will achieve those purposes may vary in different circumstances.'[44] This understanding was confirmed in more recent decisions too.[45]

However, the duty to conduct an investigation arises 'in all cases of killing and other suspicious deaths, whether the perpetrators were private persons or State agents or are unknown.'[46] The obligation to investigate also applies to cases arising from an alleged infringement of the right to life that did not result in the death of the person but in life-threatening injuries.[47] In *Razvozzhayev v. Russia & Ukraine and Udaltsov v. Russia*, the Court made clear that the requirements regarding the official investigation are similar whether treatment contrary to the Convention (in this case

---

41 ECtHR, Judgment, 24 February 2005, *Isayeva v Russia*, Application No. 57950/00, para. 209.

42 *Id.*, para. 210–214.

43 *Id.*, para. 212.

44 *Id.*, para. 210.

45 ECtHR, Judgment, 28 January 2020, *Nicolaou v Cyprus*, Application No. 29068/10, paras. 132 ff.; ECtHR, Judgment, 3 October 2019, *Fountas v Greece*, Application No. 50283/13, para. 67 ff.

46 ECtHR, Judgment, 26 May 2020, *Makuchyan and Minasyan v Azerbaijan and Hungary*, Application No. 17247/13, para. 154; see also ECtHR, Judgment, 26 July 2007, *Angelova and Iliev v Bulgaria*, Application Nos. 55523/00, para. 93.

47 See e.g. ECtHR, Judgment, 12 May 2020, *Danciu and others v Romania*, Application No. 48395/16, para. 80.

Article 3 ECHR) was inflicted by private individuals or through State agents.[48]

In *Labita v. Italy*, the Court confirmed that the procedural requirements arising from Article 3 ECHR in conjunction with Article 1 of the Convention are similar to those under Article 2 ECHR. In this sense, the Court stated that:

> where an individual makes a credible assertion that he has suffered treatment infringing Article 3 at the hands of the police or other similar agents of the State, that provision, read in conjunction with the State's general duty under Article 1 of the Convention [...] requires by implication that there should be an effective official investigation. As with an investigation under Article 2, such investigation should be capable of leading to the identification and punishment of those responsible [...]. Otherwise, the general legal prohibition of torture and inhuman and degrading treatment and punishment would, despite its fundamental importance [...], be ineffective in practice and it would be possible in some cases for agents of the State to abuse the rights of those within their control with virtual impunity.[49]

Consequently, the same standards as regarding the procedural limb of Article 2 ECHR apply.

In this context, it should also be noted that the failure to comply with the procedural obligation to conduct an effective investigation into the fate of missing persons may constitute inhumane treatment of such persons' relatives, and thus a violation of Article 3 of the Convention.[50] In *El Masri v. The former Yugoslav Republic of Macedonia*, the Court found that the lack of an adequate investigation impacted the 'right to the truth.'[51] In this case, the procedural obligation to investigate arose from a violation of Article 3 ECHR. The Court made clear that the investigation was fundamental 'not only for the applicant and his family, but also for other victims of

---

48 ECtHR, Judgment, 19 November 2019, *Razvozzhayev v Russia & Ukraine and Udaltsov v Russia*, Application Nos. 75734/12, 2695/15, 55325/15, para. 171.

49 ECtHR, Judgment (GC), 6 April 2000, *Labita v Italy*, Application No. 26772/95, para. 131.

50 ECtHR, Judgment (GC), 10 May 2001, *Cyprus v Turkey*, Application No. 25781/94, paras. 157f.

51 ECtHR, Judgment (GC), 13 December 2012, *El Masri v The former Yugoslav Republic of Macedonia*, Application No. 39630/09, para. 191.

similar crimes and the general public, who had the right to know what had happened.'[52]

Finally, in a case concerning Article 2 ECHR, the Court emphasised the need for a vigorous and impartial investigation where an act is racially motivated, 'having regard to the need to reassert continuously society's condemnation of racism and to maintain the confidence of minorities in the ability of the authorities to protect them from the threat of racist violence.'[53] More recently, both in cases concerning Articles 2 and 3 of the Convention, the Court stated that domestic- and gender-based violence call for an investigation to be pursued with vigour.[54]

2. *Criticism of the Court's Approach to Criminal Law Measures*

Against this backdrop, some authors have argued that positive obligations as interpreted in the jurisprudence of the Court generally, and the ECtHR's approach to criminal law measures specifically, indicate a potential 'coercive overreach.'[55] The potential for 'coercive overreach', Natasa Mavronicola argues, arises from the ECtHR leaning towards conflating State responsibility for the breach of the negative obligations under Article 2 ECHR with individual criminal liability.[56] According to this author, the Court's 'tendency to seek punitive redress and its occasional apparent endorsement of arguments equating Article 2 breaches with criminal

52 *Ibid.*

53 See ECtHR, Judgment (GC), 6 May 2003, *Menson v The United Kingdom*, Application No. 47916/99, para. 1.

54 ECtHR, Judgment, 4 August 2020, *Tërshana v Albania*, Application No. 48756/14, para. 160; ECtHR, Judgment, 9 July 2019, *Volodina v Russia*, Application No. 41261/17, para. 92 (on Article 3).

55 Mavronicola, 'Taking Life and Liberty Seriously' (2017) 80(6) *MLR*, 1026 (building on the more general account of Lazarus, 'Positive Obligations and Criminal Justice: Duties to Protect or Coerce?' in Zedner and Roberts (eds) *Principles and Values in Criminal Law and Criminal Justice: Essays in Honour of Andrew Ashworth* (2012), 135 (149)). For arguments on procedural obligations as burdens on the State, see Chevalier-Watts, 'Effective investigations under Article 2 of the European Convention on Human Rights: Securing the Right to Life or an Onerous Burden on a State?' (2010) 21 *EJIL* 701, 709 ff. (concluding that procedural obligations are not too burdensome on the State).

56 Mavronicola, 'Taking Life and Liberty Seriously' (2017) 80(6) *MLR*, 1026 (1037 ff.).

offences via positive obligations is bordering on supranational criminal law-making.'[57]

These are legitimate concerns arising from the Court's involvement with criminal law. For example, in *Nikolova and Velichkova v. Bulgaria*, the Court took issue with the length of a criminal sentence.[58] This seems to conflict with the 'obligation of means, not result' doctrine of the Court and could therefore be conceived as 'coercive overreach'.[59] This case, however, remains the exception. As a matter of fact, the Court has been careful not to refer to an obligation to punish.[60] In finding a need to put in place criminal law provisions, investigate human rights violations and prosecute alleged perpetrators, the Court has maintained a nuanced approach in order not to interfere with procedural safeguards, justifications and excuses under domestic criminal law. In this sense, the ECtHR made clear that the Convention does not confer upon anyone the individual right to have someone prosecuted, not to mention to have someone punished.[61] In *Öneryildiz v. Turkey*, for example, the Court stated that Article 2 ECHR does not entail a right 'to have third parties prosecuted or sentenced for a criminal offence [...] or an absolute obligation for all prosecutions to result in conviction, or indeed in a particular sentence [...]'.[62] Similarly, in *Perez v. France*, the Court stated 'that the Convention does not confer any right [...] to "private revenge" or an *actio popularis*.'[63]

More importantly, in *Mosendz v. Ukraine*, the Court elaborated on the distinction between domestic criminal law and international law:

> It should be specified that criminal-law liability under national legislation is distinct from a State's international-law responsibility under the Convention. In determining whether there has been a breach of Arti-

---

57 *Id.*, 1040.

58 ECtHR, Judgment, 20 December 2007, *Nikolova and Velichkova v Bulgaria*, Application No. 7888/03, para. 60 ff.

59 The term 'coercive overreach' in this context stems from Lazarus, 'Positive Obligations and Criminal Justice: Duties to Protect or Coerce?' in Zedner and Roberts (eds) *Principles and Values in Criminal Law and Criminal Justice: Essays in Honour of Andrew Ashworth* (2012), 135, and was applied to the ECtHR by Mavronicola, 'Taking Life and Liberty Seriously' (2017) 80(6) *MLR*, 1026.

60 Seibert-Fohr, *Prosecuting Serious Human Rights Violations* (2009), 115; Roberti di Sarsina, *Transitional Justice and a State's Response to Mass Atrocity* (2019), 77.

61 ECtHR, Judgment (GC), 30 November 2004, *Öneryildiz v Turkey*, Application No. 48939/99, para. 96.

62 *Ibid.*

63 ECtHR, Judgment (GC), 12 February 2004, *Perez v France*, Application No. 47287/99, para. 70.

> cle 2, the Court does not assess the criminal responsibility of those directly or indirectly concerned. Its competence is confined to the State's international responsibility under the Convention, the provisions of which are to be interpreted and applied on the basis of the object and purpose of the Convention and in the light of the relevant principles of international law. In other words, the responsibility of a State under the Convention, arising for the acts of its organs, agents and servants, is not to be confused with the domestic legal issues of individual criminal responsibility under examination in the national criminal courts. The Court is not concerned with reaching any findings as to guilt or innocence in that sense.[64]

In light of this, the claim that the jurisprudence of the Court resembles criminal law making cannot be sustained. Nevertheless, it appears that the Court's jurisprudence is lacking in clarity, especially when it comes to the obligation of States Parties in response to unintentional breaches of the right to life. In this specific area, the absence of a systematic approach has recently surfaced in the abovementioned joint concurring opinion of Judges Paulo Pinto de Albuquerque and María Elósegui in *Vovk and Bogdanov v. Russia*.[65]

3. Unintentional Infliction of Death or Life-Threatening Injuries

Perhaps the least established aspect of the Court's jurisprudence on criminal law measures relates to unintentionally inflicted harm. This category covers a wide spectrum, from the loss of life due to medical negligence by private actors to gross negligence on account of State authorities. In these cases, there is a level of uncertainty as to whether criminal investigation and prosecution is required.

In *Banel v. Lithuania*, the Court held that a State might be held responsible for a violation of Article 2 ECHR as a result of the domestic legal system's inability to secure accountability for negligent acts endangering

64 ECtHR, Judgment, 17 January 2013, *Mosendz v Ukraine*, Application No. 52013/08, para. 95.

65 ECtHR, Judgment, 11 February 2020, *Vovk and Bogdanov v Russia*, Application No. 15613/10, Joint Concurring Opinion of Judges Pinto de Albuquerque and Elósegui.

or resulting in a loss of human life.[66] It is undisputed that the positive obligations require States Parties to have in place a judicial system that is capable of establishing the facts including the cause of death and holding accountable those who are responsible and providing appropriate redress to the victim.[67] However, it is not always clear whether criminal proceedings are required to fulfil these requirements. As a rule, in cases arising from non-intentional death or life-threatening injuries, Article 2 ECHR does not necessarily require criminal law remedies.[68] However, under 'exceptional circumstances', civil remedies might be insufficient. The Court found that to be the case 'when lives have been lost as a result of events occurring under the responsibility of the public authorities and where the negligence attributable to those authorities went beyond an error of judgment or carelessness.'[69] In *Öneryildiz v. Turkey*, the Court stated that in such cases of gross negligence on the side of public authorities, the same principles apply as in cases arising from the use of lethal force.[70] In these cases, 'the fact that those responsible for endangering life have not been charged with a criminal offence or prosecuted may amount to a violation of Article 2.'[71] The Court considered such circumstances to apply to a large number of cases concerning, *inter alia*, the public health sector,[72] military activities[73] and waste collection sites.[74] In *Sinim v. Turkey*, the Court con-

66 ECtHR, Judgment, 18 June 2013, *Banel v Lithuania*, Application No. 14326/11, para. 70.

67 ECtHR, Guide on Article 2 of the European Convention on Human Rights, Right to Life, updated 31 August 2020, 41.

68 ECtHR, Judgment, 6 June 2017, *Sinim v Turkey*, Application No. 9441/10, para. 62; see also ECtHR, Judgment (GC), 17 January 2002, *Calvelli and Ciglio v Italy*, Application No. 32967/96, para. 51.

69 See e.g. ECtHR, Judgment, 27 January 2015, *Asiye Genç v Turkey*, Application No. 24109/07, para. 73; ECtHR, Judgment, 6 June 2017, *Sinim v Turkey*, Application No. 9441/10, para. 62; ECtHR, Judgment, 11 February 2020, *Vovk and Bogdanov v Russia*, Application No. 15613/10, para. 64; ECtHR, Judgment (GC), 30 November 2004, *Öneryildiz v Turkey*, Application No. 48939/99, para. 93.

70 ECtHR, Judgment (GC), 30 November 2004, *Öneryildiz v Turkey*, Application No. 48939/99, para. 93.

71 *Ibid.*

72 ECtHR, Judgment, 9 April 2019, *Mehmet Şentürk and Bekir Şentürk v Turkey*, Application No. 13423/09, para. 104; ECtHR, Judgment, 27 January 2015, *Asyie Genç v Turkey*, Application No. 24109/07, para. 73.

73 ECtHR, Judgment, 4 February, *Oruk v Turkey* 2014, Application No. 33647/04, paras. 56 ff.; ECtHR, Judgment, 11 February 2020, *Vovk and Bogdanov v Russia*, Application No. 15613/10, para. 74.

74 ECtHR, Judgment (GC), 30 November 2004, *Öneryildiz v Turkey*, Application No. 48939/99, para. 71.

sidered a criminal investigation necessary although public authorities were not involved in the dangerous activity.[75] However, the Court continues to consider these cases the exception to the norm whereby civil remedies are sufficient in the case of unintentional infliction of death.[76] In *Nicolae Virgiliu Tănase v. Romania*, the Court held that once it has been established that death or a life-threatening injury has not been inflicted intentionally, civil remedies are to be considered sufficient, 'regardless of whether the person presumed responsible for the incident is a private party or a State agent.'[77]

The Judges Paulo Pinto de Albuquerque and María Elósegui strongly criticised the approach taken in *Nicolae Virgiliu Tănase v. Romania*, and the Court's comparatively lenient approach to negligence situations as being 'both incompatible with international law and contrary to Council of Europe member State practice'.[78] Pointing to General Comment No. 36 of the United Nations Human Rights Committee on the right to life,[79] the judges argued that there is a trend in international law towards remedying unintentional threats to life.[80] In addition, they pointed to the practice of the Member States of the Council of Europe, which generally provide for criminal law remedies in cases of death or injuries due to medical negligence. The judges went even further in their criticism:

> [i]n spite of remaining linguistically attached to the statement of principle in *Calvelli and Ciglio v. Italy*, according to which the Convention did not necessarily require the provision of a criminal-law remedy when the right to life had been infringed unintentionally, the Court has on several occasions made it clear that criminal remedies would be necessary, such as when human-caused harm resulted from operation of waste-collection sites and military activities [...]. As a matter of

---

75 ECtHR, Judgment, 6 June 2017, *Sinim v Turkey*, Application No. 9441/10, para. 62.

76 ECtHR, Judgment, 28 January 2010, *Zinatullin v Russia*, Application No. 10551/10, para. 35.

77 ECtHR, Judgment (GC), 25 June 2019, *Nicolae Virgiliu Tănase v Romania*, Application No. 41720/13, para. 163.

78 ECtHR, Judgment, 11 February 2020, *Vovk and Bogdanov v Russia*, Application No. 15613/10, Joint Concurring Opinion of Judges Pinto de Albuquerque and Elósegui.

79 Human Rights Committee, 30 October 3018, CCPR/C/GC/36, paras. 20, 27, 28.

80 ECtHR, Judgment, 11 February 2020, *Vovk and Bogdanov v Russia*, Application No. 15613/10, Joint Concurring Opinion of Judges Pinto de Albuquerque and Elósegui.

> fact, it seems that the exception has become the rule, since the Court has found more often than not that the lack of criminal remedies constituted a violation of Article 2.[81]

In light of the forceful arguments made in this concurring opinion, it remains to be seen how the Court's jurisprudence in negligence cases will develop. Currently, there is a certain degree of uncertainty[82] due to the fact that it is not entirely clear under what circumstances civil law remedies suffice. In *Nicolae Virgiliu Tănase v. Romania*, the Court stated that civil remedies suffice once it has been established that death was inflicted unintentionally. However, when it is not clear whether death or injuries are inflicted intentionally or unintentionally, the Court might have to draw the line between negligence and intentional conduct, and thus engage with a question at the heart of criminal law. This could be perceived as yet another interference in domestic matters of criminal law.

C. *The Rationales behind the Obligations to Criminalise, Investigate, and Prosecute*

In order to better understand the rationale behind the obligations to criminalise, investigate, and prosecute, the concept of 'procedural protection' should be employed.[83] As explained earlier, procedural obligations stem from the substantive right in question combined with the obligation to secure to everyone the rights and freedoms under Article 1 ECHR. They are considered to be 'separate and autonomous' from the substantive obligations, and thus independent from a finding of a substantive breach.[84] A finding that the substantive right has not been violated does not preclude

---

81 *Ibid.*

82 Mavronicola also raises this issue, although not in relation to the *Nicolae Virgiliu Tănase* case: Mavronicola, 'Taking Life and Liberty Seriously' (2017) 80(6) *MLR*, 1026 (1045).

83 See Seibert-Fohr, *Prosecuting Serious Human Rights Violations* (2009), 118; see also Schabas, *The European Convention on Human Rights: A Commentary* (2015), 191; Roberti di Sarsina, *Transitional Justice and a State's Response to Mass Atrocity* (2019), 78.

84 ECtHR, Judgment (GC), 9 April 2009, *Šilih v Slovenia*, Application No. 71463/01, para 159; Schabas, *The European Convention on Human Rights: A Commentary* (2015), 134; Roberti di Sarsina, *Transitional Justice and a State's Response to Mass Atrocity* (2019), 78; See also ECtHR,' Guide on Article 2 of the European Convention on Human Rights, Right to Life', updated 31 August 2020, https://www.echr.coe.int/Documents/Guide_Art_2_ENG.pdf, 33.

an applicant from lodging a complaint under Article 13 ECHR, and the Court may still find a violation of the procedural obligations.[85]

Seibert-Fohr convincingly argues that in search of the rationale behind criminal law measures in the Court's jurisprudence, one should distinguish between different aspects of criminal law. Criminalisation and enforcement of criminal law are usually regarded as 'matters of general human rights protection' by the Court, whereas protection of an individual victim leads to a focus on the investigation.[86] Whereas there is no right to have a third party prosecuted or punished, the Court found that the victim is entitled to an investigation.[87] However, the Court itself does not distinguish clearly between these aspects.

In *X. and Y. v. The Netherlands*, the Court clearly explains why positive obligations sometimes require recourse to criminal law.[88] In this case, the Court made clear that 'effective deterrence is indispensable' when fundamental values, and in this case 'essential aspects of private life', are at stake. Deterrence 'can be achieved only by criminal law provisions; indeed, it is by such provisions that the matter is normally regulated.'[89] However, criminalisation is not enough to achieve effective deterrence. Criminal law must be enforced in order to have a deterrence effect. In an atmosphere of impunity, legal protection of the right to life is ineffective.[90]

Deterrence and general prevention are considered the main rationale behind the obligations to criminalise, investigate, and prosecute, while special crime prevention and the intention to protect society from specific perpetrators are rather the exception. Special prevention appears to be the central rationale in *Mastromatteo v. Italy*, where the Court stated that a prison sentence has the function 'to protect society for example by preventing a criminal from re-offending and thus causing further harm.'[91]

Deterrence considerations can also play a role when it comes to individual rights violations. In *Mahmut Kaya v. Turkey*, the Court held that inadequate criminal procedures in the past had perpetuated an atmosphere

---

85 Schabas, *The European Convention on Human Rights: A Commentary* (2015), 551 f.; Roberti di Sarsina, *Transitional Justice and a State's Response to Mass Atrocity* (2019), 78.

86 Seibert-Fohr, *Prosecuting Serious Human Rights Violations* (2009), 116.

87 *Id.*, 124.

88 ECtHR, Judgment, 26 March 1985, *X and Y v The Netherlands*, Application No. 8978/80, para. 27.

89 *Ibid.*

90 See Seibert-Fohr, *Prosecuting Serious Human Rights Violations* (2009), 118.

91 ECtHR, Judgment (GC), 24 October 2002, *Mastromatteo v Italy*, Application No. 37703/97, para. 72.

of impunity, and thus enabled the violation of the rights of the victim in the case at hand.[92] In short, the lack of effective enforcement of existing criminal law provisions in previous cases explains why the Court found that the protection offered to the applicant was lacking. However, this rationale remains the exception, as the Court made clear that it only applies in a narrow set of circumstances. In the above case, the Court considered that a pattern of inadequate investigations and prosecutions in the past 'undermined the effectiveness of the protection afforded by the criminal law' and 'permitted or fostered a lack of accountability of members of the security forces for their actions which [...] was not compatible with the rule of law in a democratic society respecting the fundamental rights and freedoms guaranteed under the Convention.'[93]

However, deterrence is not the only rationale behind the obligations to investigate and prosecute serious human rights violations. In some instances, the Court found that the protection of the rule of law required criminal prosecution.[94] The rationale of protecting the rule of law originated from *Öneryildiz v. Turkey* and was confirmed in recent cases.[95] In that case, the Court stated that 'the national courts should not under any circumstances be prepared to allow life-endangering offences to go unpunished. This is essential for maintaining public confidence and ensuring adherence to the rule of law and for preventing any appearance of tolerance of or collusion in unlawful acts.'[96] Furthermore, in analysing the

---

92 ECtHR, Judgment, 28 March 2000, *Mahmut Kaya v Turkey*, Application No. 22535/93, para. 96.

93 *Id.*, para. 98.

94 ECtHR, Judgment, 28 January 2010, *Zinatullin v Russia*, Application No. 10551/10, para. 37; see also ECtHR, Judgment, 30 June 2020, *Satybalova and Others v Russia*, Application No. 79947/12, para. 71; ECtHR, Judgment, 2 April 2020, *Kukhalashvili and Others v Georgia*, Application Nos. 8938/07, 41891/07, para. 129.

95 ECtHR, Judgment (GC), 30 November 2004, *Öneryildiz v Turkey*, Application No. 48939/99, para. 96; see also ECtHR, Judgment, 28 January 2010, *Zinatullin v Russia*, Application No. 10551/10, para. 37; ECtHR, Judgment, 30 June 2020, *Satybalova and Others v Russia*, Application No. 79947/12, para. 71; ECtHR, Judgment, 2 April 2020, *Kukhalashvili and Others v Georgia*, Application Nos. 8938/07, 41891/07, para. 129.

96 ECtHR, Judgment (GC), 30 November 2004, *Öneryildiz v Turkey*, Application No. 48939/99, para. 96; see also ECtHR, Judgment, 28 January 2010, *Zinatullin v Russia*, Application No. 10551/10, para. 37; ECtHR, Judgment, 30 June 2020, *Satybalova and Others v Russia*, Application No. 79947/12, para. 71; ECtHR, Judgment, 2 April 2020, *Kukhalashvili and Others v Georgia*, Application Nos. 8938/07, 41891/07, para. 129.

requirements for an effective investigation, the Court referred to 'public confidence in the State's monopoly on the use of force.'[97] Where State agents are involved, the Court additionally stresses the importance of investigation to hold them accountable for deaths occurring under their responsibility.[98]

Seibert-Fohr observes that, although in the context of individual complaints, 'prosecution as a matter of general human rights protection as shared interest of society' is the main rationale utilised by the Court to justify the need for criminal law measures. This aligns with the trend in the Court's jurisprudence to 'use individual complaints to test compliance with the Convention more generally.'[99]

As anticipated, the Court has so far ruled out the existence of an individual right of a victim to have a perpetrator prosecuted or punished.[100] In that regard, the ECtHR has refused to adopt the 'right to justice' doctrine developed and applied by the Inter-American Court of Human Rights.[101] Nevertheless, in the jurisprudence of the ECtHR, victims are recognised to have a right to an investigation (framed as 'remedial right'),[102] capable of leading to the identification and punishment of those responsible, which is generally derived from the right to a remedy enshrined in Article 13 ECHR.[103] Such an investigation is a necessary precondition for the victim to obtain redress. More recently, however, there is a trend towards finding the legal basis of the obligations to investigate and prosecute in the substantive right affected, especially the right to life.[104]

---

97 ECtHR, Judgment (GC), 15 May 2007, *Ramsahai and Others v The Netherlands*, Application No. 52391/99, para. 325.

98 ECtHR, Judgment, 4 May 2001, *Hugh Jordan v The United Kingdom*, Application No. 24746/94, paras. 105, 144.

99 See Seibert-Fohr, *Prosecuting Serious Human Rights Violations* (2009), 119.

100 See Roberti di Sarsina, *Transitional Justice and a State's Response to Mass Atrocity* (2019), 78.

101 See e.g. ECtHR, Judgment (GC), 26 October 1999, *Erikson v Italy*, Application No. 37900/97; ECtHR, Judgment (GC), 12 February 2004, *Perez v France*, Application No. 47287/99; ECtHR, Judgment (GC), 30 November 2004, *Öneryildiz v Turkey*, Application No. 48939/99, para. 96. See also Seibert-Fohr, *Prosecuting Serious Human Rights Violations* (2009), 123 f.; Roberti di Sarsina, *Transitional Justice and a State's Response to Mass Atrocity* (2019), 74.

102 Seibert-Fohr, *Prosecuting Serious Human Rights Violations* (2009), 124 ff.

103 See e.g. ECtHR, Judgment, 24 February 2005, *Isayeva v Russia*, Application No 57950/00, paras. 228 ff.; Roberti di Sarsina, *Transitional Justice and a State's Response to Mass Atrocity* (2019), 79.

104 *Ibid.*, citing ECtHR, Judgment (GC), 15 May 2007, *Ramsahai and Others v The Netherlands*, Application No. 52391/99, paras. 356, 362.

In sum, the ECtHR has made clear that States parties have positive 'procedural' obligations to criminalise, investigate, and prosecute stemming from the substantive provisions read in conjunction with Article 1 or stemming from Article 13. It has also developed precise and strict standards for securing the implementation of these obligations, especially in its jurisprudence relating to infringements of the right to life and the prohibition of torture. The obligations to criminalise, investigate, and prosecute are mainly considered as measures of general human rights protection, which aim to guarantee non-repetition and ensure deterrence to the benefit of the society at large. However, the distinction between the concept of prevention and the concept of remedy is blurred in the jurisprudence of the Court.[105] Since the concept of prevention is tied to protecting society at large and the concept of remedy is tied to the individual victim, this trend indicates an increasing conflation of individual, remedial rights and additional preventative obligations on State Parties.

D. *Conclusion*

In 2009, Anja Seibert-Fohr identified 'a trend towards gradually assuming additional criminal law obligations under the European Convention.'[106] It is true that – as Judge Françoise Tulkens acknowledges – a State can potentially be held accountable by the ECtHR for failures at 'each step of the criminal law process', from criminalisation of certain acts, to execution of the sentence.[107] This tendency is confirmed and reinforced in the most recent jurisprudence of the Court, as it aligns with a general trend towards human rights protection through criminal law.[108]

Despite the legitimate concerns raised against an expansion of the ECtHR's jurisprudence regarding criminal measures and acknowledging that States Parties should retain a margin of appreciation in determining the means to secure the rights protected by the Convention, it cannot be said that the Court's increasing engagement with the procedural obligations to criminalise, investigate, and prosecute constitutes an undue restriction on a State's prerogatives. In this regard, it should be stressed that the extension of the scope of criminal law measures in the jurisprudence of the

---

105 Seibert-Fohr, *Prosecuting Serious Human Rights Violations* (2009), 149.

106 *Id.*, 146.

107 Tulkens, 'The Paradoxical Relationship between Criminal Law and Human Rights' (2011), 9 *JICJ*, 577 (586 f.).

108 See Seibert-Fohr, *Prosecuting Serious Human Rights Violations* (2009), 146.

Court is limited to the most fundamental and basic rights, i.e. the right to life, freedom from torture, and the protection of liberty and security. The Court's willingness to scrutinise the overall administration of justice may produce overly prescriptive results, but this should not deter States Parties as they should cooperate with the Court in ensuring the rights enshrined in the ECHR, including their effective protection. However, the conflation of remedial and preventative concepts in the Court's jurisprudence is problematic. It shows that the Court has not yet reached a definitive understanding of the interplay between international human rights law and domestic criminal law. This emerges especially in cases arising from the unintentional infringements of the right to life.

Bibliography

Chevalier-Watts, Juliet: Effective Investigations under Article 2 of the European Convention on Human Rights: Securing the Right to Life or an Onerous Burden on a State?, EJIL 2010, 701ff.

Gioia, Andrea: The Role of the European Court of Human Rights in Monitoring Compliance with Humanitarian Law in Armed Conflict, in: Ben-Naftali, Orna (ed), International Humanitarian Law and International Human Rights Law (2011), 201ff.

Jackson, Miles: Amnesties in Strasbourg, Oxf. J. Leg. Stud. 2018, 451ff.

Lazarus, Liora: Positive Obligations and Criminal Justice: Duties to Protect or Coerce?, in: Zedner, Lucia/Roberts, Julian V. (eds), Principles and Values in Criminal Law and Criminal Justice: Essays in Honour of Andrew Ashworth (2012), 135ff.

Mallinder, Louise: Investigations, Prosecutions and Amnesties under Articles 2 & 3 of the European Convention on Human Rights, Transitional Justice Institute, Research Paper No. 15–05 (2015), https://papers.ssrn.com/sol3/papers.cfm?abstract_id=2668106.

Mavronicola, Natasa: Taking Life and Liberty Seriously, MLR 2017, 1026ff.

Roberti di Sarsina, Jacopo: Transitional Justice and a State's Response to Mass Atrocity (2019).

Schabas, William: The European Convention on Human Rights: A Commentary (2015).

Seibert-Fohr, Anja: Prosecuting Serious Human Rights Violations (2009).

Tulkens, Françoise: The Paradoxical Relationship between Criminal Law and Human Rights, JICJ 2011, 577ff.

The European Court of Human Rights and Article 18 – An Indicator for the State of Democracy in Europe?

Christiane Schmaltz

A. *Introduction – An Alarming Tendency*

On 27 July 2019, the Moscow police, following a day of mostly peaceful protests, took more than 1,000 people into custody. One week later, there were again peaceful protests and again hundreds of arrests. The people were taking to the streets because the electoral commission had denied opposition candidates a place on the ballot for the election to Moscow's city council. Allegedly, the signatures the candidates had collected were fake.[1]

It seems likely that most – if not all – of these 1,000 and more arrests were not the result of a reasonable suspicion that the arrested had committed an offence as prescribed by Article 5 of the Convention. Even more, it is obvious that the protestors were detained to prevent them from voicing their support for the opposition candidates. In the words of the European Court of Human Rights in Strasbourg, such a police crackdown on protests as in Moscow will inevitably have a 'chilling effect'[2] on political expression. It will suppress the activity of individuals taking part in such actions and thereby destroy what is most valuable in a democratic society – free expression and public discourse.

These episodes illustrate the topic of this chapter and lead straight into the heart of the issue – the prohibition to limit rights set forth in the European Convention on Human Rights (ECHR) for any purpose other than those stipulated in the convention. This is enshrined in Article 18 of

1 See Bershidsky, 'Putin reminds Russians he can do suppression', Bloomberg L.P., 29 July 2019, https://www.bloombergquint.com/business/moscow-protests-vladimir-putin-s-suppression-potential; Bigalke, Mit aller Macht, Süddeutsche Zeitung, 28 July 2019, https://www.sueddeutsche.de/politik/russland-mit-aller-macht-1.4542891.

2 See ECtHR, Judgment, 15 May 2014, *Taranenko v Russia*, Application No. 19554/05, para. 95; ECtHR, Judgment (GC), 2 February 2017, *Navalnyy v Russia*, Application No. 29580/12 and 4 more, Joint Partly Dissenting Opinion of Judges López Guerra, Keller and Pastor Vilanove, para. 4.

the ECHR. The provision has achieved an inglorious and rather alarming prominence since the Strasbourg Court has begun to repeatedly hand down judgments finding a violation of this article.

There are many aspects relevant to Article 18 ECHR. This chapter will provide a brief introduction to the provision (B.) including an overview of the recent jurisprudence of the Strasbourg Court[3] (C.) and will then outline some thoughts on a somewhat bolder approach to Article 18 ECHR and its application. In doing so, the chapter will draw on ideas already voiced by a number of judges in separate opinions.[4] The focus of this chapter will be the scope of application of Article 18 ECHR, namely its application in conjunction with Article 6 ECHR (D.), as well as questions of proof (E.). It will conclude with a critique of the practice of the Court to sometimes refrain from a separate examination of the alleged violation of Article 18 ECHR (F.).

As this chapter aims to discuss questions surrounding Article 18, which have in the author's view not yet been – sufficiently – clarified by the Court, it will not address the specific issue of the predominant purpose test established by the Grand Chamber in *Merabishvili v. Georgia*[5]. This test addresses the question of how to deal with restrictions of rights or freedoms under Article 18 ECHR which are applied both for an ulterior purpose and a purpose prescribed by the Convention ('plurality of purposes').[6] In *Merabishvili v. Georgia*, the Court ruled that in such cases the restriction will run counter to Article 18 ECHR only if the ulterior purpose was predominant, whereas there will be no violation of Article 18 ECHR if the prescribed purpose was the main one, even if the restriction also pursues

---

3 Jurisprudence up to 31 December 2020 has been taken into account.

4 See e.g. ECtHR, Judgment, 30 April 2013, *Tymoshenko v Ukraine*, Application No. 49872/11, Joint Dissenting Opinion of Judges Jungwiert, Nußberger and Potocki; ECtHR, Decision, 23 February 2016, *Navalnyy and Ofitserov v Russia*, Application No. 46632/13, 28671/14, Joint Partly Dissenting Opinion of Judges Nicolaou, Keller and Dedov; ECtHR, Judgment, 11 October 2016, *Kasparov v Russia*, Application No. 53659/07, Partly Dissenting Opinion of Judge Keller; ECtHR, Judgment (GC), 2 February 2017, *Navalnyy v Russia*, Application No. 29580/12 and 4 more, Joint Partly Dissenting Opinion of Judges López Guerra, Keller and Pastor Vilanova; ECtHR, Judgment, 17 October 2017, *Navalnyy v Russia*, Application No. 101/15, Joint Partly Dissenting Opinion of Judges Keller and Dedov; ECtHR, Judgment, 16 November 2017, *Ilgar Mammadov v Azerbaijan (No. 2)*, Application No. 919/15, Joint Dissenting Opinion of Judges Nußberger, Tsotsoria, O'Leary and Mits.

5 ECtHR, Judgment (GC), 28 November 2017, *Merabishvili v Georgia*, Application No. 72508/13.

6 *Id.*, para. 292.

another purpose.[7] The question of which purpose is predominant depends on all the circumstances of the particular case[8] and thus does not lend itself to an abstract discussion like the one in this chapter.

B. *Article 18 ECHR – Autonomous Application Linked with Substantive Convention Guarantees*

Article 18 ECHR is titled 'Limitation on use of restrictions on rights' and is found at the very end of the first section of the Convention. It reads:

> 'The restrictions permitted under this Convention to the said rights and freedoms shall not be applied for any purpose other than those for which they have been prescribed.'

Together with Article 17 ECHR, which prohibits the abuse of rights, Article 18 ECHR serves as an additional safeguard to the 'Rights and freedoms' contained in the first section of the Convention. Both provisions underline that the restriction of rights permitted under the Convention serves a particular purpose and may neither go beyond this purpose nor serve a different one. Hence, limitations of rights are permissible only if they themselves remain within the limits provided for in the Convention. While this might seem evident, Article 18 ECHR goes beyond the obvious.[9] It seeks to prevent an abuse of restrictions for purposes contrary to the Convention and thus creates an autonomous role for its application[10].

Article 18 ECHR presupposes the possibility of lawful restrictions of a right. It is therefore long-standing case law of the Court that it cannot be pleaded alone, but only in conjunction with a substantive Convention guarantee, which contains explicit or inherent restrictions. Nonetheless, Article 18 ECHR has – as already mentioned – an independent scope of application. That independence is underlined by the fact that the finding of a violation of Article 18 ECHR does not depend on the outcome of the Court's examination of an alleged breach of the other provision. Article 18

---

7 *Id.*, para. 305.

8 *Id.*, para. 307.

9 See ECtHR, Judgment (GC), 28 November 2017, *Merabishvili v Georgia*, Application No. 72508/13, para. 288.

10 See Satzger et al., 'Does Art. 18 ECHR Grant Protection Against Politically Motivated Criminal Proceedings (Part 1) – Rethinking the Interpretation of Art. 18 ECHR Against the Background of New Jurisprudence of the European Court of Human Rights' (2014) 4 *EuCLR* 91 (109 ff.).

ECHR can be breached regardless of whether the other article is found to have been breached.[11] This clearly demonstrates that Article 18 ECHR protects a legal interest separate from that protected by the right it is pleaded in conjunction with.[12]

C. *Development of the Case Law – From Uncertainty to Clarification*

For quite some time the case law of the Court on Article 18 ECHR was rather inconsistent and even a bit unpredictable: the applicable standard of proof varied, the question of how to deal with a plurality of purposes had not been answered and the scope of application was – and still is – unclear. In November 2017, the Grand Chamber clarified some of these aspects in the case of *Merabishvili v. Georgia.*[13]

The need to clarify the case law did not arise until well into the late nineteen-nineties and early two thousands. After the entry into force of the Convention in 1953, more than five decades passed before the Court found a separate breach of Article 18 ECHR for the first time in 2004.[14] Between then and December 2020, there have been another 17 cases (19 if one counts Chamber and Grand Chamber judgments separately) in which the Court held that the respondent Government had breached Article 18 ECHR. What is striking – and alarming – is the increase of judgments finding a violation of Article 18 ECHR in recent years, namely since 2016: 15 of the 20 judgments finding a violation of Article 18 ECHR were handed down over the course of four years between March 2016 and December 2020. This of course raises questions, namely whether this is an indicator for the state of democracy – or rather its demise – in Europe.

At the beginning, however, the Court finding violations of Article 18 ECHR by the Convention States remained the exception. After the first

11 ECtHR, Judgment (GC), 28 November 2017, *Merabishvili v Georgia*, Application No. 72508/13, para. 288; for an example see ECtHR, Judgment, 19 May 2004, *Gusinskiy v Russia*, Application No. 70276/01, para. 74 and 77.

12 See ECtHR, Judgment, 11 October 2016, *Kasparov v Russia*, Application No. 53659/07, Partly Dissenting Opinion of Judge Keller, para. 3; ECtHR, Judgment (GC), 2 February 2017, *Navalnyy v Russia*, Application No. 29580/12 and 4 more, Joint Partly Dissenting Opinion of Judges López Guerra, Keller and Pastor Vilanova, para. 2.

13 ECtHR, Judgment (GC), 28 November 2017, *Merabishvili v Georgia*, Application No. 72508/13, paras. 264 ff.

14 ECtHR, Judgment, 19 May 2004, *Gusinskiy v Russia*, Application No. 70276/01.

judgment in May 2004 in the case of *Gusinskiy v. Russia*[15] more than three years passed without a judgment finding a violation of Article 18 ECHR. It was not until November 2007 that the Court found that Moldova had breached Article 18 ECHR taken in conjunction with Article 5 ECHR (*Cebotari v. Moldova*[16]).

Then, four years later the number of violation judgments picked up speed. In July 2012 and April 2013, Ukraine was found to have breached Article 18 ECHR in two cases concerning criminal proceedings against former government members: *Lutsenko v. Ukraine*[17] and *Tymoshenko v. Ukraine.*[18] In May 2014, the Court found that Azerbaijan had breached Article 18 ECHR in the case of *Ilgar Mammadov v. Azerbaijan*[19] (the case led to the first judgment of the Court pursuant to Article 46 § 4 ECHR, holding that Azerbaijan had failed to fulfil its obligation under Article 46 § 1 ECHR of the Convention[20]). Further judgments against Azerbaijan followed in March 2016 (*Rasul Jafarov v. Azerbaijan*[21]) as well as in April (*Mammadli v. Azerbaijan*[22]), in June (*Rashad Hasanov et al. v. Azerbaijan*[23]) and in September 2018 (*Aliyev v. Azerbaijan*[24]). In June 2016, a new state joined the list of Article 18 ECHR violators: a Chamber held that Georgia had breached Article 18 ECHR in the case of *Merabishvili v Georgia*[25]. Upon referral, the Grand Chamber[26] confirmed the judgment and – more importantly – provided the much-needed consolidation of the case law al-

15 *Ibid.*
16 ECtHR, Judgment, 13 November 2007, *Cebotari v Moldova*, Application No. 35615/06.
17 ECtHR, Judgment, 3 July 2012, *Lutsenko v Ukraine*, Application No. 6492/11.
18 ECtHR, Judgment, 30 April 2013, *Tymoshenko v Ukraine*, Application No. 49872/11.
19 ECtHR, Judgment (GC), 22 May 2014, *Ilgar Mammadov v Azerbaijan*, Application No.15172/13.
20 *Ibid.*
21 ECtHR, Judgment, 17 March 2016, *Rasul Jafarov v Azerbaijan*, Application No. 69981/14.
22 ECtHR, Judgment, 19 April 2018, *Mammadli v Azerbaijan*, Application No. 47145/14.
23 ECtHR, Judgment, 7 June 2018, *Rashad Hasanov et al. v Azerbaijan*, Application No. 48653/13 and 3 more.
24 ECtHR, Judgment, 20 September 2018, *Aliyev v Azerbaijan*, Application No. 68762/14, 71200/14.
25 ECtHR, Judgment, 14 June 2016, *Merabishvili v Georgia*, Application No. 72508/13.
26 ECtHR, Judgment (GC), 28 November 2017, *Merabishvili v Georgia*, Application No. 72508/13.

ready mentioned. In November 2018 and April 2019, judgments involving Russia and Turkey were handed down. Two cases concerned the well-known political activist Navalnyy: the first of them was a Grand Chamber judgment[27] whereas in the second case[28] the request for referral submitted by the government was rejected by the Grand Chamber panel in September 2019.[29] In the case of *Selahattin Demirtaş v. Turkey (No. 2)*,[30] the Chamber found a violation of Article 18 in November 2018. Upon referral requests of both the government and the applicant, the Grand Chamber delivered its judgment on 22 December 2020, also finding – *inter alia* – a violation of Article 18 ECHR in conjunction with Article 5 ECHR[31]. In November 2019, February and July 2020, the Court handed down four more judgments against Azerbaijan in the cases of *Natig Jafarov v. Azerbaijan*[32], *Ibrahimov and Mammadov v. Azerbaijan*[33], *Khadija Ismayilova (no. 2) v. Azerbaijan*[34] and *Yunusova and Yunusov v. Azerbaijan (No. 2)*[35]. In addition, in December 2019 the Court held that Turkey once again had violated Article 18 ECHR in the widely discussed case of *Kavala v. Turkey*.[36]

This overview would not be complete without mentioning a few cases in which the applicants raised Article 18 ECHR complaints but in which the Court declined to either examine these complaints or found no breach of this provision. The most prominent are possibly the two *Khodorkovskiy*

---

27 ECtHR, Judgment (GC), 15 November 2018, *Navalnyy v Russia*, Application No. 29580/12 and 4 more.

28 ECtHR, Judgment, 9 April 2019, *Navalnyy v Russia (No. 2)*, Application No. 43734/14.

29 ECtHR, Press Release 308 (2019).

30 ECtHR, Judgment (GC), 20 November 2018, *Selahattin Demirtaş v Turkey (No. 2)*, Application No. 14305/17.

31 ECtHR, Judgment (GC), 22 December 2020, *Selahattin Demirtas v Turkey (No. 2)*, Application No. 14305/17.

32 ECtHR, Judgment, 7 November 2019, *Natig Jafarov v Azerbaijan*, Application No. 64581/16.

33 ECtHR, Judgment, 13 February 2020, *Ibrahimov and Mammadov v Azerbaijan*, Application No. 63571/16 and 5 more.

34 ECtHR, Judgment, 27 February 2020, *Khadija Ismayilova (No. 2) v Azerbaijan*, Application No. 30778/15.

35 ECtHR, Judgment, 16 July 2020, *Yunusova and Yunusov v Azerbijan (No. 2)*, Application No. 68817/14.

36 ECtHR, Judgment, 10 December 2019, *Kavala v Turkey*, Application No. 28749/18. The request for referral submitted by the Government was rejected by the Grand Chamber panel on 11 May 2020.

v. Russia[37] cases and the related *Yukos v. Russia*[38] case from 2011 and 2013, respectively. In all three cases, the Court found that the applicants had not put forth sufficient proof that the State had acted in bad faith. In the 2020 judgment of *Khodorkovskiy and Lebedev v. Russia (No. 2)*,[39] the Court concluded that no separate issue arose under Article 18 in conjunction with Articles 6 and 7 of the Convention and Article 4 of Protocol no. 7. With regard to an alleged breach of Article 18 in conjunction with Article 8 ECHR, the Court found no evidence of an ulterior motive as alleged by the applicants. Furthermore, there are two cases submitted – *inter alia* – by the political activist Navalnyy which led to judgments in 2016 and 2017.[40] In these cases, the Court dismissed the complaint under Article 18 ECHR taken in conjunction with Articles 6 and 7 ECHR as inadmissible *ratione materiae*. It held that Article 6 and 7 ECHR did not contain any express or implied restrictions that could form the subject of the Court's examination under Article 18 ECHR of the Convention.

This development of the case law not only illustrates the rather alarming state of democracy in Europe but also shows the Court's increasing willingness to apply Article 18 ECHR and thus hold the Convention States responsible for attempts to stifle Convention rights and freedoms. Furthermore, the high number of cases in which Article 18 complaints were raised in recent years offered the Court an opportunity to clarify and consolidate its case law on this Convention provision.

D. *Application of Article 18 in Conjunction with Article 6 – Inconsistency, but Positive Signals*

Despite of the growing body of case law on Article 18 ECHR, questions as to its application remain. One of the issues this chapter wants to focus

---

37 ECtHR, Judgment, 31 May 2011, *Khodorkovskiy v Russia*, Application No. 5829/04, paras. 254 ff.; ECtHR, Judgment, 25 July 2013, *Khodorkovskiy and Lebedev v Russia*, Application No. 11082/06, 13772/05, paras. 897 ff.

38 ECtHR, Judgment, 20 September 2011, *OAO Neftyanaya Kompaniya Yukos v Russia*, Application No. 14902/04, paras. 663 ff.

39 ECtHR, Judgment, 14 January 2020, *Khodorkovskiy and Lebedev v Russia (No. 2)*, Application No. 51111/07, 42757/07, paras. 620 ff.

40 ECtHR, Judgment, 23 February 2016, *Navalnyy and Ofitserov v Russia*, Application No. 46632/13, 28671/14, para. 130; ECtHR, Judgment, 17 October 2017, *Navalnyy v Russia*, Application No. 101/15, paras. 86 ff.

on is the scope of application of Article 18 ECHR, namely the question whether it can be raised in conjunction with Article 6 of the Convention.

It is not surprising that the most common Article pleaded in conjunction with Article 18 is Article 5 ECHR. The arrest and detention of a person is likely one of the most effective ways to exclude someone from the political forum and from public debate. However, abusing the restrictions permitted under the Convention to other rights can obviously also frustrate the consensus on democracy and the rule of law underlying the Convention. An example is the November 2018 case of *Navalnyy v Russia*[41] in which the Grand Chamber found a violation of Article 18 ECHR in conjunction with Articles 5 and 11 ECHR. Another example is the judgment in the case of *Aliyev v Azerbaijan*[42] of September 2018 in which the Court found a violation of Article 18 ECHR taken in conjunction with Articles 5 and 8 ECHR of the Convention.

Concerning the applicability of Article 6 ECHR together with Article 18 ECHR, the Court has not yet come to a coherent approach, let alone found a breach of Article 18 ECHR together with Article 6 ECHR. Instead, in the judgments of February 2016 and October 2017 (*Navalnyy and Ofitserov v. Russia*; *Navalnyy v. Russia*), the Third Section of the Court dismissed Article 18 ECHR complaints of the civil society activist Navalnyy and others as inadmissible *ratione materiae* because they had pleaded a violation only in conjunction with Articles 6 and 7 ECHR. Just one month later, in the case of *Ilgar Mammodov v. Azerbaijan (No. 2)*,[43] the Fifth Section shied away from addressing the very same question, namely whether the applicant can raise an Article 18 ECHR complaint in conjunction with Article 6 ECHR. Instead, referring to the inconsistent case law, the Chamber stated:

> Furthermore, the Court observes that the question whether Article 6 of the Convention contains any express or implied restrictions which may form the subject of the Court's examination under Article 18 of the Convention remains open [...]Taking those circumstances into account and having further regard to the submissions of the parties and its findings under Article 6 § 1 of the Convention, the Court considers

41 ECtHR, Judgment (GC), 15 November 2018, *Navalnyy v Russia*, Application No. 29580/12 and 4 more.

42 ECtHR, Judgment (GC), 20 September 2018, *Aliyev v Azerbaijan*, Application No. 68762/14, 71200/14.

43 ECtHR, Judgment, 16 November 2017, *Ilgar Mammadov v Azerbaijan (No. 2)*, Application No. 919/15, para. 262.

> that there is no need to give a separate ruling on the complaint under Article 18 in the present case.[44]

At first sight, these judgments make for quite a bleak outlook on the relationship of Articles 6 and 18 ECHR. It seems doomed: either the complaint is deemed inadmissible, or it is not examined at all. However, all of these judgments triggered strong separate opinions,[45] the authors of which pointed out that – as required by the Court's case law – Article 6 ECHR does allow for both explicit and implicit restrictions.[46] Furthermore, they drew on the drafting history as well as the purpose underlying Article 18 ECHR. One of the separate opinions concludes:

> Although the situation in Europe today cannot be compared to that in Europe in 1950, the importance of this Article has not diminished. The right to a fair trial under Article 6 is one of the guarantees with reference to which fundamental abuses by a state may likely manifest themselves. Therefore, trials before a court must never be used for 'ulterior purposes'. This is the *conditio sine qua non*; the very basis for the idea of 'fair trial' as understood in the Convention. Almost all the other guarantees are futile if this most basic guarantee is called into question or undermined.[47]

In this context, it is worthwhile to take note of the Council of Europe's Commissioner for Human Rights and her December 2018 third party

44 *Id.*, paras. 261f.

45 ECtHR, Judgment, 23 February 2016, *Navalnyy and Ofitserov v Russia*, Application No. 46632/13, 28671/14, Joint Partly Dissenting Opinion of Judges Nicolaou, Keller and Dedov; ECtHR, Judgment, 17 October 2017, *Navalnyy v Russia*, Application No. 101/15, Joint Partly Dissenting Opinion of Judges Keller and Dedov and Partly Dissenting Opinion of Judge Serghides; ECtHR, Judgment, 16 November 2017, *Ilgar Mammadov v Azerbaijan (No. 2)*, Application No. 919/15, Joint Concurring Opinion of Judges Nußberger, Tsotsoria, O'Leary and Mits.

46 ECtHR, Decision, 23 February 2016, *Navalnyy and Ofitserov v Russia*, Application No. 46632/13, 28671/14, Joint Partly Dissenting Opinion of Judges Nicolaou, Keller and Dedov, para. 6; *Navalnyy v Russia*, Application No. 101/15, Joint Partly Dissenting Opinion of judges Keller and Dedov, para. 7, and Partly Dissenting Opinion of Judge Serghides; ECtHR, Judgment, 16 November 2017, *Ilgar Mammadov v Azerbaijan (No. 2)*, Application No. 919/15, Joint Concurring Opinion of Judges Nußberger, Tsotsoria, O'Leary and Mits, para. 12.

47 ECtHR, Judgment, 16 November 2017, *Ilgar Mammadov v Azerbaijan (No. 2)*, Application No. 919/15, Joint Concurring Opinion of Judges Nußberger, Tsotsoria, O'Leary and Mits, para. 16.

intervention in the case of *Kavala v. Turkey.*[48] The Commissioner alleges possible flagrant abuses of the fair trial guarantees of Article 6 ECHR, in particular with respect to the principle of equality of arms, namely decisions to restrict access to the investigation file. She submitted:

> A particular worrying pattern reported to the Commissioner, especially for cases which attract political attention [...], is that despite restriction decisions, information from the investigation file seems to be used frequently in smear campaigns against suspects in pro-governmental media. For the Commissioner, this could be an indication that the motivation behind these decisions is the restriction of defence rights of the suspects, rather than the protection of the integrity of the investigation.[49]

Considering the separate opinions as well as the Commissioner's third-party intervention, there may be room for optimism. The next time the Court has to decide on whether Article 18 ECHR is applicable in conjunction with Article 6 ECHR it will hopefully seize the opportunity and acknowledge that there is no basis for excluding Article 6 ECHR from the scope of application of Article 18 ECHR. The Article 46 ECHR judgment in *Ilgar Mammadov v. Azerbaijan* of 20 May 2019 might possibly already point in this direction. In this judgment, the Grand Chamber found:

> It follows that the Court's finding of a violation of Article 18 in conjunction with Article 5 of the Convention in the first Mammadov judgment vitiated any action resulting from the imposition of the charges.[50]

This conclusion undeniably goes beyond the mere finding of an unfair trial. It might signal that restrictions of the fair trial guarantees of Article 6 ECHR can be applied for ulterior purposes and that this provision can thus be pleaded in conjunction with Article 18 ECHR.[51]

---

48 ECtHR, Judgment, 10 December 2019, *Kavala v Turkey*, Application No. 28749/18.

49 CommDH(2018)30, 20 December 2018.

50 ECtHR, Judgment (GC), 29 May 2019, *Ilgar Mammadov v Azerbaijan*, Application No. 15172/13, para. 189 (emphasis added).

51 See Gavron and Remezaite, 'Has the ECtHR in Mammadov 46 (4) opened the door to findings of "bad faith" in trials?', EJIL:Talk!, 4 July 2019, https://www.ejiltalk.org/has-the-ecthr-in-mammadov-464-opened-the-door-to-findings-of-bad-faith-in-trials/.

E. Burden and Standard of Proof

As regards the question of proof when examining an alleged violation of Article 18 ECHR, a starting point can be the Court's introductory statement when discussing the burden as well as the standard of proof in these cases. The Court usually states that 'the whole structure of the Convention rests on the general assumption that public authorities in the member States act in good faith'.[52] According to the Court, this assumption is rebuttable in theory, but difficult to overcome in practice.[53] Until the Grand Chamber's clarification of the case law in *Merabishvili v. Georgia*, the Court tended to use varying standards of proof in Article 18 ECHR cases, though the minimum has always been a 'very exacting standard of proof'. However, in the *Khodorkovskiy* cases the Court's approach was stricter. It required not only that the applicants must 'convincingly show' that the state actions were driven by improper motives, it also asked for 'incontrovertible and direct proof', thereby making it essentially impossible to prove bad faith.[54] The Court again applied this strict approach in a case against Poland in 2012.[55] However, in the later cases of *Ilgar Mammadov*[56] and *Rasul Jafarov v. Azerbaijan*,[57] the Court did not refer to the strict standard; it merely required convincing evidence. Unfortunately, there was no explanation for this more lenient approach.

In order to clarify these issues, the Grand Chamber's attempts to consolidate the case law with regard to the burden of proof (I.) and the standard of proof (II.) in *Merabishvili v. Georgia* will be examined. Then, it will be shown in a comparative analysis that the Court tends to apply these principles as a safeguard against undemocratic tendencies (III.).

---

52 ECtHR, Judgment, 31 May 2011, *Khodorkovskiy v Russia*, Application No. 5829/04, para. 255.

53 *Ibid.*

54 *Ibid., Id.*, 260; ECtHR, Judgment, 25 July 2013, *Khodorkovskiy and Lebedev v Russia*, Application No. 11082/06, 13772/05, para. 900, 903.

55 ECtHR, Judgment, 18 September 2012, *Dochnal v Poland*, Application No. 31622/07, para. 116.

56 ECtHR, Judgment, 22 May 2014, *Ilgar Mammadov v Azerbaijan*, Application No. 15172/13, paras. 138 ff.

57 ECtHR, Judgment, 17 March 2016, *Rasul Jafarov v Azerbaijan*, Application No. 69981/14, paras. 153 ff.

I. Burden of Proof – Open Questions and Lack of Guidance for Applicants

With regard to the burden of proof, the Grand Chamber's findings in *Merabishvili v. Georgia* are regrettably very limited. The Court only reiterated that

> as a general rule, the burden of proof is not borne by one or the other party because the Court examines all material before it irrespective of its origin, and because it can, if necessary, obtain material of its own motion.[58]

This leaves unanswered the question of whether the burden of proof can shift to the respondent Government once the applicant has established a *prima facie* case of improper motive – an interpretation the Chamber expressly refused to follow in the *Khodorkovskiy* judgment.[59] If one accepts that the Grand Chamber rubberstamped this *Khodorkovskiy* line of argument and the burden of proof does not shift to the respondent State, there is still the question of the 'onus of presentation' (*Darlegungslast*). This 'onus of presentation' is not always and necessarily identical to the 'burden of proof'. It could be argued that in Article 18 ECHR cases, the State has (at least) a so called 'secondary onus of presentation' *(sekundäre Darlegungslast)*, which obliges the State to address and rebut the allegations of the applicant in a sufficiently substantiated manner.[60] Such a doctrine exists e.g. in German civil procedural law.[61]

It is not clear whether the Grand Chamber in *Merabishvili* condoned such an obligation and hence a secondary onus of presentation of the respondent State. The statement that the Court can draw inferences from the respondent Government's conduct in the proceedings and may combine such inferences with contextual factors are open for such an inter-

58 ECtHR, Judgment (GC), 28 November 2017, *Merabishvili v Georgia*, Application No. 72508/13, para. 311.

59 ECtHR, Judgment, 31 May 2011, *Khodorkovskiy v Russia*, Application No. 5829/04, para. 257; Satzger et al., 'Does Art. 18 ECHR Grant Protection Against Politically Motivated Criminal Proceedings (Part 2) – Prerequisites, Questions of Evidence and Scope of Application' (2014) 4 *EuCLR*, 248 (253).

60 This is also what Satzger et al. most likely mean when they talk about a shifting of the burden of proof, see 'Does Art. 18 ECHR Grant Protection Against Politically Motivated Criminal Proceedings (Part 2) – Prerequisites, Questions of Evidence and Scope of Application' (2014) 4 *EuCLR* 248 (255).

61 See e.g. BGH 12.5.2010, NJW 2010, 2061; Fritsche in: Rauscher/Krüger, Münchner Kommentar ZPO I (2020) § 138 mn. 24.

pretation.[62] In addition, the Court referred to situations in which the respondent State alone had access to information capable of corroborating or refuting the applicant's allegations.[63] This will usually be the case in Article 18 ECHR cases. These vague and elusive rules give the Court certain flexibility in dealing with the individual cases; such flexibility will often be necessary to address particulars of individual cases. However, the standards formulated by the Court in this respect lack sufficient guidance for applicants – and respondent governments for that matter – when arguing Article 18 ECHR cases.

II. Standard of Proof – The Usual Approach

As regards the 'standard of proof' in Article 18 cases, the Grand Chamber has put an end to the different approaches. It decided to adhere to its usual approach regarding proof rather than to develop special rules.[64] Hence, the standard of proof is officially that of 'beyond a reasonable doubt'.[65] However, the application of this standard depends on the facts in question and the Convention right at stake.[66] Finally, in assessing the evidence, the Court is not bound by predetermined formulae for its assessment of the evidence; rather, its conclusion is based on a free evaluation of all evidence put before it.[67] Thus, the Court remains sensitive to any potential evidentiary difficulties encountered by a party.[68] Therefore, the Court will – like national courts – base its findings on a free evaluation of all evidence.

---

62 ECtHR, Judgment (GC), 28 November 2017, *Merabishvili v Georgia*, Application No. 72508/13, para. 312.

63 *Id.*, para. 313.

64 *Id.*, para. 310.

65 *Id.*, para. 314.

66 *Id.*, para. 314.

67 ECtHR, Judgment (GC), 6 July 2005, *Nachova et al v Bulgaria*, Application No. 43577/98 et al, para. 147.

68 ECtHR, Judgment (GC), 28 November 2017, *Merabishvili v Georgia*, Application No. 72508/13, para. 315.

III. Application of these Principles – A Safeguard against Undemocratic Tendencies

When looking at the application of these principles in the case law of the Court, there is something worth pointing out: the Court has repeatedly (and rightly) stated that 'high political status does not grant immunity'.[69] However, all cases in which there was no direct proof of bad faith and the applicants successfully convinced the Court that the contextual evidence produced was sufficient had been brought by either former members or heads of government (*Lutsenko v. Ukraine; Tymoshenko v. Ukraine; Merabishvili v. Georgia*) and opposition politicians (*Selahattin Demirtaş v. Turkey [No.2]*) or civil society activists (*Ilgar Mammadov v. Azerbaijan*; *Rasul Jafarov v. Azerbaijan; Mammadli v. Azerbaijan; Rashad Hasanov and others v. Azerbaijan; Navalnyy v. Russia; Yunusova and Yunusov v. Azerbaijan [No. 2]*), including human rights lawyers (*Aliyev v. Azerbaijan*). There are only two violation judgments in cases of applicants who were more into business than into politics. In these cases – *Gusinskiy v. Russia* and *Cebotary v. Moldova* – the applicants could advance more or less direct proof of bad faith of the respondent Government.

On the other hand, two other businesspersons did not succeed in convincing the Court to find a violation of Article 18 ECHR. The former heads of the Yukos Company Khodorkovskiy and Lebedev raised Article 18 ECHR complaints to no avail. The Court argued *inter alia* that 'none of the accusations against them concerned their political activities *stricto sensu*, even remotely. The applicants were not opposition leaders or public officials'.[70]

If this is more than mere coincidence, it suggests that the Court's scrutiny with regard to the standard of proof is less exacting when it comes to applications of political activists, members of the opposition or former government members. This illustrates that Article 18 ECHR as interpreted by the Court has become a safeguard against undemocratic tendencies[71] as

69 ECtHR, Judgment, 31 May 2011, *Khodorkovskiy v Russia*, Application No. 5829/04, para. 258.

70 ECtHR, Judgment, 25 July 2013, *Khodorkovskiy and Lebedev v Russia*, Application No. 11082/06, 13772/05, para. 906.

71 See Keller and Heri, 'Selective criminal proceedings and article 18 ECHR: The European Court of Human Right's untapped potential to protect democracy' (2016) *HRLJ* 1.

intended by the drafters of the Convention.[72] The partly dissenting opinion of judges López Guerra, Keller and Pastor Vilanova in the February 2017 *Navalnyy* judgment against Russia confirms this assumption.[73] The dissenting judges summarise the intention behind Article 18 as serving 'to address the abusive limitation of the rights of oppositional actors with the aim of silencing them'[74].

F. Non-Examination of Article 18 – Missed Chances to 'Raise the Red Flag'

Finally, there is another problem, which has also been the issue of separate opinions,[75] namely the Court's practice to occasionally abstain from examining the complaint under Article 18 ECHR separately. Two issues as to this practice need to be distinguished.

Sometimes the judgment lacks clear reasoning due to the refusal to separately examine the Article 18 ECHR complaint.[76] This practice is unsatisfactory because it leaves the reader puzzling as to the possible reasons for the non-examination and might easily appear arbitrary. Of course, a variety of plausible reasons come to mind, like a divided Chamber or a reluctance to relinquish jurisdiction to the Grand Chamber because of the inherent delay caused by such a referral.[77] For the sake of transparency and coherency of the case law, however, this practice should remain an excep-

---

72 Teitgen, Rapporteur, First Session of the Consultative Assembly, plenary sitting on 7 September 1949, cited according to CDH (75) 11, p. 3 [information document prepared by the Registry]; Teitgen, Rapporteur, Second Session of the Consultative Assembly, sitting on 16 August 1950, cited according to CDH (75) 11, p 9 [information document prepared by the Registry]; ECtHR, Judgment (GC), 28 November 2017, *Merabishvili v Georgia*, Application No. 72508/13, para. 154.

73 ECtHR, Judgment (GC), 2 February 2017, *Navalnyy v Russia*, Application No. 29580/12 and 4 more.

74 *Id.*, Joint Partly Dissenting Opinion of Judges López Guerra, Keller and Pastor Vilanova, para. 3.

75 E.g. ECtHR, Judgment, 21 June 2016, *Tchankotadze v Georgia*, Application No. 15256/05, Dissenting Opinion of Judge Kūris, para. 23 ff.

76 E.g. ECtHR, Judgment, 16 November 2017, *Ilgar Mammadov v Azerbaijan (No. 2)*, Application No. 919/15, para. 262; for a critique of this practice see also ECtHR, Judgment, 21 June 2016, *Tchankotadze v Georgia*, Application No. 15256/05, Dissenting Opinion of Judge Kuris, paras. 23 ff.

77 See ECtHR, Judgment, 16 November 2017, *Ilgar Mammadov v Azerbaijan (No. 2)*, Application No. 919/15, Joint Dissenting Opinion of Judges Nußberger, Tsotsoria, O'Leary and Mits.

tion. Rather, the Court should decline a separate examination of Article 18 ECHR only if the complaint is manifestly ill-founded, in particular if there is no interference with the Convention right pleaded in conjunction with Article 18 ECHR. If the act or omission by the respondent State does not even fall within the scope of protection of the Convention right or if there is at least no interference with the right, restrictions permitted under the Convention cannot have been abused.[78]

In other cases, the Court has argued that the Article 18 ECHR complaint raised the same issue that had already been dealt with in connection with a substantive Article of the Convention.[79] This practice raises even more concerns[80] because it suggests that the character of Article 18 ECHR is redundant.[81] It makes an enormous difference whether a judgment 'only' finds a violation of – for example – Article 5 ECHR or whether it also – explicitly – establishes a violation of Article 18 ECHR.

In *Merabishvili* the Grand Chamber required the Article 18 ECHR complaint to be 'a fundamental aspect of the case' to warrant separate examination.[82] This means that if the circumstances of the case clearly point to a breach of Article 18 ECHR, the Court must, in accordance with its own case law, examine this complaint separately. Only this interpretation is in conformity with the Convention. The refusal of the Court to examine and possibly find a violation of Article 18 ECHR in such cases is detrimental to the spirit of the Convention. A breach of Article 18 ECHR signals to the community of Convention States that there has not only been an 'ordinary' violation of a Convention guarantee.[83] The finding of a violation of Article 18 ECHR raises the red flag; it highlights that the respondent

---

78 See Steiger in: Pabel/Schmahl (eds), *Internationaler Kommentar zur Europäischen Menschenrechtskonvention* (2014), Art. 18 mn. 54 f.

79 E.g. ECtHR, Judgment, 18 December 1986, *Bozano v France*, Application No. 9990/82, para. 61; ECtHR, Judgment, 11 October 2016, *Kasparov v Russia*, Application No. 53659/07, para. 74 with further references; ECtHR, Judgment (GC), 2 February 2017, *Navalnyy v Russia*, Application No. 29580/12 and 4 more, para. 79.

80 See also Keller and Heri, 'Selective criminal proceedings and article 18 ECHR: The European Court of Human Right's untapped potential to protect democracy' (2016) *HRLJ* 1 (8).

81 See Steiger in: Pabel/Schmahl (eds), *Internationaler Kommentar zur Europäischen Menschenrechtskonvention* (2014), Art. 18 mn. 57 f.

82 ECtHR, Judgment (GC), 28 November 2017, *Merabishvili v Georgia*, Application No. 72508/13, para. 291.

83 Satzger et al., 'Does Art. 18 ECHR Grant Protection Against Politically Motivated Criminal Proceedings (Part 2) – Prerequisites, Questions of Evidence and Scope of Application' (2014) 4 *EuCLR* 249 (251).

State has deliberately acted against the presumption that public authorities in the member States act in good faith and in so doing has intentionally damaged the foundation of trust underlying the Convention structure.[84] It is only when the Court clearly identifies and sanctions[85] such violations that it will sound the alarm for the state of democracy and the rule of law in Europe. Only then will it truly live up to its role as the 'Conscience of Europe'.[86]

G. Conclusion – A Developing Tool in Need of Sharpening

As this chapter has shown, the Court has had ample opportunity in recent years to refine its case law on Article 18 ECHR. And it has used this opportunity, not only to consolidate and clarify the case law but also to reshape Article 18 ECHR into a more effective tool against undemocratic tendencies in a growing number of Convention States.

This chapter has also illustrated, however, that there are issues surrounding the application of Article 18 ECHR that still need to be addressed and resolved. The most pressing among them is the applicability of Article 18 in conjunction with Article 6 ECHR. It is time for the Court to acknowledge that there is no basis for excluding Article 6 from the scope of application of Article 18 ECHR. Regarding the burden of proof in Article 18 ECHR cases, it would be helpful for both applicants and respondent States if the Court gave a clear indication that it will look to the government for a rebuttal if the applicant's allegations regarding the Article 18 ECHR complaint are sufficiently substantiated. Finally, the refusal to conduct a separate examination of an Article 18 ECHR complaint should be handled

---

84 ECtHR, Judgment, 31 May 2011, *Khodorkovskiy v Russia*, Application No. 5829/04, para. 255; see Satzger et al., 'Does Art. 18 ECHR Grant Protection Against Politically Motivated Criminal Proceedings (Part 1) – Rethinking the Interpretation of Art. 18 ECHR Against the Background of New Jurisprudence of the European Court of Human Rights' (2014) *EuCLR* 91 (112).

85 Satzger et al, 'Does Art. 18 ECHR Grant Protection Against Politically Motivated Criminal Proceedings (Part 1) – Rethinking the Interpretation of Art. 18 ECHR Against the Background of New Jurisprudence of the European Court of Human Rights' (2014) *EuCLR* 91 (112).

86 Council of Europe, *The Conscience of Europe: 50 Years of the European Court of Human Rights* (2010); *cf.* also Dzehtsiarou and Tzevelekos, 'The Conscience of Europe that Landed in Strasbourg: A Circle of Life of the European Court of Human Rights' (2020) 1 *ECHR law review* 1.

with care and restraint. The Court should only choose this path if the Article 18 ECHR complaint is manifestly ill-founded.[87]

Clarification of these issues will enhance the value of Article 18 ECHR in the practice of the Court and might transform this newly discovered tool into a sharp and effective instrument for the protection of democracy in Europe.

Bibliography

Bershidsky, Leonid: Putin reminds Russians he can do suppression. A record crackdown on protests in Moscow is a warning to voters tempted to protest their increasingly hopeless situation, Bloomberg L.P., 29 July 2019, https://www.bloomberg.com/opinion/articles/2019-07-29/moscow-protests-vladimir-putin-s-suppression-potential.

Bigalke, Silke: Mit aller Macht. Bei Protesten in Moskau wurden am Samstag mehr als 1000 Menschen festgenommen – sie forderten die Zulassung von Oppositionskandidaten zur Stadtratswahl. Um die Politiker selbst hatten sich die Behörden bereits gekümmert. Süddeutsche Zeitung, 28 July 2019, https://www.sueddeutsche.de/politik/russland-mit-aller-macht-1.4542891.

Dzehtsiarou, Kanstantsin/Tzevelekos, Vassilis: The Conscience of Europe that Landed in Strasbourg: A Circle of Life of the European Court of Human Rights, ECHR law review 2020, 1 ff.

Fritsche in: Rauscher/Krüger, Münchner Kommentar ZPO I (2020).

Gavron, Jessica/Remezaite, Ramute: Has the ECtHR in Mammadov 46(4) opened the door to findings of 'bad faith' in trials?, EJIL:Talk!, 4 July 2019, https://www.ejiltalk.org/has-the-ecthr-in-mammadov-464-opened-the-door-to-findings-of-bad-faith-in-trials/.

Keller, Helen/Heri, Corina: Selective criminal proceedings and article 18 ECHR: The European Court of Human Right's untapped potential to protect democracy, HRLJ 2016, 1 ff.

Satzger, Helmut/Zimmermann, Frank/Eibach, Martin: Does Art. 18 ECHR Grant Protection Against Politically Motivated Criminal Proceedings (Part 1) – Rethinking the Interpretation of Art. 18 ECHR Against the Background of New Jurisprudence of the European Court of Human Rights, EuCLR 2014, 91 ff.

Satzger, Helmut/Zimmermann, Frank/Eibach, Martin: Does Art. 18 ECHR Grant Protection Against Politically Motivated Criminal Proceedings (Part 2) – Prerequisites, Questions of Evidence and Scope of Application, EuCLR 2014, 248 ff.

Steiger, Dominik, in: Pabel, Katharina/Schmahl, Stefanie (eds), Internationaler Kommentar zur Europäischen Menschenrechtskonvention (2014), Art. 18.

87 For an example see ECtHR, Decision, 12 January 2021, *Rarinca v Romania*, Application No. 10003/16, para 135 f.

Teitgen, Rapporteur: First Session of the Consultative Assembly, plenary sitting on 7 September 1949, CDH (75) 11, 3.

Teitgen, Rapporteur: Second Session of the Consultative Assembly, sitting on 16 August 1950, CDH (75) 11.

The Copenhagen Declaration: Wrapping up the Interlaken Reform?

Helga Molbæk-Steensig

A. *Introduction*

The European Court of Human Rights (hereafter ECtHR or the Court) is a remarkably active international court, second in output of judgments only to the European Court of Justice, an institution with more than six times the budget and jurisdiction over private and public law questions in a wide range of fields.[1] By comparison, the ECtHR deals only with cases against its 47 Member States concerning one or more of between one and two dozen fundamental rights depending on which protocols the respondent state in question has signed. Nevertheless, the Court receives tens of thousands of applications every year from the around 830 million citizens its jurisdiction encompasses, and since the 1990s it has been unable to process these cases at the rate they were lodged, leading to the build-up of a backlog of cases. Court presidents, High Contracting Parties, and academic commentators have debated this unsustainable situation since the 1990s.[2] By the year 2000, at the 50th anniversary of the signing of the European Convention on Human Rights (ECHR), the backlog had reached 15,000

1 The ECtHR's budget for 2019 was just under 70m euro, whereas the ECJ had a 2018 budget of 410m euro. The ECtHR has 47 judges whereas the ECJ has 75 judges and 11 advocates general. (Court of Justice of the European Union: Annual Report 2018: The year in Review).

2 Court President Ryssdal warned of this in his Speech 'The Coming of Age of the European Convention on Human Rights' (1996) 1, *European Human Rights Law Review*, 18; while several judicial and political actors have warned it at various meetings in the Council of Europe. Available in: Council of Europe, *Reforming the European Convention on Human Rights: A work in progress* (2009), p. 147: Michael McKenzie of the Royal Courts of Justice, England in Warsaw 2006, on page 187: Jan Sobczak, Director General of Human Rights in Belgrade 2007, on page 245: Marie-Louise Bemelmans-Videc, Member of the Parliamentary Assembly in San Marino 2007, on page 468: Terry Davis, Secretary General of the Council of Europe in Stockholm 2008.

cases.[3] A decade later that number passed the 100,000 cases mark,[4] and cases now took so long to pass through the system, that the Court would likely have been in violation of article 6, had it been a State. This was a serious concern, as the Court's legitimacy depends on its ability to provide judgments on practical and effective human rights. At the time individual applicants often had to wait a decade or more to receive closure on whether their rights had been violated. This was particularly problematic for cases where time was sensitive, including cases on the right to family life where children were involved, and cases concerning deprivation of liberty or *non-refoulement.*

The high caseload of the ECtHR was originally one of the many markers of the triumph of the Convention System. In Slaughter and Helfer's model of effective supra-national adjudication, the ECtHR is held up as an example of a success, not least because its high output of judgments and decisions had enabled it to construct a comprehensive and coherent body of case law from which principles of interpretation could be both applied and exported to other courts.[5] The high caseload supposedly showed that the Court was well-known by potential applicants in its jurisdiction, and its judgments were considered fair by both applicants (who otherwise, presumably, would have not applied to it) and Member States (who otherwise, presumably, would not continue to expand its jurisdiction).

Throughout its 60 active years, the ECtHR has also been undergoing almost continuous reform. Protocols have been negotiated to improve applicants' access to the Court (Protocols 9 and 11),[6] to increase the capacity of the Convention System (Protocols 3, 8, 11, 14),[7] to include more

3 *Ibid.*, 11: Walter Schwimmer, Secretary General of the Council of Europe pointed to this in his speech in Rome 2000.

4 Department for the Execution of Judgments of the European Court of Human Rights 2017. Pending cases: Overview 1998 – 2017, Strasbourg.

5 Helfer and Slaughter, 'Toward a Theory of Effective Supranational Adjudication' (1997) *Yale Law Journal*, 2.

6 The *Convention for the Protection of Human Rights and Fundamental Freedoms.* (2019[1950]).

7 The European Court of Human Rights was up until the coming into effect of protocol 11 in 1998 one of two institutions that undertook analysing and reporting/adjudicating on human rights applications. (interested readers can learn more on this in: Myjer, *The conscience of Europe: 50 years of the European Court of Human Rights* (2010), the Committee of Ministers also played an important role in adjudication in the first three decades of the Convention's existence. Even today, the Committee of Ministers undertakes important tasks in relation to the execution of judgments. In this article the term 'Convention System' is used when referring to not only the Court but all the branches of Convention adjudication,

fundamental rights and abolish the death penalty (Protocols 1, 4, 6, 7, 13), and to ensure the independence of the judges and functioning of the Convention System (Protocols 2, 5, 10, 11). The most recent reform, the Interlaken process which took place between 2010 and 2020, thus dealt with a problem the Convention system had faced before, namely an insufficient capacity to deliver judgments as fast as applications came in. Unlike previous reforms however, this one took place in a period where the public discourse in Europe was unfavourable to the idea of international adjudication. This makes the Interlaken process a particularly interesting lens for studying the perception of the legitimacy of the ECtHR in a changing political landscape, and since the reform has only just been concluded at the end of 2020, such a study is particularly appropriate to take on at this time.

This chapter will take on this task by providing an overview of this recently concluded reform and provide an analysis of how it was impacted by the changing political climate. Throughout the reform, the Steering Committee for Human Rights (CDDH) issued two central reports in 2015 and 2019,[8] and the Parliamentary Assembly for the Council of Europe (PACE) held regular meetings on the themes of the reform,[9] but by far the most well-known output of the reform is the five Declarations from the High-Level Conferences undertaken by the Chairmanships of the Committee of Ministers in Interlaken (Switzerland) in 2010, Izmir (Turkey) in 2011, Brighton (United Kingdom) in 2012, Brussels (Belgium) in 2015, and Copenhagen (Denmark) in 2018. These Declarations are intriguing when studying the interplay between the political and the judicial branches of the Convention System, since they represent an official mouthpiece of the Member States and therefore an opportunity to assess their views of the Court in a structured manner. International declarations of this kind are the result of a compromise between the 47 Member States and are thus often very polished documents. For two of these Declarations

including the Committee of Ministers, The Commission of Human rights (where applicable), The Court, and the Member States, as each have important tasks to take on to make the rights in the Convention effective.

8 *Contribution of the CDDH to the evaluation provided for by the Interlaken Declaration adopted by the CDDH at its 92nd meeting* (26–29 November 2019), R92Addendum2; *The longer-term future of the system of the European Convention on Human Rights* (2015). The Steering Committee for Human Rights (CDDH), CDDH(2015)R84 Addendum I.

9 A wide range of documents are available at semantic-pace.net, the most relevant ones to this chapter will be referenced separately.

however, early drafts are available for study. A draft of the Brighton Declaration from 2012 was leaked,[10] and in the case of the Copenhagen Declaration from 2018, it was deliberately made public.[11] Both drafts were controversial,[12] but to outside observers, the Copenhagen Draft was the more surprising one. While the United Kingdom had expressed critical views of the interpretation tradition of the ECtHR in the past, notably as a third-party intervener in central cases[13] and through non-compliance,[14] Denmark was an infrequent respondent and intervening state and historically one of the first to accept the Court's jurisdiction. It also had a record of winning most of its cases and promptly implementing any judgments finding violations.[15] The confrontational tenor of the Copenhagen Draft, which had not even been attempted kept confidential, was therefore unsuspected. For these reasons, and because the Copenhagen Declaration was the last Declaration in the Interlaken reform, this chapter will zoom in on the Danish context and the changes that took place from Draft to final Declaration in 2018. The reasoning for doing this is thus both general and specific. On the one hand we might assume that each of the Declarations have gone through a process similar to the Copenhagen Declaration's journey from a Draft written by national authorities coloured by national priorities, to an international Declaration adopted by 47 Member States

10 *Draft Brighton Declaration.* (23 February 2012). The Guardian originally posted the leaked draft, but it is no-longer available there. At the time of writing the 2012 draft can be accessed here: https://www.documentcloud.org/documents/321624-draft-brighton-declaration-on-echr-reform.html.

11 *Draft Copenhagen Declaration* (5 February 2018). Available here: https://menneskeret.dk/sites/menneskeret.dk/files/media/dokumenter/nyheder/draft_copenhagen_declaration_05.02.18.pdf.

12 Føllesdal and Ulfstein, 'The Draft Copenhagen Declaration: Whose Responsibility and Dialogue?' (2018). EJIL:Talk!, https://www.ejiltalk.org/the-draft-copenhagen-declaration-whose-responsibility-and-dialogue/ February 22nd 2018; Donald and Leach, 'A wolf in sheep's clothing: why the draft copenhagen declaration must be rewritten' (2018) EJIL: Talk! https://www.ejiltalk.org/a-wolf-in-sheeps-clothing-why-the-draft-copenhagen-declaration-must-be-rewritten/ February 21st 2018; Ulfstein and Føllesdal, 'Copenhagen – much ado about little?' (2018), EJIL: Talk! https://www.ejiltalk.org/copenhagen-much-ado-about-little/ April 14th 2018; Bates, 'Who should have the final word on human rights?' (2012). UK Human Rights Blog https://ukhumanrightsblog.com/2012/03/06/who-should-have-the-final-word-on-human-rights-dr-ed-bates/ March 6th 2012.

13 See e.g., ECtHR, Judgment (GC), 22 May 2012, *Scoppola v Italy (no. 3)*, Application No. 126/05.

14 See e.g., ECtHR, Judgment (GC), 6 October 2005, *Hirst v The United Kingdom (No. 2)*, Application No. 74025/01.

15 Hartmann, *Danmark og Den Europæiske Menneskerettighedskonvention* (2017), 37.

reflecting common priorities. The choice of the Copenhagen Declaration is also partly due to its process having been relatively transparent. The transparency makes it possible to study it in a way it has not been possible with earlier Declarations. At the same time, the political context in Denmark including the confrontational discourse on the ECtHR, which is visible in the Copenhagen Draft cannot be assumed to be replicated in most CoE Member States for the simple reason that the negotiated final Copenhagen Declaration does not reflect it to the same degree.

The remainder of this chapter will proceed in the following manner. First the reform history of the ECHR will be addressed briefly along with the goals of the Interlaken process and the methods suggested by key actors to achieve those goals (B). Then we explore the progress in the Interlaken reform up until the Danish Chairmanship took up the mantle in 2017–2018 (C). This will be followed by a section on the content of the Copenhagen Draft and the final Copenhagen Declaration (D), determining how this crucial last Declaration suggested solving the problems laid out in section B. Finally, the concluding remarks (E) will assess to what extent the issues that led to the initiation of the Interlaken process have been addressed. This section will also provide a bit of Danish political context to answer the question asked by the PACE in the aftermath of the Danish Chairmanship on how '*a founding member of the Council of Europe saw fit to submit a Draft Declaration that would have put in question some of the fundamental principles on which the Convention system depends*'?[16]

B. The Interlaken Reform: The Latest Chapter in a History of Reforms

The Convention System has been under continuous development since the Convention was first opened for signatures in 1950. It has grown geographically from 14 signatory states to 47, materially, with additional protocols including more rights, and its system of adjudication has changed. The ECHR was the first treaty of its kind that aimed to create a supranational jurisdiction with binding force on human rights within the borders of the state.[17] Initially, the Member States which negotiated the Convention were reluctant to give the Court jurisdiction.[18] In the 1950s,

16 Parliamentary Assembly of the Council of Europe (PACE), *Copenhagen Declaration, appreciation and follow-up*, 24 April 2018, Doc. 14539, para. 5.

17 *Travaux Préparatoires vol I.* 1975, 30.

18 Evidenced by the fact that there were not initially enough article 46 declarations to create the Court.

it was thus only the Commission on Human Rights that could hear cases from the Member states. The Commission was not a judicial body but rather a body of experts with the power to investigate and report to the Committee of Ministers. Even the Commission could initially only hear inter-state cases[19] unless the State in question had agreed to individual application explicitly (so-called Article 25 declarations). The Court only came into existence in 1959, when 8 of the original 14 signatories had delivered declarations that they would submit to the jurisdiction of the Court (so-called Article 46 declarations). In the first cases before the Court, even those launched by individuals, individual applicants could not be parties. The case went instead through the Commission, which reported to the Committee of Ministers, which could then choose to bring the case as a party before the Court. This changed gradually through the 1980s and 1990s through first the Rules of the Court and then later the optional protocol 9 in 1990 and finally protocol 11 in 1998. Protocol 11 made major changes to the Convention System: the Commission was abolished, and the Committee of Ministers no longer took on the role as party for the applicant, though it retained an important role in ensuring the execution of judgments, the jurisdiction of the Court was made mandatory, and the Court started operating full time.

Protocol 11 had been necessary because the Council of Europe (CoE) was growing. The fall of the Iron Curtain had opened the door for applications form former communist countries, and the CoE had included them as Member States and signatories to the ECHR. This meant both that the sheer amount of people under the jurisdiction of the Court was growing, and furthermore, many of the new member states were still undergoing transitions to democracy with many of the rights in the Convention still unsettled. The numbers of applications were therefore rising, and a full-time Court was needed to deal with them. Protocol 11 was, however, delayed, and by the time it came into effect, the influx of cases had already increased beyond the additional capacity it provided.[20] While major changes, as those brought on by Protocol 11, can happen only through official political intervention from the Member States, smaller changes can be made by the internal bodies in the Council of Europe. As a response, the approach by the Court in the early 2000s was two-pronged. On the one

---

19 Cases where the applicant is a state rather than an individual. More on this period in Bates, *The evolution of the European Convention on Human Rights: from its inception to the creation of a permanent court of human rights* (2010), Chapter 6.

20 Myjer, *The conscience of Europe: 50 years of the European Court of Human Rights* (2010), 55.

hand, negotiations started for protocol 14[21], while on the other, the Court explored ways it could speed up filtering and adjudication without changes to the Convention.[22] This resulted for example in the pilot judgement procedure (Rule 61 of the Rules of Court), and the priority policy (Rules 39 and 41 of the Rules of Court). The two methods also worked in tandem in that protocol 14 both changed the Court directly by allowing single judge formations for cases on admissibility, and it moved certain decisions down a constitutional level to leave more to the Rules of the Court, which are adopted by the Plenary Court (Art. 25(d) ECHR). For example, the Court could after protocol 14 temporarily influence the number of judges that sit in a chamber in cooperation with the Committee of Ministers (Art. 26(2) ECHR) and allow registry employees to function as rapporteurs in single judge formations (Art. 24 ECHR). Protocol 14 was opened for signatures in 2004 but only came into effect in 2010, and like the situation in 1998, this delay meant that by the time it came into force, the backlog had grown so much that the rationalisations it offered were not going to be sufficient to deal with the problem.[23] This time however, the delay had been political. Russia had held back on ratifying protocol 14 to put pressure on the Court for what the Duma perceived as anti-Russian discrimination after losing a large number of high-profile cases on pre-trial detention.[24] While the protocol 14 situation was solved with the Madrid Agreement, which created protocol 14bis to enact the key provisions in protocol 14 on an optional basis, which removed Russia's power to withhold ratification, this political pressure within the reform process was a premonition of the forthcoming Interlaken process.

At the event of the 60th anniversary of the Convention, Jean-Paul Costa, the President of the Court at the time, asked the Member States to take

---

21 Protocols 12 and 13 had dealt respectively with non-discrimination and the abolishment of the death-penalty rather than institutional reform.

22 The 2005 report by Lord Woolf explicitly had this purpose: Woolf, 'Review of the Working Methods of the European Court of Human Rights' (2005) *European Court of Human Rights*.

23 CoE, *Report of the Evaluation Group to the Committee of Ministers on the European Court of Human Rights*, 27 September 2001, EG Court (2001)1, 6; CoE, *European Ministerial Conference on Human Rights and Commemorative Ceremony of the 50th anniversary of the European Convention on Human Rights*. Rome, 3–4 November 2000 (2002), 27 ff.

24 For example ECtHR, Judgment, 22 December 2008, *Aleksanyan v Russia*, Application No. 46468/06. See more on this in: Bowring, 'The Russian Federation, Protocol No. 14 (and 14bis), and the Battle for the Soul of the ECHR' (2010) *Goettingen Journal of International Law*, 2(2), 605.

on the task of reforming the Court yet another time. As with protocol 14, his memorandum suggested both direct changes to the Convention and suggested moving certain decisions down a constitutional level to let the Court decide in the future in case it yet again found itself in a situation where its current working methods were insufficient to deal with the incoming cases.[25] The Interlaken process was first and foremost about solving the problem of the backlog and the unsustainable workload,[26] but the suggestions in Costa's memorandum on how to deal with this engaged with a range of other themes that caught the eye of certain Member States. In addition to requesting a larger budget to deal with the larger caseload,[27] and suggesting a case-filtering mechanism to deal with the large number of inadmissible cases,[28] Costa made a wide-reaching suggestion to have the Member States take more ownership of the application of the Convention. He suggested making the Court's judgments binding not just on the parties to the case but for all Member States and allowing citizens to invoke the Convention directly before domestic courts, which would then in turn adjudicate on the basis of the Convention and the interpretations of the ECtHR. This would improve human rights protection, stop individuals from having to take their case all the way to Strasbourg, reduce the caseload on the ECtHR, and 'make it easier for the Court to maintain an appropriate distance from national proceedings in full compliance with the principle of subsidiarity.'[29] The idea of increasing the application of the principle of subsidiarity, by incorporating to a greater degree the national level in the responsibility to provide remedy for human rights interferences, was thus part of the reform programme in the Interlaken reform from the very beginning.

C. *Progress in the Interlaken Process up until Copenhagen*

When the Member States met in Interlaken, however, their initial conclusions were less dramatic than Costa's suggestions, although they did deal with the same themes. The Interlaken Declaration included an action plan with tasks for both the Member States and the Court, including streamlin-

25 Costa, *Memorandum of the President of the European Court of Human Rights to the States with a view to preparing the Interlaken Conference* (2009), para. 4.
26 *Ibid.* para. 1.
27 *Ibid.* para. 3.
28 *Ibid.* Ch 3(a).
29 *Ibid.* Ch B.2(1 and 2).

ing of the pilot judgment procedure that promised to lower the caseload by bundling cases together that deal with the same structural problem. The action plan also prescribed that the Committee of Ministers should determine before the end of 2019 whether the reforms were sufficient to make the Court's workload sustainable or if more profound changes were needed.[30] The Izmir Declaration largely followed up on the Interlaken Declaration with a few additions. There was an early mention of the option of an advisory mechanism (later Protocol 16), the issue of interim decisions was addressed, and there was a statement that the Court should not become a fourth instance court or immigration appeals tribunal – a theme that was to become much more potent later on.[31] By 2012, when the Brighton Declaration was adopted, the improved productivity of the Court made possible by Protocol 14 as well as the internal reforms and rule changes had already resulted in a decrease of the backlog. By the time the Copenhagen Declaration was adopted, the backlog was less than half the size it was in the worst year, 2011, although the number of cases pending before a judicial formation was still a worryingly high 56,350.

Figure 1.[32]

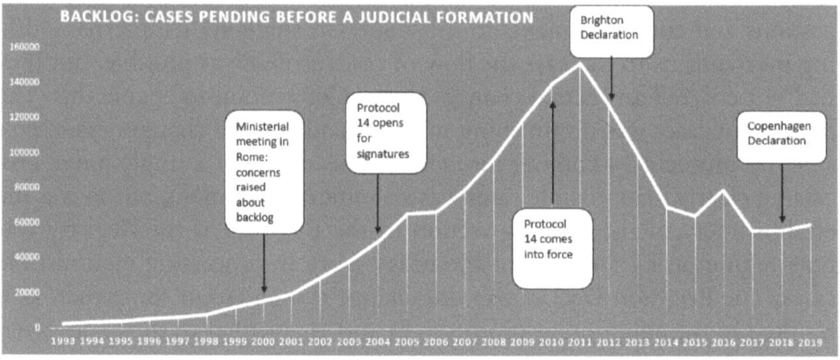

30 CoE, *High Level Conference on the Future of the European Court of Human Rights*, Interlaken Declaration, 19 February 2010, 6.

31 CoE, *High Level Conference on the Future of the European Court of Human Rights organised within the framework of the Turkish Chairmanship of the Committee of Ministers of the Council of Europe*. Izmir Declaration, Turkey 26 – 27 April 2011, para A(3).

32 This figure was created by gathering data on the backlog of cases from the yearly statistics reports of the Court from 1993–2019. For example: Rights, *Analysis of statistics 2018*, (2019).

In terms of themes, the Brighton Declaration built to some extent on the two previous Declarations, but it also contained new elements including an unprecedented critique of the judges and judgments of the Court and more detailed suggestions for how the Court should apply the principle of subsidiarity. The final Declaration's treatment of subsidiarity and the margin of appreciation is not so different from the formulations in the Court's own caselaw and was significantly toned down in comparison to the Brighton Draft.[33]

After Brighton, there was the Brussels Declaration that, in addition to repeating concerns from previous Declarations, focused on implementation at the national level. Both the Brighton and the Brussels Declarations thus had a subsidiarity focus, but where the Brighton Declaration, especially in the Brighton Draft, focused more on a 'room of manoeuvre' understanding, the Brussels Declaration and the 2015 CDDH report on the longer-term future of the Court had a stronger focus on the responsibility of States that subsidiarity entails.[34] Neither had taken up President Costa's suggestion to bring the Member States directly into the Convention adjudication system by making caselaw binding on all Member States and adjudicating more human rights cases at the national level.

By 2012, the Member States had mainly used Declarations to make suggestions and encouragements to the Court on changing its internal working mechanisms to increase the flow of cases as much as possible, but they had not enacted any actual changes to the Convention to enable this. The backlog of cases was diminishing mainly thanks to the changes made possible by protocol 14 coming into effect. The ability of a single judge processing clearly inadmissible cases was an important element, but so was the establishment of the filtering section in the Registry, as the Registry was now taking on by far most of the heavy work in processing inadmissible cases. The Brighton Declaration did change this situation somewhat, as it resulted in the adoption of protocols 15 and 16. Neither of these, however,

33 CoE, *High Level Conference on the Future of the European Court of Human Rights*, Brighton Declaration, 20 April 2012, para. 11; Glas, 'From Interlaken to Copenhagen: What Has Become of the Proposals Aiming to Reform the Functioning of the European Court of Human Rights?' (2020) 20(1) *Human Rights Law Review*, 121.

34 Kuijer, 'Margin of Appreciation Doctrine and the Strengthening of the Principle of Subsidiarity in the Recent Reform Negotiations' (2016) 36 *Human Rights Law Journal*, 339; CoE Steering Committee for Human Rights (CDDH), *The longer-term future of the system of the European Convention on Human Rights*, 11 December 2015, CDDH(2015)R84 Addendum I.

dealt directly with the problem the reform had set out to solve, namely the backlog, instead protocol 16 was to allow the Court to receive requests from high national courts for advisory opinions, while protocol 15 included a provision to shorten the deadline for making applications to the Court from six to four months and amend the preamble of the Convention to include reference to the subsidiarity-based interpretive principle of the Margin of Appreciation.[35] Both protocols could be construed to reduce the caseload indirectly. The explanatory report for protocol 15, however, mentions the acceleration of proceedings only in connection with relinquishing jurisdiction to the Grand Chamber.[36] The reduction of the time-limit for submitting applications and the removal of the exceptions for declaring cases inadmissible where the applicant has suffered 'no significant disadvantage' (Art. 35(b) ECHR) could both arguably reduce the number of incoming applications or make more cases rejectable at the administrative stage,[37] but this is not envisioned in the explanatory report. Similarly, the explanatory report to protocol 16 surprisingly does not mention the backlog or the workload of the Court at all. It argues, like the Izmir Declaration, that advisory opinions could help clarify provisions and case law, thus assisting States Parties in avoiding future violations.[38] On the other hand, the Copenhagen Declaration envisions that the coming into force of protocol 16 will add to the workload of the court.[39] Neither

35 *Protocol No. 15 amending the Convention on the Protection of Human Rights and Fundamental Freedoms.* (24.VI.2013); *Protocol No. 16 amending the Convention on the Protection of Human Rights and Fundamental Freedoms.* (2.X.2013).

36 CoE, *Explanatory Report to Protocol No. 15 amending the Convention for the Protection of Human Rights and Fundamental Freedoms*, 24 June 2013, Council of Europe Treaty Series No. 213.

37 Several commentators have assumed this for good or ill, e.g. Madsen, 'Rebalancing European Human Rights: Has the Brighton Declaration Engendered a New Deal on Human Rights in Europe?' (2017) 9(2) *Journal of International Dispute Settlement*, 199 (201); Amnesty International et al., *Joint NGO response to Protocol 15 to the European Convention on Human Rights must not result in a weakening of human rights protection*, 24 June 2013, https://www.justiceinitiative.org/uploads/f4e441ba-07dc-4061-b113-049ccf470ac5/echr-protocol15-joint-statement-06272013.pdf; Arnardóttir, 'Organised Retreat? The Move from 'Substantive' to 'Procedural' Review in the ECtHR's Case Law on the Margin of Appreciation' (2015) 5(4) *ESIL Conference Paper Series*, 1.

38 CoE, *Explanatory Report to Protocol No. 16 to the Convention for the Protection of Human Rights and Fundamental Freedoms*, 2 October 2013, Council of Europe Treaty Series No. 214.

39 CoE, Copenhagen Declaration, 13 April 2018, https://rm.coe.int/copenhagen-declaration/16807b915c, para. 46.

protocols 15 nor 16 had yet come into force by the time Denmark took over the Chairmanship of the Committee of Ministers. Protocol 16 required at least 10 ratifications while protocol 15 required all Members to ratify before it could come into effect. Protocol 16 came into effect in August 2018 shortly after the Copenhagen High-Level Conference, while protocol 15 came into force in August 2021.

D. The Copenhagen Declaration

When Denmark took over the Chairmanship there had thus been four Declarations and two amending protocols had been negotiated and were open for signature, but the overarching problem of the backlog and the unsustainably high caseload had not been solved. Furthermore, the remaining backlog consisted of more complex cases, many of them potentially well-founded and pending before a Chamber or the Grand Chamber.

Figure 2.[40]

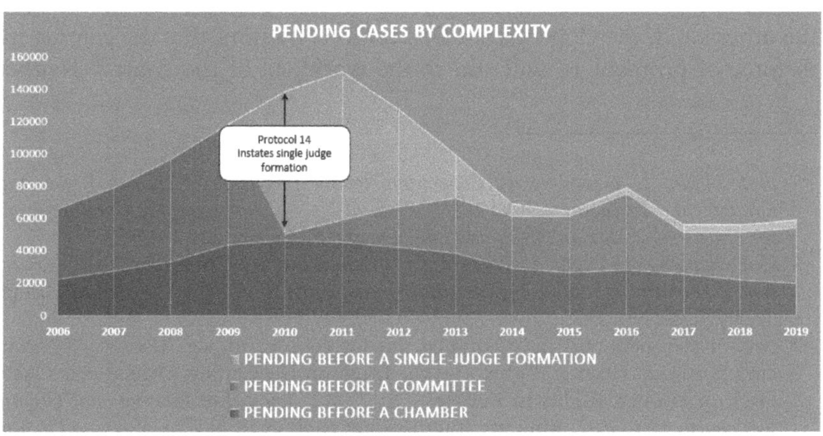

Furthermore, the 2019 deadline set in the Interlaken Declaration was approaching and the Committee of Ministers had to determine whether the existing rationalisations were sufficient or if more profound reforms were

40 Figure created using data on the yearly backlog from ECtHR statistics 2009 through 2019, including *Statistics on pending cases and executions, Overview 1998–2017* (2017).

needed to ensure the future of the Court. In terms of addressing the issues that had initiated the Interlaken process, there was thus plenty of work still to do and little time to do it.

Instead of restructuring the Court or increasing its budget, the Member States had spent a lot of energy in the negotiations of the Declarations to debate the meaning of the principle of subsidiarity and how it should be applied in the Convention system. Two distinct but connected conceptualisations had been reached in the Brighton and Brussels Declarations. Brighton's definition conceptualised subsidiarity mainly through the better-placed argument, and the Brighton Draft had even conceptualised it as a right for States, pointing to the notion of democratic mandate.[41] Meanwhile, the Brussels Declaration had focused on national implementation and conceptualised subsidiarity mainly as a duty for States to ensure the rights within their jurisdictions and to provide a remedy and adjudication if such securing of rights failed.[42] The Danish Chairmanship appeared to be more convinced by the Brighton understanding of subsidiarity as the Brighton Declaration is referenced four times as often as the Brussels Declaration in the parliamentary debates and press clippings provided as background material for the Danish parliament by the inter-ministry taskforce for the Chairmanship.[43]

The Copenhagen Draft which the Danish Chairmanship presented in February 2018 was, generally speaking, a continuation of the previous reform programme. It included many of the elements present in the Declarations before it. In addition to reaffirmations of the States Parties' commitment to the Convention, the right to individual application, and the reform process (paras. 1 ff.),[44] the Copenhagen Draft dealt with the concept

---

41 Committee of Ministers. 2012. Brighton Declaration. Brighton. Para B(11). And British Chairmanship of the Council of Europe 2012. February 23rd 2012. Draft Brighton Declaration. United Kingdom, para. 17.

42 Kuijer see note 30: 339; Donald and Leach, 'A Wolf in Sheep's Clothing: Why the Draft Copenhagen Declaration Must be Rewritten', EJIL:Talk!, 21 February 2018, https://www.ejiltalk.org/a-wolf-in-sheeps-clothing-why-the-draft-copenhagen-declaration-must-be-rewritten/.

43 Taskforce Ministry of Justice and Ministry of Foreign Affairs, *Presseklip (Background information to the Parliamentary group on Council of Europe)* (25 October 2017).

44 See also CoE, Interlaken Declaration, 19 February 2010, 1; Izmir Declaration, 1; CoE, Brighton Declaration, 20 April 2012, paras. 1 ff.; CDDH, Brussels Declaration adopted at the High-level Conference on the "Implementation of the European Convention on Human Rights, our shared responsibility" (Brussels, Belgium, 26–27 March 2015), 10 April 2015, CDDH(2015)004, 2 f.

of subsidiarity and shared responsibility (paras. 5 ff. and 22 ff.);[45] national implementation and execution of judgments (paras. 16 ff.), including the pilot judgment procedure (paras. 43, 50, 70 ff.) and the establishment and role of National Human Rights Institutions(NHRIs) (paras. 18, 21);[46] dialogue between domestic authorities and the Court (paras. 31 ff.),[47] the caseload, including the budget (paras. 43 ff.);[48] clarity and consistency of the Court's interpretation (paras. 55 ff.);[49] the selection and election of judges of the highest quality (paras. 62 ff.);[50] and finally, the accession of the EU to the Convention (para. 79).[51]

The Copenhagen Draft, however, also contained highly contentious statements on treaty interpretation, subsidiarity, and dialogue, which went on to be commented critically in the Joint NGO Response and in responses from the PACE and the Court itself. Both the PACE and the Court itself issued responses to the Copenhagen Draft, but neither gave suggestions on specific changes to the wording. The Court was more soft-spoken than the PACE, as was also pointed out by defenders of the Draft.[52] The Court still, however, in its diplomatic way, pointed out several problems with the Draft. Initially, in its introductory remarks, the Court reiterated the

45 See also CoE, Interlaken Declaration, 19 February 2010, 1 f.; Izmir Declaration, 1 f.; CoE, Brighton Declaration, 20 April 2012, paras. 3, 10 ff., 33; CDDH, Brussels Declaration, 10 April 2015, CDDH(2015)004, 2 ff.

46 See also CoE, Interlaken Declaration, 19 February 2010, 2 f., 5 f.; Izmir Declaration, 1, 3 f., 6; Brighton Declaration, 20 April 2012, paras. 7 ff., 26 ff.; CDDH, Brussels Declaration, 10 April 2015, CDDH(2015)004, 4, 6 ff.

47 See also Izmir Declaration, 5; CoE, Brighton Declaration, 20 April 2012, paras. 12(c) ff., 20(g) ff.; DDH, Brussels Declaration, 10 April 2015, CDDH(2015)004, 4 f., 7 f.

48 See also CoE, Interlaken Declaration, 19 February 2010,, 1 ff.; Izmir Declaration, 1 ff.; CoE, Brighton Declaration, 20 April 2012, paras. 5, 13 ff., 16 ff.; CDDH, Brussels Declaration, 10 April 2015, CDDH(2015)004, 2 f., 5.

49 See also CoE, Interlaken Declaration, 19 February 2010, 2; Izmir Declaration, 2; CoE, Brighton Declaration, 20 April 2012, paras. 25(c) ff.; CDDH, Brussels Declaration, 10 April 2015, CDDH(2015)004, 2 f., 5.

50 See also CoE, Interlaken Declaration, 19 February 2010, 2, 5; Izmir Declaration, 2; CoE, Brighton Declaration, 20 April 2012, paras. 21 f., 25; CDDH, Brussels Declaration, 10 April 2015, CDDH(2015)004, 2 f., 4.

51 See also CoE, Interlaken Declaration, 19 February 2010, 1; Izmir Declaration, 1, 6; CoE, Brighton Declaration, 20 April 2012, para. 36; CDDH, Brussels Declaration, 10 April 2015, CDDH(2015)004, 4.

52 Madsen and Christoffersen, 'The European Court of Human Rights' View of the Draft Copenhagen Declaration', EJIL:Talk!, 23 February 2018, https://www.ejiltalk.org/the-european-court-of-human-rights-view-of-the-draft-copenhagen-declaration/.

division of power and responsibilities in the Convention system and the importance of judicial independence.[53] This speaks to the general tenor and tendency in the Copenhagen Draft to understand subsidiarity as a right for states and diminish the importance of judicial independence.

In relation to the topic of subsidiarity, the Court was concerned by the Copenhagen Draft's mention of 'national circumstances' and 'constitutional traditions' as something that should influence interpretation.[54] The PACE clarified this in stronger language, arguing that '[t]hrough repeatedly highlighting one aspect of subsidiarity, the Draft Declaration gives the impression that the Court's role should be essentially deferential, or even subordinate to that of national authorities'.[55] Another way the Court subtly suggested a change of discourse on subsidiarity was in reference to paras. 22 ff., where the Copenhagen Draft made a series of statements on what the margin of appreciation is and how it ought to be applied. Here, the Court simply stated that it assumed that these statements attempted to derive a general position from the case law, and if that were the case, the Copenhagen Draft should have included as well the provisions involved, the exact nature of the facts, complaints and the procedural background. Furthermore, the Court retained the power to give the final ruling.[56] Discursively, this is less direct than the joint response from human rights non-governmental organisations, which stated that *'it is not for a political Declaration to seek to determine what and how judicial tools of interpretation, such as the margin of appreciation, [are applied]'*.[57] Substantively, however, the point is the same.

Both the Court and the PACE, as well as the NGOs and academics, rejected the Copenhagen Draft's attempts at gaining the right to define the margin of appreciation, and attempts at expanding the concept of subsidiarity at the Court's expense. In terms of changes, the final Copenhagen

---

53 ECtHR, Opinion on the draft Copenhagen Declaration. Adopted by the Bureau in light of the discussion in the Plenary Court on 19 February 2018, 2018, https://www.echr.coe.int/documents/opinion_draft_declaration_copenhague%20eng.pdf , para. 4.

54 ECtHR, Opinion on the draft Copenhagen Declaration, 2018, https://www.echr.coe.int/documents/opinion_draft_declaration_copenhague%20eng.pdf, paras. 9 f.

55 PACE, *Declaration on the Draft Copenhagen Declaration on the European Human Rights system in the future Europe*, 16 March 2018, AS/Per (2018) 03, para. 5.

56 ECtHR, Opinion on the draft Copenhagen Declaration, 2018, https://www.echr.coe.int/documents/opinion_draft_declaration_copenhague%20eng.pdf, para. 13.

57 Amnesty International et al., *Joint NGO Response to the Draft Copenhagen Declaration*, 13 February 2018, https://www.amnesty.eu/news/joint-ngo-response-to-the-draft-copenhagen-declaration/, 6.

Declaration retained several paragraphs on subsidiarity and the margin of appreciation, with central parts removed and key elements added. Discursively, the final Copenhagen Declaration refers to the Court's caselaw in its argumentation on the margin of appreciation rather than issuing declarative statements itself, and uses terms like 'recalling', 'reiterating', and 'welcoming' about the Court's interpretative practice, rather than 'encouraging' or 'inviting'.[58] In terms of substantive changes, a reference to the two characteristics of subsidiarity prevalent in the Brighton and Brussels Declarations was added to para. 7, and the clause 'Reiterates that strengthening the principle of subsidiarity is not intended to limit or weaken human rights protection' was added to para. 10. Furthermore, any reference singling out the field of asylum and immigration as an area where the Court should 'avoid intervening except in the most exceptional circumstances'[59] was removed. This is strong evidence that the tenor of the Declaration had softened, especially considering that the final Izmir Declaration did contain a reference to the Court not being an immigration appeals tribunal, though with a softer wording more in line with the case law than the Copenhagen Draft originally sported.[60] The contentious subsection on the need for clarity and consistency in the interpretation of the Convention was also reduced and written into the subsection on subsidiarity. The Court itself pointed out that there is no formal doctrine of precedent, while the PACE opinion more directly warned that the Copenhagen Draft's reference to national considerations could harm the universality of human rights, and the joint NGO responses directly suggested deleting the paragraphs instructing the Court how to interpret.[61]

---

58 Committee of Ministers. 2018. Copenhagen Declaration. Denmark, paras. 9–10, 29–32, 37, 47–48, 58; Danish Ministry of Justice, 5 February 2018, Draft Copenhagen Declaration Denmark, paras. 11–15, 28, 30, 38–39, 48–49, 60–61.

59 Draft Copenhagen Declaration, 5 February 2018, https://menneskeret.dk/sites/menneskeret.dk/files/media/dokumenter/nyheder/draft_copenhagen_declaration_05.02.18.pdf, paras. 25 f.

60 Izmir Declaration, 3.

61 Draft Copenhagen Declaration, 5 February 2018, https://menneskeret.dk/sites/menneskeret.dk/files/media/dokumenter/nyheder/draft_copenhagen_declaration_05.02.18.pdf, paras. 55 ff.; ECtHR, Opinion on the draft Copenhagen Declaration, 2018, https://www.echr.coe.int/documents/opinion_draft_declaration_copenhague%20eng.pdf, paras. 27 f.; PACE, Declaration on the Draft Copenhagen Declaration, 16 March 2018, AS/Per (2018) 03, paras. 3 f.; Amnesty International et al., *Joint NGO Response to the Draft Copenhagen Declaration*, 13 February 2018, https://www.amnesty.eu/news/joint-ngo-response-to-the-draft-copenhagen-declaration/, 10 f.

On the topic of dialogue between Member States and the Court, the Copenhagen Draft suggested that the case law of the Court has significant impact on domestic policy questions, wherefore the Court should engage in 'increased dialogue on the general development of case law in important areas' (paras. 32 f.) in a series of informal meetings (para. 42). These paragraphs were widely criticised.[62] The Court itself pointed out that while it is already engaged in judicial dialogue through its Superior Courts Network,[63] the appropriate forum for dialogue with governments on case law was through third-party interventions.[64] On the topic of an ongoing political dialogue among Member States, the Court pointed out that it would neither comment nor become involved in it because of its judicial independence.[65] In the final Declaration, these concerns were taken into account, and the only substantive suggestions that remained were for the Court to adapt its procedures to make it possible for other Member States to indicate their support for the referral of a Chamber case to the Grand Chamber.[66] In terms of the informal meetings for discussing case law developments, they were reduced to a single meeting following up on the Danish Chairmanship where jurisprudence could be discussed with full respect for the Court's independence and the binding nature of the judgments.[67]

Apart from the Copenhagen Draft's suggestion to create a separate mechanism for inter-state cases or cases concerning international conflict,[68] the Court did not have any particularly critical remarks concerning the Drafts' suggestions for dealing with the caseload. It did point out, however, that it had already had success with implementing a system for

62 Føllesdal and Ulfstein, 'The Draft Copenhagen Declaration: Whose Responsibility and Dialogue?', EJIL:Talk!, 22 February 2018, https://www.ejiltalk.org/the-draft-copenhagen-declaration-whose-responsibility-and-dialogue/; Amnesty International *et al.*, Joint NGO Response to the Draft Copenhagen Declaration, 13 February 2018, https://www.amnesty.eu/news/joint-ngo-response-to-the-draft-copenhagen-declaration/.

63 ECtHR, Opinion on the draft Copenhagen Declaration, 2018, https://www.echr.coe.int/documents/opinion_draft_declaration_copenhague%20eng.pdf, para. 15.

64 *Id.*, para. 16.

65 *Id.*, para. 18.

66 CoE, Copenhagen Declaration, 13 April 2018, para. 38.

67 CoE, Copenhagen Declaration, 13 April 2018, https://rm.coe.int/copenhagen-declaration/16807b915c,, para. 41.

68 ECtHR, Opinion on the draft Copenhagen Declaration, 2018, https://www.echr.coe.int/documents/opinion_draft_declaration_copenhague%20eng.pdf, para. 26, where it remarks that clarification of the idea is required before it can be properly analysed.

giving reasons for single judge decisions despite its workload, suggesting that the Copenhagen Draft made a mistake in assuming the Court to be at its maximum capacity.[69] Generally, the Joint NGO Response's concerns that the Copenhagen Draft advocated friendly settlements, unilateral declarations and dealing with the repetitive cases to 'avoid the need for the Court's adjudication', were addressed and the language in these paragraphs was changed. Para. 44 had previously argued that the Court had the capacity to deliver no more than two thousand cases per year,[70] referencing an analysis of an unknown source presented at the Expert Conference in Kokkedal,[71] – but was significantly toned down and made less concrete.[72] On the point of the budget, which in many ways is the only reliable evidence on whether there is political will to solve the problems of the caseload, the Court asked in its opinion on the Copenhagen Draft that it deliver a stronger message on allocating resources to deal with the backlog.[73] However, in this regard, there was no improvement in the final Declaration, which still only 'acknowledges the importance of retaining a sufficient budget' (para. 52).

E. Conclusion

The final Copenhagen Declaration in quantitative terms incorporated more than three out of every four substantive suggestions for changes from the Joint NGO Response, and qualitatively, the final Declaration strikes a much different tone than the Draft.[74] The PACE's follow-up report also

69 ECtHR, Opinion on the draft Copenhagen Declaration, 2018, https://www.echr.coe.int/documents/opinion_draft_declaration_copenhague%20eng.pdf, para. 19.

70 Draft Copenhagen Declaration, 5 February 2018, https://menneskeret.dk/sites/menneskeret.dk/files/media/dokumenter/nyheder/draft_copenhagen_declaration_05.02.18.pdf, para. 44. For this issue, see also Amnesty International *et al.*, Joint NGO Response to the Draft Copenhagen Declaration, 13 February 2018, https://www.amnesty.eu/news/joint-ngo-response-to-the-draft-copenhagen-declaration/, p. 9.

71 The Kokkedal Conference took place under Chatham House Rules.

72 CoE, Copenhagen Declaration, 13 April 2018, https://rm.coe.int/copenhagen-declaration/16807b915c, para. 44.

73 ECtHR, Opinion on the draft Copenhagen Declaration, 2018, https://www.echr.coe.int/documents/opinion_draft_declaration_copenhague%20eng.pdf, para. 23.

74 Molbæk-Steensig, 'Something Rotten in the State of Denmark?', Verfassungsblog, 26 April 2018, https://verfassungsblog.de/something-rotten-in-the-state-of-denma

argued that its concerns were largely addressed,[75] though it also expressed unease about the fact that a founding member had released a Draft challenging the universality of human rights and the independence of the Court.[76] Furthermore, the PACE addressed that the Declaration had failed to propose concrete solutions to the main challenge of the caseload or the non-implementation of judgments,[77] and that it still contained problematic notions on dialogue, even if 'boilerplate statements' on the Court's independence had been added.[78] At the PACE level, the narrative thus appears to be that while the Copenhagen Draft disaster was averted, the final Declaration had little concrete impact, and the Court was still lacking the support it needed from the Member States to solve the problem of receiving more cases than it could process with existing resources.

On the question of why the Danish Chairmanship would issue such a Draft – and openly – one has to look no further than the domestic political debate in the previous two decades. The far-right has been critical of all things European since the beginning of the 1990s, but in the 2000s there was a shift in the Danish debate in which the practice of criticising the Court became common place across the political spectrum.[79] While the change cannot be traced back to any one case, *Sørensen and Rasmussen v Denmark* from 2006 is often referenced by the Court's critics.[80] This case concerned the right to association and reached the conclusion that Article 11 necessarily included a right not to be a part of an association as well, which made the Danish system of exclusive agreements for labour unions a human rights violation. Danish politicians complained that this

---

rk/; Ulfstein and Føllesdal, 'Copenhagen – Much ado about little?', EJIL:Talk!, 14 April 2018, https://www.ejiltalk.org/copenhagen-much-ado-about-little/.

75 PACE, *Copenhagen Declaration, appreciation and follow-up*, 24 April 2018, Doc. 14539, para. 4.

76 *Id.*, para. 5.

77 *Id.*, para. 15.

78 *Id.*, para. 16.

79 As an example, the Taskforce's Presseklip show the debate in public newspapers whereas the Parliamentary debate: F 47 Om domstolsaktivismen ved Den Europæiske Menneskerettighedsdomstol. Denmark on. 18–06–2020 available here: https://www.ft.dk/samling/20191/forespoergsel/f47/index.htm is a good example of the political discourse.

80 Henriksen (2017), 'Demokratiet Undermineres'. *Nordjyske Stifttidende*. https://nordjyske.dk/plus/domstol-gaar-over-graensen/3f0cd5a0-05c0-4d39-9137-99bbeeb05512 and Bramsen, 'Den er gal med fortolkningen af menneskerettighederne', Netavisen Pio, 21 August 2017, https://piopio.dk/den-er-gal-med-fortolkningen-af-menneskerettighederne.; ECtHR, Judgment (GC), 11 January 2006, *Sørensen and Rasmussen v Denmark,* Application Nos. 52562/99 and 52620/99.

was directly contrary to what had been agreed during the preparations of the Convention. Furthermore, the case was unpopular among the unions and therefore also with the centre-left which had otherwise been the Court's champion. By the 2010s, immigration had become a particularly troublesome topic in Danish politics, and the Court was often criticised by the far-right as an institution keeping Denmark from expelling criminal foreigners. In the meantime, the far-right party, the Danish Peoples Party, had moved from the fringes to the centre of national politics as has occurred in many European countries. By 2017, when Denmark took over the Chairmanship, the Danish Peoples Party were part of the parliamentary majority supporting the ruling centre-right coalition. During the preparations for the Chairmanship, there were opinion pieces from across the political spectrum on how the Court had become activist and disrespectful of democratic values. The far-right suggested leaving the Convention altogether or writing it out of Danish law, a debate not unlike the Human Rights Act debate in the United Kingdom.[81] While the governing centre-right coalition had it as part of its official political framework to 'have a critical look at how the ECtHR has expanded the reach of the ECHR through its dynamic interpretation'.[82] On the centre-left, the Social Democrats also had their think pieces attacking the Court's interpretation as lacking democratic legitimacy.[83] These political statements utilised arguments from many respected academics who had published in newspapers, popularised science formats or in Danish-language academic journals. These pieces on the democratic legitimacy, judicial interpretation traditions or the reform of the Court ranged from intense normative arguments that the very concept of constitutional rights was undemocratic, and international human rights law particularly so,[84] and hard criticism

---

81 Folketinget, *Forslag til folketingsbeslutning om den europæiske menneskerettighedskonvention*, 25 October 2016, Folketinget 2016–17, Beslutningsforslag nr. B 18; Conservatives, Protecting Human Rights in the UK. The Conservatives' Proposals for Changing Human Rights Laws, 2014, https://www.amnesty.org.uk/files/protectin ghumanrightsinuk_conservativeparty.pdf?vhzrAQkxzwCH8hbjeYhhcu5B5lyPp_9 K=.

82 Regeringen, *Regeringsgrundlag Marienborgaftalen 2016: For et Friere, Rigere og Mere Trygt Danmark* (2016), 55.

83 Bramsen, Den er gal med fortolkningen af menneskerettighederne, Netavisen Pio, 21 August 2017, https://piopio.dk/den-er-gal-med-fortolkningen-af-menne skerettighederne. Parties left of the social democrats have been critical of the government's discourse in parliament, but they have not been very active on this subject in the public debate.

84 Nielsen, *Loven* (2014) 58–60.

of the interpretation of the Convention including a suggestion to leave the Convention altogether,[85] to more moderate but still critical accounts of the power and interpretation of the Court[86] or its lack of a democratic mandate.[87] We can be fairly certain that these academic arguments influenced legislatures and ministers or at least legitimised opinions they already held because politicians not only reused them verbatim but also referred to them explicitly.[88]

Two years after the Copenhagen Declaration, the Committee of Ministers formally closed the Interlaken process on the 130th meeting on 4 November 2020.[89] The decision reiterated the goals and decisions in the Declarations, concluding on the themes of subsidiarity,[90] dialogue between the national and the European level,[91] national implementation and execution,[92] selection of judges[93] and the budget.[94] In the text, the States are asked to give full effect to the principle of subsidiarity by complying with their obligation to ensure the rights of everyone within their jurisdiction.[95] There is no mention of subsidiarity as an element of democratic legitimacy. The understanding of dialogue was also limited to being within the Superior Courts Network, with no suggestion to have political declarations on the direction of the Court's case law.[96] In other words, the decision formally closing the Interlaken process includes none

85 Andersen, 'Menneskerettighedsdomstolens dynamiske fortolkninger som retspolitisk problem' (2017) 3(1) *Juristen*, 81 ff.

86 Christoffersen, *Menneskeret: En demokratisk udfordring* (2014), 117.

87 Smith, 'Menneskerettighedsdomstolen er på vildspor', *Politiken*, 1 October 2017, https://politiken.dk/debat/kroniken/art6139412/Menneskerettighedsdomstolen-er-p%C3%A5-vildspor.

88 The Minister of Justice thus referred to Christoffersen's book in *Justitsministerens svar på spørgsmål 181 Almen del* (2016). Smith's piece, Henriksen's piece, an opinion piece by Bryde Andersen and the article on Støjberg were all part of the *Presseklip (Background information to the Parliamentary group on Council of Europe)* (2017, 25 October). Available here https://www.ft.dk/samling/20171/almdel/ERD/bilag/1/1808235.pdf

89 CoE Committee of Ministers, *130th Session of the Committee of Ministers* (Videoconference, Athens, 4 November 2020). 4. Securing the long-term effectiveness of the system of the European Convention on Human Rights, CM/Del/Dec(2020)130/4, para. 1.

90 *Id.*, para. 2.

91 *Id.*, para. 10 f.

92 *Id.*, para. 8 f., 12.

93 *Id.*, para. 6.

94 *Id.*, para. 7, 13 f.

95 *Id.*, para. 2.

96 *Id.*, Preamble.

of the contentious elements from the Copenhagen Declaration or its Draft. There may be any number of reasons why the Danish representative in the Committee of Ministers did not protest these conclusions publicly. First and foremost, most states had other, pandemic-related things on their plate at the end of 2020 and might well have thought of the meeting in the Committee of Ministers as a formality. The decision was also made with little public fanfare. Furthermore, the Danish government had changed in the meantime. While more recent debates in the Danish parliament suggest that the current government is just as critical of the Court as the previous one, these debates also show that the Copenhagen Declaration was very much considered a project of the former government.[97]

The Committee of Ministers' 130th meeting's decision was informed mainly by the final report of the CDDH adopted a year earlier[98] and the Court's comments on this. Great emphasis was placed on both the CDDH's contribution and the PACE's reports and on the success of the Court in bringing down the backlog of cases significantly. However, the Court noted that the remaining backlog consists of more complex and potentially well-founded cases and that without the influx of additional resources in the form of either budget or seconded national lawyers and judges, the Court will not be able to tackle this remaining backlog. At the end of the day, during the Interlaken process, the Member States first dragged their feet and then got caught up in internal party politics, and eventually did not deliver what the Court needed to deal with the backlog and unsustainably high caseload.

Bibliography

Amnesty International/European Human Rights Advocacy Centre/European Implementation Network/Fair Trials/International Commission of Jurists/Open Society Justice Initiative/World Organisation Against Torture (OMCT)/The AIRE Centre: Joint NGO Response to the Draft Copenhagen Declaration, 13 February 2018, https://www.amnesty.eu/news/joint-ngo-response-to-the-draft-copenhagen-declaration/.

97 *Parliamentary debate: F 47 Om domstolsaktivismen ved Den Europæiske Menneskerettighedsdomstol.*, (18 June 2020), Denmark.

98 CDDH, *Contribution of the CDDH to the evaluation provided for by the Interlaken Declaration*, 29 November 2019, CDDH(2019)R92Addendum2.

Amnesty International/European Human Rights Advocacy Centre/Helsinki Foundation for Human Rights/Human Rights Watch/Interights/International Commission of Jurists/JUSTICE/Open Society Justice Initiative/REDRESS/The AIRE Centre: Joint NGO response to Protocol 15 to the European Convention on Human Rights must not result in a weakening of human rights protection, 24 June 2013, https://www.justiceinitiative.org/uploads/f4e441ba-07dc-4061-b113-049ccf470ac5/echr-protocol15-joint-statement-06272013.pdf.

Andersen, Mads Bryde: Menneskerettighedsdomstolens dynamiske fortolkninger som retspolitisk problem, Juristen 2017, 81 ff.

Arnardóttir, Oddný Mjöll: Organised Retreat? The Move from 'Substantive' to 'Procedural' Review in the ECtHR's Case Law on the Margin of Appreciation, ESIL Conference Paper Series 2015, 1 ff.

Bates, Ed: The evolution of the European Convention on Human Rights: from its inception to the creation of a permanent court of human rights (2010).

Bates, Ed: Who should have the final word on human rights?, UK Human Rights Blog, 6 March 2012.

Bowring, Bill: The Russian Federation, Protocol No. 14 (and 14bis), and the Battle for the Soul of the ECHR, Goettingen Journal of International Law 2010, 589 ff.

Bramsen, Trine: Den er gal med fortolkningen af menneskerettighederne, Netavisen Pio, 21 August 2017, https://piopio.dk/den-er-gal-med-fortolkningen-af-menneskerettighederne.

Brems, Eva/Lavrysen Laurens: Procedural Justice in Human Rights Adjudication: The European Court of Human Rights, Human Rights Quarterly 2013, 176 ff.

Costa, Jean-Paul: Memorandum of the President of the European Court of Human Rights to the States with a view to preparing the Interlaken Conference (2009).

Christoffersen, Jonas: Menneskeret: En demokratisk udfordring (2014).

Danish Ministry of Justice: Draft Copenhagen Declaration Denmark, 5 February 2018.

Donald, Alice/Leach, Philip: A Wolf in Sheep's Clothing: Why the Draft Copenhagen Declaration Must be Rewritten, EJIL:Talk!, 21 February 2018, https://www.ejiltalk.org/a-wolf-in-sheeps-clothing-why-the-draft-copenhagen-declaration-must-be-rewritten/.

Folketinget: Forslag til folketingsbeslutning om den europæiske menneskerettighedskonvention, Folketinget 2016–17, Beslutningsforslag nr. B 18, 25 October 2016.

Føllesdal, Andreas/Ulfstein, Geir: The Draft Copenhagen Declaration: Whose Responsibility and Dialogue?, EJIL:Talk!, 22 February 2018, https://www.ejiltalk.org/the-draft-copenhagen-declaration-whose-responsibility-and-dialogue/.

Glas, Lize R.: From Interlaken to Copenhagen: What Has Become of the Proposals Aiming to Reform the Functioning of the European Court of Human Rights?, Human Rights Law Review 2020, 121 ff.

Hartmann, Jacques. Danmark og Den Europæiske Menneskerettighedskonvention (2017).

Helfer, Laurence/Slaughter, Anne-Marie: Toward a Theory of Effective Supranational Adjudication, Yale Law Journal 1997, 273ff.

Institut for menneskerettigheder: Draft Copenhagen Declaration, 5 February 2018, https://menneskeret.dk/sites/menneskeret.dk/files/media/dokumenter/nyheder/draft_copenhagen_declaration_05.02.18.pdf.

Kuijer, Martin: Margin of Appreciation Doctrine and the Strengthening of the Principle of Subsidiarity in the Recent Reform Negotiations, Human Rights Law Journal 2016, 339 ff.

Madsen, Mikael Rask/Christoffersen, Jonas: The European Court of Human Rights' View of the Draft Copenhagen Declaration, EJIL:Talk!, 23 February 2018, https://www.ejiltalk.org/the-european-court-of-human-rights-view-of-the-draft-copenhagen-declaration/.

Molbæk-Steensig, Helga: Something Rotten in the State of Denmark?, Verfassungsblog, 26 April 2018, https://verfassungsblog.de/something-rotten-in-the-state-of-denmark/.

Myjer, Egbert: The conscience of Europe: 50 years of the European Court of Human Rights (2010).

Nielsen, Gorm: Toftegaard: Loven (2014).

Ministry of Justice EMRK taskforce: Presseklip (Background information to the Parliamentary group on Council of Europe), 25 October 2017.

Regeringen: Regeringsgrundlag Marienborgaftalen 2016: For et Friere, Rigere og Mere Trygt Danmark (2016).

Smith, Eva: Menneskerettighedsdomstolen er på vildspor, Politiken, 1 October 2017, https://politiken.dk/debat/kroniken/art6139412/Menneskerettighedsdomstolen-er-p%C3%A5-vildspor.

Ulfstein, Geir/Føllesdal, Andreas: Copenhagen – Much ado about little?, EJIL:Talk!, 14 April 2018, https://www.ejiltalk.org/copenhagen-much-ado-about-little/.

Woolf, Harry: Review of the Working Methods of the European Court of Human Rights (2005), https://www.echr.coe.int/Documents/2005_Lord_Woolf_working_methods_ENG.pdf

B. Fundamental Human Rights Principles Facing New Challenges

How many Strikeouts are too many? The ECtHR's Evolving Approach to Repetitive Cases and the Limits of Efficiency

Edith Wagner

A. *The Increase in Strikeouts*

Three strikes and the batter is out is a fundamental rule of baseball.[1] The ideal number of strikeouts per season, however, is a topic of endless debate. Some embrace strikeouts as a trade-off for more home runs and essential part of game management; others argue that too many strikeouts spoil the game and blame the rising strikeout rate for the declining interest in major league baseball.[2] With strikeouts at an all-time high, league officials are wondering why the game is changing and what to do about it.[3] But how many strikeouts are too many? And what rules, if any, could be introduced to find the sweet spot between what is entertaining and what is efficient? To learn about the latest crisis of a quintessentially American sport in a piece about a genuinely European institution like the European Court of Human Rights ('ECtHR' or 'the Court') might strike the reader as odd. And yet, the parallels between the two are striking: the quest for efficiency, rise of statistics and constant performance evaluation led to a steady increase in strikeouts. The Court's largest strikeout so far – *Burmych and others v. Ukraine*[4] – resulted in the dismissal of 12,148 applications in one judgment.[5]

---

1 Major League Baseball, Official Playing Rules Committee, Official Baseball Rules, 2018 Edition, http://mlb.mlb.com/documents/0/8/0/268272080/2018_Official_Baseball_Rules.pdf, 126.

2 Verducci, 'There Are Too Many Strikeouts in Baseball: Here's How to Fix the Problem', Sports Illustrated, 14 June 2018, https://www.si.com/mlb/2018/06/14/strikeouts-effect-major-league-baseball.

3 Kepner, 'More Strikeouts Than Hits? Welcome to Baseball's Latest Crisis', New York Times, 16 August 2018, https://www.nytimes.com/2018/08/16/sports/baseball-mlb-strikeouts.html.

4 ECtHR, Judgment (GC), 12 October 2017, *Burmych and Others v Ukraine*, Application Nos. 46852/13 and 4 more.

5 *Ibid.*, para. 200 ff. and fourth operative provision.

With the *Burmych* judgment, the victims of the Chernobyl disaster, who make up a fair share of the applicants, lost the legal battle over the payment of social benefits under Ukrainian law for losing their health, homes and livelihood in the nuclear accident of 1986.[6] The Court did not distinguish the cases of public servants claiming outstanding salaries and other creditors seeking to collect debts from state-owned enterprises from the cases of particularly vulnerable applicants who suffer from the long-term effects of the Chernobyl disaster. Instead, the Court examined all applications through the lens of 'non-enforcement or delayed enforcement of domestic court decisions'[7] and opted for a one-size-fits-all strikeout by which it transferred the five applications that had been examined on the merits along with the 12,143 applications that are listed in the two appendices to the *Burmych* judgment to the Committee of Ministers of the Council of Europe, a body that supervises the execution of judgments at the domestic level.[8] Since the early 2000s, Ukraine had been condemned repeatedly – not least by way of a pilot judgment in *Ivanov v. Ukraine*[9] – for the many flaws in the Ukrainian legal system that make it practically impossible to enforce rulings against the Ukrainian State.[10] Ukraine never complied with the Court's findings and the *Ivanov* pilot judgment remained just as unenforced as the decisions of Ukrainian courts which, in turn, led to even more applications challenging the violation of Article 6 para. 1 European Convention on Human Rights ('ECHR' or 'the Convention') before the ECtHR.

So far, the mass strikeout in *Burmych* has been examined from the perspective of individual justice and the rights of the applicants,[11] as well as

6 Act No. 796 of 28 February 1991 on the status and social security of citizens suffering from the consequences of the Chernobyl catastrophe, as amended by Act No. 231-V of 5 October 2006, Act No. 2321-IV of 12 January 2005, Act No. 1767-IV of 15 June 2004, Act No. 429-IV of 16 January 2003, Act No. 2638-III of 11 July 2001, Act No. 2400-III of 26 April 2001, Act No. 230 of 6 June 1996, Vidomosti Verkhovnoj Rady, No. 16, 1991, 414–439.

7 ECtHR, Judgment (GC), 12 October 2017, *Burmych and Others v Ukraine*, Application Nos. 46852/13 and 4 more, para. 3.

8 Appendix I lists the 7,641 applications which had already been communicated to the Ukrainian Government; Appendix II the 4,502 non-communicated applications.

9 ECtHR, Judgment, 15 October 2009, *Yuriy Nikolayevich Ivanov v Ukraine*, Application No. 40450/04.

10 ECtHR, Judgment (GC), 12 October 2017, *Burmych and Others v Ukraine*, Application Nos. 46852/13 and 4 more, para. 148.

11 Kindt, 'Giving up on individual justice? The effect of state non-execution of a pilot judgment on victims' (2018) 36 *Netherlands Quarterly of Human Rights*, 173.

regarding its compatibility with the Convention and the implications for the relationship between the Court and the Committee of Ministers.[12] What is still missing in the academic discussion is the impact of strikeouts on the Court, in particular its legitimacy and perceived fairness, along with a critical appraisal of the Court's quest to deal more efficiently with repetitive cases through procedures like the strikeout of applications under Article 37 para. 1 lit. c ECHR. Just like in baseball, the opinion on strikeouts is divided: the majority of the Grand Chamber saw the discontinuation of the proceedings as a worthy trade-off to adjudicate more non-repetitive cases and praised it as efficient case management,[13] while the dissenting judges argued that the Court was 'shooting itself in the foot' by boosting the Court's statistical record without insisting on compliance with the existing obligations of Ukraine under the Convention.[14] But even if we accept the use of strikeouts to deal more efficiently with repetitive cases, how many strikeouts are too many? And can the Court find the sweet spot between what is efficient and what is legitimate when striking down cases in bulk?

To address these questions, the article is divided into four parts. After an overview of the challenges entailed by repetitive cases, the increase in strikeouts at the Court and the evolving procedural approach to the Ukrainian 'non-enforcement' cases, the article embarks on a critical appraisal of the Court's reasoning in the *Burmych* judgment. This is followed by a general inquiry into some of the broader questions that arise under the *Burmych* judgment: the absolute prioritization of non-repetitive over repetitive cases that are essentially a symptom of long-term non-compliance and the sociological legitimacy of the ECtHR. The further development of the Convention, so the conclusion, is just as important to keep the Convention 'alive' as holding the member states accountable for failing to comply with their existing obligations under the Convention.

---

12 Ulfstein and Zimmermann, 'Certiorari through the Back Door? The Judgment by the European Court of Human Rights in Burmych and Others v. Ukraine in Perspective' (2018) 17 *The Law and Practice of International Courts and Tribunals*, 289.

13 ECtHR, Judgment (GC), 12 October 2017, *Burmych and Others v Ukraine*, Application Nos. 46852/13 and 4 more, para. 174 f.

14 *Id.*, Joint Dissenting Opinion of Judges Yudkivska, Sajó, Bianku, Karakaş, De Gaetano, Laffranque and Motoc, para. 202.

B. Strikeouts and Repetitive Cases

In order to gain a better understanding of the Court's ruling in *Burmych*, it is necessary to take a moment to reflect on repetitive cases and the increase in strikeouts at the Court. The strikeout of applications is regulated by Article 37 para. 1 ECHR:

> The Court may at any stage of the proceedings decide to strike an application out of its list of cases where the circumstances lead to the conclusion that: (a) the applicant does not intend to pursue his application; or (b) the matter has been resolved; or (c) for any other reason established by the Court, it is no longer justified to continue the examination of the application. However, the Court shall continue the examination of the application if respect for human rights as defined in the Convention and the protocols thereto so requires.

A strikeout is relatively unproblematic if the applicant decides on her own motion not to continue the case or if the legal issues that had given rise to the application have been resolved. When ruling on the discontinuation of the proceedings under Article 37 para. 1 lit. c ECHR, the Court has considerable discretion which raises difficult questions as to when it is indeed justified to dismiss an application that is well-founded, let alone an entire group of more than 10,000 cases.

Unlike in baseball, the Court does not keep a public strikeout record. However, it is possible to come to an estimate of how many applications are struck down by the Court each year. A strikeout under Article 37 para. 1 ECHR is normally performed by decision unless the Grand Chamber, which must hand down judgments under Article 43 para. 3 ECHR, is ruling on the matter.[15] That means the approximate number of applications that were subject to a strikeout under Article 37 para. 1 ECHR can be obtained by subtracting the number of inadmissibility decisions from the total number of applications in which a decision was rendered – a number that is reported in the Court's annual reports.[16] As the table below shows,

---

15 Separate decisions on admissibility have been rendered in, e.g., ECtHR, Decision, 15 June 2017, *Harkins v the United Kingdom,* Application Nos. 71537/14; ECtHR, Decision, 1 March 2010, *Demopoulos and Others v Turkey,* Application Nos.46113/99 and 7 more; ECtHR, Decision, 2 May 2007, *Behrami and Behrami v France and Saramati v France, Germany and Norway,* Application Nos. 71412/01 and 78166/01.

16 Around 90 % of all applications that are received by the Court are dismissed as inadmissible for not complying with the substantive requirements of Article 35

the number of applications in which a strikeout decision was rendered oscillates between 3,016 and 8,974 – a mean of 5,474 applications – per year and has increased significantly from 2011 onwards.[17] The increase in strikeouts must be seen in light of the reduction of the number of pending applications before the ECTHR since 2011. After reaching an all-time high of 151,600 in 2011, the number of pending cases has steadily declined since then: to 99,900 applications in 2013; 64,850 in 2015, and 56,350 in 2018.[18]

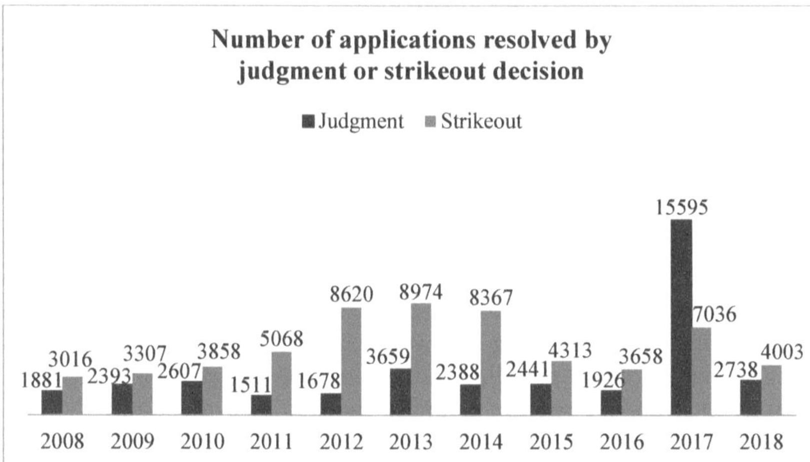

Nearly 50 % of the pending cases are so-called repetitive cases. In other words, every second case that is decided by the Court is repetitive. Just to give an example, in 2015 alone, the Court adjudicated some 30,500 repetitive cases.[19] As the name indicates, a repetitive case is a type of case that requires the Court to repeat the same findings, often many hundreds of times. Repetitive cases are a symptom of persistent systemic issues at the

ECHR, notably the six-month time limit and the exhaustion of all domestic remedies, or the formal requirements of Rule 47 of the Rules of Court.

17 Table made by the author. For data, see Annex.

18 ECtHR, Annual Report 2018, https://www.echr.coe.int/Documents/Annual_report_2018_ENG.pdf, 167; Annual Report 2015, https://www.echr.coe.int/Documents/Annual_report_2015_ENG.pdf, 187; Annual Report 2013, https://www.echr.coe.int/Documents/Annual_report_2013_ENG.pdf, 191.

19 ECtHR, Annual Report 2015, https://www.echr.coe.int/Documents/Annual_Report_2015_ENG.pdf, 5.

domestic level that affect entire groups of individuals. More often than not, the Court's case law on the underlying legal issue is well-established. Still, the Court needs to re-examine the merits given that each case is well-founded and filed by a different applicant. To adjudicate repetitive cases more efficiently, the Court's procedural toolbox has been enlarged considerably. While rulings in well-founded applications could only be handed down by a seven-judge Chamber in the past, the Court can choose between various procedures for repetitive cases: the pilot judgment procedure under Rule 61 of the Rules of Court[20], the procedure for well-established case law under Article 28 ECHR, friendly settlements under Article 39 ECHR, unilateral declarations under Rule 62a of the Rules of Court and strikeouts under Article 37 para. 1 ECHR.

I. The Widespread Disregard for the Obligations under the Convention

More often than not, repetitive cases are portrayed as a burden[21], an existential threat that diverts the Court from allegedly more meritorious non-repetitive cases that contribute to the substantive development of the Convention.[22] As convincing as this may sound at first, it is oversimplifying a highly complex reality and misses one crucial point: repetitive cases as such do not put the Court to the test. Had the Court the budget and staff it actually needed,[23] it could adjudicate both repetitive and non-repetitive cases without having to choose between a rock and a hard place: a backlog of repetitive cases or less substantive development of the Convention. What really threatens the Strasbourg system is the fact that many countries ignore their most pressing problems – be it for practical, financial or political reasons – and disregard their existing obligations under the Convention. Long-term non-compliance paired with the lack of effective local remedies lead to countless repetitive cases each year.

---

20 ECtHR, Rules of Court, 2020 https://www.echr.coe.int/Documents/Rules_Court_ENG.pdf.

21 The Court word burden is used several times across the judgment when discussing the challenges entailed by repetitive cases, see ECtHR, Judgment (GC), *Burmych and Others v Ukraine*, Application Nos. 46852/13 and 4 more, paras. 8, 134, 174, 201.

22 Sainati, 'Human Rights Class Actions: Rethinking the Pilot-Judgment Procedure at the European Court of Human Rights' (2015) 56 *Harvard International Law Journal*, 147.

23 The Court does not have its own budget. Its expenditures are borne by the Council of Europe under Article 50 ECHR.

An application with the ECtHR is often the only way to address the ailments of many European countries:

- Inadequate conditions of detention like lack of space, hygiene, or food, or ill-treatment by prison guards amounting to inhuman or degrading treatment under Art 3 ECHR.[24]
- The disenfranchisement of convicted felons violating the right to free elections under Art 3 of Protocol No. 1 to the Convention.[25]
- Various issues violating ownership rights under Art 1 of Protocol No. 1 to the Convention.[26]
- Delayed justice in civil, administrative, and criminal proceedings that violate the reasonable time requirement of the right to a fair trial under Article 6 ECHR.[27]

---

24 ECtHR, Judgment, 10 January 2012, *Ananyev and Others v Russia*, Application Nos. 42525/07 and 60800/08; ECtHR, Judgment, 8 January 2013, *Torreggiani and Others v Italy*, Applications Nos. 43517/09 and 6 more; ECtHR, Judgment, January 2015, *Neshkov and Others v Bulgaria*; Application Nos. 36925/10 and 5 more; ECtHR, Judgment, 10 March 2015, *Varga and Others v Hungary*, Application Nos. 14097/12 and 5 more; ECtHR, Judgment, 6 September 2016, *W. D. v Belgium*, Application No. 73548/13.

25 ECtHR, Judgment, 23 November 2010, *Greens and M. T. v the United Kingdom*, Application Nos. 60041/08 and 60054/08.

26 ECtHR, Judgment (GC), 22 June 2004, *Broniowski v Poland*, Application No. 31443/96; ECtHR, Judgment (GC), 19 June 2006, *Hutten-Czapska v Poland*, Application No. 35014/97; ECtHR, Judgment, 3 November 2009, *Suljagić v Bosnia and Herzegovina*; Application No. 27912/02; ECtHR, Judgment, 12 October 2010, *Maria Atanasiu and Others v Romania*, Application Nos. 30767/05 and 33800/06; ECtHR, Judgment, 31 July 2012, *Manushaqe Puto and Others v Albania*, Application Nos. 604/07 and 3 more; ECtHR, Judgment, 3 September 2013, *M. C. and Others v Italy*, Application No. 5376/11; ECtHR, Judgment (GC), 16 July 2014, *Ališić and Others v Bosnia and Herzegovina, Croatia, Serbia, Slovenia and The former Yugoslav Republic of Macedonia*, Application No. 60642/08.

27 ECtHR, Judgment, 2 September 2010, *Rumpf v Germany*, Application No. 46344/06; ECtHR, Judgment, 21 December 2010, *Vassilios Athanasiou and Others v Greece*, Application No. 50973/08; ECtHR, Judgment, 10 May 201, *Dimitrov and Hamanov v Bulgaria*, Application. Nos. 48059/06 and 2708/09; ECtHR, Judgment, 10 May 2011, *Finger v Bulgaria*, Application No. 37346/05; ECtHR, Judgment, 20 March 2012, *Ümmühan Kaplan v. Turkey*, Application. no. 24240/07; ECtHR, Judgment, 3 April 2012, *Michelioudakis v Greece*, Application No. 54447/10; ECtHR, Judgment, 30 October 2012, *Glykantzi v Greece*, Application No. 40150/09; ECtHR, Judgment, 7 July 2015, *Rutkowski and Others v Poland*, Application Nos. 72287/10, 13927/11, 46187/11; ECtHR, Judgment, 16 July 2015, *Gazsó v Hungary*, Application No. 48322/12.

- And, last but not least, the issue that lies at the heart of the *Burmych* judgment: a violation of the right to enforcement within reasonable time along with an effective domestic remedy that speeds up the enforcement and grants compensation for undue delays under Article 6 para. 1 and Article 13 ECHR.[28]

II. *Ukraine and the Chernobyl Victims*

The reason why the rulings remain unenforced in Ukraine is straightforward: the Ukrainian State owes the money and the treasury is empty. The creditors are Chernobyl victims like Lidiya Burmych that are entitled to various social payments, military servicemen and public servants that are claiming their outstanding salaries and allowances, and other creditors seeking enforcement of money judgments against enterprises that are owned by the Ukrainian State. All in all, the Court has received over 29,000 repetitive cases from applicants that had been unable to enforce the respective domestic court decision against the Ukrainian State. Since 2016, around 200 new applications were filed per month. Judgments on the merits were adopted in 3,491 cases, friendly settlements in 1,103 cases, unilateral declarations in 1,233 cases, and single judge decisions in 8,274 cases.

C. *The Court's Evolving Procedural Approach*

In order to understand the strikeout in *Burmych*, it is important to consider how the Court's procedural approach to Ukrainian non-enforcement cases evolved over time.

---

28 ECtHR, Judgment, 15 October 2009, *Yuriy Nikolayevich Ivanov v Ukraine*, Application No. 40450/04; ECtHR, Judgment (GC), 12 October 2017, *Burmych and Others v Ukraine*, Application Nos. 46852/13 and 4 more; ECtHR, Judgment, 15 January 2009, *Burdov v Russia (No. 2)*, Application No. 33509/04; ECtHR, Judgment, 28 July 2009, *Olaru and Others v Moldova*, Application Nos. 476/07, 22539/05, 17911/08, 13136/07.

I. 2001 to 2009: The First Friendly Settlement and Case-by-Case Adjudication

In 2001, in the first case addressing the non-enforcement of judgments in Ukraine – *Kaysin and Others v. Ukraine*[29] – a friendly settlement was reached and the monetary compensation paid by Ukraine. Yet, the general issue of non-enforcement remained unresolved. Between 2001 and 2004, more repetitive cases were received, and judgments were adopted on a case-by-case basis.[30]

II. 2009: The Pilot Judgment Procedure

In 2009, the Court decided to apply the pilot judgment procedure in the case *Ivanov v. Ukraine.*[31] The pilot judgment obliged Ukraine to address the structural problem – the lack of funds, the passiveness of the bailiffs, and the shortcomings in the national legislation – which made it impossible for Mr. Ivanov and 1,400 other applicants to enforce their judgments. In the aftermath of the pilot judgment, the Ukrainian Government requested two extensions of the deadline set by the Court to introduce a new local remedy. One extension was granted, the second declined,[32] and the Court agreed to adjourn the examination of the pending cases until July 15th, 2011. In June 2012, a domestic remedy was finally introduced, but turned out to be ineffective.[33]

---

29 ECtHR, Judgment, 3 May 2001, *Kaysin and Others v Ukraine*, Application No. 46144/99.

30 See, *inter alia*, ECtHR, Judgment, 29 June 2004, *Voytenko v Ukraine*, Application No. 18966/02; ECtHR, Judgment, 27 July 2004, *Romashov v Ukraine*, Application No. 67534/01; ECtHR, Judgment, 26 April 2006, *Zubko and Others v Ukraine*, Application No. 3955/04; ECtHR, Judgment, 29 November 2005, *Belanova v Ukraine*, Application No. 1093/02; ECtHR, Judgment, 15 December 2005, *Kucherenko v Ukraine*, Application No. 27347/02; ECtHR, Judgment, 20 July 2004, *Shmalko v Ukraine*, Application No. 60750/00; ECtHR, Judgment, 18 January 2005, *Poltorachenko v Ukraine*, Application No. 77317/01.

31 ECtHR, Judgment, 15 October 2009, *Yuriy Nikolayevich Ivanov v Ukraine*, Application No. 40450/04.

32 ECtHR, Judgment (GC), 12 October 2017, *Burmych and Others v Ukraine*, Application Nos. 46852/13 and 4 more, para. 16 ff.

33 *Id.*, para 27.

III. From 2012 to 2015: The Fast-Track Procedure

In July 2012, the Court resumed the examination of all adjourned non-enforcement cases, and introduced a new fast-track procedure in *Kharuk and Others v. Ukraine*[34]: the procedure for cases that concern the Court's well-established case law, commonly referred to as the WECL procedure, Article 28 para. 1 lit. b of the Convention. Under this procedure, a Committee of three judges can declare applications admissible, render judgments on the merits, and rule on just satisfaction provided that the grounds for finding a violation of the Convention are well-established in the Court's case law.

1. The Procedure for Well-Established Case Law

In the Ukrainian non-enforcement cases, the WECL procedure simplified and accelerated also the communication stage of the proceedings. The Court did not request any information on the admissibility and merits of the case from the Ukrainian Government; only factual observations were exchanged. In addition, the Court communicated the cases in groups, often several hundred cases per month, and the Registry prepared friendly settlement proposals for the entire group of cases. If the applicants agreed to settle the case, a voluntary payment was made by Ukraine, and the entire group of cases struck out. If no friendly settlement was reached, Ukraine could file a request to strike out the repetitive cases on the basis of a so-called unilateral declaration.

2. Unilateral Declarations

The Court introduced unilateral declarations in well-founded cases in *Tahsin Acar v. Turkey.*[35] The approach is now governed by Rule 62a Rules of Court.[36] In the unilateral declaration, the violation of the Convention is acknowledged and adequate redress offered. Even if the applicants want

---

34 ECtHR, Judgment, 26 July 2012, *Kharuk and others v Ukraine*, Application No. 703/05 and 115 more.

35 ECtHR, Judgment (GC), 6 May 2003, *Tahsin Acar v Turkey*, Application No. 26307/95.

36 See also ECtHR: Unilateral declarations: policy and practice, September 2012, https://www.echr.coe.int/Documents/Unilateral_declarations_ENG.pdf.

their cases to continue, the Court can strike them out so long as the continued examination is no longer justified. Aside from the missing consent on the part of the applicant, the main difference between friendly settlements and unilateral declarations is the lack of supervision during the execution stage, a lacuna in the Convention. Only the execution of friendly settlements is subject to supervision by the Committee of Ministers under Article 39 para. 4 ECHR.

In terms of efficiency, unilateral declarations are superior to judgments. They generate less work for the Court and the procedure can easily be standardised. The member states, too, are unlikely to complain when the Court allows them to file a request for a unilateral declaration. Unilateral declarations are cheaper than friendly settlements because the awards offered are usually lower than the ones calculated by the Registry in friendly settlement agreement[37] and they come with the bonus of no supervision at the execution stage. Under the current system of unilateral declarations without supervision at the execution stage, Ukraine was able to get away with long-term non-compliance. 2,234 cases had been settled through unilateral declarations between May 2015 and February 2016, but Ukraine did not always pay the sums offered under the terms of the unilateral declarations as letters by the applicants have revealed.[38]

IV. 2017: The Mass Strikeout in Burmych

In December 2015, a Chamber of the fifth section decided to relinquish jurisdiction in favour of the Grand Chamber to reconsider the Court's approach to non-enforcement cases filed against Ukraine. In a ten to seven majority decision, the Grand Chamber decided to discontinue the fast-track procedure for well-established case law in Ukrainian non-enforcement cases and ruled on the strikeout of 12,148 cases that were transferred to the execution department of the Committee of Ministers of the Council of Europe.[39] The list of reasons the Grand Chamber offered for this radical change of course was long. At the outset, the Court reiterated its findings in the *Ivanov* pilot judgment – that the structural problem was complex and required the implementation of comprehensive legislative and admin-

37 On the calculation of the awards by the Registry, see Keller et al., *Friendly Settlements before the European Court of Human Rights* (2010), 78.

38 ECtHR, Judgment (GC), 12 October 2017, *Burmych and Others v Ukraine*, Application Nos. 46852/13 and 4 more, para. 40.

39 *Id.*, operative provisions.

istrative measures involving various domestic authorities[40] – and that Ukraine had failed to implement general measures addressing the root cause. In other words, the pilot judgment in *Ivanov* had been a failure. The Court noted also that some 120,000 people were affected by unenforced judicial decisions in Ukraine – all of whom could theoretically file an application with the Court – and that such a massive influx of applications would affect the Court's ability to fulfil its mission under Article 19 in relation to other meritorious applications warranting examination.[41] Furthermore, the Court held that its judicial policy of 'wholesale delivery of rulings'[42] has neither had any meaningful impact on the overall systemic problem, nor led to any apparent progress in the execution process. The continued examination of the cases would, so the Court argued, result in more applicants turning to the Court for redress. This would transform the Court into a compensation commission for Ukrainian non-enforcement cases.[43] Finally, the Court came to the conclusion

> that nothing is to be gained, nor will justice be best served, by the repetition of its findings in a lengthy series of comparable cases, which would place a significant burden on its own resources, with a consequent impact on its considerable caseload.[44]

The majority considered the strikeout to be a win-win situation, where the applicants are 'more appropriately protected in the execution process',[45] while the Court gets to 'focus on cases raising new and serious issues of Convention compliance'.[46] This begs of course the question what is considered to be a serious issue of (non-)compliance if not the Ukrainian non-enforcement cases?

---

40 *Id.*, para. 144.
41 *Id.*, para. 149 f.
42 *Id.*, para. 152.
43 *Id.*, para. 155.
44 *Id.*, para. 174.
45 *Id.* para. 202.
46 *Id.*, para. 210.

D. Appraising the Judgment in Burmych

I. The Flawed Prioritisation of Non-repetitive over Repetitive Cases

The decision of the Grand Chamber in *Burmych* illustrates that the Court's long-standing practice of prioritising new issues over repetitive issues is flawed. How can repetitive cases be considered less important than non-repetitive cases when judgments granting social benefits that secure the survival of entire families remain unenforced? In fact, the dissenting judges

> cannot agree that the present applications and the underlying miseries are less meritorious than other cases. Who could explain to incapacitated Chernobyl victims that their decades' long misery is less meritorious than the legal qualification of a single slap on the face of a young provocateur?[47]

The clear prioritisation of non-repetitive cases stems from the Court's mission to maintain the Convention as the often-cited 'living instrument'.[48] One way, the traditional way of keeping the Convention 'alive' has been through progressive interpretive evolution. And in order to further develop the Convention, the Court needs cases that raise new legal questions. However, the Convention remains just as practically relevant when the Court reminds the member states ever so often about the problems they ignore and their duty to safeguard all the rights under the Convention within their jurisdiction, and not just the ones they agree with.

II. The Lack of Weighing and Balancing

It is a good question why the Court did not weigh and balance its institutional integrity and the efficient administration of justice under Article 19 ECHR with the right of the applicants to obtain a decision under Art 34 ECHR. While the Court goes through a long list of reasons to justify the strike out, it nowhere addresses the right of the 7,641 applicants whose cases had already been communicated to obtain a decision from the Court. Even if the Court had come to the same conclusion – that its procedural

---

47 *Id.*, Joint Dissenting Opinion of Judges Yudkivska, Sajó, Bianku, Karakaş, De Gaetano, Laffranque and Motoc, para. 9.

48 ECtHR, Judgment, 25 April 1978, *Tyrer v the United Kingdom*, Application No. 5856/72.

and institutional integrity prevails over the right of the individuals to assert their rights under the Convention – the decision would stand on a more solid legal ground and lose its defensive tone and language. The dissenting judges did not embark on a balancing test either, but found

> it particularly troubling that such a denial of the right to an individual application [...] was motivated by the bureaucratic reasons of easing the burden on the Court. [...] [L]owering the number of cases pending before the Court might make the administrative situation of the institution look brighter, this does not mean that the human rights situation in Europe is any better.[49]

III. The Substantive Evolution of the Convention

It is striking that nowhere did the Court acknowledge the fact that individual justice had been delivered in more than 14,000 cases, be it through judgments on the merits, friendly settlements, or unilateral declarations. That suggests that the Court cares about individual justice only so long as it goes hand in hand with the interpretive evolution of the Convention. Only in non-repetitive cases is it possible to interpret the Convention while delivering individual justice. But what is the point of further development if many member states find themselves unable to comply with the Convention as it stands now? If we look at Article 19 ECHR, the Court was put in place 'to ensure the observance of the engagements undertaken by the High Contracting Parties in the Convention and the Protocols thereto'. And isn't the Court doing exactly that – ensuring that Ukraine observes its engagements under the Convention – when adjudicating non-enforcement cases? So, if 'the Court's role under Article 19 cannot be converted into providing individualised financial relief',[50] why did the Court not discuss whether it should stop awarding just satisfaction under Article 41 ECHR?

---

49 ECtHR, Judgment (GC), 12 October 2017, *Burmych and Others v Ukraine*, Application Nos. 46852/13 and 4 more, Joint Dissenting Opinion of Judges Yudkivska, Sajó, Bianku, Karakas, De Gaetano, Laffranque and Motoc, para. 39.

50 *Id.*, para. 181.

IV. The Lack of a Public Hearing: Perceived Procedural Fairness and Legitimacy

Socio-legal research has shown that individuals are able to accept unfavourable outcomes without putting the legitimacy of the institution that has rendered the decision into question if the decision-making is perceived to be fair.[51] Broadly speaking, there are two competing concepts of legitimacy discussed in the literature: sociological legitimacy, on the one hand, which measures legitimacy subjectively and looks at the attitudes of the applicants and other key audiences towards the ECtHR;[52] normative legitimacy, on the other hand, which measures legitimacy in terms of whether certain standards are being met and considers the ECtHR's institutional transparency and procedural design,[53] the quality of its jurisprudence,[54] judicial independence[55] and impartiality,[56] the deliberation style,[57] overall performance and efficiency.[58] Against that backdrop, strikeouts have a disparate impact on the ECtHR's legitimacy, in theory at least. They help maximizing the Court's efficiency and thus enhance its normative legitimacy, while entailing the risk of damaging the ECtHR's sociological legitimacy if applicants that have been struck out feel treated unfairly. Put differently, strikeouts are likely to do more harm than good in the long run unless the applicants accept that they did not get the same procedural treatment as applicants in non-repetitive cases.

One way to safeguard the perceived fairness of strikeouts and mitigate the risk of damaging the Court's sociological legitimacy is to hold a public hearing. Why the judges decided to forego a public hearing, which is normally held in proceedings before the Grand Chamber,[59] is unclear.

---

51 Tyler, *Why People Obey the Law* (2006).

52 See, *inter alia*, Cohen et al., 'Legitimacy and International Courts – A Framework', in Grossman et al. (eds), *Legitimacy and International Courts* (2018), 4.

53 Berkhuysen and Van Emmerik, 'Legitimacy of European Court of Human Rights Judgments: Procedural Aspects', in Huls et al. (eds), *The Legitimacy of Highest Courts' Rulings* (2009), 435; Lasser, *Judicial Deliberations, A Comparative Analysis of Judicial Transparency and Legitimacy* (2004).

54 Sellers (ed), *Law, Reason, and Emotion* (2017).

55 Ulfstein, 'The Human Rights Treaty Bodies and Legitimacy Challenges', in Nienke Grossman et al. (eds), *Legitimacy and International Courts* (2018), 284.

56 Voeten, 'The Impartiality of International Judges: Evidence from the European Court of Human Rights' (2008) 102 *The American Political Science Review*, 417.

57 Garlicki, 'Judicial Deliberations: The Strasbourg Perspective', in Huls et al. (eds), *The Legitimacy of Highest Courts' Rulings* (2009), 389.

58 Often described as output legitimacy, Scharpf, 'Legitimacy in the multilevel European polity' (2009) 1 *European Political Science Review*, 173.

59 Nußberger, *The European Court of Human Rights* (2020), 65.

The *Burmych* judgment is silent on whether the applicants had expected a public hearing and which reasons had been considered by the judges when requesting written observations instead.[60] A public hearing would have given the applicants the chance to confront the Ukrainian Government directly and in open court, and the other victims, who appear in the two Appendices to the *Burmych* judgment and thus were not directly involved in the proceedings, the opportunity to bear witness to the pleadings by the parties. Given that all public hearings are filmed and can be viewed online on the Court's website,[61] all victims regardless of whether they had filed an application could have seen that the ECtHR had carefully considered the various arguments before closing the door to the victims of the Chernobyl disaster.

As a general rule, the Court has full discretion over whether or not to hold a hearing under Rule 59 para 5 of the Rules of Court the Court:

> Before taking a decision on admissibility, the Chamber may decide, either at the request of a party or of its own motion, to hold a hearing if it considers that the discharge of its functions under the Convention so requires. In that event, unless the Chamber shall exceptionally decide otherwise, the parties shall also be invited to address the issues arising in relation to the merits of the application.

Hearings are generally public under Article 40 ECHR, but in exceptional cases, notably when national security interests are at stake, an additional *in camera* hearing can be held to discuss confidential, secret or otherwise sensitive information.[62] The Court's public hearings tend to be rather structured and leave little room for courtroom dramatics. Rather than a trial-like confrontation between the parties, the purpose of holding a public hearing is to open the Court to the general public and allow outsiders to see the judges in action.[63]

---

60 ECtHR, Judgment (GC), 12 October 2017, *Burmych and Others v Ukraine*, Application Nos. 46852/13 and 4 more, para. 7 ("Following the Grand Chamber's decision of 16 March 2016 not to hold a hearing, the applicants and the Government each filed written observations on the admissibility and merits of the applications referred to in paragraph 1 above.").

61 Hearings held in the morning are usually available in the afternoon; hearings held in the afternoon are usually available in the evening on the Court's website (https://www.echr.coe.int) which contains a dedicated section for "Hearings" that hosts all webcasts.

62 See, *inter alia*, ECtHR, Judgment, 24 July 2014, *Al Nashiri v Poland*, Application No. 28761/11.

63 Nußberger, *The European Court of Human Rights* (2020), 65.

When it comes to strikeouts, there have been instances where the Court proceeded without a public hearing based on 'the parties' implicit undertaking not to request a rehearing of the case before the Grand Chamber'[64]. Given that the *Burmych* judgment does not address the reasons that led to the lack of a public hearing, it is impossible to tell if the judges assumed that all five applicants agreed on proceeding in writing. Public hearings are unlikely leading to additional insights in repetitive cases. However, if we accept the argument that Ukraine has the willingness but not the money to compensate all applicants, an apology from the Government during the oral hearing might have served more justice than hundreds of pages of written observations prepared by legal counsel. Depending on how oral hearings are being conducted, the Court might be able to deliver justice in repetitive cases even when striking out well-founded cases. It would be interesting to test this hypothesis and ask the applicants in the *Burmych* case including the ones listed in the two Appendices to the *Burmych* judgment if they would feel any different about the Court had they been granted an oral hearing. Should the question be answered in the affirmative, the Court could consider holding more oral hearings rather than mass producing essentially identical judgments.

E. Conclusion

I. A Call for more Realism

Through the eyes of others, the ECtHR is often viewed as 'a beacon of hope for those who feel that justice has been denied at national level'.[65] Statements like this one reveal how unrealistic our expectations about the Court often are. Even if taken to extremes, the quest for efficiency and effectiveness will not enable the Court to right all the wrongs and give the victims that are being affected by repetitive issues what they deserve: justice. Still, there is this longing for an institution that validates the

---

64 ECtHR, Judgment, 1 October 2002, *Kosa v Hungary*, Application No. 43352/98, operative part.

65 ECtHR, Annual Report 2018, Speech by Koen Lenaerts, President of the Court of Justice of the European Union, given at the opening of the judicial year, 26 January 2018, 2019, https://www.echr.coe.int/Documents/Annual_report_2018_ENG.pdf, 23 (23); Sainati, 'Human Rights Class Actions: Rethinking the Pilot-Judgment Procedure at the European Court of Human Rights' (2015) 56 *Harvard International Law Journal*, 147.

sense of injustice that is felt in many parts of Europe. The ECtHR is an unlikely candidate to assume the role of 'the conscience of Europe'[66] and fill the void that dysfunctional domestic institutions have left behind. If we look at the figures,[67] the vast majority of applicants will not get clarity, compensation or closure, but a strikeout or inadmissibility decision along with the truth that their efforts were in vain.

At the same time, scholars should not draw overly general conclusions from *Burmych* even though the judgment was handed down by the Grand Chamber. While some commentators interpret *Burmych* as denial of *certiorari* – albeit through the 'backdoor'[68] – it is unlikely that there will be more collective strikeouts without a compelling reason for doing so. After all, the *Burmych* strikeout stands at the end of a long chain of failed attempts to oblige Ukraine to safeguard the enforcement of the court decisions of the Chernobyl victims and other applicants seeking payment from the Ukrainian State. Yet one cannot help but get the impression that the Court wanted to send a message with the *Burmych* judgment: applicants should manage their expectations and be more realistic about what the Court can deliver when countries fail to solve their most pressing issues. In fact, the dissenting judges wonder why applicants suffering from the human rights violations that typically give rise to repetitive cases should bother filing an application with the Court.[69]

II. The further Development of the Convention and Compliance with Existing Obligations

The Court should reconsider the absolute prioritisation of non-repetitive over repetitive cases. One way – the traditional way – of preserving the Convention as the often-cited 'living instrument'[70] has been through

66 Myjer et al. (eds), *The Conscience of Europe, 50 Years of the European Court of Human Rights* (2010).

67 See *supra*, 3.

68 Ulfstein and Zimmermann, 'Certiorari through the Back Door? The Judgment by the European Court of Human Rights in Burmych and Others v Ukraine in Perspective' (2018) 17 *The Law and Practice of International Courts and Tribunals*, 289 (290).

69 ECtHR, Judgment (GC), 12 October 2017, *Burmych and Others v Ukraine*, Application Nos. 46852/13 and 4 more, Joint Dissenting Opinion of Judges Yudkivska, Sajó, Bianku, Karakas, De Gaetano, Laffranque and Motoc, para. 28.

70 ECtHR, Judgment, 25 April, 1978, *Tyrer v the United Kingdom*, Application No. 5856/72.

steady interpretation. However, the Convention remains just as practically relevant if the Court reminds the member states ever so often about the systemic issues that lead to widespread violations of the Convention. Repetitive cases are nothing but a symptom of long-term non-compliance with existing obligations under the Convention. Holding the member states accountable for failing to comply with the status quo is just as important to keep the Convention 'alive' as the further development of the Convention. Otherwise, the gains in efficiency are made at the expense of compliance.

III. Efficiency at the Expense of the Court's Legitimacy?

Even if the Court comes to the conclusion that efficiency must prevail – favouring procedural economy over individual justice – the Court must closely observe how a particular procedural approach impacts its perceived procedural fairness and sociological legitimacy so as to avoid the impression that applicants in repetitive cases are less important than applicants in non-repetitive cases. It is too early to tell if the Court was really 'shooting itself in the foot'[71] with the mass strikeout in *Burmych* or, quite the contrary, protecting itself from falling apart. The answer to this question depends on the invisible glue that underpins international courts: legitimacy. Legitimacy, so the theory, promotes compliance, reinforces authority, and boosts the effectiveness of international courts and tribunals.[72] Generations of legal scholars,[73] political scientists,[74] sociologists,[75] psychologists[76] and philosophers[77] have studied legitimacy, each through their own lens. In fact, there seem to be as many definitions, understandings,

---

71 ECtHR, Judgment (GC), 12 October 2017, *Burmych and Others v Ukraine*, Application Nos. 46852/13 and 4 more, Joint Dissenting Opinion, para. 39.

72 See, e.g., Grossman et al. (eds), *Legitimacy and International Courts* (2018); Wolfrum and Röben (eds), *Legitimacy in International Law* (2008).

73 See, e.g., Wolfrum and Röben (eds), *Legitimacy in International Law* (2008).

74 See, e.g., Gibson and Caldeira, 'The Legitimacy of Transnational Legal Institutions: Compliance, Support, and the European Court of Justice' (1995) 39 *American Journal of Political Science*, 459.

75 See, e.g., Luhmann, *Legitimation durch Verfahren* (2013); Weber, *Wirtschaft und Gesellschaft* (2002).

76 See, e.g. Jost and Major (eds), *The Psychology of Legitimacy, Emerging Perspectives on Ideology, Justice, and Intergroup Relations* (2001).

77 See, e.g., Buchanan, *Justice, Legitimacy, and Self-determination, Moral Foundations for International Law* (2004).

and conceptions of legitimacy as there have been scholars writing about it. It is very much an open question whether the widely drawn distinction between normative and sociological legitimacy plays in practice indeed the crucial role that it is given in theory.[78] For the time being, there is no empirical evidence to support the theoretical arguments advanced by legitimacy scholars. It would be interesting to collect data on the Court's sociological legitimacy and conduct a survey amongst the applicants of the *Burmych* case to gain new insights into their expectations before filing the application and experiences in dealing with the ECtHR. On that occasion, we should also ask the five named applicants along with the ones listed in the two Appendices to the *Burmych* judgment about strikeouts: whether they feel treated unfairly and if a public hearing had made a difference. While we can only speculate how many strikeouts they think are too many, it should not strike us as odd if their answer was 12,148.

ANNEX

Approximate number of applications in which a strikeout decision was rendered

Year	Total number of applications resolved by decision	Total number of applications resolved by judgment	Approximate number of applications resolved by strikeout decision[79]
2008[80]	30,164	1,881	3,016
2009[81]	33,067	2,393	3,307
2010[82]	38,576	2,607	3,858
2011[83]	50,677	1,511	5,068
2012[84]	86,201	1,678	8,620

78 Tyler, *Why People Obey the Law* (2006), 57.
79 The calculation is based on an average inadmissibility rate of 90 %.
80 ECtHR: Annual Report 2008, 2009, https://www.echr.coe.int/Documents/Annual_report_2008_ENG.pdf, 127.
81 ECtHR, Annual Report 2009, 2010, https://www.echr.coe.int/Documents/Annual_report_2009_ENG.pdf, 139.
82 ECtHR, Annual Report 2010, 2011, https://www.echr.coe.int/Documents/Annual_report_2010_ENG.pdf, 145.
83 ECtHR, Annual Report 2011, 2012, https://www.echr.coe.int/Documents/Annual_report_2011_ENG.pdf, 151.
84 ECtHR, Annual Report 2012, 2013, https://www.echr.coe.int/Documents/Annual_report_2012_ENG.pdf, 149.

Year	Total number of applications resolved by decision	Total number of applications resolved by judgment	Approximate number of applications resolved by strikeout decision
2013[85]	89,737	3,659	8,974
2014[86]	83,675	2,388	8,367
2015[87]	43,135	2,441	4,313
2016[88]	36,579	1,926	3,658
2017[89]	70,356	15,595	7,036
2018[90]	40,023	2,738	4,003
Mean	-	2,424[91]	5,474

Bibliography

Berkhuysen, Tom/Van Emmerik, Michael: Legitimacy of European Court of Human Rights Judgments: Procedural Aspects, in: Huls, Nick/Adams, Maurice/Bonhoff Jacco (eds), The Legitimacy of Highest Courts' Rulings (2009), 435ff.

Buchanan, Allen: Justice, Legitimacy, and Self-determination, Moral Foundations for International Law (2004).

Cohen, Harlan Grant/Follesdal, Andreas/Grossman, Nienke/Ulfstein, Geir: Legitimacy and International Courts – A Framework, in: Grossman, Nienke/Cohen, Harlan Grant/Follesdal, Andreas/Ulfstein Geir (eds), Legitimacy and International Courts (2018), 4ff.

Garlicki, Lech: Judicial Deliberations: The Strasbourg Perspective, in: Huls, Nick/Adams, Maurice/Bonhoff Jacco (eds), The Legitimacy of Highest Courts' Rulings (2009), 389ff.

85 ECtHR, Annual Report 2013, 2014, https://www.echr.coe.int/Documents/Annual_report_2013_ENG.pdf, 191.

86 ECtHR, Annual Report 2014, 2015, https://www.echr.coe.int/Documents/Annual_report_2014_ENG.pdf, 165.

87 ECtHR, Annual Report 2015, 2016, https://www.echr.coe.int/Documents/Annual_report_2015_ENG.pdf, 187.

88 ECtHR, Annual Report 2016, 2017, https://www.echr.coe.int/Documents/Annual_report_2016_ENG.pdf, 191.

89 ECtHR, Annual Report 2017, 2018, https://www.echr.coe.int/Documents/Annual_report_2017_ENG.pdf, 163.

90 ECtHR, Annual Report 2018, 2019 https://www.echr.coe.int/Documents/Annual_report_2018_ENG.pdf, 167.

91 The mean does not take into account the applications included in *Burmych and others v Ukraine* given that the strikeout was delivered by judgment.

Gibson, James L./Caldeira, Gregory A.: The Legitimacy of Transnational Legal Institutions: Compliance, Support, and the European Court of Justice, American Journal of Political Science 1995, 459 ff.

Jost, John T./Major Brenda (eds): The Psychology of Legitimacy, Emerging Perspectives on Ideology, Justice, and Intergroup Relations (2001).

Keller, Helen/Forowicz, Magdalena/Engi, Lorenz: Friendly Settlements before the European Court of Human Rights (2010).

Kepner, Tyler: More Strikeouts Than Hits? Welcome to Baseball's Latest Crisis, New York Times, 16 August 2018, https://www.nytimes.com/2018/08/16/sports/baseball-mlb-strikeouts.html.

Kindt, Eline: Giving up on individual justice? The effect of state non-execution of a pilot judgment on victims, Netherlands Quarterly of Human Rights 2018, 173ff.

Lasser, Mitchel: Judicial Deliberations, A Comparative Analysis of Judicial Transparency and Legitimacy (2004).

Luhmann, Niklas: Legitimation durch Verfahren, 9th edn. (2013).

Major League Baseball: Official Playing Rules Committee, Official Baseball Rules, 2018 Edition, 126, http://mlb.mlb.com/documents/0/8/0/268272080/2018_Official_Baseball_Rules.pdf.

Myjer, Egbert/Sharpe, Jonathan L./Spielmann, Dean (eds): The Conscience of Europe, 50 Years of the European Court of Human Rights (2010).

Nußberger, Angelika: The European Court of Human Rights (2020).

Sainati, Tatiana: Human Rights Class Actions: Rethinking the Pilot-Judgment Procedure at the European Court of Human Rights, Harvard International Law Journal 2015, 147 ff.

Scharpf, Fritz: Legitimacy in the multilevel European polity, European Political Science Review 2009, 173 ff.

Sellers, Mortimer (ed): Law, Reason, and Emotion (2017).

Tyler, Tom R.: Why People Obey the Law (2006).

Ulfstein, Geir: The Human Rights Treaty Bodies and Legitimacy Challenges, in: Grossman, Nienke/Cohen, Harlan Grant/Follesdal, Andreas/Ulfstein Geir (eds), Legitimacy and International Courts (2018), 284 ff.

Ulfstein Geir/Zimmermann, Andreas: Certiorari through the Back Door? The Judgment by the European Court of Human Rights in Burmych and Others v. Ukraine in Perspective, The Law and Practice of International Courts and Tribunals 2018, 289 ff.

Verducci, Tom: There Are Too Many Strikeouts in Baseball: Here's How to Fix the Problem, Sports Illustrated, 14 June 2018, https://www.si.com/mlb/2018/06/14/strikeouts-effect-major-league-baseball.

Voeten, Eric: The Impartiality of International Judges: Evidence from the European Court of Human Rights, The American Political Science Review 2008, 417 ff.

Weber, Max: Wirtschaft und Gesellschaft, 5th rev. edn. (2002).

Wolfrum, Rüdiger/Röben, Volker (eds), Legitimacy in International Law (2008).

Protection of Human Rights Defenders and Whistleblowers under Human Rights Law

Veronika Bílková

In October 2019, the European Union (EU) adopted a new directive on the protection of persons who report breaches of Union law, also known as the Whistleblower Protection Directive.[1] The Directive, in force since December 2019, is the first international legal instrument reflecting the increased vulnerability of those who expose certain illegal or unethical activities within a private or public organisation. This increased vulnerability is shared by other groups of persons acting in general interest, especially human rights defenders. Individuals who seek to actively defend or promote human rights might have their own human rights threatened or violated. In acknowledgement of this fact, the UN General Assembly adopted, in 1998, the UN Declaration on Human Rights Defenders.[2] These normative developments suggest that international law is neither indifferent to nor ignorant of the special needs of those who risk their well-being and sometimes also their life for the common good. This chapter identifies the challenges that human rights defenders and whistleblowers face and scrutinises how international law and regional human rights law in Europe respond to these challenges.

The chapter consists of three parts. The first part introduces the concepts of human rights defenders and of whistleblowers. It provides a definition of the two concepts and makes a comparison between them (A.). The second part explores how the increased vulnerability of human rights defenders and whistleblowers manifests itself both in their private life and in the public space (B.). The third part discusses how international law has responded to this increased vulnerability of human rights defenders and whistleblowers and identifies some gaps in these responses (C.). The chapter relies on the European Convention on Human Rights

---

1 Directive (EU) 2019/1937 of the European Parliament and of the Council of 23 October 2019 on the protection of persons who report breaches of Union law.

2 UN General Assembly, *Declaration on the Right and Responsibility of Individuals, Groups and Organs of Society to Promote and Protect Universally Recognized Human Rights and Fundamental Freedoms*, 8 March 1999, UN Doc. A/RES/53/144.

(ECHR) and the case-law of the European Court of Human Rights (ECtHR). It also draws on other human rights instruments applicable in Europe, especially those adopted within the United Nations (UN), the Council of Europe (CoE) and the European Union (EU).

A. Who are Human Rights Defenders and Whistleblowers?

This part introduces the concepts and provides definitions of human rights defenders (I.) and of whistleblowers (II.). It casts light on the origins of the two concepts and discusses whether and if so, when and in what context, they have become part of international law. It also draws a comparison between the two concepts (III.).

I. Who are Human Rights Defenders?

The term 'human rights defender' is not yet a legal term of art. It does not appear in virtually any treaty or other binding international instrument.[3] Even the so-called UN Declaration on Human Rights Defenders, however surprising it may seem, fails to use this term explicitly in its official title or its text. Notwithstanding that, references to 'human rights defenders' appear not only in materials relating to the UN Declaration,[4] but also in reports[5] and non-binding guidelines issued by international organisations[6]

---

3 One exception to this rule is the 2018 *Regional Agreement on Access to Information, Public Participation and Justice in Environmental Matters in Latin America and the Caribbean,* which refers explicitly to human rights defenders in environmental matters (Article 9). The Agreement provides no definition of the term.

4 See Wille and Spannagel, 'The history of the UN Declaration on Human Rights Defenders: its genesis, drafting and adoption', Universal Rights Group Blog, 11 March 2019, https://www.universal-rights.org/blog/the-un-declaration-on-human-rights-defenders-its-history-and-drafting-process/.

5 Inter-American Commission on Human Rights, *Criminalization of the Work of Human Rights Defenders*, 31 December 2015, OEA/Ser.L/V/II. Doc. 49/15; CoE Parliamentary Assembly, *Protecting human rights defenders in Council of Europe member States*, Report, 6 June 2018, Doc. 14567.

6 See CoE Committee of Ministers, *Declaration on Council of Europe action to improve the protection of human rights defenders and promote their activities*, 6 February 2008; Council of the EU, *Ensuring Protection – European Union Guidelines on Human Rights Defenders,* 1 December 2008, 16332/1/08.

as well as in scholarly literature.[7] In the past, several alternative terms were regularly used, such as human rights activists, human rights workers, human rights professionals, human rights monitors or (human rights) dissidents. While these terms have not completely disappeared from the vocabulary, they have become much less common over the past decades, while the term human rights defenders has prevailed. Some of these alternative terms, moreover, are only used in a specific context (e.g. the term dissident is usually reserved for those criticising and opposing political practices embraced by totalitarian or authoritarian regimes).

Due to its absence from international instruments, the term 'human rights defenders' has not received any formal legal definition so far.[8] Most international institutions, legal scholars and defenders themselves take, however, the official title and Article 1 of the UN Declaration as the primary sources of inspiration. The title refers to 'individuals, groups and organs of society /who/ promote and protect universally recognized human rights and fundamental freedoms'. Article 1 indicates that '[e]veryone has the right, individually and in association with others, to promote and to strive for the protection and realization of human rights and fundamental freedoms at the national and international levels.'

Most policy documents and non-binding guidelines on human rights defenders either quote one of these definitions directly or provide a paraphrase thereof. The UN Office of the High Commissioner for Human Rights (UN OHCHR) in its 2004 Fact Sheet on Human Rights Defenders suggests that '"human rights defender" is a term used to describe people who, individually or with others, act to promote or protect human rights'.[9] For the EU, human rights defenders are 'those individuals, groups and organs of society that promote and protect universally recognised human rights and fundamental freedoms'.[10] The OSCE quotes the UN Declaration in stating that 'human rights defenders act "individually or in association with others, to promote and to strive for the protection and realization of

7 See Bennett et al., 'Critical perspectives on the security and protection of human rights defenders' (2015) 19(7) *IJHR*, 883; Donders, 'Defending the Human Rights Defenders' (2016) 34(4) *NQHR* 282; Landman, 'Holding the Line: Human Rights Defenders in the Age of Terror' (2016) 8(2) *BJPIR* 123.

8 See Koula, 'The UN Definition of Human Rights Defenders: Alternative Interpretative Approaches' (2019) 5(1) *QMHRR* 1.

9 UN OHCHR, *Human Rights Defenders: Protecting the Right to Defend Human Rights*. Fact Sheet No. 29 (2004), 2.

10 Council of the EU, *Ensuring Protection – European Union Guidelines on Human Rights Defenders*, 1 December 2008, 16332/1/08, para. 3.

human rights and fundamental freedoms"' and adds that this can be done 'at the local, national, regional and international levels'.[11] The Parliamentary Assembly of the Council of Europe describes human rights defenders as '"those who work for the rights of others" – individuals or groups who act, in a peaceful and legal way, to promote and protect human rights'.[12]

Despite certain differences, all the definitions of human rights defenders share the same elements. These elements are three-fold. The first one relates to the actors, i.e. who human rights defenders are. They are individuals, groups of individuals or organised entities – non-governmental organisations and, in the broadest understanding, even State bodies and inter-governmental organisations.[13] A political dissident in China, the French branch of Amnesty International, the national ombuds-institution in Peru and the UN OHCHR could all qualify as human rights defenders. Thus, the term is not reserved to collective entities only and it is probably not reserved to those acting outside the official structures either. Equating human rights defenders with NGOs, as is sometimes the case, would therefore be incorrect.

The second element pertains to the activity, i.e. what human rights defenders do. Generally, they act to promote and protect human rights. More specifically, they may engage in various activities, especially those listed by the UN OHCHR in its Fact Sheet. Those activities encompass collecting and disseminating information on human rights violations, supporting victims of such violations, engaging in action to secure accountability and to end impunity, supporting better governance and government policy, contributing to the implementation of human rights treaties, and taking active part in human rights education and training.[14] Which field of human rights human rights defenders work in and whether they do so in their professional or private capacity is irrelevant for their status.

The third element concerns the mode of operation, i.e. how human rights defenders act. The UN OHCHR stresses that 'the actions taken

---

11 OSCE, *Guidelines on the Protection of Human Rights Defenders* (2014), 1.

12 CoE Parliamentary Assembly, *Protecting human rights defenders in Council of Europe member States*, 26 June 2018, Resolution 2225 (2018), para. 1.

13 For a broad definition of human rights defenders, encompassing 'certain civil servants, members of NHRIs, [...] and staff of the United Nations', see UN Economic and Social Council, *Promotion and Protection of Human Rights. Human Rights Defenders. Report submitted by the Special Representative of the Secretary-General on human rights defenders, Hina Jilani*, 23 January 2006, UN Doc. E/CN.4/2006/95, para. 29.

14 UN OHCHR, *Human Rights Defenders: Protecting the Right to Defend Human Rights. Fact Sheet No. 29* (2004), 3 ff.

by human rights defenders must be peaceful'.[15] Individuals and groups resorting to violent means thus remain outside the scope of the concept. Human rights defenders should also believe in human rights and accept the universality of these rights. Apart from that, they are not subject to any special requirements or qualifications. Thus, to quote again from the UN OHCHR Fact Sheet, 'human rights defenders can be any person or group of persons working to promote human rights [...]. Defenders can be of any gender, of varying ages, from any part of the world and from all sorts of professional or other backgrounds'.[16] This implies that 'we can all be defenders of human rights if we choose to be'.[17]

II. Who are Whistleblowers?

The term 'whistleblower' dates back to the 19th century, when it was coined in the US to describe law enforcement officials who used a whistle to alert fellow officials or the public about an emergency situation. In the 1970s-1980s, it started to be used to denote individuals who informed about certain negative phenomena in society.[18] The term entered the legal vocabulary, first at the national level, at the turn of the millennium. In 2019, the Whistleblower Protection Directive, adopted within the EU, became the first – and so far the only – international legally binding instrument dealing specifically with persons falling within this category.[19] The Directive does not use the term 'whistleblowers' in its title but invokes it repeatedly in its text. *Promiscue*, it speaks, this time both in the title and the text, about 'persons reporting on breaches of Union law', which is the most general definition of whistleblowers provided in the Directive. Article 4 specifies that the Directive shall apply to 'reporting persons working in the private or public sector who acquired information on breaches in a work-related context', giving examples of such context.

Similar definitions are provided by other international organisations, even if they do not have binding instruments on whistleblowers. The International Labour Organization (ILO) defines whistleblowing as 'the re-

---

15 *Id.*, 10.
16 *Id.*, 6.
17 *Id.*, 8.
18 See Near and Miceli, 'Organizational Dissidence: The Case of Whistle-Blowing' (1985) 4 *J. Bus. Ethics*, 1; Vaughn, *Whistleblowing Law* (2015).
19 Directive (EU) 2019/1937 of the European Parliament and of the Council of 23 October 2019 on the protection of persons who report breaches of Union law.

porting by employees or former employees of illegal, irregular, dangerous or unethical practices by employers'.[20] For the CoE, a whistleblower is 'any person who reports or discloses information on a threat or harm to the public interest in the context of their work-based relationship, whether it be in the public or private sector'.[21] International conventions dealing with the fight against corruption, while not using the term expressly, also deal with this phenomenon. The UN Convention against Corruption contains a provision on the protection of reporting persons whom it defines as 'any person who reports in good faith and on reasonable grounds to the competent authorities any facts concerning offences established in accordance with this Convention' (Article 33). The CoE Civil Law Convention on Corruption obliges States to protect 'employees who have reasonable grounds to suspect corruption and who report in good faith their suspicion to responsible persons or authorities' (Article 9).

The definition of whistleblowers again contains several elements. The first pertains to the actors, i.e. who whistleblowers are. They are all individuals who are in possession of relevant information and who report this information, regardless of whether they are active in the private or public sector. The reference to individuals or persons suggests that unlike human rights defenders, whistleblowers are natural persons, not legal entities, let alone international organisations or States. The second element concerns the activity, i.e. what whistleblowers do. They report – inside their institution or through public channels – activities that are considered illegal or immoral. Some definitions moreover require that the reported wrongdoing be of a serious nature or public interest, narrowing the acts which may qualify as whistleblowing. The third element relates to the context, i.e. where whistleblowers act. They act in a work-related context. They tend to have a privileged status within the institution that allows them to get access to confidential, inside information regarding the activities of this institution or individuals within it. As the ECtHR held in *Medžlis Islamske Zajednice Brčko*, such a privileged position entails a special duty of 'loyalty, reserve and discretion'[22] that whistleblowers have with respect to their institution and that they may break to be able to report unethical

---

20 International Labour Organization, *International Labour Organization Thesaurus* (2005) (the ILO Thesaurus is a compilation of terms relating to the world of work).

21 CoE Committee of Ministers, *Protection of Whistleblowers*, 30 April 2014, Recommendation CM/Rec(2014)7, definition a.

22 ECtHR, Judgment (GC), 27 June 2017, *Medžlis Islamske Zajednice Brčko v Bosnia and Herzegovina*, Application No. 17224/11, para. 80.

or unlawful behaviour. Those reporting wrongdoings outside the working context, based on information acquired from public sources, would not be whistleblowers. Some of them may qualify as human rights defenders.

III. What are the Shared Features and the Differences between the two Groups?

Human rights defenders and whistleblowers are two distinct categories. The differences between them relate to all the elements of the definitions identified above. First, concerning the actors: whereas whistleblowers are individuals, the circle of human rights defenders is broader, encompassing also groups, associations and, even, State bodies and organs of international organisations. Secondly, as to the activity: whistleblowers report on unlawful or unethical activities identified within their institution; human rights defenders promote and protect universally recognised human rights and fundamental freedoms. The two groups thus engage in different activities (reporting vs promoting and protecting human rights) and they operate within different normative frameworks (legal or ethical standards vs human rights).[23] Thirdly, with respect to the mode of operation and context: whistleblowers are limited to the work-related context, human rights defenders on the contrary have no *a priori* limits imposed on them, apart from the peaceful nature of their activities.

Despite these differences, human rights defenders and whistleblowers share certain important features. They both act in general interest, helping prevent actions that are harmful not only (and not necessarily) to concrete human rights defenders or whistleblowers but to other persons, institutions and even the society at large. The nature of their activities makes human rights defenders and whistleblowers alike increasingly vulnerable to human rights and other abuses carried out with the purpose of silencing them. Due to this increased vulnerability, the two groups are both in need of special legal protection and have already been provided with such protection in international law, albeit mostly through soft law instruments. Although the concrete forms of abuses that human rights defenders and

23 There are, however, overlaps between the two categories. See CoE Parliamentary Assembly, *Protection of "whistle-blowers"*, 29 April 2010, Resolution 1729 (2010), which notes that the definition of protected disclosures 'shall include all bona fide warnings against various types of unlawful acts, including all serious human rights violations which affect or threaten the life, health, liberty and any other legitimate interests of individuals as subjects of public administration or taxpayers, or as shareholders, employees or customers of private companies' (para. 6.1.1).

whistleblowers suffer differ somewhat from each other as does the legal framework applicable to them, the common characteristics which they share explain why this chapter brings the two categories together.

B. *How does the Increased Vulnerability of Human Rights Defenders and Whistleblowers Manifest Itself?*

Human rights defenders and whistleblowers engage in activities that are not welcomed by everyone.[24] These activities tend to be particularly unpopular with those who get criticised for their participation in human rights abuses (by human rights defenders) or are reported on for their illegal or immoral activities (by whistleblowers). Since such persons or institutions are often in a position of power, they may seek to take steps that would prevent human rights defenders and whistleblowers from continuing their actions or punish them for carrying these actions out. Such steps may involve violations of human rights and various other abuses.[25] The increased vulnerability to such violations and abuses manifest itself in three main areas. These areas relate to private life and safety (I.), the activities in the public space (II.), and the economic and social status, including the position at work (III.).

I. *Private Life and Safety*

Human rights defenders and whistleblowers may be subject to interferences with their private life and safety.[26] The degree of their vulnerability depends on the type of activities they engage in, the nature of wrongdoings/wrongdoers they expose, the political system of the country where

---

24 See also OSCE, *Human Rights Defenders in the OSCE Region: Challenges and Good Practices* (2008).

25 In the classical approach, human rights may only be violated by acts carried out by or attributable to States. Under the doctrine of horizontal effects, States may also be held accountable for acts of private actors if they fail to take adequate measures to prevent or repress such acts. See Alston (ed), *Non-State Actors and Human Rights* (2005); Lane, 'The Horizontal Effect of International Human Rights Law in Practice: A Comparative Analysis of the General Comments and Jurisprudence of Selected United Nations Human Rights Treaty Monitoring Bodies' (2018) 5 *EJCL*, 5.

26 See OSCE, *Guidelines on the Protection of Human Rights Defenders* (2014), 3 ff.; Alford, *Whistleblowers: Broken Lives and Organizational Power* (2002).

they live as well as their own personal features and social status. While all human rights defenders and whistleblowers are vulnerable, some are more vulnerable than others. For instance, women may face an increased risk of rape and sexual harassment, people with dependent children may be vulnerable to blackmailing through their children, etc. It is important to keep in mind that interferences may go on for a protracted period of time. Even relatively minor nuisances, which would not do much harm on their own, may, if they occur on a regular basis, have a heavy impact on the targeted persons and their families.

The most extreme forms of threats concern life and physical integrity as protected by Articles 2, 3 and 5 of the ECHR. The 2019 global report by the NGO Front Line Defenders indicates that more than 300 human rights defenders were killed all over the world that year alone.[27] Most of them were attacked by (allegedly) unknown perpetrators, abducted and subsequently murdered, or simply disappeared without any traces.[28] Hundreds of defenders get seriously injured, kidnapped, mistreated and subjected to inhuman treatment or even torture.[29] While less commonly, whistleblowers become targets of violent actions threatening their life as well.[30] Human rights defenders and whistleblowers alike are also exposed to death threats addressed to them or to members of their family.[31] Death threats, in fact, seem to be one of the most 'popular' means of intimidating persons who engage in 'undesirable' activities. Easy to make, especially with the recent spread of social media, they also tend to be taken much less seriously by law enforcement agencies than actual attacks. Yet, as noted by the UN OHCHR, 'death threats […] can oblige human rights defenders to change their daily routines completely, as well as those of their immediate family, or even to leave their country to seek temporary asylum abroad'.[32]

---

27 See Front Line Defenders, *Front Line Defenders Global Analysis 2019* (2020), 7.

28 For instance, in recent years, the investigative journalists Daphne Caruana Galizia (2017) and Ján Kuciak (2018) have been killed in Malta and Slovakia, respectively.

29 Front Line Defenders, *Front Line Defenders Global Analysis 2019* (2020).

30 The Times of India, RTI activists abducted and tortured, 26 December 2013.

31 UN General Assembly, *Final warning: death threats and killings of human rights defenders. Report of the Special Rapporteur on the situation of human rights defenders, Mary Lawlor*, 24 December 2020, UN Doc. A/HRC/46/35; mLIVE, Michigan man made death threat to Trump whistleblower's attorney, feds say, 22 February 2020, https://www.mlive.com/news/saginaw-bay-city/2020/02/michigan-man-made-death-threat-to-trump-whistleblowers-attorney-feds-say.html.

32 UN OHCHR, *Human Rights Defenders: Protecting the Right to Defend Human Rights. Fact Sheet No. 29* (2004), 11.

Female human rights defenders and whistleblowers are more likely to be exposed to sexual abuses including rape than their male counterparts, though the latter are not immune to this type of abuse either.[33] Abuses may be committed by public officials, violent non-state actors but also, not unfrequently, by members of their own family or community, seeking to discipline and silence 'trouble-makers'. Human rights defenders and whistleblowers focusing on certain issues, typically women's reproductive rights or LGBT+ rights, or reporting on certain types of abuses, such as rape and sexual violence, are particularly vulnerable to sexual abuse.[34] Other forms of harassment are also commonplace, and they often go unreported or if reported, un-investigated. Individuals get repeatedly monitored without obvious reasons, have fines imposed on them for trivial transgressions, have to present themselves at regular intervals to the police, have their private mails, emails and phone calls read and wiretapped, etc.[35] These practices not only interfere with the private life, but they may also have an impact on the state of the mental and physical health of those targeted and their families.

Closely related to these abuses are the encroachments upon personal liberty.[36] Arbitrary arrests and detentions are not uncommon, and they often occur in the absence of official charges. Sometimes, fake trials or trials for acts that should not constitute criminal offences in a democratic society (social parasitism, distributing prohibited books, etc.) are arranged, resulting in humiliating sanctions (forcible commitment to psychiatric institutions, re-education through labour, etc.).[37] This applies to human rights defenders and to whistleblowers alike. The latter may face charges of betrayal of state secrets, high treason, espionage, collusion with the

---

33 UN General Assembly, *Situation of human rights defenders. Note by the Secretary-General*, 16 July 2020, UN Doc. A/75/165, para. 48; Hunt, 'The Challenges Women Whistleblowers Face' (2010) 3(2) *International Business Research*, 3.

34 Mulé, 'LGBTQI-identified human rights defenders: courage in the face of adversity at the United Nations' (2018) 26(1) *Gender and Development*, 89.

35 See Inter-American Commission on Human Rights, *Report on the Situation of Human Rights Defenders in the Americas*, 17 March 2006, OEA/Ser.L/V/II.124/Doc. 5 rev.1, paras. 164 ff.

36 CoE, *Human Rights Defenders in the Council of Europe Area: Current Challenges and Possible Solutions. Report from the Round-Table with human rights defenders organised by the Office of the CoE Commissioner for Human Rights (Helsinki, 13–14 December 2018)*, 29 March 2019, CommDH(2019)10, paras. 14 ff.

37 Inter-American Commission on Human Rights, *Report on the Situation of Human Rights Defenders in the Americas*, 17 March 2006, OEA/Ser.L/V/II.124/Doc. 5 rev.1, paras. 174 ff.

enemy or similar charges which tend to entail high penalties. For instance, Edward Snowden, who leaked highly classified information from the US National Security Agency in 2013, has been charged with theft of government property, unauthorised communication of national defence information and wilful communication of classified intelligence information to an unauthorised person.[38] In some instances, whistleblowers are charged with common offences and it might be difficult to say whether the prosecution is politically motivated. This is the case of another well-known whistleblower, Julian Assange, the founder of WikiLeaks, wanted in Sweden in connection with the accusations of rape and sexual molestation.[39]

Many measures directed against human rights defenders and whistleblowers target their private and family life. Defamation campaigns are a popular instrument used to question the moral integrity and tarnish the reputation of those who have engaged in undesired criticism. Human rights defenders[40] and whistleblowers[41] are labelled as traitors, subversive elements, lazy and parasitic individuals or, in the recent years, as terrorists. They are accused of betraying their country and serving foreign interests and described as immoral persons. Their private space is often disrespected – their homes and business premises get surveyed and searched, their private or business communication read or wiretapped, their personal data may be stored for extended periods of time.[42] The pressure is often directed not only against human rights defenders and whistleblowers themselves but also against members of their family, including underage children.

38 Davis, 'Is Edward Snowden Protected By International Law?', Huffington Post, 17 July 2013, https://www.huffpost.com/entry/edward-snowden-international-law_n_3544679.

39 See Melzer, *State Responsibility for the Torture of Julian Assange, Speech by Nils Melzer, UN Special Rapporteur on Torture, at the German Bundestag in Berlin, 27 November 2019 (English translation)*, 16 December 2019, https://medium.com/@njmelzer/state-responsibility-for-the-torture-of-julian-assange-40935ea5d7c3.

40 UN General Assembly, *Situation of human rights defenders. Note by the Secretary-General*, 10 August 2012, UN Doc. A/67/292, paras. 15 f.

41 Papandrea, 'Leaker Traitor Whistleblower Spy: National Security Leaks and the First Amendment' (2014) 94(2) *Boston Univ Law Rev*, 449.

42 See Frost, *World Report on the Situation of Human Rights Defenders*, December 2018.

II. Activities in the Public Space

Human rights defenders and, to a lesser extent, whistleblowers face human rights abuses not only in their private life but also in the public space. Virtually all civil and political rights may get interfered with by State agents or non-state actors acting with the State's express or implicit support.[43] Free speech and access to information, protected under Article 10 of the ECHR, are among such rights. Since human rights defenders and whistleblowers say or write things that are not pleasant to hear or read by those concerned, the attempts to prevent them from being able to get access to information and to spread this information and attempts to punish them, if they succeed to do so, are common.[44] As the ultimate aim of measures directed against human rights defenders and whistleblowers is to silence them, their exercise of the right to freedom of expression is virtually always at stake. Steps taken to silence human rights defenders and whistleblowers do not only interfere with the rights of those persons but also with the legitimate interest of the general public to know about illegal and immoral activities carried out in the public or private sector. Media play a particularly important role in this field, both as actors monitoring human rights in the country and as a means through which information about human rights abuses and other wrongdoings may be made accessible to the general public.[45]

Another right, which is often interfered with in this context, is the right to freedom of association, guaranteed by Article 11 of the ECHR. As we have seen, while whistleblowers are natural persons, human rights defenders may be, and often are, collective entities, typically NGOs. Such entities may get targeted by various legal, administrative and other measures that make it difficult for them to engage in their standard activities. For example, their creation becomes subject to various burdensome conditions that are not easy to meet. Once established, they have more obligations than

43 States may be held responsible for human rights abuses by non-state actors that are attributable to them. They may also be held responsible for their own failure to prevent human rights abuses committed by non-state actors. See also Hessbruegge, 'Human Rights Violations Arising from Conduct of Non-State Actors' (2005) 11 *Buff Hum Rts L Rev*, 21.

44 See UN General Assembly, *Promotion and protection of the right to freedom of opinion and expression. Note by the Secretary-General*, 8 September 2015, UN Doc. A/70/361.

45 Mitchell, 'Journalists as Human Rights Defenders: International Protection of Journalists in Contexts of Violence and Impunity' in Shaw and Selvarajah (eds), *Reporting Human Rights, Conflicts, and Peacebuilding* (2019), 221.

other legal persons, e.g., the obligation to report about their activities or financial situation more frequently.[46] They are also often cut from certain sources of funding, especially funding from abroad. Or, if they are allowed to receive such funding, they may have to use problematic labels such as 'foreign agents'.[47] Their premises get regularly checked for unclear reasons and their internal documents are confiscated. Finally, the organization may get dissolved for minor transgressions, for instance for the failure to produce a certain document in time or minor discrepancies in the financial or membership reports.[48]

Other forms of interferences concern the rights to freedom of assembly, freedom of movement, freedom of religion, or freedom to vote and take part in public affairs. All these rights are guaranteed in the ECHR (Articles 10 and 11) and its Protocols (Article 3 of Protocol No. 1, Article 2 of Protocol No. 4). Individuals taking part in 'undesired' activities are prevented from holding public meetings or taking part in them. Alternatively, they are detained during such meetings and accused of various transgressions.[49] Human rights defenders also get prevented from travelling to places where they could investigate or simply witness human rights abuses. They may also be prohibited to leave the country or, on the contrary, forced to do so, and then prevented from returning.[50] Defenders may also face difficulties in access to religious services. Quite often, they find it uneasy to exercise the right to vote and the right to take part in public affairs.[51] The public authorities do not only fail to consult them and civil society more broadly about questions of public interest, but they also actively seek to prevent them from being able to take part in any public discussions. Whistleblow-

---

46 Amnesty International, *Global assault on NGOs reaches crisis point as new laws curb vital human rights work*, 21 February 2019.

47 Venice Commission, *Report on funding of associations*, 18 March 2019, CDL-AD(2019)002. See also Pfeffer, Why Breaking the Silence Became the Most Hated Group in Israel, Haaretz, 17 December 2015.

48 Venice Commission-OSCE/ODIHR, *Joint Guidelines on Freedom of Association*, 17 December 2014, CDL-AD(2014)046.

49 Front Line Defenders, Arrests of human rights defenders threaten rights to freedom of assembly and expression in Hong Kong, 20 April 2020, https://www.frontlinedefenders.org/en/statement-report/arrests-human-rights-defenders-threaten-rights-freedom-assembly-and-expression-hong.

50 Front Line Defenders, #Travel Ban, 2021, https://www.frontlinedefenders.org/en/violation/travel-ban.

51 Front Line Defenders, Judicial harassment of human rights defenders in the lead-up to presidential elections, 19 May 2020, https://www.frontlinedefenders.org/en/statement-report/judicial-harassment-human-rights-defenders-lead-presidential-elections.

ers might have similar difficulties in the access to the management of the institutions within which they operate.

III. Economic and Social Status

Human rights abuses committed against human rights defenders and whistleblowers are not limited to civil and political rights. Curtailing their economic, social and cultural rights, recognized and protected in the International Covenant on Economic, Social and Cultural Rights, the European Social Charter and, partly, the ECHR, might be as effective a way to dissuade them from engaging in their activities or to sanction them for doing so.[52] Human rights defenders and whistleblowers, as well as members of their family, have their property confiscated or destroyed, get evicted from their homes and may be, as mentioned above, banned from accepting funding from certain sources. Preventing their or their family members' access to health or social services and to schools is also rather frequent and may be particularly 'efficient' in countries where these services are provided predominantly or exclusively by the State. For instance, in the pre-1990 communist regimes, children of dissidents were denied access to universities and could have difficulties with access to certain social benefits.[53]

Human rights defenders and whistleblowers are also vulnerable to retaliatory measures at work. Here, their respective positions differ. Whereas human rights defenders usually do not have any special work relationship to those whose activities they criticise, whistleblowers, who report on wrongdoing committed by their colleagues, superiors or their institution, do have such a relation. That renders them exposed to an increased risk of retaliation by their employers. Whistleblowers may be sanctioned for disciplinary offences or lack of loyalty, deposed from their current position or dismissed altogether, and they may have troubles finding a new job. For instance, Jeffrey Wigand, an American biochemist and the head of research and development at a major tobacco company, who exposed on TV the toxicity of the tobacco produced by his company, was immediately fired

52 UN Committee on Economic, Social and Cultural Rights, *Human rights defenders and economic, social and cultural rights*, 29 March 2017, UN Doc. E/C.12/2016/2.

53 See Powell, 'Controlling Dissent in the Soviet Union' (1972) 7(1) *Government and Opposition*, 85.

(and received anonymous death threats).[54] Human rights defenders may be exposed to such threats as well, especially in countries where the State is the main employer and where assigning a low-paid job with no social prestige is used as a sanction.[55] Yet, while for whistleblowers, work-related measures are the main instrument of pressure, for human rights defenders, they are usually but one from a more extensive set of such instruments.

IV. Increased Vulnerability of Human Rights Defenders and Whistleblowers

As we have seen in the previous subparts, human rights defenders and whistleblowers are vulnerable to human rights abuses committed or tolerated by States. These abuses may affect them in many areas of their lives – they may have their privacy disrespected, their safety jeopardized, their activities in the public space disrupted and their voices silenced. They may also lose their job, be deprived of property or be denied access to education, health care and social services. They may be targeted directly or through family members or friends. In all cases, the aim is to prevent them from monitoring, and reporting on, human rights violations and from disclosing facts about illegal or immoral activities, or to retaliate against them for having done so. Moreover, as the OHCHR recalls, the 'violations of the rights of human rights defenders have been compounded by a culture of impunity which exists in many countries in relation to acts committed against human rights defenders'.[56] The same holds true, albeit to a lesser extent, for whistleblowers who may be left unprotected from the wrath of the person or institution whose wrongdoings they have reported. The increased vulnerability of the two categories has not gone unnoticed. It is at the source of several international instruments, and it has found reflection in international case-law that will be discussed in the next part.

---

54 Lyman, 'A Tobacco Whistle-Blower's Life Is Transformed', New York Times, 15 October 1999 https://www.nytimes.com/1999/10/15/us/a-tobacco-whistle-blower-s-life-is-transformed.html.

55 Maldives Independent, Rilwan and Yameen's relatives fired for joining protest march, 16 August 2017, https://maldivesindependent.com/society/rilwan-and-yameens-relatives-fired-for-joining-protest-march-132039.

56 UN OHCHR, *Human Rights Defenders: Protecting the Right to Defend Human Rights. Fact Sheet No. 29* (2004), 13.

C. Legal Regulations Applicable to Human Rights Defenders and Whistleblowers

In principle, human rights defenders and whistleblowers enjoy the same legal protection as other individuals or, in case of NGOs, as other associations. The full range of human rights granted in general human rights instruments, such as the ECHR, apply to them. In addition, over the past three decades, several instruments dealing specifically with these two groups have been adopted. These instruments, often non-binding in nature (soft law). do not introduce any new human rights. What they do, rather, is to specify how general human rights are to be implemented, applied and interpreted in the specific context of human rights defenders and whistleblowers. International human rights bodies, such as the ECtHR, have also contributed to this specification. Although human rights defenders and whistleblowers are exposed to similar human rights abuses, due to the differences between them, described in Part A, legal standards applicable to them are not, and cannot be, completely identical. This part provides an overview of such standards, focusing first on human rights defenders (I) and then on whistleblowers (II).

I. Legal Standards Applicable to Human Rights Defenders

There is no legally binding instrument that would focus specifically on human rights defenders. The most authoritative, albeit non-binding source is the 1998 UN Declaration on Human Rights Defenders.[57] The Declaration was elaborated over a 14-year period, which had begun in 1984 when the UN Human Rights Commission had decided to establish an open-ended working group on this topic.[58] The final text was adopted by the UN General Assembly, without vote, on 9 December 1998, on the occasion of the 50th anniversary of the Universal Declaration of Human Rights. It is based on legal standards that are contained in binding treaties, mainly the UN International Covenants on Civil and Political Rights and on Economic, Social and Cultural Rights. The Commentary on the Declaration, drafted

---

57 UN General Assembly, *Declaration on the Right and Responsibility of Individuals, Groups and Organs of Society to Promote and Protect Universally Recognized Human Rights and Fundamental Freedoms*, 8 March 1999, UN Doc. A/RES/53/144.

58 UN Commission on Human Rights, *Report on the Fortieth Session (6 February-16 March 1984)*, UN Doc. E/1984/14(SUPP)-E/CN.4/1984/77, 108.

by the UN Special Rapporteur on Human Rights Defenders, confirms that 'the Declaration specifies how the rights included in major human rights instruments apply to human rights defenders and their work'.[59] It also stresses that the Declaration 'was adopted by consensus [...], which consequently represents States' strong commitment towards its implementation'.[60]

The UN Declaration starts from the premise that 'everyone has the right, individually and in association with others, to promote and to strive for the protection and realization of human rights and fundamental freedoms at the national and international levels' (Article 1). The promotion and protection of human rights is thus not left to States, international institutions or members of any special profession. It is, as the official title of the Declaration expresses, the right and responsibility of everyone. The substantive provisions of the UN Declaration (Articles 2–18) specify the rights that human rights defenders enjoy as well as the duties that arise with respect to these rights. The duties mostly fall upon States, though occasionally, other actors are addressed as well. For instance, Article 11 calls upon those 'who, as a result of [their] profession, can affect the human dignity, human rights and fundamental freedoms of others' to 'respect those rights and freedoms and comply with relevant national and international standards of occupational and professional conduct or ethics'. The provision applies, for instance, to judges, advocates, police officers or medical staff.

The rights of human rights defenders listed in the Declaration include the rights to form associations; to meet or assemble peacefully; to seek, obtain, receive and hold information relating to human rights; to make complaints about official policies and acts relating to human rights and to have such complaints reviewed; or to solicit, receive and utilise resources for the purpose of protecting human rights. The Declaration thus mainly focuses on challenges that human rights defenders face in the public space. The other human rights abuses listed in Part B of this chapter, such as the interference with private life or the denial of economic and social rights, are either not addressed at all, or only indirectly.[61] The duties of States are

59 UN OHCHR, *Commentary to the Declaration on the Right and Responsibility of Individuals, Groups and Organs of Society to Promote and Protect Universally Recognized Human Rights and Fundamental Freedoms* (2011), 5 footnote 1.

60 *Ibid.*

61 The indirect protection could be granted, for instance, through the right to benefit from an effective remedy and to be protected in the event of the violation of human rights (Article 9(1) of the UN Declaration).

drafted in more general terms, encompassing the duty to protect, promote and implement all human rights; the duty to provide an effective remedy for persons who claim to be victims of a human rights violation; the duty to conduct prompt and impartial investigations of such alleged violations; or the duty to take all necessary measures to ensure the protection of everyone against any violence, threats, retaliation or other arbitrary action as a consequence of his or her legitimate exercise of the rights referred to in the Declaration. Some of these obligations, e.g. the duty to protect, promote and implement human rights, are broad enough to extend to all abuses that human rights defenders might suffer.

The UN Declaration is the most important international instrument concerning human rights defenders. It is not, however, the only one. In the 2000s, the Council of the EU and the CoE Committee of Ministers issued non-binding documents on the same topic, which, in fact, elaborate upon the Declaration. The two documents – the 2004 EU Guidelines on Human Rights Defenders[62] and the 2008 Declaration on Council of Europe action to improve the protection of human rights defenders and promote their activities[63] – both concentrate on the responsibilities that the relevant organisation, its member States and some other actors have with respect to human rights defenders.

The 2008 CoE Declaration takes a traditional approach, focusing on the responsibilities 'at home', i.e. in each CoE member State's respective territory. The Declaration condemns attacks on and violations of human rights of human rights defenders in the member States. It calls upon these States to take measures to prevent, stop and/or sanction such attacks and violations and to generally 'create an environment conducive to the work of human rights defenders' (para. 2-i). The 2004 EU Guidelines, on the contrary, deal with the situation of human rights defenders 'outside', i.e. in non-EU States. It is a tool of the common foreign and security policy, which is supposed to help the EU work 'towards the promotion and protection of human rights defenders in third countries' (para. 7). The EU does not have a similar instrument to help it work towards this goal 'at home'. It is probably assumed that such an instrument is not really needed or that the area is adequately covered by existing instruments (the ECHR

62 Council of the EU, *Ensuring Protection – European Union Guidelines on Human Rights Defenders*, 1 December 2008, 16332/1/08. See also Bennett, 'European Union Guidelines on Human Rights Defenders: a review of policy and practice towards effective implementation' (2015) 19(7) *IJHR*, 908.

63 CoE Committee of Ministers, *Declaration on Council of Europe action to improve the protection of human rights defenders and promote their activities*, 6 February 2008.

and the UN and CoE Declarations). Whether this assumption is warranted is open to debate.

In addition to these instruments, various resolutions on human rights defenders have been adopted by the UN, the CoE and other international organisations.[64] The UN Special Rapporteur on the situation of human rights defenders, whose mandate was established in 2000, has also played an important role in this area. Through his/her regular reports, s/he has drawn attention to the challenges faced by human rights defenders, proposed measures that should be taken to improve the situation and provided examples of best practice.[65] Particularly interesting among these reports are those submitted in February 2016 and July 2018. The former[66] identifies instances of good practices in the protection of human rights defenders at the local, national, regional and international levels. The focus lies in three areas, namely strengthening the resources and capacities of defenders, fostering an enabling environment for the defence of their rights and supporting their protection. The report contains a set of seven principles on which the protection of human rights defenders shall be based (rights-based approach, diversity, gender sensitivity, holistic security, interconnectedness, participation, flexibility).[67] The latter report[68] analyses the outcomes of a global survey covering 140 States, which was carried out at the occasion of the 20th anniversary of the adoption of the UN Declaration. The survey showed that although measures aimed at increasing the protection of human rights defenders had been adopted in many parts of the world, new challenges had also arisen, and defenders remained under serious threats. The Special Rapporteur formulated a set of recommendations, addressed to various actors at the national and international level,

64 See, for instance, UN General Assembly, *Promotion of the Declaration on the Right and Responsibility of Individuals, Groups and Organs of Society to Promote and Protect Universally Recognized Human Rights and Fundamental Freedoms: protecting women human rights defenders*, 18 December 2013, UN Doc. A/RES/68/181; CoE Parliamentary Assembly, *The situation of human rights defenders in Council of Europe member States*, 27 June 2012, Resolution 1891 (2012).

65 See UN OHCHR, *Special Rapporteur on the situation of human rights defenders*, 2021, https://www.ohchr.org/EN/Issues/SRHRDefenders/Pages/SRHRDefendersIndex.aspx.

66 UN Human Rights Council, *Report of the Special Rapporteur on the situation of human rights defenders. Note by the Secretariat*, 1 February 2016, UN Doc. A/HRC/31/55.

67 *Id.*, para. 111.

68 UN General Assembly, *Situation of human rights defenders. Note by the Secretary-General*, 23 July 2018, UN Doc. A/73/215.

that should help counter these threats and that encompass, unsurprisingly, the full respect of the UN Declaration.

Over the years, international human rights bodies have been repeatedly confronted with cases involving human rights defenders. The ECtHR has been at the frontline of this effort. Through its case-law, it has contributed to the clarification of the legal standards applicable in this area. As of January 2021, the HUDOC database renders 45 decisions that contain explicit references to human rights defenders. Certain other decisions that do not use the term deal with the group as well.[69] Most of the decisions are directed against four countries – Russia (22), Azerbaijan (7), Armenia (6) and Turkey (4). The provisions of the ECHR most frequently concerned are Articles 3 (prohibition of torture and inhuman treatment), 5 (right to liberty and security), 6 (right to a fair trial) and 13 (right to effective remedies). In virtually all cases where the application was not declared inadmissible, the ECHR has found at least one violation of the ECtHR – Articles 3 and 5 come at the top of the violated provisions, followed by Articles 6, 13 and also 10 (freedom of expression) and 11 (freedom of assembly and association).

Among the best-known cases are those concerning the situation in Azerbaijan. In the *Aliyev* Case (2008),[70] the Court considered the application of a leading Azeri human rights defender, who had been arrested and charged with financial offences. It found violations of Articles 3 (inhuman and degrading conditions of detention), 5 (unlawful deprivation of liberty), 8 (search and seizure at the applicant's home and office with no legitimate purpose) and also 18 (restrictions imposed for other than legitimate purposes) of the ECHR. The Court referred several times to international instruments on human rights defenders. It stressed that it attached

> particular importance to the special role of human-rights defenders in promoting and defending human rights, including in close cooperation with the Council of Europe, and their contribution to the protection of human rights in the member States.[71]

Noting that the facts showed that there had been a larger campaign against human rights defenders in Azerbaijan, it also called upon the country to

69 This is for instance the case in *Alekhina and Others v Russia* in which the ECtHR considered the application of the group 'Pussy Riot'. See ECtHR, Judgment, 17 July 2018, *Mariya Alekhina and Others v Russia*, Application No. 38004/12.

70 ECtHR, Judgment, 20 September 2018, *Aliyev v Azerbaijan*, Application Nos. 68762/14 and 71200/14.

71 *Id.*, para. 208.

adopt general measures to improve the situation of human rights defenders and protect them from retaliatory prosecutions and misuse of criminal law. More recent case-law shows that so far these measures have not been adopted and human rights defenders remain at risk in Azerbaijan.[72]

The special position of human rights defenders has been further elaborated upon by the ECtHR in *Kavala v Turkey* (2019).[73] The decision contains over 50 references to the term and quotes several CoE instruments adopted in this area, including the 2008 CoE Declaration. The case concerned a Turkish human rights defender and philanthropist who challenged his arbitrary arrest and placement in pre-trial detention carried out in the aftermath of the 2016 failed coup. The applicant argued that he was specifically targeted as a human rights defender and that his detention pursued the purposes of silencing him and dissuading others from engaging in the promotion and protection of human rights. Turkey contested this argument suggesting that while the applicant was indeed a human rights defender, his detention was in no way linked to this qualification. The ECtHR sided with the applicant concluding that

> it has been established beyond reasonable doubt that the measures complained of in the present case pursued an ulterior purpose, [...] namely that of reducing the applicant to silence. Further, [...] the contested measures were likely to have a dissuasive effect on the work of human-rights defenders.[74]

In light of this conclusion, the Court found violations of Articles 5 and 18 of the ECHR.

The decisions suggest that the ECtHR recognises the special position of human rights defenders, their increased vulnerability and the need to consider their cases in light of the chilling effect that measures taken against them might have on civil society at large. This approach has translated into a rather extensive use of Article 18 of the ECHR, through which the Court casts doubt as to whether measures directed again human rights defenders pursued legitimate aims or, rather, were adopted for ulterior purposes, those of intimidating civil society and silencing dissenting voices. At the same time, the Court has not found it necessary to discuss the concept of human rights defenders at any length and it has also only rarely referred

---

72 See ECtHR, Judgment, 16 July 2020, *Yunusova and Yunusov v Azerbaijan (No. 2)*, Application No. 68817/14.

73 ECtHR, Judgment, 10 December 2019, *Kavala v Turkey*, Application No. 28749/18.

74 *Id.*, para. 232.

to international instruments on human rights defenders. For instance, the UN Declaration on Human Rights Defenders is mentioned in a single case[75] and even there, it is just listed in the section providing an overview of international material on human rights defenders. This suggests that for the moment, international instruments on the one hand and the ECtHR case-law on the other operate more as two parallel and largely independent tracks pursuing the common goal of enhancing legal protection of human rights defenders, than as pieces of a uniform and internally coherent protective system.

II. Legal Standards Applicable to Whistleblowers

Whereas the protection of human rights defenders has received attention for more than two decades now, the protection of whistleblowers has started to be taken seriously only recently. Despite this fact, there already is a legally binding instrument, albeit a regional one, applicable to whistleblowers. It is the EU Whistleblower Protection Directive[76] adopted in 2019. A directive is an EU legal act that binds the member States as to the goals they have to achieve but leaves it up to them to choose the means to do so.[77] Yet, some directives are so detailed that the space left to States is relatively limited. This is the case with the EU Whistleblower Protection Directive.

The purpose of the Directive is 'to enhance the enforcement of Union law and policies in specific areas by laying down common minimum standards providing for a high level of protection of persons reporting breaches of Union law' (Article 1). These standards should guide States in the implementation and should serve as the minimum common denominator, which nonetheless is not so minimum after all. The Directive sets up rules for both internal and external reporting and follow-up as well as for public disclosure. These procedures are understood as gradual, subsidiary steps in the reporting/disclosing process. Whistleblowers should, unless this is

75 ECtHR, Judgment, 20 September 2018, *Aliyev v Azerbaijan*, Application Nos. 68762/14 and 71200/14, para. 88.

76 Directive (EU) 2019/1937 of the European Parliament and of the Council of 23 October 2019 on the protection of persons who report breaches of Union law. See also Popescu, 'A Critical Analysis of Whistleblower Protection in the European Union' (2015) 7 *JOPAFL*, 135.

77 The majority of the provisions of the Directive shall be implemented by 17 December 2021.

impossible or impractical, first act within their institution, then through external channels (authorities designated in individual countries) and only as a last step reveal their information directly to the public.

In addition to providing basic rules on the mechanisms that should be put in place for whistleblowers to be able to act, the Directive also contains a special chapter on protection measures. This chapter calls upon States to take the necessary measures to prohibit, prevent and sanction any form of retaliation against whistleblowers, regardless of whether they act in the public or private sector. The examples of such retaliatory acts provided in Article 19 are quite diverse and include demotion, dismissal, a negative employee reference, coercion, harassment and psychiatric or medical referrals. Thus, although the provision primarily relates to the position at work, it takes account of the sanctions that whistleblowers may be exposed to outside their institution, e.g. in their private life. The Directive moreover confirms that whistleblowers shall not incur liability in respect of their activities (Article 21). If they face criminal, civil or disciplinary charges, they have the right to a fair trial (Article 22). They also have the right to effective remedies, which should apply to any case of human rights abuse that they become victims of. States have the duty to 'ensure that the rights and remedies [...] cannot be waived or limited by any agreement, policy, form or condition of employment, including a pre-dispute arbitration agreement' (Article 24), which makes the rights of whistleblowers to remedies 'non-derogable' in the work-related context. Although the Directive only applies to breaches of EU law, it is the first binding international instrument on whistleblowers and, as such, it constitutes an important milestone in the international protection of this group.

Independently of the EU, the Council of Europe has paid attention to whistleblowers, albeit without adopting a binding instrument. In 2010, the CoE Parliamentary Assembly adopted a resolution on whistleblowing, which sets the basic principles on which legislation related to whistleblowers should be based.[78] The Resolution stresses that whistleblowing should be regulated both in the private and public sectors and that States should opt for a broad definition of the term. The legislation should focus on 'providing a safe alternative to silence',[79] making sure that channels of re-

78 CoE Parliamentary Assembly, *Protection of "whistle-blowers"*, 29 April 2010, Resolution 1729 (2010). For more details, see Lewis, 'The Council of Europe Resolution and Recommendation on the Protection of Whistleblowers' (2010) 39(4) *Industrial Law Journal*, 432.

79 CoE Parliamentary Assembly, *Protection of "whistle-blowers"*, 29 April 2010, Resolution 1729 (2010), para. 6.2.

porting are available and that whistleblowers are protected against retaliation. In 2014, the Recommendation on the Protection of Whistleblowers[80] was issued by the CoE Committee of Ministers. The recommendation has many similarities to the 2019 EU Directive, which certainly took inspiration from it. Yet, it is much less detailed, and it does not impose any legal obligations.

The ECtHR has dealt with the protection of whistleblowers in a limited number of cases (some 10 decisions in the HUDOC database). The best-known ones are *Guja v Moldova* (2008)[81] and *Medžlis Islamske Zajednice Brčko v Bosnia and Herzegovina* (2011),[82] decided both by the Grand Chamber. The cases concerned the right to freedom of expression. In the former case, a civil servant was dismissed after revealing information of public interest on attempts by high-ranking politicians to influence the judiciary. In the latter case, several NGOs were fined for failing to verify the truthfulness of allegations they made in a letter addressed to local government concerning a candidate for a post as director of a public radio station. The Court concluded that the interference with Mr. Guja's right, i.e. his dismissal, constituted a violation of Article 10 of the ECHR. The interference with the NGOs' right, i.e. the fine imposed on them, was, on the contrary, compatible with the ECHR. The Court also indicated that whereas Mr. Guja could qualify as a whistleblower, the NGOs could not as they 'were not in any subordinated work-based relationship with the BD public radio […] which would make them bound by a duty of loyalty, reserve and discretion towards the radio'.[83]

The ECtHR case-law has thus contributed to clarifying who whistleblowers are (and are not) and which measures may (and may not) be taken in response to their acts. The Court has made it clear that the two questions are closely related, i.e. the qualification of the applicant as a whistleblower affects the assessment of the legality of the interference with his/her rights. In *Guja*, the ECtHR introduced the main considerations that should guide this assessment, ensuring it reflects the special duty of loyalty, reserve and discretion that whistleblowers have towards their institution. Due to this duty,

80 CoE Committee of Ministers, *Protection of Whistleblowers*, 30 April 2014, Recommendation CM/Rec (2014) 7.

81 ECtHR, Judgment (GC), 12 February 2008, *Guja v Moldova*, Application No. 14277/04.

82 ECtHR, Judgment (GC), 27 June 2017, *Medžlis Islamske Zajednice Brčko v Bosnia and Herzegovina*, Application No. 17224/11.

83 *Id.*, para. 80.

> Disclosure should be made in the first place to the person's superior or other competent authority or body. It is only where this is clearly impracticable that the information could, as a last resort, be disclosed to the public.[84]

In *Medžlis Islamske Zajednice Brčko*, where the applicants were not found to be whistleblowers, the ECtHR did not see any need to 'enquire into the kind of issue which has been central in the [...] case-law on whistle-blowing',[85] namely the obligation of the whistleblower to use the internal channels of reporting prior to going public. Similar to human rights defenders, the Court has only shown interest in international instruments on whistleblowers when it has referred to them in the section providing an overview of relevant international material. The conclusion reached in the previous section, that international instruments and the ECtHR case-law develop more in parallel than in interplay, thus seems applicable here as well.

D. *Conclusions*

Human rights defenders and whistleblowers show an increased vulnerability to human rights abuses. Due to the nature of activities, they engage in – monitoring and criticising human rights violations (human rights defenders) and disclosing information about unlawful or immoral activities within an institution (whistleblowers) –, they, or their family members, are subject to interferences with their private life, face threats to their safety, are prevented from engaging in activities in the public space, are denied the enjoyment of economic or social rights and have difficulties at work. Human rights defenders and whistleblowers enjoy the same human rights as any other individuals or legal persons. Yet, their increased vulnerability has made it necessary to specify how these rights should be implemented, applied and interpreted in their particular cases. For human rights defenders, this has happened through several non-binding instruments, especially the 1998 UN Declaration on Human Rights Defenders. For whistleblowers, the binding EU Whistleblower Protection Directive has recently been adopted, albeit only in the EU's regional framework.

---

84 ECtHR, Judgment (GC), 12 February 2008, *Guja v Moldova*, Application No. 14277/04, para. 73.

85 ECtHR, Judgment (GC), 27 June 2017, *Medžlis Islamske Zajednice Brčko v Bosnia and Herzegovina*, Application No. 17224/11, para. 80.

The two groups also feature in the case-law of the ECtHR, which has drawn particular legal consequences from the applicant qualifying as a human rights defender or a whistleblower. The former qualification makes the Court more careful in assessing the aims (allegedly) pursued by the interference with the applicants' rights and more willing to resort to Article 18 of the ECHR. The latter qualification makes the Court, in the assessment of the case, resort to special consideration whether 'internal channels of reporting' were exhausted by a whistleblower prior to him/her going public. When drawing these legal consequences, the ECtHR could easily rely on the available international instruments.[86] Article 17 of the UN Declaration on Human Rights Defenders which stresses that restrictions on human rights of defenders may be adopted 'solely for the purpose of securing due recognition and respect for the rights and freedoms of others and of meeting the just requirements of morality', could underpin the use of Article 18 of the ECHR. The need to 'exhaust [...] internal channels of communication', stressed in CoE instruments, could be relied upon in cases concerning whistleblowing..[87] Yet, the ECtHR invokes neither of these provisions.

The legal standards applicable to human rights defenders and whistleblowers have thus developed through two parallel tracks – in international instruments and in case-law. The two tracks, fortunately, largely overlap in their scope and content. One may only hope that in the future, these two tracks will not depart from each other but will rather support each other more actively and explicitly in pursuing the common goal of improving the legal (and other) protection of persons who risk their well-being and sometimes also their life for the common good. One may also hope that the legal regime will take into account the full range of threats that human rights defenders and whistleblowers face, providing them with a truly comprehensive protection in all the three areas identified above (private life, public life, work) in which their increased vulnerability manifests itself.

86 The ECHR is only entitled to apply the ECtHR. Yet, it can rely on other legal instruments when interpreting the ECtHR, within the principle of systemic integration. See Rachovitza, 'The Principle of Systemic Integration in Human Rights Law' (2017) 66(3) *International and Comparative Law Quarterly*, 557.

87 CoE Parliamentary Assembly, *Protection of "whistle-blowers"*, 29 April 2010, Resolution 1729 (2010), para. 6.2.

Bibliography

Alford, C. Fred: Whistleblowers: Broken Lives and Organizational Power (2002).

Alston, Philip (ed): Non-State Actors and Human Rights (2005).

Amnesty International: Global assault on NGOs reaches crisis point as new laws curb vital
human rights work, 21 February 2019.

Bennett, Karen: European Union Guidelines on Human Rights Defenders: a review of policy
and practice towards effective implementation, The International Journal of Human Rights 2015, 908ff.

Bennett, Karen/Ingleton, Danna/Nah, Alice M./Savage, James: Critical perspectives on the security and protection of human rights defenders, The International Journal of Human Rights 2015, 883ff.

Davis, Carlo: Is Edward Snowden Protected By International Law?, Huffington Post, 17 July 2013, https://www.huffpost.com/entry/edward-snowden-international-law_n_3544679.

Donders, Yvonne: Defending the Human Rights Defenders, Netherlands Quarterly of Human Rights 2016, 282ff.

Front Line Defenders: Arrests of human rights defenders threaten rights to freedom of assembly and expression in Hong Kong, 20 April 2020, https://www.frontlinedefenders.org/en/statement-report/arrests-human-rights-defenders-threaten-rights-freedom-assembly-and-expression-hong.

Front Line Defenders: Front Line Defenders Global Analysis 2019 (2020).

Front Line Defenders: Judicial harassment of human rights defenders in the lead-up to presidential elections, 19 May 2020, https://www.frontlinedefenders.org/en/statement-report/judicial-harassment-human-rights-defenders-lead-presidential-elections.

Front Line Defenders: #Travel Ban, 2021, https://www.frontlinedefenders.org/en/violation/travel-ban.

Frost, Michel: World Report on the Situation of Human Rights Defenders (2018).

Hessbruegge, Jan A.: Human Rights Violations Arising from Conduct of Non-State Actors, Buffalo Human Rights Law Review 2015, 21ff.

Hunt, Linda: The Challenges Women Whistleblowers Face, International Business Research 2010, 3ff.

International Labour Organization: International Labour Organization Thesaurus (2005).

Inter-American Commission on Human Rights: Criminalization of the Work of Human Rights Defenders, OEA/Ser.L/V/II. Doc. 49/15, 31 December 2015.

Inter-American Commission on Human Rights: Report on the Situation if Human Rights Defenders in the Americas, OEA/Ser.L/V/II.124/Doc. 5 rev.1, 17 March 2006.

Koula, Aikaterini Christina: The UN Definition of Human Rights Defenders: Alternative Interpretative Approaches, Queen Mary Human Rights Review 2019, 1ff.

Landman, Todd: Holding the Line: Human Rights Defenders in the Age of Terror, The British Journal of Politics and International Relations 2016, 123ff.

Lane, Lottie: The Horizontal Effect of International Human Rights Law in Practice: A Comparative Analysis of the General Comments and Jurisprudence of Selected United Nations Human Rights Treaty Monitoring Bodies, European Journal of Comparative Law and Governance 2018, 5ff.

Lewis, David B.: The Council of Europe Resolution and Recommendation on the Protection of Whistleblowers, Industrial Law Journal 2010, 432ff.

Lyman, Rick: A Tobacco Whistle-Blower's Life Is Transformed, New York Times, 15 October 1999, https://www.nytimes.com/1999/10/15/us/a-tobacco-whistle-blower-s-life-is-transformed.html.

Maldives Independent, Rilwan and Yameen's relatives fired for joining protest march, 16 August 2017, https://maldivesindependent.com/society/rilwan-and-yameens-relatives-fired-for-joining-protest-march-132039.

Melzer, Nils: State Responsibility for the Torture of Julian Assange, Speech at the German Bundestag in Berlin, 27 November 2019 (English translation), 16 December 2019, https://medium.com/@njmelzer/state-responsibility-for-the-torture-of-julian-assange-40935ea5d7c3.

Mitchell, Tamsin: Journalists as Human Rights Defenders: International Protection of Journalists in Contexts of Violence and Impunity, in: Shaw, Ibrahim Seaga/Selvarajah, Senthan (eds), Reporting Human Rights, Conflicts, and Peacebuilding (2019), 221ff.

mLIVE: Michigan man made death threat to Trump whistleblower's attorney, feds say, 22 February 2020, https://www.mlive.com/news/saginaw-bay-city/2020/02/michigan-man-made-death-threat-to-trump-whistleblowers-attorney-feds-say.html.

Mulé, Nick J.: LGBTQI-identified human rights defenders: courage in the face of adversity at the United Nations, Gender and Development 2018, 89ff.

Near, Janet P./Miceli, Marcia P.: Organizational Dissidence: The Case of Whistle-Blowing, Journal of Business Ethics 1985, 1ff.

OSCE: Guidelines on the Protection of Human Rights Defenders (2014).

OSCE: Human Rights Defenders in the OSCE Region: Challenges and Good Practices (2008).

Papandrea, Mary-Rose: Leaker Traitor Whistleblower Spy: National Security Leaks and the First Amendment, Boston University Law Review 2014, 449ff.

Pfeffer, Anshel: Why Breaking the Silence Became the Most Hated Group in Israel, Haaretz, 17 December 2015.

Piccone, Ted: The contribution of the UN's special procedures to national level implementation of human rights norms, The International Journal of Human Rights 2011, 206ff.

Popescu, Ada-Iuliana: A Critical Analysis of Whistleblower Protection in the European Union, Journal of Public Administration, Finance and Law 2015, 135ff.

Powell, David E: Controlling Dissent in the Soviet Union, Government and Opposition 1972, 85ff.

Rachovitza, Adamantia: The Principle of Systemic Integration in Human Rights Law, International and Comparative Law Quarterly 2017, 557ff.

The Times of India, RTI activists abducted and tortured, 26 December 2013.

UN Commission on Human Rights: Report on the Fortieth Session, UN Doc. E/1984/14(SUPP)-E/CN.4/1984/77, 6 February-16 March 1984.

UN Committee on Economic, Social and Cultural Rights: Human rights defenders and economic, social and cultural rights, UN Doc. E/C.12/2016/2, 29 March 2017.

UN General Assembly: Declaration on the Right and Responsibility of Individuals, Groups and Organs of Society to Promote and Protect Universally Recognized Human Rights and Fundamental Freedoms, UN Doc. A/RES/53/144, 8 March 1999.

UN General Assembly: Final warning: death threats and killings of human rights defenders. Report of the Special Rapporteur on the situation of human rights defenders, Mary Lawlor, UN Doc. A/HRC/46/35, 24 December 2020.

UN General Assembly: Promotion and protection of the right to freedom of opinion and expression. Note by the Secretary-General, UN Doc. A/70/361, 8 September 2015.

UN General Assembly: Promotion of the Declaration on the Right and Responsibility of Individuals, Groups and Organs of Society to Promote and Protect Universally Recognized Human Rights and Fundamental Freedoms: protecting women human rights defenders, UN Doc. A/RES/68/181, 18 December 2013.

UN General Assembly: Situation of human rights defenders. Note by the Secretary-General, UN Doc. A/67/292, 10 August 2012.

UN General Assembly: Situation of human rights defenders. Note by the Secretary-General, UN Doc. A/75/165, 16 July 2020.

UN General Assembly: Situation of human rights defenders. Note by the Secretary-General, UN Doc. A/73/215, 23 July 2018.

UN Human Rights Council: Report of the Special Rapporteur on the situation of human rights defenders. Note by the Secretariat, UN Doc. A/HRC/31/55, 1 February 2016.

UN Economic and Social Council, Promotion and Protection of Human Rights. Human Rights Defenders. Report submitted by the Special Representative of the Secretary-General on human rights defenders, Hina Jilani, UN Doc. E/CN.4/2006/95, 23 January 2006.

UN OHCHR: Commentary to the Declaration on the Right and Responsibility of Individuals, Groups and Organs of Society to Promote and Protect Universally Recognized Human Rights and Fundamental Freedoms (2011).

UN OHCHR: Declaration on Human Rights Defenders (2020), https://www.ohchr.org/en/issues/srhrdefenders/pages/declaration.aspx.

UN OHCHR: Human Rights Defenders: Protecting the Right to Defend Human Rights, Fact Sheet No. 29 (2004).

UN OHCHR: Special Rapporteur on the situation of human rights defenders (2020), https://www.ohchr.org/EN/Issues/SRHRDefenders/Pages/SRHRDefendersIndex.aspx.

Vaughn, Robert G.: Whistleblowing Law (2015).

Venice Commission: Report on funding of associations, CDL-AD(2019)002, 18 March 2019.

Venice Commission-OSCE/ODIHR: Joint Guidelines on Freedom of Association, CDL-AD(2014)046, 17 December 2014.

Wille, Petter/Spannagel, Janika: The history of the UN Declaration on Human Rights Defenders: its genesis, drafting and adoption, Universal Rights Group Blog, 11 March 2019, https://www.universal-rights.org/blog/the-un-declaration-on-human-rights-defenders-its-history-and-drafting-process/.

The ECtHR's Jurisprudence on the Prohibition of Collective Expulsions in Cases of Pushbacks at European Borders: A Critical Perspective

Hanaa Hakiki[*]

There is surely no more burning issue in European politics today than the refoulement *of migrants at land borders or in transit zones and the resulting State liability for human-rights breaches during immigration and border-control operations.*
Judge Pinto de Albuquerque[1]

A. *Introduction*

This article will focus first on the definition of the prohibition of collective expulsions provided by the European Convention for Human Rights ('ECHR') and through the European Court of Human Right's jurisprudence ('ECtHR') (A). Second, it will look at the exception to the applicability of the prohibition as defined by the Grand Chamber in *N.D. and N.T. v. Spain*[2] (B). Third, the article will place the prohibition of collective expulsions as interpreted by Strasbourg in the wider framework of international human rights law (C).

Article 4 protocol 4 of the ECHR reads 'collective expulsion of aliens is prohibited'. It was opened for signature in 1965 and has since been ratified by all state parties except Greece, Turkey, Switzerland and the United Kingdom. Initially, drafters intended article 4 protocol 4 ECHR to address the expulsion of legally residing non-nationals[3] – now covered

* This article is the result of collective work, including research by Kristina Fried and comments by Carsten Gericke.

1 ECtHR, Judgment, 11 December 2018, *M.A. and Others v Lithuania*, Application No. 59793/17, Dissenting Opinion, para. 1.

2 ECtHR, Judgment (GC), 13 February 2020, *N.D. and N.T. v Spain*, Application Nos. 8675/15 and 8697/15.

3 The first Assembly draft of article 4 protocol 4 ECHR meant to restrict the possibility of expelling lawfully residing non-nationals to cases where (i) the lawful residency had lasted less than two years and (ii) there was a threat to national security

under article 1 protocol 7 ECHR – but they then decided to word the provision in very broad terms.[4]

Non-nationals claimed their rights under the prohibition of collective expulsions soon after its first ratifications.[5] Some of these early cases had already raised the issue of non-nationals' access to protection at borders.[6] It was thus foreseeable that the intensification of European policies of border externalisation would lead to a greater relevance of the prohibition of collective expulsions in front of Strasbourg. In the last two decades European states have attempted to escape their legal obligation *vis à vis* refugees[7] and migrants through the general use of fast-track readmission agreements on the one hand and the systematic use of irregular, summary and violent expulsions[8] on the other hand. An almost negligible number of those

---

or public order. However, the Committee of experts unanimously decided it was necessary to include an absolute prohibition on the collective expulsion of non-nationals. Further, the Committee noted that the expulsion of lawfully residing non-nationals was already addressed in another convention, deemed better to encroach upon States' discretion. See Council of Europe, *Collected Edition of the "Travaux Préparatoires" of Protocol No. 4* (1976), 428 and 506 f.

4 For more details on the drafting process leading up to the current provision, please see Riemers, *The Prohibition of Collective Expulsion in Public International Law* (2020), 8 ff. and 76.

5 The first case in which article 4 protocol 4 ECHR was claimed was European Commission of Human Rights, Decision, 5 February 1973, *X v Sweden*, Application No. 5525/72. The applicant was a stateless person facing expulsion to the United States after being convicted of theft. In fact, from the very first cases invoking this provision, the greatest majority of article 4 protocol 4 ECHR claims arise in pure immigration cases, with only a handful arising in the context of an ethnic minority facing forced displacement. Indeed the only such cases were ECtHR, Judgment, 5 February 2002, *Conka v Belgium*, Application No. 51564/99 and ECtHR, Judgment (GC), 3 July 2014, *Georgia v Russia (I)*, Application No. 13255/07 followed by two cases in which the latter decision was applied, namely ECtHR, Judgment, 20 December 2016, *Shioshvili and Others v Russia*, Application No. 19356/07 and ECtHR, Judgment, 20 December 2016, *Berdzenishvili and Others v Russia*, Application No. 14594/07. See also ECtHR, Guide on Article 4 of Protocol No. 4 to the European Convention on Human Rights, 31 August 2020, https://www.echr.coe.int/Documents/Guide_Art_4_Protocol_4_ENG.pdf, para. 10.

6 See European Commission of Human Rights, Decision, 14 October 1992, *M. v Denmark*, Application No. 17392/90, where the provision was claimed by GDR citizens seeking to move to the Federal Republic of Germany through the Danish embassy in East Berlin.

7 See Hathaway and Gammeltoft-Hansen, 'Non-Refoulement in a World of Cooperative Deterrence' (2015) 53 n. 2, *Colum. J. Transnat'l L.*, 235.

8 European Union Agency for Fundamental Rights, *Fundamental Rights Report 2019* (2019), 131.

subjected to such practices manage to take their cases to the ECtHR. This resulted in article 4 protocol 4 ECHR jurisprudence addressing a number of border situations, including fast-track (in)admission procedures on islands,[9] refusals of entry at land border points,[10] non-disembarkation at ports[11] as well as summary push backs at land borders[12] and on the high sea.[13]

The prohibition of collective expulsion of non-nationals is to be found in a number of international treaties[14] and is accepted as a general principle of international law.[15] Though distinct from the principle of *non-refoulement* – a cornerstone of the post-World War II refugee law regime – the prohibition of collective expulsions is intimately linked to it.[16] The UN Committee Against Torture ('UN CAT') considers it part of the principle of *non-refoulement*, inasmuch as it guarantees and enables its applicability in practice.[17] Indeed, the prohibition of collective expulsion is the proce-

---

9 ECtHR, Judgment (GC), 15 December 2016, *Khlaifia and Others v Italy*, Application No. 16483/12; ECtHR, Judgment, 25 June 2020, *Moustahi v France*, Application No. 9347/14.

10 ECtHR, Judgment, 24 March 2020, *Asady and Others v Slovakia*, Application No. 24917/15; ECtHR, Judgement, 23 July 2020, *M.K. and others v Poland*, Application No. 40503/17; ECtHR, Judgment, 8 July 2021, *D.A. and others v Poland*, Application No. 51246/17.

11 ECtHR, Judgment, 21 October 2014, *Sharifi and Others v Italy and Greece*, Application No. 16643/09.

12 ECtHR, Judgment (GC), 13 February 2020, *N.D. and N.T. v Spain*, Application Nos. 8675/15 and 8697/15; ECtHR, Judgment, 8 July 2021, *Shahzad v Hungary*, Application No. 12625/17.

13 ECtHR, Judgment (GC), 23 February 2012, *Hirsi Jamaa and Others v Italy*, Application No. 27765/09.

14 Article 4 Protocol 4 ECHR; Article 19(1) of the EU Charter on Fundamental Rights; Article 12(5) of the African Charter for Human and Peoples' Rights; Article 22(9) of the American Convention on Human Rights; Article 26(2) of the Arab Charter on Human Rights; Article 22(1) of the International Convention on the Rights of Migrant Workers.

15 See for example UN General Assembly, International Law Commission, *Third report on the expulsion of aliens. By Mr. Maurice Kamto, Special Rapporteur*, 19 April 2007, UN Doc. A/CN.4/581, para. 115.

16 See also Riemers, *The Prohibition of Collective Expulsion in Public International Law* (2020), 248 ff.

17 CAT, *General Comment No. 4 (2017) on the implementation of article 3 of the Convention in the context of article 22*, 9 February 2018, UN Doc. CAT/C/GC/4, paras. 13 and 18; UN High Commissioner on Refugees ['UNHCR'], *Submission by the Office of the United Nations High Commissioner for Refugees in the cases of N.D. and N.T. v Spain (Appl. Nos 8675/15 and 8697/15) before the European Court of Human Rights*, 15 November 2015, https://www.refworld.org/cgi-bin/texis/vtx/rw

dural guarantee which allows all national and international protection mechanisms – including but not limited to those under refugee law[18] – to be claimed, considered and ultimately implemented.

B. *The Prohibition of Collective Expulsion and Strasbourg: A Basic Definition*

The prohibition of collective expulsion is drafted as an absolute prohibition in protocol 4 ECHR.[19] In this section, we will look at how the Court has defined 'expulsion' (I), 'alien' (II) and 'collective' and which safeguards arise from the prohibition (III).

I. Expulsion

The first definition of 'expulsion' in the context of article 4 protocol 4 ECHR was given by the Commission as, 'any measure [...] compelling aliens [...] to leave the country.'[20] This definition will subsequently be taken over by the Court.[21]

---

main?docid=59d3a81f4, para. 11; see also UNHCR's oral submissions during the the ECtHR's Grand Chamber in N.D. and N.T. vs. Spain, https://www.echr.coe.int/Pages/home.aspx?p=hearings&w=867515_26092018&language=lang&c=&py=2018.

18 UN Office of the High Commissioner for Human Rights ['OHCHR'], *OHCHR intervention before the European Court of Human Rights in the case of N.D. and N.T v Spain*, 9 October 2015, para. 19, https://www.refworld.org/type,AMICUS,OHCHR,ESP,57a876f34,0.html.

19 This is confirmed in Council of Europe, *Collected Edition of the "Travaux Préparatoires" of Protocol No. 4* (1976), 428: 'The Working Party was also unanimous regarding the absolute prohibition of collective expulsion.', www.echr.coe.int/Library/DIGDOC/Travaux/ECHRTravaux-P4-BIL2907919.pdf.

20 European Commission of Human Rights, Decision, 3 October 1975, *Becker v Denmark*, Application No. 7011/75 was the third decision ever taken in an article 4 protocol 4 ECHR case.

21 ECtHR, Judgment, 23 February 1999, *Andric v Sweden*, Application No. 45917/99 is the first claim under article 4 protocol 4 ECHR considered by the Court. ECtHR, Judgment, 5 February 2002, *Čonka v Belgium*, Application No. 51564/99 is the first case considered on merits by the Court under article 4 protocol 4, resulting in a finding of violation. ECtHR, Judgment, 20 September 2007, *Sultani v France*, Application No. 45223/05 is the second case considered on the merits but where the Court concluded there had been no violation.

The definition was further developed in the first case to reach the Grand Chamber regarding article 4 protocol 4 ECHR, namely *Hirsi Jamaa and Others v. Italy*.[22] In this case, a group of refugees and migrants was intercepted on the high sea by Italian officials. They were made to board an Italian military ship, but instead of being transferred to Italy and/or given access to the Italian asylum procedure, they were handed over to Libyan officials who took them back to Libya. The Grand Chamber referred back to the *travaux préparatoires*,[23] where the drafters of the 4th protocol explained that 'expulsion' should be interpreted, 'in the generic meaning, in current use (to drive away from a place).'[24] Though this definition was provided by the drafters in relation to the prohibition of expulsion of nationals (article 3 protocol 4 ECHR), the Grand Chamber concluded that it ought to be understood as applying to all articles of protocol 4 ECHR.[25]

Thus, in *Hirsi Jamaa and Others v. Italy*, the Grand Chamber established that a collective expulsion, or a 'driving away', could occur not only from a country or a territory, but from anywhere where a state's jurisdiction was confirmed.[26] The Grand Chamber pointed out that its reasoning was in line with its previous jurisprudence on jurisdiction.[27] The Grand Chamber nonetheless addressed explicitly the implications of the applicability of the prohibition of collective expulsions on the high sea. In doing so, it relied on the interpretative principles of good faith and effectiveness. The Court considered that, in a context where state parties increasingly carry out border control operations outside of their territory, these principles called for 'expulsion' to include an act of driving away from the high sea.[28]

This definition was confirmed by all subsequent Grand Chamber judgments on article 4 protocol 4 ECHR.[29] In a number of cases, the Court has

---

22 ECtHR, Judgment (GC), 23 February 2012, *Hirsi Jamaa and Others v Italy*, Application No. 27765/09.

23 Council of Europe, *Collected Edition of the "Travaux Préparatoires" of Protocol No. 4* (1976).

24 ECtHR, Judgment (GC), 23 February 2012, *Hirsi Jamaa and Others v Italy*, Application No. 27765/09, para. 174.

25 *Ibid.*

26 *Id.*, para. 172 ff. See also Riemers: *The Prohibition of Collective Expulsion in Public International Law* (2020), 81.

27 ECtHR, Judgment (GC), 23 February 2012, *Hirsi Jamaa and Others v Italy*, Application No. 27765/09, para. 176 ff.

28 *Id.*, para. 171 ff.

29 See for example ECtHR, Judgment (GC), 15 December 2016, *Khlaifia and Others v Italy*, Application No. 16483/12, para. 243; ECtHR, Judgment (GC), 13 February 2020, *N.D. and N.T. v Spain*, Application Nos. 8675/15 and 8697/15, para. 137.

reiterated that the formal name attributed by the state party to the act of driving away is irrelevant.[30] Thus, whether the act is labelled by national authorities as an expulsion, a removal, a return, a refusal of entry,[31] a denial of admission[32] or a rescue operation,[33] it will still constitute an expulsion for the purposes of article 4 protocol 4 ECHR.[34]

Finally, in establishing whether an expulsion occurred in cases where no procedure or process whatsoever occurred and the state party denies the occurrence of the expulsion, the Court defined a specific evidentiary threshold. In *N.D. and N.T v. Spain*, the Grand Chamber confirmed that for disputed summary expulsions, the burden of proof shifts once the applicants provide *prima facie* evidence of their account.[35] On the facts of that particular case, the Grand Chamber considered that such *prima facie* evidence existed given (i) that the applicants' account as to their overall individual circumstances was coherent, (ii) that the state party had not

30 ECtHR, Judgment (GC), 13 February 2020, *N.D. and N.T. v Spain,* Application Nos. 8675/15 and 8697/15, para. 137.

31 *Ibid.*; ECtHR, Judgment (GC), 15 December 2016, *Khlaifia and Others v Italy,* Application No. 16483/12, paras. 226 and 243; ECtHR, Judgment (GC), 23 February 2012, *Hirsi Jamaa and Others v Italy,* Application No. 27765/09.

32 As was argued in ECtHR, Judgment, 21 October 2014, *Sharifi and Others v Italy and Greece,* Application No. 16643/09, para. 193.

33 As was argued in ECtHR, Judgment (GC), 23 February 2012, *Hirsi Jamaa and Others v Italy,* Application No. 27765/09, para. 79.

34 As noted by the Grand Chamber in ECtHR, Judgment (GC), 13 February 2020, *N.D. and N.T. v Spain,* Application Nos. 8675/15 and 8697/15, para. 175 f., this is in line with the International Law Commission ('ILC')'s Draft articles on the expulsion of aliens. Indeed, though article 2 of the draft articles excludes 'non-admission' from the definition of 'expulsion,' commentary (5) clarifies that, 'the measures taken by a State to compel an alien already present in its territory, *even if unlawfully present*, to leave it are covered by the concept of "expulsion" as defined in draft article 2, subparagraph (a) [emphasis added].' See ILC, Draft articles on the expulsion of aliens, with commentaries (2014), https://legal.un.org/ilc/texts/instruments/english/commentaries/9_12_2014.pdf. Thus the notion of 'admission' and 'non-admission' under the draft articles differ significantly from that of 'admission' and 'non-admission' under the Schengen Border Code, as referred to in relation to the 'Entry conditions for third country nationals' (article 6(1)(c)) and to 'Border checks on persons' (article 8(3)(v)).

35 ECtHR, Judgment (GC), 13 February 2020, *N.D. and N.T. v Spain,* Application Nos. 8675/15 and 8697/15, para. 85. In doing so, the Grand Chamber relied on a line of jurisprudence, quoting ECtHR, Judgment (GC), 13 December 2012, *El Masri v the former Yugoslav Republic of Macedonia*, Application No. 39630/09 and ECtHR, Judgment (GC), 23 June 2016, *Baka v Hungary*, Application No. 20261/12.

denied the occurrence of a collective expulsion on the relevant date and (iii) that such practice had been entrenched in national law.[36]

II. Collective

The term 'collective' under article 4 protocol 4 ECHR does not call for a quantitative or characterising approach,[37] but rather a procedural one. Indeed when the drafters first included the prohibition in their draft article, they added a paragraph reading, 'Decisions of expulsion shall only be taken in individual cases; collective expulsion shall not, in any circumstances, be permitted.'[38] Though the final text simply reads, 'collective expulsion of aliens is prohibited', both the Commission and the Court stayed true to the procedural essence of the prohibition and defined as 'collective' any expulsion measure not taken on the basis of an individualised examination.[39]

The Grand Chamber in *Hirsi Jamaa and Others v. Italy* further specified the requirement of an individualised examination, requesting that the evidence shows 'the existence of sufficient guarantees ensuring that the

36 ECtHR, Judgment (GC), 13 February 2020, *N.D. and N.T. v Spain*, Application Nos. 8675/15 and 8697/15, para. 86 ff.

37 *Id.*, para. 194, where any quantitative or characteristic requirements were expressly excluded by the Court's Grand Chamber; see also ECtHR, Judgment, 25 June 2020, *Moustahi v France*, Application No. 9347/14, para. 129.

38 Council of Europe, *Collected Edition of the "Travaux Préparatoires" of Protocol No. 4* (1976), 430, para. 56.

39 The Commission was first to define such an individual examination in European Commission of Human Rights, Decision, 3 October 1975, *Becker v Denmark*, Application No. 7011/75 as one which formed the basis of and preceded the expulsion measure ('a measure taken after and on the basis of…') and was 'a reasonable and objective examination of the particular cases of each individual alien of the group.' The Court took this approach in its first decision on article 4 protocol 4 ECHR in ECtHR, Judgment, 23 February 1999, *Andric v. Sweden*, Application No. 45917/99, para.1, where it defined a collective expulsion measure as one not 'taken on the basis of a reasonable and objective examination of the particular case of each individual alien of the group.' This line of jurisprudence was subsequently confirmed. See, *mutatis mutandi*, ECtHR, Judgment, 5 February 2002, *Conka v Belgium*, Application No. 51564/99, para. 59; ECtHR, Judgment (GC), 15 December 2016, *Khlaifia and Others v Italy*, Application No. 16483/12; ECtHR, Judgment (GC), 13 February 2020, *N.D. and N.T. v Spain*, Application Nos. 8675/15 and 8697/15, para. 193. Interestingly, the Grand Chamber in ECtHR, Judgment (GC), 23 February 2012, *Hirsi Jamaa and Others v Italy*, Application No. 27765/09, para. 166, took the definition provided in *Becker v Denmark* with the inclusion of 'taken after' as a requirement.

individual circumstances of each of those concerned were actually the subject of a detailed examination.'[40] This definition was subsequently applied in chamber judgments.[41] However, the Grand Chamber in *Khlaifia and Others v. Italy* will shift its approach, by ruling out the necessity for an individual interview and defining a much less protective two-fold test. In that judgment, the Grand Chamber deemed it enough for the non-national to have 'a genuine and effective possibility of submitting arguments against his or her expulsion' and when such opportunity is deemed to have existed and arguments where raised, for those arguments to be 'examined in an appropriate manner by the authorities of the respondent State.'[42]

It may be tempting to see in this approach sheer common-sense and pragmatism. Yet this reasoning disguises a crucial change: it is no longer for state parties to prove that they provided enough safeguards for an individualised examination to occur, but for the applicants to prove that they did not have any opportunity to oppose their expulsion. In light of the complete imbalance of power at borders between state parties and (here detained) applicants, in practice this shift is likely to translate into a merely theoretical and illusory existence of the safeguards provided for by article 4 protocol 4 ECHR.[43] In fact, in *Khlaifia and Others v. Italy* the Grand Chamber considered that identification processes were sufficient, though the state party was unable to produce any document proving that the identity checks had actually taken place – let alone evidence as to whether they met the safeguards defined under article 4 protocol 4 ECHR.[44] The Grand Chamber even advanced that another such opportunity to raise arguments against the expulsion had existed when the applicants had met

40 ECtHR, Judgment (GC), 23 February 2012, *Hirsi Jamaa and Others v Italy*, Application No. 27765/09, para. 185.

41 ECtHR, Judgment, 21 October 2014, *Sharifi and Others v Italy and Greece*, Application No. 16643/09, para. 214.

42 ECtHR, Judgment (GC), 15 December 2016, *Khlaifia and Others v Italy*, Application No. 16483/12, para. 248. See also Gericke: 'Zwischen effektivem Menschenrechtsschutz und Realpolitik. Die jüngere Rechtsprechung des EGMR zum Rechtsschutz an den EU-Außengrenzen' (2020), 12/2020, Asylmagazin, Zeitschrift für Flüchtlings-und Migrationsrecht, 14 (15); Riemers: *The Prohibition of Collective Expulsion in Public International Law* (2020), 171 f. and 190.

43 *Id.*, Partly Dissenting Opinion of Judge Serghides, para. 12.

44 The applicants had submitted that the identity checks had happened with no translation or legal advice, whilst the state party maintained that translators were present. *Id.*, para. 245 ff.

with Tunisian diplomatic officials before being deported back to Tunisia, their origin country.[45]

Ultimately, the Grand Chamber in *Khlaifia and Others v. Italy* was of the view that in any event the applicants had no arguments to raise against their expulsion.[46] Yet one could argue that determining the applicability of a procedural safeguard by assessing its usefulness *ex post facto* contradicts the *raison d'être* of procedural safeguards, which is to ensure that sufficient guarantees are in place for a certain process – here an individualised examination – to take place.[47]

III. Alien

The provision prohibiting collective expulsions was drafted very broadly by the all-encompassing term of 'aliens' with no distinction. In order to dissipate all doubts, the Committee of Experts drafting the provision further highlighted,

> The term 'aliens' shall here be taken to mean all those who have no actual right to nationality in a State, whether they are passing through a country or reside or are domiciled in it, whether they are refugees or entered the country on their own initiative, or whether they are stateless or possess another nationality. The collective expulsion of nationals is prohibited under article 3 [protocol 4 ECHR].[48]

This last sentence is a final testament as to the Committee's concern that everyone – nationals, non-nationals, stateless persons, refugees, non-refugees – should be protected from collective expulsions.

The Committee's definition is remarkable in its intention to clarify that such protection should not depend on status (residency, nationality or refugee status) or on the way of entry ('on their own initiative') or on the

45 ECtHR, Judgment (GC), 15 December 2016, *Khlaifia and Others v Italy*, Application No. 16483/12, para. 250; Gericke: 'Zwischen effektivem Menschenrechtsschutz und Realpolitik. Die jüngere Rechtsprechung des EGMR zum Rechtsschutz an den EU-Außengrenzen' (2020), 12/2020, Asylmagazin, Zeitschrift für Flüchtlings-und Migrationsrecht, 14 (15 f.)

46 *Id.*, para. 253.

47 In fact in more recent judgments, the Court has gone back to the original definition of collective as a lack of individual assessment. See ECtHR, Judgment, 8 July 2021, *Shahzad v Hungary*, Application No. 12625/17, para. 58.

48 Council of Europe, *Collected Edition of the "Travaux Préparatoires" of Protocol No. 4* (1976), 505, para. 34.

reasons of one's presence in a territory ('to seek refuge or not'). The *travaux préparatoires* reveal that in the Committee's eyes, this all-encompassing absolute prohibition came as a firm limit to state parties' acknowledged discretion to expel (residing) non-nationals.[49]

Though in its jurisprudence the Court has confirmed such a broad scope,[50] in its latest judgment, the Grand Chamber drew much from article 3 ECHR in its analysis as to the applicability of article 4 protocol 4 ECHR, thus blurring the line between the two.[51] In practice, the Court has not yet found a violation of article 4 protocol 4 ECHR in cases where it considered that there was no substantial protection need and/or no related claim under article 3 ECHR.[52] Arguably, such an approach contradicts the explicit intention of the drafters and effectively completely abrogates the safeguards provided for by article 4 protocol 4 ECHR. Indeed, as will be addressed in (C), article 3 ECHR provides more extensive procedural and substantive safeguards against expulsions, especially if also combined with article 13 ECHR. Thus, if only applied to cases also presenting a claim under article 3 ECHR, article 4 protocol 4 ECHR becomes utterly superfluous.[53]

---

49 In the same section, the Committee explains that the initial provision drafted by the Assembly, which would have limited the grounds on which non-nationals could be expelled, was completely abandoned, as 'only the State concerned should be competent [...] to judge of the reasons which, applying its internal law, could motivate expulsion and that such judgement should not be subject to the bodies provided for by the Convention.' Council of Europe, *Collected Edition of the "Travaux Préparatoires" of Protocol No. 4* (1976), 506, para. 36.

50 ECtHR, Judgment (GC), 13 February 2020, *N.D. and N.T. v Spain*, Application Nos. 8675/15 and 8697/15, para. 185 ff., where the Grand Chamber notes that 'expulsion' means 'any forcible removal of an alien from a State's territory, irrespective of the lawfulness of the person's stay, the length of time he or she has spent in the territory, the location in which he or she was apprehended, his or her status as a migrant or an asylum-seeker and his or her conduct when crossing the border.'

51 *Id.*, in particular paras. 184 ff. and 198 f.

52 Thus, the only two cases where there was no standing claim under article 3 ECHR, the Court concluded that there was no violation of article 4 protocol 4 ECHR. See ECtHR, Judgment (GC), 15 December 2016, *Khlaifia and Others v Italy*, Application No. 16483/12 and ECtHR, Judgment (GC), 13 February 2020, *N.D. and N.T. v Spain*, Application Nos. 8675/15 and 8697/15.

53 This was confirmed by the Court in ECtHR, Judgment, 20 July 2021, *D. v Bulgaria*, Application No. 29447/17, para. 139.

C. *The 'Own Culpable Conduct' Exception*

In *N.D. and N.T. v. Spain*, the Grand Chamber defined a new exception[54] to the prohibition of collective expulsions under article 4 protocol 4 ECHR. It found that in certain circumstances, a collective expulsion will not be in violation of article 4 protocol 4 ECHR.

This exception is to be considered in a three-fold step.[55] First it applies in certain situations as defined in the judgment (1). Second, in those cases, the Court will assess whether the state party, 'provided genuine and

---

54 In ECtHR, Judgment (GC), 13 February 2020, *N.D. and N.T. v Spain*, para. 200, the Court claimed to ground this new exception on 'well-established case-law'. This qualification was strongly questioned by a number of legal scholars, as the jurisprudence on this point is limited to two admissibility decisions, namely ECtHR, Decision, 16 June 2005, *Berisha and Haljiti v the former Yugoslav Republic of Macedonia*, Application No. 18670/03 and in ECtHR, Decision, 1 February 2011, *Dritsas and Others v Italy*, Application No. 2344/02. These cases have factually little in common between them as to what was deemed to constitute 'own culpable conduct'. Moreover, the extension of 'own culpable conduct' from acts of the applicants which had impeded attempts by the state party to examine cases individually (in the previously mentioned cases) to behaviour generally judged by the Court as justifying stripping applicants from their rights under article 4 protocol 4 ECHR (in N.D. and N.T. v. Spain) was also heavily criticised. See for example Pichl and Schmalz, '"Unlawful" may not mean rightless', Verfassungsblog, 14 February, https://verfassungsblog.de/unlawful-may-not-mean-rightless/; Riemers: *The Prohibition of Collective Expulsion in Public International Law* (2020), 72; Ciliberto: 'A Brand-New Exclusionary Clause to the Prohibition of Collective Expulsion of Aliens: The Applicant's Own Conduct in *N.D. and N.T. v Spain*' (2021) 21 Hum. Rights Law Rev., 203 (210). This position of the Court was also strongly condemned by ECtHR judge Pinto de Albuquerque in ECtHR, Judgment (GC), 21 January 2021, *Georgia v Russia (II)*, Application No. 38263/08, Partly Dissenting Opinion of the Judge Pinto de Albuquerque, para. 19, 'The fallacy of the Court's line of argument is even more patent when it is stretched ad absurdum to deny the right of access to human rights to criminals or other "disruptive" people, whatever that might mean.'

55 ECtHR, Judgment (GC), 13 February 2020, *N.D. and N.T. v Spain*, Application Nos. 8675/15 and 8697/15, para. 201; ECtHR, Judgment, 8 July 2021, *Shahzad v Hungary*, Application No. 12625/17, para. 59.
Elsewhere the test is defined as two-fold, with a precondition of applicability (which is the first step in the present article). See Gericke: 'Zwischen effektivem Menschenrechtsschutz und Realpolitik. Die jüngere Rechtsprechung des EGMR zum Rechtsschutz an den EU-Außengrenzen' (2020), 12/2020, Asylmagazin, Zeitschrift für Flüchtlings-und Migrationsrecht, 14 (19); Ciliberto: 'A Brand-New Exclusionary Clause to the Prohibition of Collective Expulsion of Aliens: The Applicant's Own Conduct in *N.D. and N.T. v Spain*' (2021) 21 *Hum. Rights Law Rev.*, 203 (211 ff.).

effective access to means of legal entry, in particular border procedures.' Third, if such was the case, the Court will consider whether there were cogent reasons for the applicants not to use such means of legal entry. In light of their inter-connectedness, the second and third step will be considered together here (2). The final section will assess the impact of this new exception on the Court's approach to article 4 protocol 4 ECHR (3).

I. Conditions of Applicability

In *N.D. and N.T. v. Spain*, the Grand Chamber stated that the exception applied when applicants, 'cross a land border in an unauthorised manner, deliberately take advantage of their large numbers and use force, is such as to create a clearly disruptive situation which is difficult to control and endangers public safety.'[56]

Thus, the applicability of the 'own culpable conduct' exception may be limited to irregular crossings of land borders. Many of the elements constituting the exception's applicability requirements remain to be clarified. First the expression 'large numbers' is unclear. The use elsewhere in the judgment of the term '*en masse*'[57] suggests the need for a rather significant number of persons. In *N.D. and N.T. v.* Spain, the Court recorded that the group was of approximately 600 individuals.[58]

Second, the Court refers to a deliberate 'use of force' several times in the judgment[59] without defining the content of the expression. On the particular facts of the case, the Court described a 'storming' of the border fence[60] and it found the requirement to be fulfilled. However, the terminology of 'use of force' is traditionally used to depict the non-consensual and violent administration of force onto a person. In fact the term appears once only in the Convention, in relation to article 2 ECHR and the right to life.[61] In the Court's guides on its jurisprudence, the term exclusively appears

56 *Id.*, para. 201.
57 *Id.*, para. 166.
58 *Id.*, para. 24.
59 *Id.*, paras. 201, 210 f. and 231.
60 *Id.*, paras. 227 and 231.
61 Article 2(2) ECHR, 'Deprivation of life shall not be regarded as inflicted in contravention of this Article when it results from the use of force which is no more than absolutely necessary: (a) in defence of any person from unlawful violence; (b) in order to effect a lawful arrest or to prevent the escape of a person lawfully detained; (c) in action lawfully taken for the purpose of quelling a riot or insurrection.'

in relation to the use of force by law-enforcement officers or in armed conflicts.[62] In *N.D. and N.T. v. Spain*, the judgment does not mention that the two applicants were violent towards other persons. It seems to be the act of climbing a border fence which was labelled as 'use of force'. A stricter definition has been used by the Court since, when in *Shahzad v Hungary*, the Court discarded the applicability of the 'own culpable conduct' exception on the ground that there was no indication of use of force or resistance by the applicant or any other men, as these had followed the orders of the officers.[63]

Third, the use by the Court of the word 'deliberately' suggests that an intention is required, though it is unclear whether the intention is only to 'take advantage of large numbers', or also to use force, or even to 'create a clearly disruptive situation which is difficult to control and endangers public safety.' In *N.D. and N.T. v. Spain*, the individual intentions of the applicants were not assessed by the Court, as pointed out by former ECtHR judge Pinto de Albuquerque,

> The suggested rationale of the Court is one of guilt by association, whereby all Africans climbing the border fences in Melilla act in the same manner, share the same intention and are in the same personal situation. In *N.D. and N.T. v. Spain*, the specific intentions of the applicants to disrupt and endanger public safety were never established and no evidence was ever put forward regarding any concrete violent acts committed by them or any other person crossing on that day. When reading the judgment, one gets the impression that the principle of individual responsibility has been completely obfuscated.[64]

---

62 Examples include the forceful taking of someone into custody: ECtHR, Guide on Article 13 of the European Convention on Human Rights, 30 April 2020, https://www.echr.coe.int/Documents/Guide_Art_13_ENG.pdf, para. 99; the infliction of physical harm: ECtHR, Guide on Article 2 of the European Convention on Human Rights, 31 August 2020, https://www.echr.coe.int/Documents/Guide_Art_2_ENG.pdf, para. 4; killings: ECtHR, Guide on Article 13 of the European Convention on Human Rights, 30 April 2020, https://www.echr.coe.int/Documents/Guide_Art_13_ENG.pdf, para. 86; the use of high-pressure water and teargas and driving into a crowd with armoured vehicles: ECtHR, Guide on Article 11 of the European Convention on Human Rights, 31 August 2020, https://www.echr.coe.int/Documents/Guide_Art_11_ENG.pdf, para. 82.

63 ECtHR, Judgment, 8 July 2021, *Shahzad v Hungary*, Application No. 12625/17, para. 61.

64 ECtHR, Judgment (GC), 21 January 2021, *Georgia v Russia (II)*, Application No. 38263/08, Partly Dissenting Opinion of the Judge Pinto de Albuquerque, para. 20.

II. Genuine and Effective Access to Means of Legal Entry and Cogent Reasons

This section analyses the second and third applicability requirements of the 'own culpable conduct' exception. In *N.D. and N.T. v. Spain*, the Grand Chamber found that genuine and effective access to means of legal entry existed, namely the possibility to claim asylum at border points and the possibility to apply for humanitarian visas at embassies and consular missions.[65]

Though the Grand Chamber did not spell out a definition in *N.D. and N.T. v. Spain*, jurisprudential definitions of 'genuine and effective' (1) and of 'effective' (2) have already been developed in the broader context of access to rights.

1. 'Genuine and Effective' in the Court's Jurisprudence on Access to Rights

The term 'genuine and effective' was introduced by the Grand Chamber in its assessment of claims under article 4 protocol 4 ECHR in *Khlaifia and Others v. Italy*[66] and used again in *N.D. and N.T. v. Spain*.[67] The term has

65 ECtHR, Judgment (GC), 13 February 2020, *N.D. and N.T. v Spain*, Application Nos. 8675/15 and 8697/15, para. 212. This factual finding was unanimously criticised by commentators. See Pichl and Schmalz, '"Unlawful" may not mean rightless', Verfassungsblog, 14 February, https://verfassungsblog.de/unlawful-may-not-mean-rightless/; Oviedo Moreno, 'A Painful Slap from the ECtHR and an Urgent Opportuniy for Spain' Verfassungsblog, 14 February 2020, https://verfassungsblog.de/a-painful-slap-from-the-ecthr-and-an-urgent-opportunity-for-spain/; Lübbe, 'The Elephant in the Room', Verfassungsblog, 19 February 2020, https://verfassungsblog.de/the-elephant-in-the-room/; Thym, 'A Restrictionist Revolution?', Verfassungsblog, 17 February 2020, https://verfassungsblog.de/a-restrictionist-revolution/; Papageorgopoulos, 'N.D. and N.T. v. Spain: do hot returns require cold decision-making?', EDAL – European Database of Asylum Law, 28 February 2020, https://www.asylumlawdatabase.eu/en/journal/nd-and-nt-v-spain-do-hot-returns-require-cold-decision-making. The finding was even qualified as 'chimerical' by the Spanish judges association Juezas y Jueces para la Democracia. See Juezas y Jueces para la Democracia, *Comunicado de JJpD acerca de la decisión del TEDH sobre las devoluciones en caliente: EUROPA SE BLINDA*, 14 February 2020, http://www.juecesdemocracia.es/2020/02/14/comunicado-jjpd-acerca-la-decision-del-tedh-las-devoluciones-caliente-europa-se-blinda/.

66 ECtHR, Judgment (GC), 15 December 2016, *Khlaifia and Others v Italy*, Application No. 16483/12, para. 248.

67 ECtHR, Judgment (GC), 13 February 2020, *N.D. and N.T. v Spain*, Application Nos. 8675/15 and 8697/15, para. 198.

not been defined by the Court.[68] In attempting to understand its meaning, this section will consider its use and content in relation to other articles of the ECHR and its protocols.

The term initially stems from the Court's assessment of states' obligations under article 6 ECHR.[69] In that context, the Court has traditionally opposed 'genuine and effective' to a 'possibility [which] seems to be rather hypothetical.'[70] Thus, in considering whether there was a 'genuine and effective' access to a procedure in the context of article 6 ECHR, the Court assesses whether an applicant has 'a realistic opportunity' to engage in proceedings 'in a concrete and effective way.'[71]

Importantly, the obligation to ensure genuine and effective access entails a proactive position of the state – including an obligation of due

68 The term was further used by the Court in ECtHR, Judgement, 23 July 2020, *M.K. and others v Poland*, Application No. 40503/17, para. 203 and in ECtHR, Judgment, 24 March 2020, *Asady and Others v Slovakia*, Application No. 24917/15, para. 65, but no definition was provided.

69 It is first used in a partly dissenting opinion in ECtHR, Judgment (GC), 16 September 1996, *Süssmann v Germany*, Application No. 20024/92, Partly Dissenting Opinion of Judges Jambrek and Pettiti, para. 10: 'First, any modern Constitution is based upon respect of the rule of law and of the fundamental human rights and freedoms, while the principles of fair and speedy trial are prerequisites for their genuine and effective respect.' The term was then first used by the Court in a judgment in relation to states' obligations to secure 'the genuine and effective enjoyment of the rights guaranteed under article 6 ECHR' in ECtHR, Judgment, 18 December 2001, *R.D. v Poland*, Application No. 29692/96, para. 44.

70 ECtHR, Judgment, 13 March 2007, *Laskowska v Poland*, Application No. 77765/01, para. 60; also in relation to article 10 ECHR, see for example ECtHR, Judgement, 24 April 2018, *Fatih Tas v Turkey (No. 4)*, Application No. 51511/08, para. 33.

71 See for example ECtHR, Judgment, 18 December 2001, *R.D. v. Poland*, Application No. 29692/96, para. 51; ECtHR, Judgment, 22 March 2007, *Staroszczyk v Poland*, Application No. 59519/00, para. 138; ECtHR, Judgment, 27 June 2006, *Tabor v. Poland*, Application No. 12825/02, para. 43.

diligence[72] – rather than a mere negative obligation not to interfere.[73] Furthermore, in considering the extent of the applicant's responsibility for any obstacles encountered in accessing a procedure in a concrete and effective way, the Court considers what is to be reasonably and justifiably expected from them.[74]

The approach of the Grand Chamber in *N.D. and N.T. v. Spain* differs greatly. In relation to the 'own culpable conduct' exception, obstacles which may completely hinder access to the relevant means of legal entry are disregarded if not deemed to be the responsibility of the respondent state.[75] Also, the Grand Chamber did not include any assessment as to whether it would be reasonable to expect applicants to attempt to use the identified means of legal entry.[76]

72 See for example ECtHR, Judgment, 17 June 2008, *Bobrowski v Poland*, Application No. 64916/01, para. 47: 'In discharging that obligation of fairness, the State must, moreover, display diligence so as to secure to those persons the genuine and effective enjoyment of the rights guaranteed under Article 6'; ECtHR, Judgment, 13 January 2009, *Miroslaw Orzechowsi v Poland*, Application No. 13526/07; ECtHR, Judgment, 19 May 2009, *Antonicelli v Poland*, Application No. 2815/05; ECtHR, Judgment, 17 July 2012, *Muscat v Malta*, Application No. 24197/10; ECtHR, Judgment, 26 July 2018, *Bartaia v Georgia*, Application No. 10978/06, para. 34; ECtHR, Judgment, 04 April 2019, *Kunert v Poland*, Application No. 8981/14.

73 In relation to access to rights under article 11 ECHR, see ECtHR, Judgment, 20 October 2005, *Ouranio Toxo and others v Greece*, Application No. 74989/01, para. 37; ECtHR, Judgment, 16 July 2019, *Zhdanov and Others v Russia*, Application No. 12200/08, para. 162. In relation to access to rights under article 10 ECHR, see ECtHR, Judgment (GC), 12 September 2011, *Palomo Sanchez and Others v Spain*, Application No. 28955/06.

74 ECtHR, Judgment, 04 April 2019, *Kunert v Poland*, Application No. 8981/14, para. 36; ECtHR, Judgment, 03 July 2012, *Siwiec v Poland*, Application No. 28095/08, para. 52 f.; ECtHR, Judgment, 26 May 2016, *Wieslaw Berecki v Poland*, Application No. 46366/12, para. 25.

75 ECtHR, Judgment (GC), 13 February 2020, *N.D. and N.T. v Spain*, Application Nos. 8675/15 and 8697/15, para. 201.

76 As noted by Ciliberto, similarly, the requirement to exhaust effective domestic remedies (addressed in the next section) does not need to be fulfilled when doing so would be 'dangerous or impossible'. See Ciliberto: 'A Brand-New Exclusionary Clause to the Prohibition of Collective Expulsion of Aliens: The Applicant's Own Conduct in *N.D. and N.T. v Spain*' (2021) 21 Hum. Rights Law Rev., 203 (216).

2. *'Effective' in the Court's Jurisprudence on Access to Rights before Domestic Courts*

The term 'effective' is also the subject of a well-established jurisprudence to assess whether the domestic legal system provides for effective access to the rights and safeguards enshrined within the ECHR. In that sense, such jurisprudence clarifies how the Court has defined what constitutes an effective access to rights. This jurisprudence is thus relevant to consider what constitutes effective access to means of legal entry.[77]

Effectiveness entails availability in law and in practice.[78] To be available in law, a measure needs to have a sufficiently clear legal basis.[79] Measures that are entirely discretionary cannot provide effective access.[80] In assessing whether a measure is available in practice, the Court considers whether it has been successfully used in the past[81] and whether it offers reasonable prospects of success.[82] Whether obstacles from the availability of a remedy in practice fall under the responsibility of the respondent state is irrelevant.[83]

Again, the approach of the Court in *N.D. and N.T. v. Spain* departs from this line of jurisprudence. First, in assessing the accessibility of asylum applications at border crossings, the Court dismissed the relevance of racial profiling by Moroccan authorities as none of the evidence 'suggest[ed] that the Spanish Government was in any way responsible for this state of affairs.'[84] Further the Grand Chamber concluded that the extremely

77 See also *id.*,213 ff.

78 ECtHR, Judgment (GC), 6 January 2011, *Paksas v Lituania*, Application No. 34932/04, para. 75; ECtHR, Judgment (GC), 01 March 2006, *Sejdovic v Italy*, Application No. 56581/00, para. 45.

79 ECtHR, Judgment (GC), 8 June 2006, *Sürmeli v Germany*, Application No. 75529/01, para. 110 ff.

80 ECtHR, Judgment (GC), 26 October 2000, *Hassan & Tchaouch v Bulgaria*, Application No. 30985/96, para. 100; ECtHR, Judgment, 12 May 2000, *Khan v United Kingdom*, Application No. 35394/97, para. 45 ff.

81 ECtHR, Judgment, 28 November 2006, *Apostol v Georgia*, Application No. 40765/02, para. 39.

82 ECtHR, Judgment (GC), 17 September 2009, *Scoppola v Italy (no. 2)*, Application No. 10249/03, para. 71; ECtHR, Judgment, 18 January 2011, *Mikolajova v Slovakia*, Application No. 4479/03, para. 34.

83 As pointed out in Ciliberto: 'A Brand-New Exclusionary Clause to the Prohibition of Collective Expulsion of Aliens: The Applicant's Own Conduct in *N.D. and N.T. v Spain*' (2021) 21 Hum. Rights Law Rev., 203 (216).

84 ECtHR, Judgment (GC), 13 February 2020, *N.D. and N.T. v Spain*, Application Nos. 8675/15 and 8697/1, para. 218.

low rate of success as to access to the border point was of no relevance,[85] despite it indicating extremely low prospects of success.

Moreover, in relation to the accessibility of humanitarian visas, the respondent state's evidence consisted of an internal letter from the ministry to ambassadors which, in light of an unclear legal situation,[86] clarified that they held discretionary power to grant humanitarian visas.[87] The Grand Chamber considered that this entirely discretionary measure mentioned in a non-public document fulfilled the 'genuine and effective' test.[88]

III. Impact of the 'Own Culpable Conduct' Exception on the Applicability of Article 4 Protocol 4 ECHR at Borders

As pointed out by commentators,[89] this newly defined exception raises more questions than it provides answers. A few weeks after the publication of the Grand Chamber's judgement, Greek authorities were shooting refugees and migrants with rubber bullets and gas canisters to push them back into Turkey.[90] These dramatic events painstakingly illustrated three points. First, unless all are identified and processed, it is impossible to know if a collective expulsion is also a *refoulement* or not. Second, the issue of access to rights by refugees and migrants at land borders will not disappear simply because a new legal exception is created to minimise – if not abrogate – state parties' obligations under article 4 protocol 4

85 *Id.*, para. 213, where the Court grounds its finding that there was a genuine and effective access to border crossings on the registration of six applications 'at the Beni-Enzar border' from black African applicants over a period of eight months.

86 As pointed out by the Grand Chamber, Spanish refugee law practitioners (authors of the AIDA report referred to) considered this possibility to be inexistent. *Id.*, para. 224.

87 *Id.*, paras. 38 and 224.

88 *Id.*, para. 227.

89 Markard, 'A Hole of Unclear Dimensions: Reading ND and NT v. Spain', 1 April 2020, https://eumigrationlawblog.eu/a-hole-of-unclear-dimensions-reading-nd-and-nt-v-spain/.

90 Christides et al., 'The Killing of a Migrant at the Greek-Turkish Border', SPIEGEL International, 8 May 2020, https://www.spiegel.de/international/europe/greek-turkish-border-the-killing-of-muhammad-gulzar-a-7652ff68-8959-4e0d-9101-a1841a944161.

ECHR. Third, the judgment was read by governments as a *carte blanche* to forcefully push refugees and migrants back.[91]

Since the publication of the *N.D. and N.T. v. Spain* judgment, five further chamber judgements on article 4 protocol 4 ECHR have been issued by the Court. Four address the expulsions of persons seeking asylum at land border crossings,[92] whilst one concerns the expulsions of children after a boat interception.[93] In the first border crossing case, the applicants' claim was dismissed on evidentiary grounds.[94] In the two remaining cases, violations of the prohibition of collective expulsions were found.[95] In all of these judgments, *N.D. and N.T. v. Spain* was barely mentioned.

This could be explained by the fact that none of these cases concerns irregular land border crossings, confirming that the 'own culpable conduct' exception is truly limited to that particular type of unauthorised crossing. A further reason could be that the exception as defined by the Grand Chamber in *N.D. and N.T. v. Spain* is so intricate and unclear that it does not, in fact, provide much guidance as to how such cases should be assessed. Though the Grand Chamber in *N.D. and N.T. v. Spain* adopted a politically conservative approach and dismissed the claim, a legally rigorous application of that same exception could have led to the opposite outcome. Therefore, the position of the Court as to access to

91 Goldner Lang, 'Which Connection between the Greek Turkish Border, the Western Balkans Route and the ECtHR's judgment in ND and NT?' 4 September 2020, http://eumigrationlawblog.eu/2750-2/. It was pointed out that though article 4 protocol 4 ECHR is not applicable in the Greek context (because Greece has not ratified protocol 4), a link was immediately made in the political sphere between the Grand Chamber decision in *N.D. and N.T. v Spain* and the situation at the Greek-Turkish border. See Gericke: 'Zwischen effektivem Menschenrechtsschutz und Realpolitik. Die jüngere Rechtsprechung des EGMR zum Rechtsschutz an den EU-Außengrenzen' (2020), 12/2020, Asylmagazin, Zeitschrift für Flüchtlings- und Migrationsrecht, 14 (19).

92 ECtHR, Judgment, 24 March 2020, *Asady and Others v Slovakia*, Application No. 24917/15; ECtHR, Judgement, 23 July 2020, *M.K. and others v Poland*, Application No. 40503/17; ECtHR, Judgment, 8 July 2021, *Shahzad v Hungary*, Application No. 12625/17; ECtHR, Judgment, 8 July 2021, *D.A. and others v Poland*, Application No. 51246/17.

93 ECtHR, Judgment, 25 June 2020, *Moustahi v France*, Application No. 9347/14.

94 ECtHR, Judgment, 24 March 2020, *Asady and Others v Slovakia*, Application No. 24917/15.

95 ECtHR, Judgement, 23 July 2020, *M.K. and others v Poland*, Application No. 40503/17; ECtHR, Judgment, 25 June 2020, *Moustahi v France*, Application No. 9347/14.

rights under article 4 protocol 4 at land borders is still to be defined as the jurisprudence develops.

Practically, the judgment offers no guidance to border guards. Indeed, the 'own culpable conduct' test calls for complex assessments as to the individual circumstances of the applicants and their endeavours to enter a territory in an authorised manner. Thus an individualised examination is still necessary, arguably an examination more complex than if the exception did not apply.[96] In reality border guards are likely to make sweeping assumptions of collective circumstances, which are equally unlikely to reach the Court for an *ex post facto* assessment half a decade later.[97] In that sense, the judgment as it stands is an invitation to push refugees and migrants back. Further the jurisprudence of the Court is now no longer in line with international human rights law.

D. *The Prohibition of Collective Expulsions: A Comparative Conclusion*

I. *The Prohibition of Collective Expulsions within the ECHR Framework*

The prohibition of collective expulsions is one of the rights which one could invoke in relation to an expulsion.[98] This section will outline the

96 Indeed, when article 4 protocol 4 ECHR calls for the identification of a person and an opportunity to challenge the expulsion, the 'own culpable conduct' exception requires a detailed questioning as to previous attempts to access means of legal entry, reasons why these were not used and an assessment as to whether these reasons are cogent or not. See also Gericke: 'Zwischen effektivem Menschenrechtsschutz und Realpolitik. Die jüngere Rechtsprechung des EGMR zum Rechtsschutz an den EU-Außengrenzen' (2020), 12/2020, Asylmagazin, Zeitschrift für Flüchtlings-und Migrationsrecht, 14 (19).

97 For a critical analysis of the Court's ex post facto assessment in article 4 protocol 4 ECHR cases, see Riemers, *The Prohibition of Collective Expulsion in Public International Law* (2020), 190 ff.

98 Hence article 1 protocol 7 ECHR is specifically applicable to non-nationals having obtained residency in the state party. Further articles 2 (right to life) and 8 (right to family life) can also be invoked to challenge expulsions. See for example ECtHR, Judgment (GC), 23 March 2016, *F.G. v Sweden*, Application No. 43611/11, for article 2 ECHR and ECtHR, Judgment (GC), 13 December 2012, *De Souza Ribeiro v France*, Application No. 22689/07, for article 8 ECHR. The Court even indicated that in some cases, expulsions could raise issues under article 6 ECHR when the applicant would be facing 'flagrant denial of a fair trial' in ECtHR, Judgment (GC), 7 July 1989, *Soering v United Kingdom*, Application No. 14038/88, para. 113.

safeguards provided by other articles under the ECHR and its protocols, with a focus on the most relevant ones, namely (1) the prohibition of torture and inhuman or degrading treatment under article 3 ECHR and (2) the right to an effective remedy under article 13 ECHR

1. *Article 3 ECHR and the Prohibition of Torture and Inhuman or Degrading Treatment*

Where article 4 protocol 4 ECHR was drafted to apply to all non-nationals, article 3 ECHR only applies to those who face an imminent risk of torture, inhuman or degrading treatment directly or indirectly upon expulsion.

Though both article 3 and article 4 protocol 4 ECHR are framed in absolute terms, the safeguards afforded by article 3 ECHR are much more protective. Indeed, this provision prohibits state parties from knowingly surrendering a person to another state when there are substantial grounds to believe that the person runs a real risk of exposure to torture or inhuman or degrading treatment or punishment.[99] The individual assessment required is thus better defined. In fact article 3 ECHR imposes an obligation on states to assess such risk on their own initiative when they ought to know of it, for example when information about a real and concrete risk of treatment in breach of article 3 ECHR is available from numerous public sources.[100] Therefore, state parties cannot defend claims under article 3 ECHR by alleging that an applicant did not raise the risks which she would be imminently exposed to upon expulsion.

---

99 ECtHR, Judgment (GC), 7 July 1989, *Soering v United Kingdom*, Application No. 14038/88; ECtHR, Judgment (GC), 20 March 1991, *Cruz Varas and Others v Sweden*, Application No. 15576/89, para. 69 ff.; ECtHR, Judgment (GC), 28 February 2008, *Saadi v Italy*, Application No. 37201/06, para. 124 f.

100 See, *mutatis mutandis*, ECtHR, Judgment (GC), 15 November 1996, *Chahal v United Kingdom*, Application No. 22414/93, para. 104 f.; ECtHR, Judgment, 11 July 2000, *Jabari v Turkey*, Application No. 40035/98, para. 40 f.; ECtHR, Judgment (GC), 21 January 2011, *M.S.S. v Belgium and Greece*, Application No. 30696/09, para. 359; ECtHR, Judgment (GC), 23 February 2012, *Hirsi Jamaa and Others v Italy*, Application No. 27765/09, para.133; ECtHR, Judgment (GC), 21 November 2019, *Ilias and Ahmed v Hungary*, Application No. 47287/15, para. 141.

2. *Article 13 ECHR and the Right to an Effective Remedy*

The most significant difference between article 13 and article 4 protocol 4 ECHR is that, whilst the prohibition of collective expulsions can be claimed as a free-standing right, article 13 ECHR is an instrumental right which can only be claimed in connection with another ECHR right.[101]

When claimed in connection with article 3 ECHR – and unlike when claimed in connection with article 4 protocol 4 ECHR,[102] article 13 ECHR requires from domestic remedies to have automatic suspensive effect.[103] Further, in those cases article 13 ECHR affords the right to a close, rigorous and independent scrutiny of the claim by the authorities[104] in a reason-

101 ECtHR, Guide on Article 13 of the European Convention on Human Rights, 31 August 2020, https://www.echr.coe.int/Documents/Guide_Art_13_ENG.pdf.

102 In ECtHR, Judgment (GC), 15 December 2016, *Khlaifia and Others v Italy*, Application No. 16483/12, para. 279, the Grand Chamber reversed previous jurisprudence, following which for claims under article 13 in connection to article 4 protocol 4 ECHR, a remedy would not be effective against an expulsion if it did not carry automatic suspensive effect. See ECtHR, Judgment (GC), 13 December 2012, *De Souza Ribeiro v France*, Application No. 22689/07, para. 82; ECtHR, Judgment (GC), 23 February 2012, *Hirsi Jamaa and Others v Italy*, Application No. 27765/09, para.199; ECtHR, Judgment, 5 February 2002, *Conka v Belgium*, Application No. 51564/99, para. 76 ff.

103 ECtHR, Judgment (GC), 15 December 2016, *Khlaifia and Others v Italy*, Application No. 16483/12, paras. 276 and 281; ECtHR, Judgment (GC), 13 December 2012, *De Souza Ribeiro v France*, Application No. 22689/07, para. 82; ECtHR, Judgment (GC), 23 February 2012, *Hirsi Jamaa and Others v Italy*, Application No. 27765/09, paras. 199 ff.; ECtHR, Judgment, 5 February 2002, *Conka v Belgium*, Application No. 51564/99, para. 79 ff.; ECtHR, Judgment, 26 April 2007, *Gebremedhin [Gaberamadhien] v France*, Application No. 25389/05, paras. 58 and 66.

104 ECtHR, Judgment (GC), 23 February 2012, *Hirsi Jamaa and Others v Italy*, Application No. 27765/09, para. 198; ECtHR, Judgment (GC), 13 December 2012, *De Souza Ribeiro v France*, Application No. 22689/07, para. 82; ECtHR, Judgment (GC), 15 November 1996, *Chahal v United Kingdom*, Application No. 22414/93, para. 151; ECtHR, Judgment, 11 July 2000, *Jabari v Turkey*, Application No. 40035/98.

ably prompt fashion,[105] as well as the right to sufficient information,[106] including that to interpreters and legal advisers.[107]

In all expulsion cases – including those where article 13 is claimed in connection with article 4 protocol 4 ECHR, the right to an effective remedy guarantees access to a domestic remedy before the execution of the expulsion.[108] In other words, a hasty expulsion which does not allow an applicant to avail herself of a remedy and the relevant judicial authority to examine and rule before the expulsion will be in breach of article 13 ECHR.

II. The Prohibition of Collective Expulsions in Other Regional Human Rights Instruments

The prohibition of collective expulsions is also guaranteed within the (1) American and (2) African human rights systems.

---

105 ECtHR, Judgment (GC), 13 December 2012, *De Souza Ribeiro v France*, Application No. 22689/07, para.82; ECtHR, Judgment, 3 June 2004, *Bati and Others v Turkey*, Application No. 33097/96, para. 136; ECtHR, Judgment (GC), 21 January 2011, *M.S.S. v Belgium and Greece*, Application No. 30696/09, para. 320.

106 ECtHR, Judgment (GC), 23 February 2012, *Hirsi Jamaa and Others v Italy*, Application No. 27765/09, para. 203 ff.; ECtHR, Judgment (GC), 21 January 2011, *M.S.S. v Belgium and Greece*, Application No. 30696/09, para. 304.

107 ECtHR, Judgment (GC), 23 February 2012, *Hirsi Jamaa and Others v Italy*, Application No. 27765/09, para. 202; ECtHR, Judgment, 21 October 2014, *Sharifi and Others v Italy and Greece*, Application No. 16643/09, para. 168; ECtHR, Judgment (GC), 21 January 2011, *M.S.S. v Belgium and Greece*, Application No. 30696/09, para. 301.

108 ECtHR, Judgment, 25 June 2020, *Moustahi v France*, Application No. 9347/14, para. 161; ECtHR, Judgment (GC), 13 December 2012, *De Souza Ribeiro v France*, Application No. 22689/07, para. 94 f.; ECtHR, Judgment, 15 May 2012, *Labsi v Slovakia*, Application No. 33809/08, para. 139; ECtHR, Judgment (GC), 15 December 2016, *Khlaifia and Others v Italy*, Application No. 16483/12, para. 280. This is in line with jurisprudence from the UN Treaty Bodies on this point. See in particular UN CAT, *Communication No. 63/1997, Josu Arkauz Arana v France*, 9 November 1999, UN Doc. CAT/C/23/D/63/1997, para. 6.1; UN CAT, *Communication No. 300/2006, Tebourski v France*, 11 May 2005, UN Doc. CAT/C/38/D/300/2006, para. 7.3 f.; UN Human Rights Committee ('UN HRC'), *Communication No. 193/1985, Giry v France*, 20 July 1990, UN Doc. CCPR/C/39/D/193/1985; UN HRC, *Communication No. 289/1988, Wolf v Panama*, 26 March 1992, U.N. Doc. CCPR/C/44/D/289/1988, para. 5.2.

1. The American Convention on Human Rights

The prohibition of collective expulsions of aliens is stipulated under article 22(9) of the American Convention in exactly the same words as under article 4 protocol 4 ECHR. The prohibition is one of the procedural and substantial guarantees protecting non-nationals – irrespective of legal status – from arbitrary expulsions.[109]

The first two cases in which the Inter-American Commission considered group expulsions were *The Haitian Center for Human Rights et al. v. United States* ('the Haitian Interdiction Case')[110] and *John Doe et al. v. Canada*.[111] Both cases were not considered under the American Convention but rather under the American Declaration of the Rights and Duties of Man – which does not contain a prohibition of collective expulsion – as the respondent states in the respective cases had only ratified the latter. The Haitian Interdiction Case addressed a U.S. policy by which boats from Haiti were intercepted in the high sea by U.S. authorities and forced back to Haiti,[112] thus not only impeding access to protection in the U.S. but also in other countries.[113] In the Haitian Interdiction Case, the Commission found that the U.S. had jurisdiction over those intercepted, grounding its finding in a UNHCR Amicus Brief on the jurisdictional scope of the *non-refoulement* principle.[114] The Commission concluded that the U.S. policy was *inter alia* in breach of the right to resort to the courts, the right to equality before the law and the right to seek and receive asylum.[115] In *John Doe et al. v. Canada*, the Commission considered the Canadian 'direct

109 Additional procedural guarantees which have been successfully claimed include the right to a fair trial, including judicial guarantees and protection under article 8 and the right to non-discrimination under article 1(1). Substantial rights successfully claimed by non-nationals include the right to life (article 4) and humane treatment (article 5). See Inter-American Court of Human Rights ('IACtHR'), 24 October 2012, *Case of Nadege Dorzema et al. v Dominican Republic*, Series C No. 251, para. 66; IACtHR, 28 August 2014, *Case of Expelled Dominicans and Haitians v Dominican Republic*, Series C No. 282, para. 406 f.

110 Inter-American Commission for Human Rights ('IAComHR'), *The Haitian Center for Human Rights et al. v United States*, 13 March 1997, Report No. 51/96.

111 IAComHR, *John Doe et al. v Canada*, 21 July 2011, Report No. 78/11.

112 For more details on this policy, see Gutekunst, 'Interdiction of Haitian Migrants on the High Sea: a Legal and Policy Analysis' (1984) 10 *Yale Journal of International Law*, 150.

113 IAComHR, *The Haitian Center for Human Rights et al. v United States*, 13 March 1997, Report No. 51/96, para. 161.

114 *Id.*, para. 157.

115 *Id.*, paras. 183–8.

back policy,' by which persons who sought asylum at the Canadian-U.S. border were sent back to the U.S. until their asylum interview date, but without assurances that the U.S would not deport them further. In this case, the Commission also found violations of the right to seek asylum and to resort to courts, as well as the right to protection from possible chain *refoulement*.[116]

It is against this backdrop of cases that the Inter-American Court found its first violation of the prohibition of collective expulsions under article 22(9) of the American Convention in *Case of Nadege Dorzema et al. v. Dominican Republic*.[117] The case addressed the violent summary expulsions by Dominican officers of a group of Haitian migrants who had entered the Dominican Republic irregularly. In its assessment of the state's obligations under article 22(9), the Court found that the prohibition of collective expulsions was part of a set of rights expressed under article 22 which constituted an essential condition to the free development of human beings.[118] Furthermore, the Court highlighted that the essential criterion to the characterisation of a collective expulsion was not the number of non-nationals expelled but the lack of an individualised expulsion proceedings.[119] Then the Court defined minimal procedural guarantees to be applied without any discrimination as to status. These include: the right to be formally and expressly informed of the grounds for expulsion; the right to state one's case and contest the state's case; the right to legal assistance, interpretation and consular representation; the right to have an unfavourable decision reviewed by a competent authority; and the right to a notified and reasoned decision.[120]

The second case in which the Court found a violation of article 22(9) of the Convention is the *Case of Expelled Dominicans and Haitians v. Dominican Republic*.[121] The case addressed a 1990s systematic practice of expulsion of Haitians and Dominicans of Haitian descent from the Dominican Republic.[122] The Court noted that these expulsions, 'affected

116 IAComHR, *John Doe et al. v Canada*, 21 July 2011, Report No. 78/11, para. 128.
117 IACtHR, 24 October 2012, *Case of Nadege Dorzema et al. v Dominican Republic*, Series C No. 251.
118 *Id.*, para. 169.
119 *Id.*, para. 172 ff.
120 *Id.*, para. 175.
121 IACtHR, 28 August 2014, *Case of Expelled Dominicans and Haitians v Dominican Republic*, Series C No. 282.
122 *Id.*, para. 171.

nationals and aliens alike, both documented and undocumented [...].'[123] Before addressing the prohibition of collective expulsions, the Court summarised its view on applicable standards in expulsion proceedings. Drawing from its Advisory Opinion on the Juridical Condition and Rights of the Undocumented Migrants,[124] the Court highlighted that, 'due process must be guaranteed to everyone, regardless of their migratory status.'[125] In this section, the Court reiterated the procedural safeguards it had listed in Nadege Dorzema.[126] In considering the prohibition of collective expulsions, the Court once more highlighted that the prohibition, 'stems from the considerations on due process of law in immigration proceedings.'[127] It confirmed that the essence of the prohibition was to guarantee, 'an objective analysis of the individual circumstances of each alien.' In doing so the Court referred to the ECtHR's definition of a collective expulsion from the cases of *Andric v. Sweden*[128] and *Conka v. Belgium*.[129]

The American Convention contains procedural and substantive rights which can be invoked to ensure that non-nationals have their cases individually considered before being expelled.[130] Yet the Inter-American Court of Human Rights has clearly connected the prohibition of collective expulsions to the right to due process, whilst underscoring that such due process rights are not to be underestimated for being only procedural. To the contrary, they constitute core human rights.

---

123 *Id.*, para. 330.

124 IACtHR, 17 September 2003, *Juridical Condition and Rights of the Undocumented Migrants*, Advisory Opinion, Series A No.18.

125 IACtHR, 28 August 2014, *Case of Expelled Dominicans and Haitians v Dominican Republic*, Series C No. 282, para. 351.

126 *Id.*, para. 356.

127 *Id.*, para. 361. This connection between the right to due process and the prohibition of collective expulsions had already been made by the Court in IACtHR, 24 October 2012, *Case of Nadege Dorzema et al. v Dominican Republic*, Series C No. 251, para. 176.

128 ECtHR, Judgment, 23 February 1999, *Andric v Sweden*, Application No. 45917/99.

129 ECtHR, Judgment, 5 February 2002, *Conka v Belgium*, Application No. 51564/99.

130 For example, in IACtHR, 24 October 2012, *Case of Nadege Dorzema et al. v Dominican Republic*, Series C No. 251, para. 66, the Court also found violations of the right to judicial guarantee under article 8(1) and to judicial protection under article 25 (an equivalent of the right to an effective remedy under article 13 ECHR) of the American Convention, *inter alia*.

2. *The African Charter on Human and Peoples' Rights*

Article 12(5) of the African Charter ('the Charter') stipulates that 'the mass expulsion of non-nationals shall be prohibited. Mass expulsion shall be that which is aimed at national, racial, ethnic or religious groups.' This provision has two particularities. First, it uses the word 'mass' rather than 'collective'.[131] Second it defines characteristic discriminatory grounds for the expulsion to qualify as *en masse*. In practice, the African Commission on Human and Peoples' Rights does not impose such requirements when applying this article.

Here again, the prohibition is one of many procedural and substantial guarantees protecting non-nationals – irrespective of legal status – from arbitrary expulsions.[132]

The Commission's first finding of a violation of the prohibition of mass expulsions addressed the mass expulsion of Burundian refugees from Rwanda.[133]

Then the Commission found a violation of article 12(5) of the Charter in relation to the apprehension, detention and expulsion over a period of

---

131 As pointed out by Riemers, this difference is not significant and in fact the French version of the Charter uses the word 'collective'. See Riemers, *The Prohibition of Collective Expulsion in Public International Law* (2020),17 ff.

132 The main and most crucial additional procedural guarantee as acknowledged by the ACPHR jurisprudence is the right to appeal to a competent national organ (article 7). This stands in contrast to the position under the ECHR and the ECtHR's jurisprudence, where the applicability of the right to a fair hearing under article 6 ECHR has been excluded for immigration issues. See ECtHR, Judgment (GC), 5 October 2000, *Maaouia v France*, Application No. 39652/98, para. 35; Substantial rights successfully claimed by non-nationals in the context of their arbitrary expulsions include the prohibition of discrimination (article 2), the right to life and integrity (article 4), the right to human dignity and the prohibition of torture, cruel, inhuman or degrading treatment (article 5), the right to family life (article 18). See African Commission for Human and Peoples' Rights ('ACHPR'), *Organisation Mondiale Contre la Torture and Others v Rwanda*, October 1996, 27/89; ACHPR, *African Institute for Human Rights and Development v Guinea*, 23 November to 7 December 2004, 249/2002; ACHPR, *Rencontre africaine pour la défence des droits de l'Homme (RADDHO) v Zambia*, 31 October 1997, 71/92; ACHPR, *Union Inter-Africaine des Droits de l'Homme et al. v Angola*, 11 November 1997, 159/96.

133 ACHPR, *Organisation Mondiale Contre la Torture and Others v Rwanda*, October 1996, 27/89. The Commission also found a violation of article 12(5) of the Charter further to the mass expulsion of refugees in ACHPR, *African Institute for Human Rights and Development v Guinea*, 23 November to 7 December 2004, 249/2002.

two months of over 500 non-nationals which the respondent state claimed were staying irregularly on its territory. Thus in *Rencontre Africaine pour la Défense des Droits de l'Homme (RADDHO) v. Zambia*,[134] though the Commission agreed that the respondent state had the right to expel non-nationals staying irregularly, it held that such expulsions had to comply with certain requirements.[135] In particular, the Commission found violations of the prohibition of mass expulsion. Importantly the Commission ruled that the fact that these non-nationals had been apprehended, served with detention orders and detained in different places and at different times over a period of two months did not exclude that the expulsions were *en masse* because the respondent state could not 'prove that the deportees were given the opportunity to seek appeal against the decision on their deportation.'[136] In many ways, the situation of the applicants was factually similar to the one in the ECtHR case of *Khlaifia and Others v. Italy*,[137] but unlike the ECtHR, the African Commission allocated responsibility to the state to prove that the applicants could have challenged their deportations in practice. A further crucial finding was that the Commission defined the characteristic discriminatory grounds very broadly, finding that it was enough that, 'West Africans constituted the majority of those expelled.'[138]

This jurisprudence was reaffirmed shortly after, in a third case, relating to a practice of mass expulsions of West Africans from Angola.[139] In *Union Inter-Africaine des Droits de l'Homme et al. v. Angola*, the Commission found a violation of article 12(5) of the Charter. In doing so, it specifically addressed the expulsion of undocumented migrants and highlighted that it could not happen without any procedural guarantees.[140] Importantly the Commission stated that mass/collective expulsions, 'constitute a special

134 ACHPR, *Rencontre africaine pour la défence des droits de l'Homme (RADDHO) v Zambia*, 31 October 1997, 71/92.

135 *Id.*, para. 23.

136 *Id.*, para. 27 f.

137 ECtHR, Judgment (GC), 15 December 2016, *Khlaifia and Others v Italy*, Application No. 16483/12.

138 ACHPR, *Rencontre africaine pour la défence des droits de l'Homme (RADDHO) v Zambia*, 31 October 1997, 71/92, para. 26.

139 *Id.*, para. 11. This jurisprudence was further confirmed in ACPHR, *Institute for Human Rights and Development in Africa v Angola*, 7 to 22 May 2008, 292/04, paras. 35 f. and 67 ff.

140 ACHPR, *Union Inter-Africaine des Droits de l'Homme et al. v Angola*, 11 November 1997, 159/96, para. 20.

violation of human rights'[141] which 'calls into question a whole series of rights recognized and guaranteed in the Charter'.

E. Conclusion

The prohibition of collective expulsions as initially intended by the drafters of the 4th protocol to the ECHR ensures a very minimal and basic right, namely the right to be treated as an individual – as a legal subject rather than a mere object of the law.[142] By denying its applicability to undocumented migrants crossing borders irregularly,[143] the Strasbourg Court may be denying their very humanity. It certainly places its jurisprudence in an interpretative dissonance with its American and African counterparts. This dissonance results partially from the perception and treatment of undocumented migrants – as often opposed to refugees – by these institutions. Where Strasbourg takes a punitive stance,[144] both the Inter-American Court and the African Commission consider undocumented migrants as a particularly vulnerable category requiring specific protection.[145]

Scholars have examined the failure of international human rights law to protect the basic rights of undocumented migrants, thus echoing Hannah Arendt's analysis on 'the right to have rights.'[146] In a concurring judgement on access to rights at borders, former ECtHR judge Pinto de Albuquerque stated, 'To allow people to be rejected at land borders and returned without assessing their individual claims amounts to treating

141 *Id.*, para. 19.

142 In that sense, the prohibition of collective expulsions is one of the concrete expressions of the right to juridical personality, as first embodied under article 6 of the Universal Declaration of Human Rights but also within article 16 of the Convention for Civil and Political Rights.

143 See ECtHR, Judgment (GC), 15 December 2016, *Khlaifia and Others v Italy*, Application No. 16483/12; ECtHR, Judgment (GC), 13 February 2020, *N.D. and N.T. v Spain*, Application Nos. 8675/15 and 8697/15.

144 Pichl and Schmalz, '"Unlawful" may not mean rightless', Verfassungsblog, 14 February 2020, https://verfassungsblog.de/unlawful-may-not-mean-rightless.

145 IACtHR, 24 October 2012, *Case of Nadege Dorzema et al. v Dominican Republic*, Series C No. 251, para. 152; ACHPR, *Open Society Justice Initiative v Côte d'Ivoire*, 25 February 2016, 318/06, para. 141.

146 See Ramji-Nogales, '"The Right to Have Rights": Undocumented Migrants and State Protection' (2015) 63 *Kansas Law Review*, 1045.

them like animals. Migrants are not cattle that can be driven away like this.'[147]

This principle is deeply grounded in post-World War II values. In the late 1940s, René Cassin advocated for the inclusion of the right to legal personality in order to avoid historical repetitions by which humans, 'were once considered as instruments, as chattels, not as beings who could have rights.'[148] Sadly, Cassin's concerns remain relevant. In this case the failure of human rights to protect the whole of humanity does not find its cause in imperfect legal provisions, but rather in the historical and social constructs – and bias – of those interpreting the law.

Bibliography

Christides, Giorgos/Lüdke, Steffen/Popp, Maximilian: The Killing of a Migrant at the Greek-Turkish Border', SPIEGEL International, 8 May 2020, https://www.spiegel.de/international/europe/greek-turkish-border-the-killing-of-muhammad-gulzar-a-7652ff68-8959-4e0d-9101-a1841a944161.

Ciliberto, Giulia: A Brand-New Exclusionary Clause to the Prohibition of Collective Expulsion of Aliens: The Applicant's Own Conduct in N.D. and N.T. v Spain, Hum. Rights Law Rev. 2021, 203ff.

Gericke: Zwischen effektivem Menschenrechtsschutz und Realpolitik. Die jüngere Rechtsprechung des EGMR zum Rechtsschutz an den EU-Außengrenzen, Asylmagazin, Zeitschrift für Flüchtlings-und Migrationsrecht 2020, 14ff.

Goldner Lang, Iris: Which Connection between the Greek Turkish Border, the Western Balkans Route and the ECtHR's judgment in ND and NT?, 4 September 2020, http://eumigrationlawblog.eu/2750-2/.

Gutekunst, Claire P.: Interdiction of Haitian Migrants on the High Sea: a Legal and Policy Analysis, Yale Journal of International Law 1984, 150ff.

Hathaway, James C./Gammelthoft-Hansen, Thomas: Non-Refoulement in a World of Cooperative Deterrence, Colum. J. Transnat'l L. 2015, 235ff.

ILC, Draft articles on the expulsion of aliens, with commentaries (2014), https://legal.un.org/ilc/texts/instruments/english/commentaries/9_12_2014.pdf.

147 ECtHR, Judgment, 11 December 2018, *M.A. and Others v Lithuania*, Application No. 59793/17, Dissenting Opinion, para. 54.

148 UN Economic and Social Council, *Record of the Eighth Meeting of the Drafting Committee of the Commission on Human Rights*, 17 June 1947, UN Doc. E/CN.4/AC.1.SR.8, 7 f.

Juezas y Jueces para la Democracia: Comunicado de JJpD acerca de la decisión del TEDH sobre las devoluciones en caliente: EUROPA SE BLINDA, 14 February 2020, http://www.juecesdemocracia.es/2020/02/14/comunicado-jjpd-acerca-la-decision-del-tedh-las-devoluciones-caliente-europa-se-blinda/.

Lübbe, Anna: The Elephant in the Room, Verfassungsblog, 19 February 2020, https://verfassungsblog.de/the-elephant-in-the-room/.

Markard, Nora: A Hole of Unclear Dimensions: Reading ND and NT v. Spain, 1 April 2020, https://eumigrationlawblog.eu/a-hole-of-unclear-dimensions-reading-nd-and-nt-v-spain/.

Oviedo Moreno, Carlos: A Painful Slap from the ECtHR and an Urgent Opportuniy for Spain, Verfassungsblog, 14 February 2020, https://verfassungsblog.de/a-painful-slap-from-the-ecthr-and-an-urgent-opportunity-for-spain/.

Papageorgopoulos, Stavros: N.D. and N.T. v. Spain: do hot returns require cold decision-making?, EDAL – European Database of Asylum Law, 28 February 2020, https://www.asylumlawdatabase.eu/en/journal/nd-and-nt-v-spain-do-hot-returns-require-cold-decision-making.

Pichl, Maximilan/Schmalz, Dana: "Unlawful" may not mean rightless, Verfassungsblog, 14 February 2020, https://verfassungsblog.de/unlawful-may-not-mean-rightless/.

Ramji-Nogales, Jaya: "The Right to Have Rights": Undocumented Migrants and State Protection, Kansas Law Review 2015, 1045ff.

Riemers, Lena: The Prohibition of Collective Expulsion in Public International Law (2020).

Thym, Daniel: A Restrictionist Revolution?, Verfassungsblog, 17 February 2020, https://verfassungsblog.de/a-restrictionist-revolution/.

UN CAT: General Comment No. 4 (2017) on the implementation of article 3 of the Convention in the context of article 22, UN Doc. CAT/C/GC/4, 9 February 2018.

UN General Assembly, International Law Commission: Third report on the expulsion of aliens. By Mr. Maurice Kamto, Special Rapporteur, UN Doc. A/CN.4/581, 19 April 2007.

UN Economic and Social Council: Record of the Eighth Meeting of the Drafting Committee of the Commission on Human Rights, UN Doc. E/CN.4/AC.1.SR.8, 17 June 1947.

UNHCR: Submission by the Office of the United Nations High Commissioner for Refugees in the cases of N.D. and N.T. v. Spain (Appl. Nos 8675/15 and 8697/15) before the European Court of Human Rights, 15 November 2015, https://www.unhcr.org/protection/operations/5f9ab8794/unhcr-interventions-european-court-human-rights.html.

Protecting Democratic Elections Against Online Influence via "Fake News" and Hate Speech – The French Loi Avia and Loi No. 2018–1202, the German Network Enforcement Act and the EU's Digital Services Act in Light of the Right to Freedom of Expression

Dominik Steiger[1]

This book chapter will focus on different legislatures' efforts to protect the integrity of their elections against 'fake news' and hate speech. These efforts are a reaction to an unprecedented rise of private dissemination of 'fake news' and hate speech in general and Russian undertakings to undermine the legitimacy of elections worldwide in particular. Elections must be protected as they are 'a characteristic principle of democracy'[2] and consequently 'of prime importance in the Convention system.'[3] Equally of prime importance for democracy is 'freedom of expression [which] constitutes one of the essential foundations of a democratic society and one of the basic conditions for its progress and for each individual's self-fulfilment.'[4] While '[f]ree elections and freedom of expression, particularly freedom of political debate, together form the bedrock of any democratic system [and] are inter-related and operate to reinforce each other',[5] tensions also exist between them that need to be resolved. After having introduced the facts that are foundational for these tensions (A.), this chapter will resolve them by turning to the law (B.). The focus will be on Article 10 of the European Convention of Human Rights ('ECHR') and the European Court of Human Rights' ('ECtHR') pertinent case law.

---

1 The author thanks Laura Lepsy for her valuable help.
2 ECtHR, Judgement, 2 March 1987, *Mathieu-Mohin and Clerfayt v Belgium*, Application No. 9267/81, para. 47.
3 *Ibid.*
4 ECtHR, Judgment, 8 July 1986, *Lingens v Austria*, Application No. 9815/82, para. 41.
5 ECtHR, Judgment, 21 February 2017, *Orlovskaya Iskra v Russia,* Application No. 42911/08, para. 110.

A. The Facts: Old Habits of Influencing Elections Die Hard – And How Legislatures Deal With It

Elections are supposed to be secret, free, and fair.[6] As the cornerstone of every democratic society, even authoritarian states that want to keep a democratic appearance invest much energy and money in holding elections and upholding the impression that these elections are secret, free, and fair. Since elections decide who will be in power for the years to come, much is at stake, and, thus, the temptation to influence the outcome of elections is high.

I. A Very Short History of Influencing Elections

It comes as no surprise that influencing elections is not a new phenomenon and has been undertaken by all kinds of states and in all kinds of times. For example, in the early 18th century, Russia and other major powers regularly influenced the elections of the King of Poland.[7] In the 1796 US presidential campaign, France tried to intimidate voters by publishing official notes addressed to the US Secretary of State in a newspaper that barely concealed that France was threatening the use of force against the US, if Thomas Jefferson was not elected US President.[8] The political opponent's, *i.e.* John Adams', side judged that '[i]n short there never was so barefaced and disgraceful an interference of a foreign power in any free country.'[9] The United States, according to some estimates, influenced 81 presidential elections worldwide between 1947 and 2000, inter alia by using bribes and 'fake news':[10] 'We've used posters, pamphlets, mailers, banners – you name it. We've planted false information in foreign newspa-

---

6 Art. 3 of Protocol No. 1 ECHR; ECtHR, Judgement (GC), 6 October 1976, *X v UK*, Application No. 7140/75; ECtHR, Judgment, 2 March 1987, *Mathieu-Mohin and Clerfayt v Belgium*, Application No. 9267/81, para. 54; Inter-Parliamentary Union, Inter-Parliamentary Council at its 154th session in Paris, *Declaration on Criteria for Free and Fair Elections*, 26 March 1994, http://archive.ipu.org/cnl-e/154-free.htm.

7 Roberts, 'Peter the Great in Poland' (1927) 5 *The Slavonic Review*, 537 (550).

8 DeConde, 'Washington's Farewell, the French Alliance, and the Election of 1796' (1957) 43 *The Mississippi Valley Historical Review*, 641 (653).

9 *Ibid.*

10 Shane, 'Russia Isn't the Only One Meddling in Elections. We Do It, Too', The New York Times, 17 February 2018, https://www.nytimes.com/2018/02/17/sunday-review/russia-isnt-the-only-one-meddling-in-elections-we-do-it-too.html.

pers. We've used what the British call 'King George's cavalry': suitcases of cash.'[11]

II. Today's Story of Influencing Elections – Manipulating the Democratic Process via "Fake News" and Hate Speech

While some of the means of influencing elections have changed today, the deed as such still continues. Democratic states, on the one hand, mainly – but not exclusively[12] – do this overtly. For example, Germany supports democratic initiatives, e.g., via its political foundations and the US via tax-funded groups such as the National Democratic Institute and the International Republican Institute. While this is seen as problematic in some states such as Russia and Hungary, which have adopted so called "foreign agent laws" that aim at minimizing financial and other support to political actors,[13] there is a difference between this kind of overt influence and the influence of elections that this book chapter is about: these organisations, in principle, do not try to get certain candidates elected but to empower citizens to make use of their democratic rights.[14] Instead of manipulating the democratic process, they foster it. Authoritarian States, on the other

---

11 *Ibid.*

12 *Ibid*; Levin, 'Partisan electoral interventions by the great powers: Introducing the PEIG Dataset' (2019) 36 *Conflict Management and Peace Science*, 88; Tharoor, 'The long history of the U.S. interfering with elections elsewhere', The Washington Post, 13 October 2016, https://www.washingtonpost.com/news/worldviews/wp/2016/10/13/the-long-history-of-the-u-s-interfering-with-elections-elsewhere/.

13 For Russia see Tysiachniouk et al., 'Civil Society under the Law 'On Foreign Agents': NGO Strategies and Network Transformation' (2018) 70 *Europe-Asia Studies*, 615; for Hungary see Bárd, 'The Hungarian "Lex NGO" before the CJEU: Calling an Abuse of State Power by its Name', Verfassungsblog, 27 January 2020, https://verfassungsblog.de/the-hungarian-lex-ngo-before-the-cjeu-calling-an-abuse-of-state-power-by-its-name/.

14 Shane, 'Russia Isn't the Only One Meddling in Elections. We Do It, Too.', The New York Times, 17 February 2018, https://www.nytimes.com/2018/02/17/sunday-review/russia-isnt-the-only-one-meddling-in-elections-we-do-it-too.html. See for a distinction between process-oriented election intervention (for or against democracy) and actor-oriented election intervention (for or against a particular candidate): Bubeck et al., 'Why Do States Intervene in the Elections of Others? The Role of Incumbent–Opposition Divisions' (2020) *British Journal of Political Science*, 1 (2). For a similar distinction also see Shulman and Bloom, 'The legitimacy of foreign intervention in elections: The Ukrainian response' (2012) 38 *Review of International Studies*, 445 (450 f.).

hand, tend to influence foreign elections via covert operations that make use of information in a devious way and use "fake news" and hate speech to manipulate the electorate.[15]

1. "Fake News" and the Difference between Mis-, Dis- and Mal-Information

The International Organization in which the European Court of Human Rights is embedded – i.e., the Council of Europe – differentiates three different types of 'fake news'.[16] The first type is called misinformation and is understood to be false information not created with the intent of causing harm. Misinformation may thus be a pure mistake or satire.[17] The second type is called disinformation and is equally understood to be false information, but one which is deliberately created to cause harm.[18] Lastly, the third type is mal-information, which is information based on reality, and thus in principle is true, but shared in order to inflict harm.[19] This form of 'fake news' is the most dangerous one as it is based on reality but distorts it.[20] An aphorism by *William Blake*, coined already in 1807, describes well how much influence this last category of 'fake news' may have: '*A truth that's told with bad intent / Beats all the lies you can invent.*'[21]

2. Hate Speech: Spreading Hatred based on Intolerance

Closely connected to 'fake news' is the problem of hate speech. Some 'fake news' might be hate speech and vice versa – e.g., the denial of the holocaust. 'Fake news' might also lead to hate speech by others and might intended to do so. While the ECHR does not know the term hate speech, the ECtHR uses it[22] and understands it to encompass 'all forms

---

15 See Cardenal et al., *Sharp power: rising authoritarian influence* (2017).

16 CoE, *Information Disorder: Toward an interdisciplinary framework for research and policy making*, September 2017, CoE report DGI (2017) 09.

17 *Id.*, 16.

18 *Id.*, 20.

19 *Ibid.*

20 Baade, 'Fake News and International Law' (2019) 29 *EJIL*, 1357 (1358 ff.).

21 *Ibid.*; Blake, 'Auguries of Innocence', *The Pickering Manuscript* (1807), line 23 f., available at www.blakearchive.org/copy/bb126.1?descId=bb126.1.ms.15.

22 See e.g. ECtHR, Judgement (GC), 16 June 2015, *Delfi AS v Estonia*, Application No. 64569/09, e.g. paras. 151, 152, 154, 155, 156, 157, 158; See also ECtHR, Judgement, 4 December 2003, *Gündüz v Turkey*, Application No. 35071/97, e.g.

of expression which spread, incite, promote or justify hatred based on intolerance.'[23]

3. *The Recent Rise of "Fake News" and Hate Speech in the Context of Elections*

In the last years, the dissemination of disinformation, mal-information and hate speech in general has been unprecedented.[24] This is inseparably connected to the rise of the internet. While the upsurge of 'fake news' and hate speech is already a worrisome development, from a democratic point of view, this becomes even worse when the cornerstone of democracy, i.e., elections, is the target of disinformation, mal-information and hate speech.

The impact of 'fake news' and hate speech on the 2016 US presidential election has been considerable.[25] European elections have been the target of 'fake news' and hate speech as well. For example, the UK House of Commons Digital, Culture, Media and Sports Committee, in its 2018 Interim Report on Disinformation and 'Fake News' found that '156,252 Russian accounts [were] tweeting about #Brexit and that they posted over 45,000 Brexit messages in the last 48 hours of the campaign.'[26] In short,

---

paras. 21, 22, 40, 44, 51; ECtHR, Judgement, 9 May 2018, *Stomakhin v Russia*, Application No. 52273/07, e.g. paras. 6, 70, 71, 72, 96, 117; ECtHR, Decision, 12 May 2020, *Lilliendahl v Iceland*, Application No. 29297/18, e.g. paras. 4, 13, 17, 32, 33, 34, 35, 39.

23 ECtHR, Judgement, 4 December 2003, *Gündüz v Turkey*, Application No. 35071/97, para. 40; ECtHR, Judgement, 5 December 2019, *Tagiyev and Huseynov v Azerbaijan*, Application No. 13274/08, para. 38

24 For an exploration see e.g. Martens et al., 'The digital transformation of news media and the rise of disinformation and fake news', JRC Digital Economy Working Paper No. 2018–02, https://www.econstor.eu/bitstream/10419/202231/1/jrc-dewp201802.pdf.

25 The United States District Court for the District of Columbia 16.02.2018 – Case 1:18-cr-00032-DLF – *United States of America v Internet Research Agency LLC A/K/A Mediasintez*, www.justice.gov/file/1035477/download, para. 32; Scola, 'How chatbots are colonizing politics', Politico, 10 November 2016, www.politico.com/story/2016/10/chatbots-are-invading-politics-229598; Robertson et al., 'How to Hack an Election', Bloomberg Businessweek, 31 March 2016, www.bloomberg.com/features/2016-how-to-hack-an-election/; Steiger, 'International Law and New Challenges to Democracy in the Digital Age: Big Data, Privacy and Interferences with the Political Process' in Witzleb et al. (eds), *Big Data, Political Campaigning and the Law: Privacy and Democracy in the Age of Micro-Targeting* (2020), 71 (73).

26 DCMSC, HC 363, Disinformation and 'fake news': Interim Report, 29 July 2018, https://publications.parliament.uk/pa/cm201719/cmselect/cmcumeds/363/36302.htm, para. 162.

Russia followed the US election campaign playbook by using *personae* who pretended to be ordinary citizens and posted offensive and often divisive comments aimed at sowing 'mistrust and confusion and to sharpen existing divisions in society, [which] may also have destabilising effects on democratic processes.'[27] Further, Russia deployed social bots, i.e. automated software programs that perform tasks within social networks and pretend to be human beings and behave like trolls, programmed to post controversial and divisive comments on websites and on Facebook, or use fake Twitter accounts and other means to magnify comments of trolls and make their work more effective.[28]

Also, the notorious company Cambridge Analytica, is said to have worked for Brexit.[29] The by now dissolved company and its methods, which have survived the dissolution of the company,[30] are able to have a tremendous impact on elections, as was shown in the 2016 US presidential election. Here, the company used direct marketing tools in order to manipulate voters. This manipulation became possible via an algorithm that used data available via Facebook[31] to create a so called Ocean Score that divided people into five basic types.[32] It is said that the algorithm already knows you better than a friend by taking into account only 70 Facebook

---

27 CoE Committee of Ministers, *1309*[th] Meeting, CM/Rec(2018)2, preamble para. 3.

28 Gorodnichenko et al., 'Social Media, Sentiment and Public Opinions: Evidence from #Brexit and #Uselection' (2018) NBER Working Paper No. 24631.

29 Scott, 'Cambridge Analytica did work for Brexit groups, says ex-staffer', Politico, 30 July 2019, https://www.politico.eu/article/cambridge-analytica-leave-eu-ukip-brexit-facebook/; but see BBC News, 'Cambridge Analytica 'not involved' in Brexit referendum, says watchdog', 7 October 2020, https://www.bbc.com/news/uk-politics-54457407; Gehrke, 'UK probe finds no evidence that Cambridge Analytica misused data to influence Brexit', Politico, 7 October 2020, https://www.politico.eu/article/no-evidence-that-cambridge-analytica-misused-data-to-influence-brexit-report/; U.K. Information Commissioner's Office (ICO), RE: ICO investigation into use of personal information and political influence, 2 October 2020, https://ico.org.uk/media/action-weve-taken/2618383/20201002_ico-o-ed-l-rtl-0181_to-julian-knight-mp.pdf, para. 7.

30 Goldhill, 'A 'big data' firm sells Cambridge Analytica's methods to global politicians, documents show', Quartz, 14 August 2019, https://qz.com/1666776/data-firm-ideia-uses-cambridge-analytica-methods-to-target-voters/.

31 See generally Fuster and Scherrer, Big data and smart devices and their impact on privacy, Directorate-General for Internal Policies of the Union Study, September 2015, http://www.europarl.europa.eu/RegData/etudes/STUD/2015/536455/IPOL_STU(2015)536455_EN.pdf, 10 f.

32 See generally John et al., 'Paradigm Shift to the Integrative Big Five Trait Taxonomy' in John et al. (eds), *Handbook of Personality: Theory and Research* (3rd edn., Guildford Press 2008) 114 (114–117).

likes.[33] With 150 likes, it knows you better than your parents and with 300 likes it knows you better than your partner.[34] With this knowledge, personalized ads, called dark posts because they could only be seen by the target person and will often not even be disclosed as an ad, were directed at Facebook users, often with a racist undertone or with at least misleading information.[35] A comparison between ordinary commercials and these micro-targeted dark posts shows the effectiveness of this tool: click rates increase by 60 % compared to non-personalised advertising.[36] The conversion rate, which indicates the percentage of those who click and those who actually become buyers, rises by an extraordinary 1,400 %.[37]

In the French presidential election campaign of 2017, disinformation shared on Twitter included assertions that Emmanuel Macron was homosexual or an agent for financial interests of the United States.[38] This election campaign included also the most notorious hack in a European election context: The – probably – Russian hacks by the hacker group APT 28, also called Fancy Bear, into the servers of the Emmanuel Macron's presidential campaign led to the subsequent release of 21,000 e-mails and nine gigabytes of stolen files, aimed to influence the French election.[39] While the publication of the material in principle has to be understood as a mal-information attack, according to the campaign managers, the leaked material included fake material,[40] and thus also disinformation. Because of the very quick response by the Macron campaign, it is being assumed that it itself planted the fake material in order to be prepared for and be able to counter any possible leaks.[41]

---

33 Quenqua, 'Facebook Knows You Better Than Anyone Else', The New York Times, 19 January 2015, <www.nytimes.com/2015/01/20/science/facebook-knows-you-better-than-anyone-else.html>.

34 *Ibid.*

35 *Cf.* Grassegger and Krogerus, 'Cambridge Analytica / Big data and the Future of Democracy: The Matrix world behind the Brexit and the US Elections', Diplomat Magazine, 5 March 2017, www.diplomatmagazine.nl/2018/03/22/cambridge-analytica-big-data-and-the-future-of-democracy-the-matrix-world-behind-the-brexit-and-the-us-elections/.

36 *Ibid.*

37 *Ibid.*

38 Brattberg and Maurer, Russian Election Interference – Europe's Counter to Fake News and Cyber Attacks, Carnegie Endowment for International Peace, May 2018, https://carnegieendowment.org/files/CP_333_BrattbergMaurer_Russia_Elections_Interference_FINAL.pdf, 10 f.

39 *Ibid.*

40 *Id.*, 11.

41 *Ibid.*

In the European Election of 2019, 500 suspicious pages and groups on Facebook were named that emitted disinformation. 32 million people followed these groups; 67 million people liked, commented, or shared them; and the content received 533 million views.[42] Facebook banned 77 pages und groups and blocked 230 accounts.[43]

The aim of foreign interference is to sow discord and division,[44] and they are quite successful in inspiring individuals in partaking. Hate speech against politicians for example is massively on the rise, especially against female politicians.[45] In Germany, for instance, the number of criminal offences against politicians increased from 1,674 in 2019 to 2,629 in 2020, which is a rise of 57 %.[46] A multitude of these crimes were insults and threats uttered in the anonymity of the internet.[47] 64 % of the female Members of German Parliament who participated in a 2021 survey by the weekly news magazine SPIEGEL said they experienced misogynistic hatred expressed in messages, mostly online.[48] Small extremist groups reportedly used hate postings to exert control over online discussions and in that way influenced the outcome of elections.[49] For example, in the time leading up to the 2017 German federal elections, Reconquista Germania, a right-wing troll factory, gained 7,000 members within a few weeks and succeeded in placing seven of its hashtags among the top 20 hashtags in Germany only

42 Lomas, 'Facebook found hosting masses of far right EU disinformation networks', Tech Crunch, 22 May 2019, https://techcrunch.com/2019/05/22/facebook-found-hosting-masses-of-far-right-eu-disinformation-networks/.

43 *Ibid.*

44 Ohlin, *Election Interference – International Law and the Future of Democracy* (2020), 14.

45 Knight, 'Germany: Hate speech, threats against politicians rise', Deutsche Welle, 9 February 2021, https://www.dw.com/en/germany-hate-speech-threats-against-politicians-rise/a-56512214.

46 Deutscher Bundestag, Drucksache 19/26419, 3 February 2021, Antwort der Bundesregierung auf die Kleine Anfrage der Abgeordneten Ulla Jelpke, Dr. André Hahn, Gökay Akbulut, weiterer Abgeordneter und der Fraktion DIE LINKE.– Drucksache 19/26017 -Straftaten gegen Amts- und Mandatsträger.

47 *Id.*, 5.

48 SPIEGEL online, 'SPIEGEL-Umfrage unter Parlamentarierinnen – Frauenfeindlichkeit im Bundestag durch AFD gestiegen', 12 February 2021, https://www.spiegel.de/politik/deutschland/bundestag-frauenfeindlichkeit-durch-afd-gestiegen-a-4c8c425c-6b08-4ac5-b049-61ad65d1240c.

49 CoE, ECRI Report on Germany (sixth monitoring cycle), 17 March 2020, https://rm.coe.int/ecri-report-on-germany-sixth-monitoring-cycle-/16809ce4be, para. 38.

two weeks before the election.[50] Also 'fake news' played a role before the 2017 German federal election: Buzzfeed News found that seven of the ten most commented, linked, and liked articles about Angela Merkel on Facebook could be classified as disinformation.[51] While other studies rather suggest that the circulation of disinformation played a comparatively small role in the German elections,[52] they problematize that once disinformation is spread, it cannot easily be corrected: only in one out of ten cases did the corrected information achieve a greater circulation than the disinformation.[53] To conclude, dis- and mal-information attacks are obviously real, as is a rise in hate speech. Especially since not only Russia but also China and Iran are stepping up their hybrid and disinformation warfare capabilities,[54] it seems to be mandatory that Europe finds effective – and legal – answers to this threat.

III. Fighting Back – European States' and the EU's Response to Counter Election Influence

Politics and academia have not been oblivious to the phenomena identified above. Since 2017, States around the world have introduced legislation

---

50 Köhler and Ebner, 'Strategies and tactics: communication strategies of jihadists and right-wing extremists' in Baldauf et al. (eds), *Hate Speech and Radicalisation Online – The OCCI Research Report* (2019), 18 (24), https://www.isdglobal.org/wp-content/uploads/2019/06/ISD-Hate-Speech-and-Radicalisation-Online-English-Draft-2.pdf.

51 Schmehl and Lytvynenko, '7 Out Of The 10 Most Viral Articles About Angela Merkel On Facebook Are False', Buzzfeed News, 27 July 2017, https://www.buzzfeednews.com/article/karstenschmehl/top-merkel-news.

52 Schwarz and Holnburger, 'Disinformation: what role does disinformation play for hate speech and extremism on the internet and what measures have social media companies taken to combat it?' in Baldauf et al. (eds), *Hate Speech and Radicalisation Online – The OCCI Research Report* (2019), 35 (36), https://www.isdglobal.org/wp-content/uploads/2019/06/ISD-Hate-Speech-and-Radicalisation-Online-English-Draft-2.pdf.

53 *Ibid.*; Sängerlaub et al., Fakten statt Fakes – Verursacher, Verbreitungswege und Wirkungen von Fake News im Bundestagswahlkampf 2017, Stiftung Neue Verantwortung, März 2018, https://www.stiftung-nv.de/sites/default/files/snv_fakten_statt_fakes.pdf, 79.

54 Shearer, The Evolution of Hybrid Warfare and Key Challenges, Statement Before the House Armed Services Committee, 22 March 2017, https://csis-website-prod.s3.amazonaws.com/s3fs-public/congressional_testimony/170322_shearer_testimony_evolution_of_hybrid_warfare.pdf.

to combat 'fake news' and hate speech on the internet in order to protect democracy.[55] They do so by creating new obligations for online intermediaries with regard to the speech that is published on their platforms. While the idea behind these new rules is, in principle, to protect the democratic discourse, these laws have been criticized for impeding the right to freedom of expression.[56] Furthermore, in some legislations, there have been accusations that the laws serve to silence dissent and hinder democratic discourse.[57] The most outstanding examples of current legislation aimed at countering hate speech and 'fake news' will form the focus of the following legal analysis. These are, namely, two French laws, 'Loi Avia' and 'Loi No. 2018–1202' respectively (1.), the German Network Enforcement Act ('GNEA') (2.), and the proposed EU Digital Services Act (3.).

55 For an overview see Funke and Flamini, A guide to anti-misinformation actions around the world, Poynter, https://www.poynter.org/ifcn/anti-misinformation-actions/; Haciyakupoglu et al., Policy Report Countering Fake News – A Survey of Recent Global Initiatives, Rajaratnam School of International Studies, March 2018, https://www.rsis.edu.sg/wp-content/uploads/2018/03/PR180307_Countering-Fake-News.pdf; Article 19, Responding to 'hate speech': Comparative overview of six EU countries, 2018, https://www.article19.org/wp-content/uploads/2018/03/ECA-hate-speech-compilation-report_March-2018.pdf.; Laub, Hate Speech on Social Media: Global Comparisons, Council on Foreign Relations, 11 April 2019, https://www.cfr.org/backgrounder/hate-speech-social-media-global-comparisons.

56 See for Germany e.g.: Hong, 'The German Network Enforcement Act and the Presumption in Favour of Freedom of Speech', Verfassungsblog, 22 January 2018, https://verfassungsblog.de/the-german-network-enforcement-act-and-the-presumption-in-favour-of-freedom-of-speech/; Peukert, 'Put it back: Ein Vorschlag für ein NetzDG, das die Meinungsfreiheit wahrt', Verfassungsblog, 14 June 2018, https://verfassungsblog.de/put-it-back-ein-vorschlag-fuer-ein-netzdg-das-die-meinungsfreiheit-wahrt/; Lang, 'Netzwerkdurchsetzungsgesetz und Meinungsfreiheit' (2018) 143 *AöR*, 220 (225 f.); for France: Wienfort, 'Blocking Overblocking – Frankreichs Verfassungsrat kippt das Gesetz gegen Hasskriminalität im Netz', Verfassungsblog, 20 June 2020, https://verfassungsblog.de/blocking-overblocking/; Smith, 'Fake news, French Law and Democratic Legitimacy: Lessons for the United Kingdom?' (2019) 11 *Journal of Media Law*, 52 (53).

57 For example in Russia, see International Press Institute, New 'fake news' law stifles independent reporting in Russia on Covid-19, 8 May 2020, https://ipi.media/new-fake-news-law-stifles-independent-reporting-in-russia-on-covid-19/; Pollicino, 'Fundamental Rights as Bycatch – Russia's Anti-Fake News Legislation', Verfassungsblog, 28 March 2019, https://verfassungsblog.de/fundamental-rights-as-bycatch-russias-anti-fake-news-legislation/.

1. *The French Approach: Generally Combatting Hate Speech; "Fake News" only in Election Times*

The French legislator chose to enact two different laws, one directed against hate speech in general (a) and the other against fake news in election times (b).

a) Loi Avia Against Hate Speech: Not Enough Time and Too Much Discretion

The Loi Avia, the French law to combat hate speech,[58] which was declared unconstitutional by the French Conseil Constitutionnel,[59] obliged all online intermediaries, understood in a very broad sense to include any provider of online communication services or storage, independent of the number of users, to remove all posts with terrorist or child pornography content within one hour after notice by an administrative authority (art 1er (I) 1° (b)). Other manifestly illegal content, which was explicitly listed, such as content condoning the commission of certain crimes or incitement to discrimination, hatred or violence (art 1er (II)), had to be taken down within 24 hours after the online intermediary had been notified about the post (art 1er (II), so called notice and takedown procedure). Article 4 required an internal complaint handling system against takedown decisions as well as against decisions not to take down certain posts. The Conseil Supérieur de l'Audiovisuel would have supervised this process. In the case of non-compliance, the online intermediaries, in the case of art 1er (II) only professional online platform operators whose activity on French territory exceeded a certain monetary threshold that was to be determined by decree, faced fines of up to 250,000 € (art 1er (II)). In case of violations of art 1er (I), up to one year of imprisonment was foreseen.

The Conseil Constitutionnel mainly differentiated between the two different paragraphs of Article 1: for the unconstitutionality of paragraph I, the main reasons given were that the one-hour time limit did not allow for any judicial review of the administrative takedown decision, that a request

58 Assemblée Nationale, Proposition de loi nº 388, adoptée par l'Assemblée nationale, en nouvelle lecture, visant à lutter contre les contenus haineux sur internet, 13 Mai 2020, https://www.assemblee-nationale.fr/dyn/15/textes/l15t0388_texte-adopte-seance#.

59 Conseil Constitutionnel, 18 June 2020, Décision no 2020–801 DC – JORF, n° 0156 du 25/06/2020, Texte 2 sur 181, para. 8, para. 19.

to review the decision would not have any suspensive effect, and that finally the law foresaw no requirement that the content had to be "manifestly illegal" and thus allowed the administrative authority too much discretion.[60]

With regard to paragraph II, the Conseil Constitutionnel held it to be problematic that, instead of a court order, a notice by any individual sufficed to obligate the online intermediary to act; underlined the difficulties for online intermediaries in ascertaining whether a post is obviously unlawful, especially within such a short time limit, and that the norm lacked specific possibilities for online intermediaries to be exempted from liability.[61] These reasons read together with the high penalties that would be incurred already for the first infringement[62] would lead online intermediaries to block content that had been flagged by users as manifestly illegal just to be on the safe side.[63] The Law Avia, , according to the Conseil Constitutionnel, thus violated the right to freedom of expression in a disproportionate manner.

b) Loi No. 2018–1202 Against the Manipulation of Information: A much more Differentiated and Precise Approach

The Loi No. 2018–1202, which entered into force in November 2018, is directed against 'fausses informations' ('false information'), in the sense of 'inaccurate or misleading allegations or imputations of a fact likely to affect the integrity of [a] forthcoming election.'[64] If such false information whose 'incorrect or misleading nature is apparent',[65] is disseminated deliberately, artificially or automatically, and on a mass scale via an online public communication service that has more than five million visitors per month or is paid 100 € for each piece of content that is related to a debate of general interest, has been subjectively transmitted to cause harm and ob-

60 *Id.*, para. 7.
61 *Id.*, para. 19.
62 *Id.*, para. 18.
63 *Id.*, para. 19
64 Loi no 2018–1202 du 22 décembre 2018 relative à la lutte contre la manipulation de l'information, JORF n° 0297 du 23 décembre 2018, Texte 2 sur 191, art. 1er 2°; original wording: "allégations ou imputations inexactes ou trompeuses d'un fait de nature à altérer la sincérité du scrutin à venir".
65 Conseil Constitutionnel, 20 December 2018, Décision no 2018–773 DC- JORF, n°0297 du 23 décembre 2018, Texte 5 sur 191, para. 23.

jectively possesses the apparent effect of undermining the reliability of the election,[66] a judge may order its removal or the blockage of certain websites. The judge has to act within 48 hours after such a request – which can be filed by everyone during the three months before elections. The Conseil Constitutionnel in December 2018 held that the law struck a 'balance [between] the constitutional principle of the honesty of elections with the constitutional freedom of expression.'[67] Decisive arguments of the Conseil Constitutionnel in favor of the constitutionality of Loi No. 2018-1202 were, *inter alia*, that it only applies in the three months before elections;[68] that instead of a notice and takedown procedure[69] a judge has to order the takedown of the posts; the preconditions that allow the judge to act are precisely framed; that the fines, which may be imposed on the users and the platforms alike, only reach up to 75,000 €[70]; and that the online intermediaries are rather narrowly defined. These arguments also indirectly highlight the differences between the two French Laws and show why the first law violates the right to freedom of expression and the other does not.

2. *The German Approach: Generally Combatting Hate Speech and – less so – "Fake News"*

The GNEA's[71] express motivation is to combat hate speech and other unlawful content including punishable 'fake news'.[72] These terms, however, do not feature in the text. Instead, the GNEA obligates online intermediaries with more than two million registered users in Germany to help in enforcing – hence the name 'Network Enforcement Act'– certain sections of the German Criminal Code, in particular, the prohibition of public

66 *Ibid.*
67 *Id.*, paras. 17, 25.
68 *Id.*, paras. 8, 9, 19.
69 *Id.*, para. 21.
70 *Id.*, para. 7.
71 Gesetz zur Verbesserung der Rechtsdurchsetzung in sozialen Netzwerken (Netzwerkdurchsetzungsgesetz – NetzDG) vom 1. September 2017, BGBl Jahrgang 2017 Teil 1 Nr. 61; for an overview see Lauber-Rönsberg, 'Hate Speech – ein Überblick über rechtliche Rahmenbedingungen, ihre Durchsetzung und das neue NetzDG' (2017) 13 *Aptum*, 100.
72 Deutscher Bundestag, Drucksache 18/12727, 18. Wahlperiode, 14 June 2017, Gesetzentwurf der Bundesregierung Entwurf eines Gesetzes zur Verbesserung der Rechtsdurchsetzung in sozialen Netzwerken (Netzwerkdurchsetzungsgesetz – NetzDG), 1 f.

incitement to crime or incitement to hatred.[73] A closer look reveals that, while hate speech is indeed targeted by the GNEA, 'fake news' is only marginally touched upon: of the 21 sections of the Criminal Code that are explicitly named by the GNEA, only the defamation of religions, religious and ideological associations, insults, and the general prohibition of defamation encompass an element of falsehood. While some types of disinformation, e.g., those that refer to financial dependencies of politicians, might be subsumed under these norms, many other types of disinformation, especially politically misleading ones, such as that Chancellor Angela Merkel 'hopes' for 12 million immigrants by 2060,[74] will not. While the GNEA is not specifically designed to protect elections, it aims to protect a 'free, open and democratic society'[75] by civilizing the public discourse.

Posts that contravene these prohibitions have to be taken down within seven days by the online intermediary after having received the complaint (§ 3 (2) Nr. 3 GNEA). If the post is manifestly unlawful, it must be blocked or taken down within 24 hours (§ 3 (2) Nr. 3 GNEA).[76]

There are some similarities between the GNEA and the Loi Avia, such as the notice and takedown procedure, the difficulties to determine whether a post is manifestly unlawful or not and that no specific grounds for online intermediaries to exempt themselves from liability exist.[77] However, there are important differences: while the GNEA regulates that social media companies face fines of up to five million Euros, it only requires

73 Gesetz zur Verbesserung der Rechtsdurchsetzung in sozialen Netzwerken (Netzwerkdurchsetzungsgesetz – NetzDG) vom 1. September 2017, BGBl Jahrgang 2017 Teil 1 Nr. 61, § 1 (3).

74 Röttger, 'Nein – Merkel „hofft“ nicht auf 12 Millionen Einwanderer', Correctiv, 5 March 2018, https://correctiv.org/fakten-check/2018/03/05/nein-merkel-hofft-nicht-auf-12-millionen-einwanderer/.

75 Deutscher Bundestag, Drucksache 18/12727, 18. Wahlperiode, 14 June 2017, Gesetzentwurf der Bundesregierung Entwurf eines Gesetzes zur Verbesserung der Rechtsdurchsetzung in sozialen Netzwerken (Netzwerkdurchsetzungsgesetz – NetzDG), 1.

76 Katsirea, '"Fake news": reconsidering the value of untruthful expression in the face of regulatory uncertainty' (2018) 10 *Journal of Media Law*, 159 (181).

77 Assemblée Nationale, Proposition de loi nº 388, adoptée par l'Assemblée nationale, en nouvelle lecture, visant à lutter contre les contenus haineux sur internet, 13 May 2020, https://www.assemblee-nationale.fr/dyn/15/textes/l15t0388_texte-adopte-seance#; Gesetz zur Verbesserung der Rechtsdurchsetzung in sozialen Netzwerken (Netzwerkdurchsetzungsgesetz – NetzDG) vom 1. September 2017, BGBl Jahrgang 2017 Teil 1 Nr. 61.

that these fines are paid for systematic violations of their obligations.[78] Furthermore, the time frame is not as strict and the GNEA even allows for the possibility to prolong the time frame under specific circumstances.[79] One of the major shortcomings of the original 2017 GNEA is that, even though online intermediaries are obligated to give reasons for their decision (§ 3 (2) Nr. 5 GNEA), no remedies were provided against the social media companies in case they block or delete a post, not even an internal complaint mechanism as installed by the art 4 Loi Avia. However, German lawmakers just recently tackled this shortcoming . In June 2021, an amendment to the GNEA, obliged online intermediaries to install an internal complaint-handling system[80] and an out-of-court settlement procedure.[81] Furthermore, German civil law courts have successfully obligated Facebook to restore deleted or blocked posts on the basis of the German Civil Law Code ('put-back').[82] The basis for such put-back claims are the private law contracts between online intermediaries and users, including the terms and conditions, but also the right to freedom of expression.[83] While online intermediaries are not directly bound by human rights, the German constitutional doctrine of indirect third party effect or horizontal effect ('mittelbare Drittwirkung') allows for some indirect impact of human rights within private law relationships.[84]

---

78 Gesetz zur Verbesserung der Rechtsdurchsetzung in sozialen Netzwerken (Netzwerkdurchsetzungsgesetz – NetzDG) vom 1. September 2017, BGBl Jahrgang 2017 Teil 1 Nr. 61, § 4.

79 Peukert, 'Put it back: Ein Vorschlag für ein NetzDG, das die Meinungsfreiheit wahrt', Verfassungsblog, 14 June 2018, https://verfassungsblog.de/put-it-back-ein-vorschlag-fuer-ein-netzdg-das-die-meinungsfreiheit-wahrt/.

80 Gesetz zur Änderung des Netzwerkdurchsetzungsgesetzes vom 03. Juni 2021, BGBl Jahrgang 2021 Teil 1 Nr. 29, § 3b.

81 *Id.*, § 3c.

82 Kettemann and Tiedeke, 'Back up: can users sue platforms to reinstate deleted content?' (2020) 9 *Internet Policy Review*, 1 (10 f.); Peukert, 'Gewährleistung der Meinungs- und Informationsfreiheit in sozialen Netzwerken. Vorschlag für eine Ergänzung des NetzDG um sog. Put-back-Verfahren' (2018) *MMR*, 572.

83 Kalbhenn and Hemmert-Halswick, 'Der Regierungsentwurf zur Änderung des NetzDG – Vom Compliance-Ansatz zu Designvorgaben' (2020), *MMR*, 518 (519).

84 BVerfG, Decision, 11 April 2018, 1 BvR 3080/09, http://www.bverfg.de/e/rs20180411_1bvr308009.html; OLG München Decision, 17 July 2018 – 18 W 858/18, *Juris*; OLG Dresden Decision, 8 August 2018 – 4 W 577/18, https://www.debier.de/debier-datenbank/?dbnr=olgd0004W-2018-00577; BVerfG, Decision, 22 May 2019, 1 BvQ 42/19, http://www.bverfg.de/e/qk20190522_1bvq004219.html; OLG Oldenburg, Judgement, 1 July 2019, – 13 W 16/19; OLG München Judgement, 7 January 2020 – 18 U 1491/19 Pre, *Juris*; Schleswig-Holsteinisches Oberlandesgericht Judgement, 26 February 2020 – 9 U 125/19, *Juris*; see also

3. The EU Approach: Adding an Additional Layer to the Protection of Elections

Purely national approaches to regulate the internet seem to be rather outdated given the internet's ubiquity. Consequently, in December 2020, the EU Commission has proposed a new comprehensive EU regulation, i.e., a directly applicable set of legally binding rules that will take precedence over national law (Article 288 (2) TFEU), in order to regulate online intermediaries.

a) Personal and Material Scope of Application

The Digital Services Act Draft[85] ('DSA-Draft') aims to contribute to the proper functioning of the internal market for intermediary services and to help in creating a safe, predictable, and trusted online environment where fundamental rights are effectively protected (Article 1 (2) lit. b) DSA-Draft). The DSA-Draft differentiates between 'online platforms', i.e., a provider of a hosting service that, at the request of a recipient of the service, stores and disseminates information to the public (Article 2 lit. h) DSA-Draft) and 'very large online platforms', i.e., those platforms that provide their services to more than 45 million active users (Article 25 (1) DSA). The draft further differentiates between illegal content, which 'means any information that [...] is not in compliance with Union law or the law of a Member State' (Art. 2 lit g) DSA-Draft), and manifestly illegal content that is, according to recital 47 DSA-Draft, information 'where it is evident to a layperson, without any substantive analysis, that the content is illegal.' While hate speech will be such manifestly illegal content, 'fake news' as 'harmful content' (recital 52 DSA-Draft) often will not – but the DSA-Draft has found an additional way on how to deal with 'fake news' (see below d).

Kettemann and Tiedeke, 'Back up: can users sue platforms to reinstate deleted content?' (2020) 9 *Internet Policy Review*, 1 (9).

85 European Commission, *Proposal for a Regulation of the European Parliament and of the Council on a Single Market for Digital Services (Digital Services Act) and amending Directive 2000/31/EC*, 15 December 2020, COM (2020) 825 final.

b) (Excluding) Liability of Online Platforms

The DSA itself does not regulate that *illegal content* has to be taken down. It only obliges online platforms to suspend, for a reasonable period of time and after having issued a prior warning, the provision of their services to recipients of the service that frequently provide *manifestly illegal content* (Article 20 DSA-Draft). However, since Article 5 (1) lit. b) DSA-Draft excludes online platforms' liability only before they have been notified of illegal content, platforms are under an indirect obligation to take down illegal content 'expeditiously' after having been notified, or else they will be liable for it. Additionally, Article 8 DSA-Draft institutes procedural rules for situations in which national judicial or administrative authorities issue orders with regard to illegal content: online intermediaries need to be transparent about the actions taken and the authorities need to issue a statement of reasons explaining, *inter alia*, why the information is illegal content and inform about the redress available to the provider of the service and to the recipient of the service who published the content.

c) Notice and Takedown Procedure and Legal Remedies

With regard to the notice and takedown procedure, online platforms shall put mechanisms in place that allow them to be notified of illegal content (Article 14 DSA-Draft). If a takedown decision has been made, the platform has to inform the user whose post has been blocked or whose access has been disabled of the decision and provide the user with a clear and specific statement of reasons (Article 15 DSA-Draft). Users have the right to access an effective internal complaint-handling system (Article 17 DSA-Draft), which, if the post is not illegal, obliges the platform to reverse its decision without undue delay,[86] and to access an out-of-court dispute settlement body which shall be established with the Digital Services Coordinator of the Member State. Further judicial remedies based on domestic law are not prejudiced by this multi-step approach (Article 18 DSA-Draft).

86 Kaesling, 'Evolution statt Revolution der Plattformregulierung' (2021) *ZUM*, 177 (182).

d) "Fake News" and Advertisement Regulation

While the depicted rules will mainly help against hate speech, 'fake news' will often not be illegal but 'only' harmful. Here, the DSA-Draft adds a further layer of protection, if and insofar 'fake news' come via paid (political) advertisements as in the case of Cambridge Analytica. The nexus between 'fake news' and advertisements is highlighted by the DSA-Draft itself as it obligates online intermediaries to be transparent about their activities in this area by, *inter alia*, having

> to facilitate supervision and research into emerging risks brought about by the distribution of advertising online, for example in relation to illegal advertisements or manipulative techniques and disinformation with a real and foreseeable negative impact on public health, public security, civil discourse, political participation and equality (recital 63 DSA-Draft).

Article 24 DSA provides that advertising shall be marked as such, that the person on whose behalf the advertisement is displayed shall be named and that the main parameters used to determine the recipient to whom the advertisement is displayed are indicated, including means of profiling (recital 52 DSA-Draft). Moreover, the Commission has already announced a legislative act on political advertisement.[87]

e) Further Duties of Very Large Online Platforms

This standard is further raised for very large online platforms that have to compile and make publicly available the content of the advertisement and the natural or legal person on whose behalf the advertisement is displayed; the period during which the advertisement was displayed; whether the advertisement was intended to be displayed specifically to one or more particular groups of recipients of the service and if so, the main parameters used for that purpose; the total number of recipients of the service reached and, where applicable, aggregate numbers for the group or groups of recipients at whom the advertisement was targeted specifically (Article 30 DSA-Draft).

---

87 European Commission, *Communication from the Commission to the European Parliament, the Council, the European Economic and Social Committee and the Committee of the Regions*, 3 December 2020, COM(2020) 790 final, 6.

Another way to combat 'fake news' – and also hate speech – comes via very large online platforms' special duties to identify, analyse, assess and mitigate so called 'significant systemic risks' that include any intentional manipulation of the platforms' services, including by means of inauthentic use or automated exploitation of the service, which has or might have a negative effect on the protection of, *inter alia*, civic discourse or electoral processes (Articles 26 ff. DSA-Draft).

f) Fines and Penalties

While Member States shall lay down the rules on penalties applicable to infringements (Article 42 DSA-Draft), very large online platforms may have to pay fines imposed by the EU Commission not exceeding 6 % of their total turnover (Article 59 DSA-Draft). Like the GNEA, but different from the Loi Avia, these fines may not be imposed for failing to take down single illegal posts but for more systematic omissions like not installing a functional notice and takedown procedure or failing to identify, analyse, assess and mitigate so called 'significant systemic risks' (Art. 26 DSA-Draft).

g) Summary – Regulating "Fake News" and Hate Speech, Not Only in Election Times

To conclude, the DSA-Draft regulates mainly hate speech but also 'fake news' – and not only in election times. It does not only foresee different remedies against over-blocking by containing a right of redress that is directed against the platform itself, it also installs a specific dispute settlement between the user and the platform and tackles the problem of 'fake news' and manipulation via advertisements. The electoral process is identified as particularly vulnerable. Fines are severe and can be as high as 6 percent of the yearly turnover, which, in the case of Facebook could be nearly 5 billion US Dollar.

4. Conclusion: Regulating Online Intermediaries in Different Ways

While the new regulations concentrate on online intermediaries, they also indirectly affect individuals. The French approach concentrates on hate speech on the one hand and 'fake news' on the other hand. Its 'fake news' legislation is specifically tailored to fight disinformation during election times. The takedown of disinformation has to be ordered by a judge. The German approach, just like the unconstitutional French approach to hate speech, relies on users notifying the online intermediaries about certain content. They have to decide whether content is legal, illegal – which needs to be taken down within a week – or manifestly illegal – which needs to be taken down within 24 hours. This duty mainly applies to hate speech and only marginally to 'fake news'. Specific procedural rules to mitigate over-blocking do not yet exist but are in the making. Lastly, the European DSA-Draft not only tackles the problem of hate speech but also of micro-targeting and disinformation and foresees specific remedies against the deletion of posts and the blockage of individual access to online intermediaries. Just as the GNEA and the Loi Avia, the DSA-Draft obligates the online intermediaries to decide whether certain speech is lawful or not and thus 'formalize[s] the role of social media platforms as the governors of […] speech.'[88] Since all approaches are aimed at suppressing speech, it is questionable whether they are in conformity with the right to freedom of expression.

B. The Law: Applying the ECHR to Laws Regulating "Fake News" and Hate Speech

In order to answer the question of whether these rules are in conformity with the ECHR, the first question to be answered is who is protected and who is bound by human rights (I.), then the material scope of the ECHR's substantive protection needs to be determined (II.), and lastly interferences with the right to freedom of expression need to be justified (III.). Here, *inter alia*, the right to freedom of expression must be balanced with the right to free elections.

I. Who is Protected and Who is Bound by the ECHR? Of Individuals and States, the EU, Companies, and Bots

Elections are influenced by individuals, by companies, and also by third States. In order to protect democracy from such interferences, States have

88 Helberger, 'The Political Power of Platforms: How Current Attempts to Regulate Misinformation Amplify Opinion Power' (2020) 8 *Digital Journalism*, 842 (844).

started to regulate online intermediaries, i.e., companies. These regulations have an indirect effect on those influencing elections, i.e., individuals, companies, and also third States. But neither are all of these actors protected nor are all of them bound by the ECHR.

1. *Individuals – Protected by the ECHR*

First and foremost, private individuals are protected by the ECHR. The regulations on hate speech and 'fake news' certainly have an impact on the freedom of expression of individuals as they obligate companies to take action against specific forms of online speech. While this is only an indirect effect – since the online intermediaries are specifically targeted, not the users of their service – this effect is so closely connected to the regulation of the state that the freedom of expression of the individual users might be interfered with.

2. *Companies and Bots – Protected and Indirectly Bound by the ECHR*

Further, a company that uses online intermediaries in order to express itself is protected by the ECHR.[89] But what about the online intermediaries? Here, it seems questionable whether they may rely on freedom of expression guarantees as it is not their speech act that is being interfered with but their users'. However, the ECtHR held that online intermediaries may rely on the right of freedom of expression.[90] Again, the situation is different

---

89 *Cf.* ECtHR, Judgment, 22 May 1990, *Autronic AG v Switzerland*, Application No. 12726/87, para. 47.

90 ECtHR, Judgment, 18 December 2012, *Ahmet Yildirim v Turkey*, Application No. 3111/10, paras. 49 f.; ECtHR, Judgment (GC), 20 January 2020, *Magyar Kétfarkú Kutya Párt (MKKP) v Hungary*, Application No. 201/17, paras. 87 f., 91; ECtHR, Decision, 19 September 2017, *Tamiz v UK*, Application No. 3877/14, para. 90; ECtHR, Decision, 19 February 2013, *Neij and Sunde Kolmisoppi v Sweden*, Application No. 40397/12; ECtHR, Judgment (GC) 16 June 2015, *Delfi AS v Estonia*, Application No. 64569/09, para. 118; ECtHR, Judgment, 2 February 2016, *MTE v Hungary*, Application No. 22947/13, para. 45; ECtHR, Decision, 7 February 2017, *Pihl v Sweden*, Application No. 74742/14, para. 29; ECtHR, Judgment, 19 March 2019, *Høiness v Norway*, Application No. 43624/14, para. 68; see also Lauber-Rönsberg 'Persönlichkeitsschutz in der EMRK und im EU-Recht, § 57. Europäische Menschenrechtskonvention' in Götting et al. (eds), *Handbuch des Persönlichkeitsrechts* (2019), 1197 (mn. 87).

for bots that are often used in disinformation and hate speech contexts as amplifiers. They may not rely on the right to freedom of expression.[91]

Lastly, online intermediaries are not directly bound by human rights obligations. Individuals thus cannot claim that their right to freedom of expression has been violated by an online intermediary. However, indirectly, human rights may play a role in these purely private relationships as human rights are applied to private individuals via a State's 'duty to protect'.[92] According to this duty, a State must, under certain circumstances, protect individuals from *de facto* human rights violations by other private actors, *inter alia* by creating 'a safe and enabling environment for everyone to participate in public debate and to express opinions and ideas without fear.'[93] Another way to indirectly bind online intermediaries is via the German Federal Constitutional Court's indirect third party effect doctrine.[94] Lastly, the UN Guiding Principles on Business and Human Rights hold that companies have a responsibility to respect human rights, including freedom of expression.[95]

3. *States and the EU – Bound but not Protected by the ECHR*

If certain posts are attributed to a State, there will be no protection by the ECHR: States are bound, not protected by human rights treaties. Since attribution in cyber space, however, often is a very difficult if not an impossible task,[96] in case of doubt, the post will have to be understood as

---

91 Sardo, 'Categories, Balancing, and Fake News: The Jurisprudence of the European Court of Human Rights' (2020) *Canadian Journal of Law & Jurisprudence*, 435 (455).

92 Akandji-Kombe, *Positive Obligations under the European Convention on Human Rights* (2007), 14.

93 CoE Committee of Ministers, *Recommendation to member States on the roles and responsibilities of internet intermediaries,* 7 March 2018, CM/Rec(2018)2, para. 6.

94 See e.g. BVerfG, Decision, 11 April 2018, 1 BvR 3080/09, mn. 31 ff., http://www.bverfg.de/e/rs20180411_1bvr308009.html; see also Engle, 'Third Party Effect of Fundamental Rights (Drittwirkung)' (2009) 5 *Hanse Law Review*, 165; Kettemann and Tiedeke, 'Back up: can users sue platforms to reinstate deleted content?' (2020) 9 *Internet Policy Review*, 1 (8 ff.).

95 UNGA, *Report of the Special Representative of the Secretary-General on the issue of human rights and transnational corporations and other business enterprises*, 21 March 2011, A/HRC/17/31, 13 ff.

96 Krieger, 'Krieg gegen anonymous – Völkerrechtliche Regelungsmöglichkeiten bei unsicherer Zurechnung im Cyberwar' (2012) 50 *AVR*, 1 (3); Zimmermann, 'International Law and „Cyber Space"' (2014) 3 *ESIL Reflections*, 1 (3).

having emanated from a private individual and thus the ECHR's personal scope applies.

While France and Germany as High Contracting Parties have to obey their treaty obligations, the EU is not a High Contracting Party (yet[97]). Nevertheless, it is indirectly bound because of Article 6 (3) TEU and since all the EU member states are High Contracting Parties of the ECHR. Furthermore, the guarantees on freedom of expression in the Charter of Fundamental Rights of the European Union are basically equivalent to the regulations in the ECHR. Lastly, from the point of view of the ECHR, the ECtHR in its *Bosphorus* decision has clarified that it reserves scrutiny even in cases in which the EU exercises exclusive competence.[98]

4. *Summary – Personal Application as a Mainly Procedural Question, not a Material Question*

The repercussions of the involvement of so many different actors are mainly situated on the procedural level – e.g., who may claim a human rights violation; against whom can a human rights violation be claimed; with whom lies the burden of proof – but not on the material level. It is decisive that States as well as the EU have to comply with human rights obligations and have to refrain from violations of freedom of expression of individuals and online intermediaries alike. Whether this is the case is the subject matter of the next section.

II. *The Scope of the ECHR's Substantive Protection in Light of the French, German and EU Legislation Regulating Online Speech*

While the French legislation is concerned with hate speech on the one hand and disinformation on the other hand, the German and the EU legislation are mainly directed against hate speech and only partly touch upon disinformation. Since the legal rules in question are aimed at the deletion of online speech, we first need to turn to general questions of the application of Article 10 ECHR to the online world (1.). In a second

97 See Art. 6 (2) TEU and also CJEU, Opinion 2/13, 18 December 2014, *Opinion pursuant to Article 218 (11) TFEU*, ECLI:EU:C:2014:2454, para. 153.

98 ECtHR, Judgment (GC), 30 June 2005, *Bosphorus v Ireland*, Application No. 45036/98, para. 153.

step, the material scope of the right to freedom of expression (2.) will be examined. Lastly, the right to receive information (3.) deserves special attention.

1. Freedom of Expression on the Internet – Offline Rules also Apply Online

Although some might argue that in cyberspace 'code is law'[99] and that cyberspace exists outside any state's sovereignty,[100] the ECtHR very early on held that the rules that apply offline, in principle, also apply online.[101] At the same time, it understood that these rules need to be applied keeping in mind the peculiarities of the online world.[102] It held

> that in the light of its accessibility and its capacity to store and communicate vast amounts of information, the Internet plays an important role in enhancing the public's access to news and facilitating the dissemination of information in general[103]

and that it 'provides an unprecedented platform for the exercise of freedom of expression.'[104] The Court also underlined the importance of the Internet for political speech as it

---

99 Lessig, *Code: And Other Laws of Cyberspace* (1999), 6; Lessig, *Code: And Other Laws of Cyberspace, Version 2.0* (2006), 1.

100 Barlow, A Declaration of the Independence of Cyberspace, Electronic Frontier Foundation, 8 February 1996, https://www.eff.org/cyberspace-independence : "Governments of the Industrial World, you weary giants of flesh and steel, I come from Cyberspace, the new home of Mind. On behalf of the future, I ask you of the past to leave us alone. You are not welcome among us. You have no sovereignty where we gather."

101 ECtHR, Judgment, 1 July 2008, *Liberty v UK*, Application No. 58243/00, 64 ff.

102 Kettemann and Benedek, 'Freedom of expression online' in Susi (ed), *Human Rights, Digital Society and the Law: A Research Companion* (2019), 58 (62).

103 See ECtHR, Judgment, 18 December 2012, *Ahmet Yildirim v Turkey*, Application No. 3111/10, para. 48; ECtHR, Judgments, 10 March 2009, *Times Newspapers Ltd. (Nos. 1 and 2) v The United Kingdom*, Application No. 3002/03 and 23676/03, para. 27; ECtHR, Judgment, 19 January 2016, *Kalda v Estonia*, Application No. 17429/10, para. 44; ECtHR, Judgment, 23 June 2020, *Engels v Russia*, Application No. 61919/16, para. 25; ECtHR, Judgment, 4 December 2018, *Magyar Jeti Zrt v Hungary*, Application No. 11257/16, para. 66.

104 See ECtHR, Judgment, 18 December 2012, *Ahmet Yildirim v Turkey*, Application No. 3111/10, para. 48; and ECtHR, Judgment, 10 March 2009, *Times Newspapers Ltd. (Nos. 1 and 2) v The United Kingdom*, Application No. 3002/03 and 23676/03, para. 27.

> has now become one of the principal means by which individuals exercise their right to freedom to receive and impart information and ideas, providing as it does essential tools for participation in activities and discussions concerning political issues and issues of general interest.[105]

This very positive view of the internet is contrasted with the Court's understanding that 'the risk of harm posed by content and communications on the Internet to the exercise and enjoyment of human rights and freedoms, particularly the right to respect for private life, is certainly higher than that posed by the press.'[106] Other dangers recognized by the Court are '[d]efamatory and other types of clearly unlawful speech, including hate speech and speech inciting violence [which] can be disseminated like never before, worldwide, in a matter of seconds, and sometimes remain persistently available online.'[107]

All in all, the Court approaches the internet in a cautious manner, highlighting its positive aspects for making use of human rights on the one hand and being aware of its dangers for human rights on the other hand. While this seems to be the right approach in general, in the end it remains crucial how the Court finds the right balance between the different rights at stake in this new and still partly unchartered space.

2. *The Material Scope of Freedom of Expression*

Freedom of expression is understood broadly by the ECtHR and

> is applicable not only to 'information' or 'ideas' that are favourably received or regarded as inoffensive or as a matter of indifference, but also to those that offend, shock or disturb the State or any sector

105 ECtHR, Judgment, 1 December 2015, *Cengiz and others v Turkey*, Application No. 48226/10 and 14027/11, para. 49; ECtHR, Judgment, 18 December 2012, *Ahmet Yildirim v Turkey*, Application No. 3111/10, para. 54; ECtHR, Judgment, 4 December 2018, *Magyar Jeti Zrt v Hungary*, Application No. 11257/16, para. 66.

106 ECtHR, Judgment (GC), 16 June 2015, *Delfi AS v Estonia*, Application No. 64569/09, para. 133; ECtHR, Judgment, 5 May 2011, *Editorial Board of Pravoye Delo and Shtekel v Ukraine*, Application No. 33014/05, para. 63; ECtHR, Judgment, 4 December 2018, *Magyar Jeti Zrt v Hungary*, Application No. 11257/16, para. 66; ECtHR, Judgment, 7 November 2017, *Egill Einarsson v Iceland*, Application No. 24703/15, para. 46.

107 ECtHR, Judgment (GC), 16 June 2015, *Delfi AS v Estonia*, Application No. 64569/09, para. 11.

> of the population. Such are the demands of pluralism, tolerance and broadmindedness without which there is no democratic society.[108]

Both, value judgments ('opinions' and 'ideas') and factual allegations ('information') are generally protected, no matter whether the factual allegations are true or false.[109] Disinformation is thus protected[110] as can be seen in the case *Perinçek v. Switzerland*.[111] Here, the Court had to decide about a Swiss Court's decision to sentence the Chairman of the Turkish Workers' Party, Doğu Perinçek, for different statements made about Armenian Genocide. Mr. Perinçek inter alia said that 'the allegations of the 'Armenian genocide' are an international lie.' While the genocide is a proven historic fact, the Court nevertheless concluded that Mr. Perinçek's right to freedom of expression had been interfered with and in the end even had been violated.

However, if 'fake news' is connected with hate speech, i.e. 'all forms of expression which spread, incite, promote or justify hatred based on intolerance,'[112] e.g. in the case of Holocaust denial, it may not be protected anymore. The ECtHR has 'no doubt that, like any other remark direct-

---

108 ECtHR, Judgment, 7 December 1976, *Handyside v UK*, Application No. 5493/72, para. 49.

109 Value judgement can neither be "true" nor "false" as there is no way to prove them, ECtHR, Judgment, 8 July 1986, *Lingens v Austria*, Application No. 9815/82, para. 46; ECtHR, Judgment, 29 March 2005, *Ukranian Media Group v Ukraine*, Application No. 72713/01, para. 41. See also Grabenwarter, *European Convention on Human Rights: Commentary* (2014), Art. 10, mn. 31 with further references.

110 Grabenwarter, *European Convention on Human Rights: Commentary* (2014), Art. 10, mn. 5; Rainey et al., *Jacobs, White, and Ovey: The European Convention on Human Rights* (7th edn. 2017), 490; ECtHR, Judgment, 7 May 2002, *Mc Vicar v United Kingdom*, Application No. 46311/99, para. 87; see also ECtHR, Judgment, 25 July 2019, *Brzezinski v Poland*, Application No. 47542/07, para. 58. But see for a different view Pollicino, 'Judicial Protection of Fundamental Rights in the transition from the world of atoms to the word of bits: The case of freedom of speech' (2019) 25 *Eur Law J*, 155 (158 f.); Kettemann and Benedek, 'Freedom of expression online' in Susi (ed), *Human Rights, Digital Society and the Law: A Research Companion* (2019), 58 (Fn. 39), referring to ECtHR, Decision, 3 June 2014, *Schuman v Poland*. Application No. 52517/13. Here, however, the Court found misinformation to be protected by Article 10 ECHR and did not express itself on neither dis- nor mal-information.

111 ECtHR, Judgment (GC), 15 October 2015, *Pernicek v Switzerland*, Application No. 27510/08.

112 ECtHR, Judgment, 4 December 2003, *Gündüz v Turkey*, Application No. 35071/97, para. 40.

ed against the Convention's underlying values, expressions that seek to spread, incite or justify hatred based on intolerance, including religious intolerance, do not enjoy the protection afforded by Article 10 of the Convention.'[113] While this sounds like a very clear statement, the Court is not consequently following this approach. Glorifying terrorism for example is not considered to be hate speech,[114] neither was the denial of the Armenian Genocide in *Perinçek v. Switzerland*.[115] Equally, in *Kühnen v. Germany*,[116] which was about denial of the Holocaust, the Court afforded Article 10 ECHR protection. However, in *Garaudy v. France*, which was also about the denial of the Holocaust, the Court found that Article 10 ECHR does not protect the speech in question.[117] In order to avoid such contradictions, hate speech should fall under the general protection of Article 10 ECHR as well. Of course, interferences in such cases will mostly be justified.[118]

Advertisements, whether political or commercial, are also protected by Article 10 ECHR.[119] When dealing with commercial advertisements, State parties enjoy a wide margin of appreciation. The ECtHR only scrutinizes whether a proportionality test was undertaken by national courts but does not carry one out itself.[120] This however changes in case the advertisement is a political one.[121]

---

113 *Ibid.* also ECtHR, Judgment (GC), 23 September 1994, *Jersild v Denmark*, Application No. 15890/89, para. 35.

114 ECtHR, Judgment, 2 October 2008, *Leroy v France*, Application No. 36109/03.

115 ECtHR, Judgment (GC) 15 October 2015, *Pernicek v Switzerland*, Application No. 27510/08, partly concurring partly dissenting opinion Judge Nußberger.

116 European Commission of Human Rights, Decision, 12 May 1988, *Kühnen v. Federal Republic of Germany*, Application No 12194/86.

117 ECtHR, Decision, 7 July 2003, *Garaudy v France*, Application No. 65831/01.

118 See Schiedermair, in Pabel and Schmahl (eds), *Internationaler Kommentar zur Europäischen Menschenrechtskonvention* (2010), Art. 10 EMRK, mn. 29 with further references.

119 ECtHR, Judgment, 20 November 1989, *Markt Intern Verlag GmbH and Klaus Beerkann v Germany*, Application No. 10572/83, para. 26; ECtHR, Judgment, 23 June 1994, *Jacubowski v Germany*, Application No.15088/89, para. 25; ECtHR, Judgment, 11 December 2003, *Krone Verlag GmbH & Co KG (No. 3) v Austria*, Application No. 39069/97, paras. 33 ff.; ECtHR, Decision, 23 October 2007, *Brzank v Germany*, Application No. 7969/04; (all misleading advertisments); ECtHR, Judgment, 28 June 2001, *VgT Verein gegen Tierfabriken v Switzerland*, Application No. 24699/94, para. 48, (see Grabenwarter, *European Convention on Human Rights: Commentary* (2014), Art. 10, mn. 19.

120 Id., mn 42.

121 ECtHR, Judgment, 5 March 2009, *Hachette Filipacchi Presse Automobile a Dupuy v France*, Application No. 13353/05, para. 63; ECtHR, Judgment, 28 June 2001,

The French, German, and proposed EU legislation are directed against hate speech, dis- and mal-information and also partly regulate advertisements. While dis- and mal-information as well as advertisements are protected by Article 10 ECHR, the scope of protection is unclear for hate speech. As argued, hate speech should also be protected by the material scope of Article 10 ECHR. Thus, the laws in question interfere with the right to freedom of expression.

3. *Right to Receive Information*

Article 10 ECHR does not only protect the right to express oneself but also the right to receive information from third parties. This may, in principle, also allow users of online intermediaries to challenge the takedown of posts or the blocking of profiles. The ECtHR up until now only had to decide on cases where access to entire platforms had been disabled. Here, the Court held that at least in cases where the applicant was not only passive but also an active user and the speech was political and not (easily) obtainable somewhere else,[122] the right to receive information had been interfered with. In principle, this approach can be transferred to the deletion of single posts. Since the French, the German, and the proposed EU legislation aim at blocking certain content that shall thus not be received by third parties, they also lead to interferences with the right to receive information.

III. *Freedom of Expression v. Protection of Elections – Justifying the French, German, and EU Legislation Regulating Online Speech*

Neither freedom of expression nor the right to receive information is absolute, interferences may be justified (Article 10 (2) ECHR). States are allowed to interfere with the right to freedom of expression and receive information in order to protect elections as long as this interference is prescribed by law (1.) and done in a proportionate manner (2.).

VgT Verein gegen Tierfabriken v Switzerland, Application No. 24699/94, paras. 69 ff.

122 ECtHR, Judgment, 1 December 2015, *Cengiz and others v Turkey*, Application No. 48226/10 and 14027/11, para. 51; see also ECtHR, Judgment, 18 December 2012, *Ahmet Yildirim v Turkey*, Application No. 3111/10; ECtHR, Decision, 11 March 2014, *Akdeniz v Turkey*, Application No. 20877/10.

1. Protection of Elections as a Legitimate Aim Prescribed by Law

The interference must not only be prescribed by law (b.) but also follow a specific and legitimate aim (a.).

a) Protection of Elections as a Legitimate Aim

The ECHR does not expressly provide the protection of elections as a specific aim that allows for interferences with human rights. Article 10 (2) ECHR, however, foresees that the rights of others may serve as a legitimate aim for an interference. Article 3 (1) of the First Optional Protocol to the ECHR provides for such a right as it guarantees a right to free elections. Elections are 'a characteristic principle of democracy',[123] without them there is no democracy. Thus, the protection of democracy also might serve as a legitimate aim. In addition, Article 10 (2) ECHR refers to a 'democratic society'. While the limitation clause is not primarily concerned with the legitimate aim but with the standard of proportionality, it nevertheless indirectly shows that the protection of democracy is able to justify interferences with human rights. This is especially true as democracy is the only form of government foreseen by the Convention:[124]

> Democracy constitutes a fundamental element of the 'European public order.' [T]he Convention establishes a very clear connection between the Convention and democracy by stating that the maintenance and further realisation of human rights and fundamental freedoms are best ensured on the one hand by an effective political democracy and on the other by a common understanding and observance of human rights. [D]emocracy is the only political model contemplated by the Convention and, accordingly, the only one compatible with it.[125]

---

123 ECtHR, Judgment, 2 March 1987, *Mathieu-Mohin and Clerfayt v Belgium*, Application No. 9267/81, para. 47.

124 ECtHR, Judgment (GC), 13 February 2003, *Refah Partisi (The Welfare Party) and others v Turkey*, Application Nos. 41340/98, 41342/98, 41343/98 and 41344/98, para. 86.

125 ECtHR, Judgment (GC), 16 March 2006, *Zdanoka v Latvia*, Application No. 58278/00, para. 98.

b) Prescribed by Law, especially Foreseeability and Effective Judicial Review

The interference must be prescribed by law. This requirement does not only demand the formal existence of a law but also certain material pre-conditions, 'the quality of the law in question,'[126] namely the accessibility and foreseeability of the domestic law as well as its compatibility with the rule of law.[127] Blocking of entire websites has been held to be a violation of Article 10 ECHR, *inter alia*, in the cases *Cengiz and others v. Turkey* and *Yildirim v. Turkey*.[128] These cases are instructive insofar as they highlight that the applicants have to be able to regulate their own conduct according to legal rules and that domestic law must afford a measure of legal protection against arbitrary interference by public authorities with the rights guaranteed by the Convention.[129] Thus, 'a legal framework is required, ensuring both tight control over the scope of bans and effective judicial review to prevent any abuse of power.'[130] This includes that the national

126 ECtHR, Judgment, 1 December 2015, *Cengiz and others v Turkey*, Application No. 48226/10 and 14027/11, para. 59; ECtHR, Judgment, 18 December 2012, *Ahmet Yildirim v Turkey*, Application No. 3111/10, para. 57.

127 *Ibid.*

128 ECtHR, Judgment, 1 December 2015, *Cengiz and others v Turkey*, Application No. 48226/10 and 14027/11; ECtHR, Judgment, 18 December 2012, *Ahmet Yildirim v Turkey*, Application No. 3111/10; ECtHR, Judgment, 23 June 2020, *Bulgakov v Russia*, Application No. 20159/15, paras. 34 ff.; ECtHR, Judgment, 23 June 2020, *Engels v Russia*, Application No. 61919/16, paras. 31 ff.; ECtHR, Judgment, 23 June 2020, *Kharitonov v Russia*, Application No. 10795/14, paras. 43 f.; ECtHR, Judgment, 23 June 2020, *OOO Flavus and others v Russia*, Application No. 12468/15 and 2 others, para. 40–42.

129 ECtHR, Judgment, 18 December 2012, *Ahmet Yildirim v Turkey*, Application No. 3111/10, para. 59; ECtHR, Judgment, 1 December 2015, *Cengiz and others v Turkey*, Application No. 48226/10 and 14027/11, para. 65; see also ECtHR, Judgment, 26 April 1979, *The Sunday Times v UK*, Application No. 6538/74, para. 49; ECtHR, Judgment (GC), 17 February 2004, *Maestri v Italy*, Application No. 39748/98, para. 30; (see, among other authorities, ECtHR, Judgment, 28 June 2001, *VgT Verein gegen Tierfabriken v Switzerland*, Application No. 24699/94, para. 52; ECtHR, Judgment (GC), 16 June 2015, *Delfi AS v Estonia*, Application No. 64569/09, para. 120; ECtHR, Judgment, 15 May 2018, *Unifaun Theatre Productions Limited and Others v Malta*, Application No. 37326/13, para. 78; ECtHR, Judgment, 23 June 2020, *Bulgakov v Russia*, Application No. 20159/15, paras. 35–37; ECtHR, Judgment, 23 June 2020, *Engels v Russia*, Application No. 61919/16, paras. 31 f.

130 ECtHR, Judgment, 18 December 2012, *Ahmet Yildirim v Turkey*, Application No. 3111/10, para. 64; see also ECtHR, Judgment, 1 December 2015, *Cengiz and*

law obligates the national courts to weigh the competing interests at stake and to strike a balance between them.[131] While the laws in question are all laws in a formal manner (or, for the DSA-Draft, will be), it is questionable whether the exact duties of the individuals concerned as well as of the online intermediaries are foreseeable (aa.) and whether an effective judicial review exists (bb.).

aa) Foreseeability: What is Manifestly Illegal Content?

The GNEA defines rather precisely its illegal content by referring to well-established national criminal law. The DSA equally refers to other norms as does the Loi Avia, and the definitions and requirements in Loi No. 2018–1202 are very precise. However, the differentiation between illegal content and manifestly illegal content in the DSA-Draft, the GNEA and the Loi Avia has been criticized as being too imprecise.[132] While the differentiation does not change the duty to take down posts as such, it makes a difference whether a post has to be taken down within 24 hours or within seven days as prescribed by the GNEA and the unconstitutional French Loi Avia. It also makes a difference whether a profile will be suspended – and not only a singular post deleted – if manifestly illegal content is posted on

---

others v Turkey, Application No. 48226/10 and 14027/11, para. 62; ECtHR, Judgment, 30 April 2019, *Kablis v Russia*, Application Nos. 48310/16 and 59663/17, paras. 67, 80; ECtHR, Judgment, 17 July 2001, *Association Ekin v France*, Application No. 39288/98, para. 58. See also CJEU, Judgment, 27 March 2017, *UPC Telekabel Wien*, Case C-314/12, ECLI:EU:C:2014:192, para. 57, where the CJEU held that "the national procedural rules must provide a possibility for internet users to assert their rights before the court once the implementing measures taken by the internet service provider are known."

131 ECtHR, Judgment, 18 December 2012, *Ahmet Yildirim v Turkey*, Application No. 3111/10, para. 64.

132 For DSA see Frosio and Geiger, 'Taking Fundamental Rights seriously in the Digital Services Act's Platform Liability Regime' (2020) available at SSRN: https://papers.ssrn.com/sol3/papers.cfm?abstract_id=3747756 *SSRN*, 37; for GNEA see Bassini,'Fundamental rights and private enforcement in the digital age' (2019) 25 *Eur Law J*, 182 (195); Claussen, 'Fighting hate speech and fake news. The Network Enforcement Act (NetzDG) in Germany in the context of European legislation' (2018) *Rivista di Diritto dei Media*, 110 (123); Ladeur and Gostomzyk, 'Das Netzwerkdurchsetzungsgesetz und die Logik der Meinungsfreiheit' (2017) 21 *K&R*, 390 (391). For the Loi Avia see Conseil Constitutionnel 18.6.2020 – Décision no 2020–801 DC – JORF, n° 0156 du 25/06/2020, Texte 2 sur 181, para. 7.

a frequent basis as foreseen by the DSA-Draft. The difficult differentiation between illegal and manifestly illegal might lead to over-blocking and thus might have 'a chilling effect'[133] on the right of freedom of expression. In order to contravene such an over-blocking, it is necessary that, just as in the GNEA and the DSA-Draft, fines are not imposed for a single failure to block manifestly illegal content but only for systematic failure to do so. Furthermore, fines should be imposed not only for under-blocking but also for over-blocking.[134]

bb) Effective Judicial Review: Some Work to be Done

With regard to effective judicial review, Loi No. 2018–1202 is certainly lawful as only court injunctions lead to a duty to take down a certain post. The other three laws are based on a notice and takedown procedure, which is seen as highly critical *per se* as private parties and not the State decide about the legality or illegality of a specific speech.[135] While it is true that online intermediaries 'are less well-placed than courts to consider the lawfulness of comments on their website domains [and that] qualifying speech as hate speech is a very difficult and delicate exercise, not only for domestic courts, but also for the European Court of Human Rights,'[136]

---

133 See e.g. ECtHR, Judgment, 10 July 2014, *Axel Springer AG v Germany (No.2)*, Application No. 48311/10, para. 76.

134 Hong, 'The German Network Enforcement Act and the Presumption in Favour of Freedom of Speech', Verfassungsblog, 22 January 2018, https://verfassungsblog.de/the-german-network-enforcement-act-and-the-presumption-in-favour-of-freedom-of-speech/.

135 See e.g. Bassini,'Fundamental rights and private enforcement in the digital age' (2019) 25 *Eur Law J*, 182; Helberger, 'The Political Power of Platforms: How Current Attempts to Regulate Misinformation Amplify Opinion Power' (2020) 8 *Digital Journalism*, 842; Kalbhenn and Hemmert-Halswick, 'Der Regierungsentwurf zur Änderung des NetzDG – Vom Compliance-Ansatz zu Designvorgaben' (2020), *MMR*, 518 (519); Guggenberger, 'Das Netzwerkdurchsetzungsgesetz – schön gedacht, schlecht gemacht' (2017) *ZRP*, 98 (100); Lang, 'Netzwerkdurchsetzungsgesetz und Meinungsfreiheit – Zur Regulierung privater Internet-Intermediäre bei der Bekämpfung von Hassrede' (2018) 143 *AöR*, 220 (225); UNHCR, OSCE, OAS, AU 'Joint Declaration on Freedom of Expression and „Fake News, Disinformation and Propaganda', FOM. GAL/3/17, 3 March 2017, preambular clause 12.

136 Voorhoof and Lievens, 'Offensive Online Comments – New ECtHR Judgement', ECHR Blog, 15 February 2016, https://www.echrblog.com/2016/02/offensive-online-comments-new-ecthr.html.

one also needs to keep in mind that online intermediaries are making this decision a million times a day.[137] This is due to their adherence to community standards on the one hand and due to their liability for illegal content after they have been notified about it on the other hand.

While online intermediaries are able to make such decisions, they need to be supervised by courts. The original GNEA neither foresaw any effective judicial review nor installed an internal dispute settlement mechanism. The Loi Avia at least installs an internal dispute settlement mechanism. While German courts have ordered posts to be reinstated and profiles to be unblocked,[138] this right is based on the private law contract between the online intermediary and the user, which is only informed by the right to freedom of expression.[139] This is a rather weak remedy that has partly been fortified by the 2021 bill amending the GNEA through providing for out of court settlements.[140] Furthermore, the original GNEA already made it easier for legal processing to take place by obligating online intermediaries to name a person authorized to receive service (§ 5 GNEA). Before that, the absence of such a specific rule has led to factual difficulties in starting civil court proceedings against online intermediaries. Still, even the amended GNEA does not stipulate any specific legal remedies in case a post or a user (profile) has been blocked or deleted.

While the original GNEA was deficient but has been improved in 2021, the DSA-Draft is much more developed. It explicitly calls for different forms of dispute settlement mechanisms and installs an elaborate multi-step system in order to make sure that users may take redress against the deletion of posts and suspension of profiles. Article 18 (1) DSA-Draft explicitly states that national remedies are not prejudiced by the out-of-court settlements. Such proceedings are made much easier by the online intermediaries' duty to name a legal representative in each member state (Article 11 DSA-Draft). They may, *inter alia*, have to receive service for the on-

137 Lang, 'Netzwerkdurchsetzungsgesetz und Meinungsfreiheit – Zur Regulierung privater Internet-Intermediäre bei der Bekämpfung von Hasserde' (2018) 143 *AöR*, 220 (239).

138 Kettemann and Tiedeke, 'Back up: can users sue platforms to reinstate deleted content?' (2020) 9 *Internet Policy Review*, 1 (10 f.); Peukert, 'Gewährleistung der Meinungs- und Informationsfreiheit in sozialen Netzwerken. Vorschlag für eine Ergänzung des NetzDG um sog. Put-back-Verfahren' (2018) *MMR*, 572.

139 XY; see Kalbhenn and Hemmert-Halswick, 'Der Regierungsentwurf zur Änderung des NetzDG – Vom Compliance-Ansatz zu Designvorgaben' (2020), *MMR*, 518 (519).

140 Gesetz zur Änderung des Netzwerkdurchsetzungsgesetzes vom 03. Juni 2021, BGBl Jahrgang 2021 Teil 1 Nr. 29, § 3c.

line intermediary and may even be held individually liable (Article 11 (3) DSA-Draft). Furthermore, with regard to the duty to balance different interests, the DSA-Draft states in Recital 105 that it should be interpreted and applied in accordance with those fundamental rights, including the freedom of expression.[141] Lastly, very large online platforms are obligated to take into account the effect of their actions on freedom of expression (Article 26 (1) lit b. DSA-Draft). Such provisions are missing in the national laws and should be explicitly added.

cc) Summary: DSA-Draft as a Model for National Legislation

While there is some doubt with regard to the foreseeability of the laws since they use a differentiation between illegality and manifest illegality, such doubts can be overcome by imposing fines not for single failures to block manifestly illegal content but only for systematic failure to do so and by instituting internal review procedures and strengthening judicial review. Here, the DSA-Draft is a model for national legislation.

2. *The Right Balance between Protecting Elections and Ensuring Freedom of Expression*

Lastly, the proportionality test limits the power of the public authorities to interfere with human rights by requiring the public authority to use the least intrusive means and to balance the competing interests.[142]

a) Different Rights and Interests to be taken into Account

For the balancing act, different rights and interests have to be taken into account, *inter alia* whether the act in question is a statement of fact or a

141 See also Article 1 (2) DSA-Draft.

142 ECtHR, Decision, 29 June 2006, *Weber and Saravia v Germany*, Application No. 54934/00, 106; see ECtHR, Judgment (GC), 7 February 2012, *Axel Springer AG v Germany*, Application No. 39954/08, para. 84; and ECtHR, Judgment (GC), *Von Hannover v Germany (no. 2)*, 7 February 2012, Application Nos. 40660/08 and 40641/08, para. 106 and the cases cited therein.

value judgment,[143] the form of the expression,[144] whether it is a commercial speech act or political speech act,[145] the function and context of the expression, its place and its time,[146] its objective,[147] its object,[148] the severity of the state's interference[149] as well as the human rights of other non-state actors involved.[150] In essence, 'the Court consistently gives a higher level of protection to publications and speech which contribute towards social and political debate, criticism, and information – in the broadest sense.'[151]

b) Dis- and Mal-Information and Hate Speech

Dis- and mal-information may fall in the category of commercial speech acts if they are created not for political purposes but in order to generate traffic that in turn will lead to revenue through advertisements.[152] Com-

---

143 ECtHR, Judgment, 8 July 1986, *Lingens v Austria*, Application No. 9815/82, para. 46.

144 ECtHR, Judgment, 10 January 2013, *Ashby Donald and others v France*, Application No. 36769/08, para. 39; ECtHR, Decision, 19 February 2013, *Neij and Sunde Kolmisoppi v Sweden*, Application No. 40397/12; ECtHR, Judgment, 5 March 2009, *Hachette Filipacchi Presse Automobile a Dupuy v France*, Application No. 13353/05, para. 63; ECtHR, Judgment, 28 June 2001, *VgT Verein gegen Tierfabriken v Switzerland*, Application No. 24699/94, paras. 69 ff.

145 ECtHR, Judgment, 26 April 1979, *Sunday Times v The United Kingdom*, Application No. 6538/74; ECtHR, Judgment, 8 July 1986, *Lingens v Austria*, Application No. 9815/82.

146 ECtHR, Judgment (GC), 15 October 2015, *Pernicek v Switzerland*, Application No. 27510/08, paras. 242 ff.

147 'This is based on the idea that a free political debate is of fundamental importance for a democracy.', Grabenwarter, *European Convention on Human Rights: Commentary* (2014), Art. 10, mn. 36.

148 ECtHR, Judgment, 11 April 2006, *Brasilier v France*, Application No. 71343/01, para. 41; ECtHR, Judgment, 21 February 2012, *Tusalp v Turkey*, Application Nos. 32131/08 and 41617/08, para. 45; ECtHR, Judgment, 23 April 1992, *Castells v Spain*, Application No. 11798/85, para. 46; Grabenwarter, *European Convention on Human Rights: Commentary* (2014), Art. 10, mn. 36 with further reference.

149 ECtHR, Judgment (GC), 15 October 2015, *Pernicek v Switzerland*, Application No. 27510/08, paras. 272 f.

150 Rainey et al., *Jacobs, White, and Ovey: The European Convention on Human Rights* (7th edn. 2017), 486 f.

151 *Id*, 428; ECtHR, Judgment, 2 October 2008, *Leroy v France*, Application No. 36109/03, para. 41: "debate of public interest".

152 See e.g. Hughes and Waismel-Manor, 'The Macedonian Fake News Industry and the 2016 US Election' (2021) 54 *Political Science & Politics*, 19.

mercial speech acts are afforded less protection; the margin of appreciation is wider. But dis- and mal-information may also be political acts. While information as well as value judgments are protected, false information or misleading information is less protected than value judgments and correct information, as sufficient steps need to be taken to verify the truth.[153]

In cases of hate speech, even if the Court considered that hate speech fell within the scope of application of Article 10 ECHR,[154] the States' interference was always justified.[155]

c) The Online Speech Case Law of the ECtHR

In the four cases that involved online intermediaries and the takedown of (defamatory) speech and possible Article 10 ECHR violations, the ECtHR in principle applied its offline jurisprudence to the online world. In none of the cases could the online intermediary in question be classified as a social media company. Rather, users' comments on news websites and private blogs[156] were at question, and the ECtHR understood the sites to be publishers.[157] Nevertheless, these cases provide decisive guidance in how the ECtHR might decide cases involving social media companies and the deletion of speech. This is especially true since the Court in 2020 had to decide a case in which the applicants contended that they had suffered discrimination on the grounds of their sexual orientation because the public authorities refused to launch a pre-trial investigation into hateful comments left on the first applicant's Facebook page. The Court explicitly 'reject[ed] the Government's argument that comments on Facebook are less dangerous than those on the Internet news portals.'[158]

---

153 ECtHR, Judgment, 14 February 2008, *Rumyna Ivanova v Bulgaria*, Application No. 36207/03, paras. 64 ff.

154 See above p. 191.

155 ECtHR, Judgment (GC), 16 June 2015, *Delfi AS v Estonia*, Application No. 64569/09; ECtHR, Judgment, 10 July 2008, *Soulas and others v France*, Application No. 15948/03, paras. 43; 47; ECtHR, Judgment, 13 September 2005, *I.A. v Turkey*, Application No. 42571/98, paras. 29, 32.

156 ECtHR, Decision, 7 February 2017, Application No. 74742/14, *Pihl v Sweden*.

157 ECtHR, Judgment (GC), 16 June 2015, *Delfi AS v Estonia*, Application No. 64569/09, para. 129. But see ECtHR, Judgment (GC), 16 June 2015, *Delfi AS v Estonia*, Application No. 64569/09, dissenting opinion of Judges Sajó and Tsotsoria, para. 27.

158 ECtHR, Judgment, 14 January 2020, *Beizara and Levickas v Lithuania*, Application No. 41288/15, para. 127.

aa) *Delfi v. Estonia* (2015) – Demanding a Notice and Takedown Procedure ….

In the first case, *Delfi v. Estonia*, the ECtHR held that States may hold providers of a professionally managed and commercial news portal liable for certain posts, in this case '[d]efamatory and other types of clearly unlawful speech, including hate speech and speech inciting violence',[159] without violating Article 10 ECHR. The news portal Delfi was asked by the victim of threatening and offensive comments to take down the posts and pay damages. While Delfi took down the posts, it refused to pay any damages. In the ensuing civil action, Delfi was held liable and ordered to pay damages. Important aspects in the balancing test include that while the company immediately deleted the incriminated comments after having been notified about them, the comments were still six weeks online; that the comments were 'of a clearly unlawful nature'[160] by being qualified as 'hate speech or incitements to violence';[161] that information posted on the Internet will remain public and 'accessible forever';[162] that Delfi created the original content as well as the electronic infrastructure for the posts;[163] and that the portal allowed the authors to remain anonymous. The Court also took into consideration that the compensation Delfi was ordered to pay, 320 €, was rather low.[164] With this decision, the ECtHR clarified that online intermediaries' liability for users' speech interferes with Article 10 ECHR but will be justified in cases of hate speech.

The Court was highly criticized for this judgment, which, in the opinion of the critics, did not do enough to protect freedom of expression.[165] One main point of critique was that contrary to Article 15 of the EU's E-Commerce Directive, which is the blueprint for Article 5 DSA-Draft and excludes any online intermediaries' duty to generally monitor content

159 ECtHR, Judgment (GC), 16 June 2015, *Delfi AS v Estonia*, Application No. 64569/09, para. 110.
160 *Id.*, para. 140.
161 *Ibid.*
162 *Id.*, para. 92.
163 *Id.*, para. 116.
164 *Id.*, para. 160.
165 See van der Sloot 'The Practical and Theoretical Problems with 'Balancing': Delfi, Coty and the Redundancy of the Human Rights Framework' (2016) 23 *Maastricht Journal of European and Comparative Law*, 439; Brunner, 'The Liability of an Online Intermediary for Third Party Content: The Watchdog Becomes the Monitor: Intermediary Liability after Delfi v Estonia' (2016) 16 *Human Rights Law Review*, 163.

and instead establishes a 'notice and takedown procedure', the decision can compel online intermediaries to use automatic filter technology to monitor online speech. The use of such filters, however, is said to have a chilling effect on freedom of expression as it will lead to over-blocking and risks undermining freedom of speech.[166] Consequently, none of the laws in question require an automated filtering system to take down illegal posts before notice.[167]

bb) *MTE and Index.hu ZRT v. Hungary* (2016) – .... But not in all Cases

In contrast to *Delfi*, in its next case on online intermediaries' liability for speech of third parties, *MTE and Index.hu ZRT v. Hungary*, the ECtHR found a violation of Article 10 ECHR because Hungarian courts held two online intermediaries liable for defamatory speech of third parties. While not explicitly deviating from the standards developed in *Delfi*, the Court clearly supported a more liberal view with regard to freedom of speech.

The Court, *inter alia*, underlined that 'the notice-and-takedown-system could function in many cases as an appropriate tool for balancing the rights and interests of all those involved'.[168] Contrary to *Delfi*, it was a legal person that sued the applicants;[169] the applicant MTE was a 'non-profit self-regulatory association of Internet service providers' without commercial interests; the applicants were not notified of the comments but were sued directly – and took down the comments after they learned about the lawsuit; and lastly, and most importantly, the posts in the *MTE* and *Index.hu* were 'devoid of [their] pivotal elements of hate speech and incitement of violence'[170] and thus did not constitute clearly unlawful speech.

166 Voorhoof, 'The Court's subtle approach for online media platform's liability for user-generated content since the 'Delfi Oracle'', Strasbourg Observers, 10 April 2020, https://strasbourgobservers.com/2020/04/10/the-courts-subtle-approach-of-online-media-platforms-liability-for-user-generated-content-since-the-delfi-oracle/. See also CJEU, Judgment, 16 February 2012, *SABAM v. Netlog NV*, Case C-360/10, ECLI: EU:C:2012:85.

167 For a critique of automated decision making see Frosio and Geiger, 'Taking Fundamental Rights seriously in the Digital Services Act's Platform Liability Regime' (2020) available at SSRN: https://papers.ssrn.com/sol3/papers.cfm?abstract_id=3747756 *SSRN*, 26.

168 ECtHR, Judgment, 2 February 2016, *MTE v Hungary*, Application No. 22947/13, para. 91.

169 *Id.*, para. 83.

170 *Id.*, paras. 64, 75.

The Court even held that the Internet's communication style might be a bit rougher: 'For the Court, the expressions used in the comments, albeit belonging to a low register of style, are common in communication on many Internet portals'.[171] Further, the topic of the comments was of public interest.[172] Lastly, the Hungarian judgment in question was too far reaching, not well tailored and 'effectively preclude[d] the balancing between the competing rights according to the criteria laid down in the Court's case law'[173] as it held that defamatory content must not appear at all – which created 'foreseeable negative consequences' for freedom of expression.[174]

cc) *Pihl v. Sweden* (2017) – Limited Liability for Small Blogs

In the next case, *Pihl v. Sweden*, the Court strengthened its *MTE* approach. Again, the case did not concern hate speech but 'only' defamatory speech, in the form of an online comment, which had been published anonymously on a blog. The subject of the comments, Mr. Pihl, raised an unsuccessful civil claim against a small non-profit association responsible for the blog. He claimed that it should be held liable for the comment. The Court rejected this claim and thus again argued in favour of freedom of expression. The decisive factors were that the blog had a rather small audience and was of a non-commercial nature,[175] that the post had been taken down the day after the applicant had made a complaint (the blog even apologized for the comments), and the comments had only been online 'for about nine days in total'.[176] *Pihl* thus privileges small blogs that are run on a non-profit basis. Here, the content neither has to be pre-monitored nor does an effective notice and takedown procedure need to be installed.[177]

---

171 *Id.*, para. 77.
172 *Id.*, para. 72.
173 *Id.*, para. 89.
174 *Id.*, para. 86.
175 ECtHR, Decision, 7 February 2017, *Pihl v Sweden*, Application No. 74742/14, para. 35; see also ECtHR, Decision, 19 September 2017, *Tamiz v UK*, Application No. 3877/14, para. 85.
176 ECtHR, Decision, 7 February 2017, *Pihl v Sweden*, Application No. 74742/14, para. 32.
177 Voorhof, 'Pihl v. Sweden: non-profit blog operator is not liable for defamatory users' comments in case of prompt removal upon notice', Strasbourg Observers, 20 March 2017, https://strasbourgobservers.com/2017/03/20/pihl-v-sweden-non-p

dd) *Høiness v. Norway* (2019) – Reiteration of the Court's Cautious Approach

The last case in this line is *Høiness v. Norway*, which concerned sexist comments on a news portal below the threshold of defamation and hate speech. Comparable to *Pihl*, Ms. Høiness was the victim of the comments and applied to the ECtHR as the national courts did not help her. As in *Pihl*, the ECtHR did not find a violation of the ECHR and thus argued again in favor of freedom of expression. It reiterated that it follows a cautious approach in limiting freedom of expression as long as the speech in question does not amount to hate speech or incitement to violence.[178]

d) Application of the Court's Case Law: Has the Right Balance Been Found?

Applying this case law to regulations at hand, one first has to highlight that while the ECtHR accepts automatic filtering system, at least for commercial news portals and in the case of hate speech, none of the laws obligate online intermediaries to use such systems. Here, the Court seems to be more restrictive than the legislator. Second, the Court also takes a very strict stance against hate speech and consequently allows for national rules that obligate online intermediaries to take down hate speech.[179] Third, the Court is cautious in allowing States to hold online intermediaries liable for illegal speech that falls below the threshold of hate speech.[180] Fourth, while this jurisprudence applies to online intermediaries, the Court differentiates between different intermediaries: commercial news portals are under more obligations, non-commercial news portals and small blogs[181] carry less obligations than commercial news portals and blogs with a

---

rofit-blog-operator-is-not-liable-for-defamatory-users-comments-in-case-of-prompt-removal-upon-notice/.

178 ECtHR, Judgment, 19 March 2019, *Høiness v Norway*, Application No. 43624/14, para. 69.

179 Brings-Wiesen and Damberg-Jänsch, 'Der *free flow of information* im Wandel des digitalen Zeitalters: Eine Bestandsaufnahme der internetbezogenen Rechtsprechung des EGMR zu Art. 10 EMRK' (2020) 84 *UFITA*, 284 (310 ff.).

180 See e.g. ECtHR, Judgment (GC), 15 October 2015, *Pernicek v Switzerland*, Application No. 27510/08; ECtHR, Judgment, 2 February 2016, *MTE v Hungary*, Application No. 22947/13.

181 E.g. ECtHR, Decision, 19 September 2017, *Tamiz v UK*, Application No. 3877/14, para. 85; ECtHR, Decision, 7 February 2017, *Pihl v Sweden*, Application

larger audience. Thus, 'the greater the degree of editorial control over and entrepreneurial interest in the data in question, the more likely it is that the court will find that the defences are not available.'[182] The Court, however, has not yet decided about online intermediaries that do not provide content themselves, like Facebook, YouTube, Instagram etc.[183] These online intermediaries are very large, have a very high commercial interest and possess editorial control via the algorithms that decide which content the user will see.[184] This, together with the Court's pronouncement that comments on platforms like Facebook are not less dangerous than those on the Internet news portals[185] speaks in favor of applying the depicted Court's jurisprudence, at least generally, to those service providers that the DSA-Draft calls very large online platforms.[186] Fifth, the content and the context of the speech in question matters.[187] While monitoring obligations

---

No. 74742/14, para. 31; ECtHR, Judgment, 2 February 2016, *MTE v Hungary*, Application No. 22947/13, para. 86.

182 Proops, 'Comment is (not) free – E-Commerce back in the limelight', Panopticon, 22 June 2015, https://panopticonblog.com/2015/06/22/comment-is-not-free-e-commerce-back-in-the-limelight/.

183 But see ECtHR, communicated 24 May 2019, *Gluhkov v Russia*, Application No. 42633/18, and ECtHR, communicated 9 January 2018, *Sanchez v France*, Application No. 45581/15, both communications have not yet been decided.

184 Two referrals to the CJEU have asked to clarify whether YouTube is neutral, i.e. "mere technical, automatic and passive" (CJEU, Judgment, 23 March 2010, *Google France SARL, Google Inc. v Louis Vuitton Malletier*, Joint Cases C-236/08 to C-238/08, ECLI:EU:C:2010:159, paras.42, 113.). In the sense of Art. 14 e-commerce directive: Opinion of Advocate General Saugmandsgaard Øe, 16 July 2020, *LF v Google LLC, YouTube Inc, YouTube LLC, Google Germany GmbH*, C-682/18, ECLI:EU:C:2020:586; request for a preliminary ruling from the Oberster Gerichtshof (Austria), 1 July 2019, *Puls 4 TV GmbH & Co KG v. YouTube LLC and Google Austria GmbH*, C-500/19.

185 ECtHR, Judgment, 14 January 2020, *Beizara and Levickas v Lithuania*, Application No. 41288/15, par. 127.

186 See also CJEU, Judgment, 3 October 2019, *Glawischnig-Piesczek v Facebook Ireland*, Case C-18/18, ECLI:EU:C:2019:821, paras. 19, 53, which left out the question of fundamental rights in its preliminary ruling and thus does not play a role in our context. It however showed that the CJEU allows for a national Court injunction to seek and identify identical as well as equivalent posts to the information that has been characterised as illegal – because of its defamatory nature – although this means that automated filters need to be used.

187 ECtHR, Judgment (GC), 15 October 2015, *Pernicek v Switzerland*, Application No. 27510/08, paras. 228, 239, 242 ff; ECtHR, Judgment (GC), 16 June 2015, *Delfi AS v Estonia*, Application No. 64569/09, paras. 144 ff; ECtHR, Judgment, 2 February 2016, *MTE v Hungary*, Application No. 22947/13, paras. 72 ff; ECtHR, Decision, 7 February 2017, *Pihl v Sweden*, Application No. 74742/14, para. 30; see

for hate speech for news portals do not violate Article 10 ECHR, other forms of illegal speech only allow for liability of online intermediaries under specific circumstances. The Court also takes into account whether the topic of the comments is of public interest or not.[188] Sixth, the reaction time and the measures applied by the company in order to remove a defamatory comment play a role in the balancing act.[189] Seventh, a proper balancing between the competing rights involved has to take place.[190] Eighth, and lastly, the liability of the actual authors of the comments as an alternative to the intermediary's liability, and the consequences of the domestic proceedings for the company need to be considered.[191]

The essence of the ECtHR jurisprudence is thus that a domestic law that holds a content provider of a certain size and with commercial interests liable for third party postings that amount to hate speech and incitement to violence does not violate Article 10 of the ECtHR. Illegal posts that fall below that threshold in principle need to be taken down without delay on receiving constructive knowledge of their existence in order to avoid liability. Certain conditions, however, apply.

Taking all these points into consideration, the GNEA and the DSA-Draft rules that apply to large online intermediaries that have a large commercial motivation and obligate them only to take down illegal con-

---

also Lauber-Rönsberg 'Persönlichkeitsschutz in der EMRK und im EU-Recht – § 57. Europäische Menschenrechtskonvention' in Götting et al. (eds), *Handbuch des Persönlichkeitsrechts* (2019), 1197 (mn. 87).

188 ECtHR, Judgment (GC), 15 October 2015, *Pernicek v Switzerland*, Application No. 27510/08, paras. 197, 230, 241; ECtHR, Judgment, 2 February 2016, *MTE v Hungary*, Application No. 22947/13, para. 72; see also Lauber-Rönsberg 'Persönlichkeitsschutz in der EMRK und im EU-Recht – § 57. Europäische Menschenrechtskonvention' in Götting et al. (eds), *Handuch des Persönlichkeitsrechts* (2019), 1197 (mn. 46 ff.).

189 ECtHR, Judgment (GC), 16 June 2015, *Delfi AS v Estonia*, Application No. 64569/09, paras. 152 ff.; ECtHR, Judgment, 2 February 2016, *MTE v Hungary*, Application No. 22947/13, paras. 80 ff; ECtHR, Decision, 7 February 2017, *Pihl v Sweden*, Application No. 74742/14, para. 32.

190 ECtHR, Judgment (GC), 7 February 2012, *Von Hannover v Germany (no. 2)*, Application Nos. 40660/08 and 40641/08, para. 106; ECtHR, Judgment (GC), 16 June 2015, *Delfi AS v Estonia*, Application No. 64569/09, para. 139; ECtHR, Judgment, 19 March 2019, *Høiness v Norway*, Application No. 43624/14, para. 65.

191 ECtHR, Decision, 7 February 2017, *Pihl v Sweden*, Application No. 74742/14, para. 28; see also ECtHR, Judgment, 19 March 2019, *Høiness v Norway*, Application No. 43624/14, para. 67.

tent[192] – not harmful content or unwanted content – are in principle proportionate. This is especially true with regard to hate speech. The laws in question, however, should clarify that online intermediaries have to take into consideration the importance of freedom of expression like the DSA-Draft already does. Highly problematic was that the GNEA foresaw not even out of court remedies against the deletion of posts and users profiles by social media companies, leading to possible over-blocking and thus to a chilling effect of the GNEA on freedom of expression. This has partly been rectified by the 2021 amendment. In its former version, however, the GNEA seemed not to be in conformity with the ECHR.[193] Recognizing a freedom to receive information claim would help against over-blocking as would a fine against over-blocking, and not only under-blocking.[194] The Loi Avia was also not formulated in a way that would stop over-blocking – one of the reasons it was declared unconstitutional. Another reason was the highly problematic strict time frame, which constitutes one of the major differences to the GNEA.[195] The Loi Avia has a chilling effect on free speech that is out of balance. The Loi 2018–1202 on the other hand, while directed against speech that is in principle not illegal but wrong, holds up to the Court's requirements, especially because it is so narrowly construed.

---

192 See Wischmeyer, 'Making social media an instrument of democracy' (2019) 25 *Eur Law J*,169 (176), who argues that these takedowns are marginal compared to those based on the "community standards."

193 Claussen, 'Fighting hate speech and fake news. The Network Enforcement Act (NetzDG) in Germany in the context of European legislation' (2018) *Rivista di Diritto dei Media*, 110 (124 ff.); Gersdorf, 'Hate Speech in sozialen Netzwerken – Verfassungswidrigkeit des NetzDG-Entwurfs und grundrechtliche Einordnung der Anbieter sozialer Netzwerke', (2017) *MMR*, 439 (446).

194 Hong, 'The German Network Enforcement Act and the Presumption in Favour of Freedom of Speech', Verfassungsblog, 22 January 2018, https://verfassungsblog.de/the-german-network-enforcement-act-and-the-presumption-in-favour-of-freedom-of-speech/.

195 See also CoE Committee of Ministers, *Recommendation to member States on the roles and responsibilities of internet intermediaries*, 7 March 2018, CM/Rec(2018)2, para. 1.3.7.: 'State authorities may hold intermediaries co-responsible with respect to content that they store if they do not act expeditiously to restrict access to content or services as soon as they become aware of their illegal nature, including through notice-based procedures. State authorities should ensure that notice-based procedures are not designed in a manner that incentivises the take-down of legal content, for example due to inappropriately short timeframes'.

IV. Conclusion: Regulating Online Intermediaries while Ensuring Freedom of Expression

Human rights law ensures freedom of expression of individuals as well as of online intermediaries. At the same time, it allows for certain interferences in order to protect democracy. As long as the regulation is proportionate, online intermediaries may be obligated to counter "fake news" and hate speech, stop the manipulation and censorship of its users and break up their echo chambers and filter bubbles. The Loi Avia does not meet the ECHR's standard. This is different for the other three laws. While the original GNEA was problematic, the amended versions seems to be in conformity with the ECHR. Also, the proposed DSA-Draft and the French Loi 2018–1202 – which is well balanced because it restricts its negative effects on freedom of speech to the three months before elections – are in conformity with the ECHR. These are also the laws that protect elections against manipulation via online tools. In order for democracy to survive and strive, it needs to be protected – as do human rights, especially the right to freedom of expression. Neither can live without the other as democracy and human rights are two sides of the same coin. The preamble's understanding, that human rights are 'the foundation of justice and peace in the world and are best maintained on the one hand by an effective political democracy and on the other by a common understanding and observance of the Human Rights upon which they depend', is as true today as it was in 1950.

Bibliography

Akandji-Kombe, Jean-François: Positive Obligations under the European Convention on Human Rights (2007), 14 ff.

Article 19: Responding to 'hate speech': Comparative overview of six EU countries (2018), https://www.article19.org/wp-content/uploads/2018/03/ECA-hate-speech-compilation-report_March-2018.pdf.

Baade, Björnstjern: Fake News and International Law, EJIL 2018, 1357 ff.

Bárd, Petra: The Hungarian "Lex NGO" before the CJEU: Calling an Abuse of State Power by its Name, Verfassungsblog, 27 January 2020, https://verfassungsblog.de/the-hungarian-lex-ngo-before-the-cjeu-calling-an-abuse-of-state-power-by-its-name/.

Barlow, John Perry: A Declaration of the Independence of Cyberspace, Electronic Frontier Foundation, 8 February 1996, https://www.eff.org/cyberspace-independence.

Bassini, Marco: Fundamental rights and private enforcement in the digital age, Eur. Law J. 2019, 182 ff.

BBC News: Cambridge Analytica 'not involved' in Brexit referendum, says watchdog, 7 October 2020, https://www.bbc.com/news/uk-politics-54457407.

Blake, William: Auguries of Innocence, The Pickering Manuscript (1807), www.blakearchive.org/copy/bb126.1?descId=bb126.1.ms.15.

Brattberg, Erik/Maurer, Tim: Russian Election Interference – Europe's Counter to Fake News and Cyber Attacks, Carnegie Endowment for International Peace 2018, https://carnegieendowment.org/files/CP_333_BrattbergMaurer_Russia_Elections_Interference_FINAL.pdf.

Brings-Wiesen, Tobias/ Damberg-Jänsch, Alicia: Der *free flow of information* im Wandel des digitalen Zeitalters: Eine Bestandsaufnahme der internetbezogenen Rechtsprechung des EGMR zu Art. 10 EMRK, UFITA 2020, 284 ff.

Brunner, Lisl: The Liability of an Online Intermediary for Third Party Content: The Watchdog Becomes the Monitor: Intermediary Liability after Delfi v Estonia, Human Rights Law Review 2016, 163 ff.

Bubeck, Johannes/Jäger, Kai/Marinov, Nikolay/Nanni, Federico: Why Do States Intervene in the Elections of Others? The Role of Incumbent–Opposition Divisions, British Journal of Political Science 2020, 1 ff.

Cardenal, Juan Pablo/Kucharczyk, Jacek/Mesežnikov, Grigorij/Pleschlová Gabriela: Sharp power: rising authoritarian influence (2017).

Claussen, Victor: Fighting hate speech and fake news. The Network Enforcement Act (NetzDG) in Germany in the context of European legislation, Rivista di Diritto dei Media 2018, 110 ff.

DCMSC: Disinformation and 'fake news': Interim Report, HC 363, 29 July 2018, para. 162 https://publications.parliament.uk/pa/cm201719/cmselect/cmcumeds/363/36302.htm.

DeConde, Alexander: Washington's Farewell, the French Alliance, and the Election of 1796, The Mississippi Valley Historical Review 1957, 641 ff.

Deutscher Bundestag: Antwort der Bundesregierung auf die Kleine Anfrage der Abgeordneten Ulla Jelpke, Dr. André Hahn, Gökay Akbulut, weiterer Abgeordneter und der Fraktion DIE LINKE.– Drucksache 19/26017 -Straftaten gegen Amts- und Mandatsträger, Drucksache 19/26419, 03 February 2021.

Engle, Eric: Third Party Effect of Fundamental Rights (Drittwirkung), Hanse Law Review 2009, 165 ff.

Frosio, Giancarlo/Geiger, Christophe: Taking Fundamental Rights seriously in the Digital Services Act's Platform Liability Regime (2020), https://papers.ssrn.com/sol3/papers.cfm?abstract_id=3747756.

Funke, David/ Flamini, Daniela: A guide to anti-misinformation actions around the world, Poynter 2018, https://www.poynter.org/ifcn/anti-misinformation-actions/.

Fuster, Gloria González/Scherrer, Amandine: Big data and smart devices and their impact on privacy, Directorate-General for Internal Policies of the Union Study (2015), http://www.europarl.europa.eu/RegData/etudes/STUD/2015/536455/IPOL_STU(2015)536455_EN.pdf.

Gehrke, Laurenz: UK probe finds no evidence that Cambridge Analytica misused data to influence Brexit, Politico, 7 October 2020, https://www.politico.eu/article/no-evidence-that-cambridge-analytica-misused-data-to-influence-brexit-report/.

Gersdorf, Hubertus: Hate Speech in sozialen Netzwerken – Verfassungswidrigkeit des NetzDG-Entwurfs und grundrechtliche Einordnung der Anbieter sozialer Netzwerke, MMR 2017, 439 ff.

Goldhill, Olivia: A 'big data' firm sells Cambridge Analytica's methods to global politicians, documents show, Quartz, 14 August 2019, https://qz.com/1666776/data-firm-ideia-uses-cambridge-analytica-methods-to-target-voters/.

Gorodnichenko, Yuriy/Pham, Tho/Talavera, Oleksandr: Social Media, Sentiment and Public Opinions: Evidence from #Brexit and #Uselection, NBER Working Paper No. 24631, May 2018.

Grabenwarter, Christoph: European Convention on Human Rights: Commentary (2014)Grassegger, Hannes/Krogerus, Mikael: Cambridge Analytica / Big data and the Future of Democracy: The Matrix world behind the Brexit and the US Elections, Diplomat Magazine, 5 March 2017, www.diplomatmagazine.nl/2018/03/22/cambridge-analytica-big-data-and-the-future-of-democracy-the-matrix-world-behind-the-brexit-and-the-us-elections/.

Guggenberger, Nikolaus: Das Netzwerkdurchsetzungsgesetz – schön gedacht, schlecht gemacht, ZRP 2017, 98 ff.

Haciyakupoglu, Gulizar/Hui, Jennifer Yang/ Suguna, V.S./Leong, Dymples/Bin Abdul Rahman, Muhammad Faizal: Policy Report Countering Fake News – A Survey of Recent Global Initiatives, Rajaratnam School of International Studies (2018), https://www.rsis.edu.sg/wp-content/uploads/2018/03/PR180307_Countering-Fake-News.pdf.

Helberger, Natali: The Political Power of Platforms: How Current Attempts to Regulate Misinformation Amplify Opinion Power, Digital Journalism 2020, 842 ff.

Hong, Mathias: The German Network Enforcement Act and the Presumption in Favour of Freedom of Speech, Verfassungsblog, 22 January 2018, https://verfassungsblog.de/the-german-network-enforcement-act-and-the-presumption-in-favour-of-freedom-of-speech/.

Hughes, Heather/Waismel-Manor, Israel: The Macedonian Fake News Industry and the 2016 US Election, Political Science & Politics 2021, 19 ff.

Inter-Parliamentary Union: Inter-Parliamentary Council at its 154th session in Paris. Declaration on Criteria for Free and Fair Elections, 26 March 1994, http://archive.ipu.org/cnl-e/154-free.htm.

International Press Institute: New 'fake news' law stifles independent reporting in Russia on Covid-19, 8 May 2020, https://ipi.media/new-fake-news-law-stifles-independent-reporting-in-russia-on-covid-19/.

John, Oliver/Naumann, Laura/Soto Christopher: Paradigm Shift to the Integrative Big Five Trait Taxonomy, in: John, Oliver/Pervin, Lawrence/Robins, Richard (eds), Handbook of Personality: Theory and Research, 3rd edn. (2008), 114 ff.

Kaesling, Katharina: Evolution statt Revolution der Plattformregulierung, ZUM 2021, 177 ff.

Kalbhenn, Jan Christopher/Hemmert-Halswick, Maximilian: Der Regierungsentwurf zur Änderung des NetzDG – Vom Compliance-Ansatz zu Designvorgaben, MMR 2020, 518 ff.

Katsirea, Irini: "Fake news": reconsidering the value of untruthful expression in the face of regulatory uncertainty, Journal of Media Law 2018, 159 ff.

Kettemann, Matthias/Benedek, Wolfgang: Freedom of expression online, in: Susi, Mart (ed), Human Rights, Digital Society and the Law: A Research Companion (2019), 58 ff.

Kettemann, Matthias/Tiedeke, Anna: Back up: can users sue platforms to reinstate deleted content?, Internet Policy Review 2020, 1 ff.

Knight, Ben: Germany: Hate speech, threats against politicians rise, Deutsche Welle, 9 February 2021, https://www.dw.com/en/germany-hate-speech-threats-against-politicians-rise/a-56512214.

Köhler, Daniel/Ebner, Julia: Strategies and tactics: communication strategies of jihadists and right-wing extremists, in: Baldauf, Johannes/Ebner, Julia/Guhls, Jakob (eds), Hate Speech and Radicalisation Online – The OCCI Research (2019), 18 ff. https://www.isdglobal.org/wp-content/uploads/2019/06/ISD-Hate-Speech-and-Radicalisation-Online-English-Draft-2.pdf.

Krieger, Heike: Krieg gegen anonymous – Völkerrechtliche Regelungsmöglichkeiten bei unsicherer Zurechnung im Cyberwar, AVR 2012, 1 ff.

Ladeur, Karl-Heinz/Gostomzyk, Tobias: Das Netzwerkdurchsetzungsgesetz und die Logik der Meinungsfreiheit, K&R 2017, 390 ff.

Lang, Andrej: Netzwerkdurchsetzungsgesetz und Meinungsfreiheit – Zur Regulierung privater Internet-Intermediäre bei der Bekämpfung von Hassrede', AöR 2018, 220 ff.

Laub, Zachary: Hate Speech on Social Media: Global Comparisons, Council on Foreign Relations, 11 April 2019, https://www.cfr.org/backgrounder/hate-speech-social-media-global-comparisons.

Lauber-Rönsberg, Anne: Hate Speech – ein Überblick über rechtliche Rahmenbedingungen, ihre Durchsetzung und das neue NetzDG, Aptum 2017, 100 ff.

Lauber-Rönsberg, Anne: Persönlichkeitsschutz in der EMRK und im EU-Recht – § 57. Europäische Menschenrechtskonvention, in: Götting, Horst-Peter/Schertz, Christian/Seitz, Walter (eds), Handbuch des Persönlichkeitsrechts (2019), 1197 ff.

Lessig, Lawrence: Code: And Other Laws of Cyberspace (1999), 6 ff.

Lessig, Lawrence: Code: And Other Laws of Cyberspace, Version 2.0 (2006), 1 ff.

Levin, Dov: Partisan electoral interventions by the great powers: Introducing the PEIG Dataset, Conflict Management and Peace Science 2019, 88 ff.

Lomas, Natasha: Facebook found hosting masses of far right EU disinformation networks, Tech Crunch, 22 May 2019, https://techcrunch.com/2019/05/22/facebook-found-hosting-masses-of-far-right-eu-disinformation-networks/.

Martens, Bertin/Aguiar, Luis/Gomez-Herrera, Maria/Muller-Langer, Frank: The digital transformation of news media and the rise of disinformation and fake news, JRC Digital Economy Working Paper, No. 2018–02, https://www.econstor.eu/bitstream/10419/202231/1/jrc-dewp201802.pdf.

Ohlin, Jens David: Election Interference – International Law and the Future of Democracy (2020), 14 ff.

Quenqua, Douglas: Facebook Knows You Better Than Anyone Else, The New York Times, 19 January 2015, www.nytimes.com/2015/01/20/science/facebook-knows-you-better-than-anyone-else.html.

Peukert, Alexander: Gewährleistung der Meinungs- und Informationsfreiheit in sozialen Netzwerken. Vorschlag für eine Ergänzung des NetzDG um sog. Put-back-Verfahren, MMR 2018, 572 ff.

Peukert, Alexander: Put it back: Ein Vorschlag für ein NetzDG, das die Meinungsfreiheit wahrt, Verfassungsblog, 14 June 2018, https://verfassungsblog.de/put-it-back-ein-vorschlag-fuer-ein-netzdg-das-die-meinungsfreiheit-wahrt/.

Pollicino, Oreste: Fundamental Rights as Bycatch – Russia's Anti-Fake News Legislation, Verfassungsblog, 28 March 2019, https://verfassungsblog.de/fundamental-rights-as-bycatch-russias-anti-fake-news-legislation/.

Pollicino, Oreste: Judicial Protection of Fundamental Rights in the transition from the world of atoms to the word of bits: The case of freedom of speech, Eur. Law J. 2019, 155 ff.

Proops, Anya: Comment is (not) free – E-Commerce back in the limelight, Panopticon, 22 June 2015, https://panopticonblog.com/2015/06/22/comment-is-not-free-e-commerce-back-in-the-limelight/.

Rainey, Bernadette/Wicks, Elizabeth/Ovey, Clare: Jacobs, White, and Ovey: The European Convention on Human Rights, 7th edn. (2017), 486 ff.

Roberts, Louise: Peter the Great in Poland, The Slavonic Review 1927, 537 ff.

Robertson, Jordan/Riley, Michael/Willis, Andrew: How to Hack an Election, Bloomberg Businessweek, 31 March 2016, www.bloomberg.com/features/2016-how-to-hack-an-election/.

Röttger, Tania: Nein – Merkel „hofft“ nicht auf 12 Millionen Einwanderer, Correctiv, 5 March 2018, https://correctiv.org/fakten-check/2018/03/05/nein-merkel-hofft-nicht-auf-12-millionen-einwanderer/.

Sängerlaub, Alexander/Meier, Miriam/Rühl, Wolf-Dieter: Fakten statt Fakes – Verursacher, Verbreitungswege und Wirkungen von Fake News im Bundestagswahlkampf 2017, Stiftung Neue Verantwortung 2018, 79 ff., https://www.stiftung-nv.de/sites/default/files/snv_fakten_statt_fakes.pdf.

Sardo, Alessio: Categories, Balancing, and Fake News: The Jurisprudence of the European Court of Human Rights, Canadian Journal of Law & Jurisprudence 2020, 435 ff.

Schmehl, Karsten/Lytvynenko, Jane: 7 Out Of The 10 Most Viral Articles About Angela Merkel On Facebook Are False, Buzzfeed News, 27 July 2017, https://www.buzzfeednews.com/article/karstenschmehl/top-merkel-news.

Schwarz, Karolin/Holnburger, Josef: Disinformation: What role does disinformation play for hate speech and extremism on the internet and what measures have social media companies taken to combat it?, in: Baldauf, Johannes/Ebner, Julia/Guhls, Jakob (eds), Hate Speech and Radicalisation Online – The OCCI Research (2019), 35 ff., https://www.isdglobal.org/wp-content/uploads/2019/06/ISD-Hate-Speech-and-Radicalisation-Online-English-Draft-2.pdf.

Scola, Nancy: How chatbots are colonizing politics, Politico, 10 November 2016, www.politico.com/story/2016/10/chatbots-are-invading-politics-229598.

Scott, Mark: Cambridge Analytica did work for Brexit groups, says ex-staffer, Politico, 30 July 2019, https://www.politico.eu/article/cambridge-analytica-leave-eu-ukip-brexit-facebook/.

Shane, Scott: Russia Isn't the Only One Meddling in Elections. We Do It, Too., The New York Times, 17 February 2018, https://www.nytimes.com/2018/02/17/sunday-review/russia-isnt-the-only-one-meddling-in-elections-we-do-it-too.html.

Shearer, Andrew: The Evolution of Hybrid Warfare and Key Challenges, Statement Before the House Armed Services Committee, 22 March 2017, https://csis-website-prod.s3.amazonaws.com/s3fs-public/congressional_testimony/170322_shearer_testimony_evolution_of_hybrid_warfare.pdf.

Shulman, Stephen/Bloom, Stephen: The legitimacy of foreign intervention in elections: The Ukrainian response, Review of International Studies 2012, 445 ff.

van der Sloot, Bart: The Practical and Theoretical Problems with 'Balancing': Delfi, Coty and the Redundancy of the Human Rights Framework, Maastricht Journal of European and Comparative Law 2016, 439 ff.

Smith, Rachael Craufurd: Fake news, French Law and Democratic Legitimacy: Lessons for the United Kingdom?, Journal of Media Law 2019, 52 ff.

SPIEGEL online: SPIEGEL-Umfrage unter Parlamentarierinnen – Frauenfeindlichkeit im Bundestag durch AFD gestiegen, 12 February 2021, https://www.spiegel.de/politik/deutschland/bundestag-frauenfeindlichkeit-durch-afd-gestiegen-a-4c8c425c-6b08-4ac5-b049-61ad65d1240c.

Steiger, Dominik: International Law and New Challenges to Democracy in the Digital Age: Big Data, Privacy and Interferences with the Political Process, in: Witzleb, Normann/Paterson, Moira/Richardson, Janice (eds), Big Data, Political Campaigning and the Law: Privacy and Democracy in the Age of Micro-Targeting, Abingdon (2020), 71 ff.

Tharoor, Ishaan: The long history of the U.S. interfering with elections elsewhere.

The Washington Post, 13 October 2016, https://www.washingtonpost.com/news/worldviews/wp/2016/10/13/the-long-history-of-the-u-s-interfering-with-elections-elsewhere/.

Tysiachniouk, Maria/Tulaeva, Svetlana/Henry, Laura: Civil Society under the Law 'On Foreign Agents': NGO Strategies and Network Transformation, Europe-Asia Studies 2018, 615 ff.

U.K. Information Commissioner's Office (ICO): RE: ICO investigation into use of personal information and political influence, 2 October 2020, https://ico.org.uk/media/action-weve-taken/2618383/20201002_ico-o-ed-l-rtl-0181_to-julian-knight-mp.pdf.

UNGA: Report of the Special Representative of the Secretary-General on the issue of human rights and transnational corporations and other business enterprises, A/HRC/17/31, 21 March 2011, 13 ff.

Voorhof, Dirk: Pihl v. Sweden: non-profit blog operator is not liable for defamatory users' comments in case of prompt removal upon notice, Strasbourg Observers, 20 March 2017, https://strasbourgobservers.com/2017/03/20/pihl-v-sweden-non-profit-blog-operator-is-not-liable-for-defamatory-users-comments-in-case-of-prompt-removal-upon-notice/.

Voorhoof, Dirk: The Court's subtle approach for online media platform's liability for user-generated content since the 'Delfi Oracle', Strasbourg Observers, 10 April 2020, https://strasbourgobservers.com/2020/04/10/the-courts-subtle-approach-of-online-media-platforms-liability-for-user-generated-content-since-the-delfi-oracle/.

Voorhoof, Dirk/Lievens, Eva: Offensive Online Comments – New ECtHR Judgement, ECHR Blog, 15 February 2016, https://www.echrblog.com/2016/02/offensive-online-comments-new-ecthr.html.

Wienfort, Nora: Blocking Overblocking – Frankreichs Verfassungsrat kippt das Gesetz gegen Hasskriminalität im Netz, Verfassungsblog, 20 June 2020, https://verfassungsblog.de/blocking-overblocking/.

Wischmeyer, Thomas: Making social media an instrument of democracy, Eur. Law J. 2019, 169 ff.

Zimmermann, Andreas: International Law and „Cyber Space", ESIL Reflections 2014, 1 ff.

A Culture of Justification or a Culture of Presumption? The Turn to Procedural Review and the Normative Function of Proportionality at the European Court of Human Rights

Alain Zysset

A. *Introduction*

The European Court of Human Rights ('the Court' or 'ECtHR') has recently consolidated a 'turn to procedural review' ('TPR') in its role as supreme interpreter of the European Convention on Human Rights ('ECHR'). In a nutshell, the TPR adjusts the object of the Court's scrutiny; rather than reviewing the (substantive) merits of cases independently within the proportionality assessment, the Court focuses on the quality of the domestic procedure by which the (potentially infringing) law under consideration was adopted and applied. This then informs the merits stage of evaluation.

While the literature has documented the TPR in the Court's case law, critical and evaluative accounts of the turn are still scarce. What is the broader significance of the TPR for our understanding of the Court's nature, function and legitimacy? In this article, I suggest remedying this deficit by evaluating the TPR from a theoretical and normative perspective. I concentrate on the relationship between the TPR and proportionality analysis. With a view to building an analytical framework, I employ the well-established distinction between a *culture of authority* and a *culture of justification*. In brief, a culture of authority is exemplified when a court reviews the process of creation of an infringing law as its procedural review. In contrast, the rise of proportionality assessments in constitutional and human rights review exemplifies a culture of justification because it scrutinizes a wider spectrum of reasons that may ground the interference. As we shall see, however, the TPR often has implications for the Court's proportionality analysis: I argue that the TPR indicates a reversed dynamic towards a culture of authority.

A culture of authority has two main variants. First, the Court may exemplify a culture of authority by relying on the text of the Convention and on established methods of adjudication (e.g. 'evolutive and dynamic', 'autonomous concepts', or 'practical and effective') or by allocating a margin of appreciation to the respondent state party as 'better placed' (empirically) to operate the balancing between conflicting rights and interests. Second, it may exemplify a culture of authority by relying on the quality of the procedure by which the piece of legislation is adopted by the appropriately situated decision-making body. The TPR corresponds to the second variant: the Court places the burden of legitimate authority on the domestic processes (including taking into account of ECHR standards), which may lead – but not necessarily – the Court to allocate a margin of appreciation to the respondent state.

This argument has implications for how one normatively evaluates the TPR. Indeed, it has been argued that the TPR may reinforce the democratic legitimacy of the Court's rulings, as we shall see. I argue that the TPR rather points to a worrying retreat of the Court, which I call a culture of presumption. This culture disables the core normative function of proportionality analysis, a key component of effective protection of human rights. More fundamentally, I argue, the TPR runs the risk of retreating from the very concept of human rights understood as the 'right to justification.'[1]

This chapter proceeds in two steps. In section B., I define the TPR and the context(s) of adjudication in which it operates at the Court. I specifically examine the link between the TPR and proportionality. In section C., I develop the distinction between justification and authority and explain how relevant it is to evaluate the TPR. I then argue that the TPR exemplifies the return to a culture of authority through a discussion of the normative function of proportionality.

B. The turn to procedural review ('TPR')

In this section, I introduce the main features of the TPR in the practice of the Court in recent years. This section also aims to show that while the TPR is now well understood at a descriptive level, it has not yet been comprehensively conceptualised and normatively evaluated. I aim to remedy this deficit in later sections of the article.

The TPR in the practice of the Court is now well documented in the literature. Using this growing literature, I suggest reconstructing the TPR in two steps. First, one may reconstruct the typical context(s) of the TPR – that is, where the turn from substantive to procedural review occurs (or

1 Forst, 'The Justification of Human Rights and the Basic Right to Justification: A Reflexive Approach' (2010) 120:4 *Ethics*, 711.

when they co-exist) in the reasoning of the Court. Second, one may ask about the wider implications of the TPR. In other words, what gets lost when the Court's review is predominantly procedural? This second step is properly normative and will require, I shall explain, an normative account of proportionality analysis that I offer in section C.

In terms of its context(s), the TPR predominantly concerns both the procedural obligations of an ECHR article, on the one hand, and the review of the domestic procedure and its impact on the merits of a case, on the other. The literature here has shown that the former context concerns, most importantly, Articles 5, 6, and 13 of the ECHR.[2] However, the same literature has also highlighted how procedural obligations can be read into other articles of the ECHR, in particular Articles 2, 3, 8 and Article 1 Protocol 1. The issue of the right to abortion under Article 8 of the Convention and the case of *A, B and C v. Ireland* is illustrative: while emphasising that 'the profound moral views of the Irish people as to the nature of life'[3] justifies allocating a wide margin of appreciation to the Irish state, the Court nonetheless found a violation of Article 8 on distinctively procedural grounds (for one of the applicants):

> The authorities failed to comply with their positive obligation to secure to the third applicant effective respect for her private life by reason of the absence of any implementing legislative or regulatory regime providing an accessible and effective procedure by which the third applicant could have established whether she qualified for a lawful abortion in Ireland.[4]

The latter context concerns the Court focusing on the domestic procedure of decision-making (parliamentary, administrative and judicial), which then informs and alters the substantive merits of a case. This type of procedural review, which the literature has called 'procedural review *stricto sensu*',[5] is the focus of this chapter. For that portion of the analysis, it

2 Brems, 'Procedural Protection: An Examination of Procedural Safeguards Read into Substantive Convention Rights' in Brems and Gerards (eds), *Shaping Rights in the ECHR: The Role of the European Court of Human Rights in Determining the Scope of Human Rights* (2014), 137.

3 ECtHR, Judgment (GC), 16 December 2010, *A, B and C v Ireland*, Application No. 25579/05, para. 241.

4 ECtHR, Judgment (GC), 16 December 2010, *A, B and C v Ireland*, Application No. 25579/05, para. 267.

5 Arnardóttir, 'The "Procedural Turn" under the European Convention on Human Rights and Presumptions of Convention Compliance' (2017) 15:1 *Int. J. Const. Law*, 9.

appears that the Court tends to refrain from reviewing the balancing performed by the domestic authorities between the protected provision and the norm interfering with it on its own terms, or at least assigns greater weight to the quality of the domestic procedure in that same balancing step of the proportionality test.

Refraining from or limiting the review of the balancing phase of the proportionality test is not new to the practice of the Court; it has long been shown that the Court may simply refrain from balancing or balance but still allocate a margin of appreciation to the respondent state.[6] Yet, the emphasis on domestic procedures may also operate as another, more principled approach to justify the application of the margin. As Nussberger explains, 'when States are free to decide a case in different ways without violating the Convention, the inclusiveness and transparency of the decision-making process is the most relevant element for the Court to control.'[7]

In that second context, the TPR is most operative when the Court faces an acute conflict between two protected rights with particular emphasis on Articles 8–11. This is the case for instance in *Von Hannover v. Germany (No. 2)* in which the Court had to balance freedom of expression (Article 10) against the right to private life (Article 8):

> The Court observes that, in accordance with their case-law, the national courts carefully balanced the right of the publishing companies to freedom of expression against the right of the applicants to respect for their private life. In doing so, they attached fundamental importance to the question whether the photos, considered in the light of the accompanying articles, had contributed to a debate of general interest. They also examined the circumstances in which the photos had been taken.[8]

In this case, the Court paid particular attention to whether two photographs depicting a royal family on holiday contributed to a debate of public interest, which is deemed essential to the Court's 'democratic soci-

6 Letsas, 'Two Concepts of the Margin of Appreciation' (2006) 26:4 *Oxf. J Leg. Stud.*, 705.

7 Nussberger, 'Procedural Review by the ECHR: View from the Court' in Brems and Gerards (eds) *Procedural Review in European Fundamental Rights Cases* (2017), 161 (174).

8 ECtHR, Judgment (GC), 7 February 2012, *Von Hannover v Germany (No. 2)*, Application Nos. 40660/08 and 60641/08, para. 124.

ety.'[9] In the words of Gerards, this depicts a situation where the Court 'generally has to accept the outcomes of such a (non-problematic) procedure, even if it reflects a different balance or a different choice than the Court's judges would have preferred.'[10] For positive obligations, ethical dilemmas and/or conflicts of rights, the Court often states that domestic authorities are 'better' placed to review the substantive merits of the case, which is the usual route to allocate the margin of appreciation. In *A, B and C v. Ireland*, the Court for instance concluded that:

> by reason of their direct and continuous contact with the vital forces of their countries, the State authorities are, in principle, in a better position than the international judge to give an opinion, not only on the 'exact content of the requirements of morals' in their country, but also on the necessity of a restriction intended to meet them.[11]

This justification is *epistemic* in that the Court claims not to have the necessary empirics to conduct the balancing on its own terms, which often prompts the Court to allocate the margin. That said, the TPR is also operating when it defers to domestic authorities qua *democratic* authorities. This is salient for example in *S.A.S. v. France*, where the Court faced the question of the wearing of the full-face veil in public under Article 8:

> In such circumstances, the Court has a duty to exercise a degree of restraint in its review of Convention compliance, since such review will lead it to assess a balance that has been struck by means of a democratic process within the society in question. The Court has, moreover, already had occasion to observe that in matters of general policy, on which opinions within a democratic society may reasonably differ widely, the role of the domestic policy-maker should be given special weight.[12]

---

9 Zysset, 'Freedom of expression, the right to vote, and proportionality at the European Court of Human Rights: an internal critique' (2019) 17:1 *Int. J. Const. Law*, 230.

10 Gerards, 'The Prism of Fundamental Rights' (2012) 8:2 *Eur. Const. Law Rev.*, 173 (173).

11 ECtHR, Judgment (GC), 16 December 2010, *A, B and C v Ireland,* Application No. 25579/05, para. 232.

12 ECtHR, Judgment (GC), 1 July 2014, *S.A.S. v France*, Application No. 43835/11, para. 154.

The Court held that view after having emphasised the subsidiary role of the Court's system:

> it is also important to emphasise the fundamentally subsidiary role of the Convention mechanism. The national authorities have direct democratic legitimation and are, as the Court has held on many occasions, in principle better placed than an international court to evaluate local needs and conditions. In matters of general policy, on which opinions within a democratic society may reasonably differ widely, the role of the domestic policy-maker should be given special weight.[13]

This brief overview helps identify the various pieces of the puzzle forming the context of the TPR: positive obligations, ethical dilemmas, conflicts of rights, the margin of appreciation, the proportionality test, and the principle of subsidiarity. These elements may be placed in the reversed order: the principle of subsidiarity explains and (from the Court's perspective) justifies why it concentrates on the domestic procedure as the *locus* of review, particularly when it has to review acute conflicts of rights, ethical dilemmas, and positive obligations. The margin of appreciation is only a contingent and not a necessary implication of the Court's emphasis on procedure. Subsidiarity provides the primary justification, and one may view it in the context of the amendment to the Preamble to the ECHR in Protocol 15.[14] In terms of its consequences, the potential impact on the proportionality analysis and therefore on its normative function is noteworthy. Regardless, the procedural and substantive review of the analysis can likewise co-exist and do not necessarily function as substitutes for one another. The Court may acknowledge that the domestic authority considered Convention standards but still review the substantive merits in its own terms and diverge from the domestic decision.[15]

Having described the relevant context in which the TPR operates, I suggest specifying the object of the TPR *stricto sensu*. In the broadest terms, the TPR implies that the Court focuses on the quality of the domestic

---

13 ECtHR, Judgment (GC), 1 July 2014, *S.A.S. v France*, Application No. 43835/11, para. 129.

14 "Affirming that the High Contracting Parties, in accordance with the principle of subsidiarity, have the primary responsibility to secure the rights and freedoms defined in this Convention and the Protocols thereto, and that in doing so they enjoy a margin of appreciation, subject to the supervisory jurisdiction of the European Court of Human Rights established by this Convention".

15 See in particular ECtHR, Judgment, 12 June 2012, *Lindheim and Others v Norway*, Application Nos. 13221/08 and 2139/10.

process (legislative, administrative and judicial) in enacting and applying a particular piece of legislation that may interfere with an ECHR right. Gerards speaks for instance of the 'quality of the process and deliberations underlying a certain piece of legislation.'[16] These conditions are broadly democracy- and rule of law-based and include participation, inclusiveness, pluralism, independence, transparency, and proportionality.[17] In *Animals Defender International v. UK*, which concerned the general prohibition of political advertising in broadcasting, the Court for instance insisted on the quality of the procedure across both parliamentary and judicial channels:

> The Court, for its part, attaches considerable weight to these exacting and pertinent reviews, by both parliamentary and judicial bodies, of the complex regulatory regime governing political broadcasting in the United Kingdom and to their view that the general measure was necessary to prevent the distortion of crucial public interest debates and, thereby, the undermining of the democratic process.[18]

Surely, some of these procedural requirements form part of the proportionality test itself – for example, when the Court assesses that the interfering norm was 'prescribed by law' (1st prong of the test for Articles 8–11 of the Convention). The TPR can also consist of the evidence that the domestic authority has taken into account ECHR standards (irrespective of if and how the authority might ultimately balance conflicting rights and interests). This is salient for instance in *Axel Springer v. Germany (No. 2)* in which the Court held that 'where the balancing exercise between those two rights has been undertaken by the national authorities in conformity with the criteria laid down in the Court's case-law, the Court would require strong reasons to substitute its view for that of the domestic courts'.[19]

It appears that the TPR does not consist of inherently new normative standards – rather, it is indirectly referring to well-established duties that correlate with some of the most developed provisions of the Convention, which also blurs the distinction between the two types of TPR drawn at the start of the article. The requirement of pluralism and contribution to public debate, which were central to the Court's conclusion in *Von Hanno-*

---

16 Gerards, 'Procedural Review by the ECtHR: A Typology' in in Brems and Gerards (eds) *Procedural Review in European Fundamental Rights Cases* (2017), 127 (140).

17 *Ibid.*

18 ECtHR, Judgment (GC), 22 April 2013, *Animals Defender International v The United Kingdom*, Application No. 48876/08, para. 116.

19 ECtHR, Judgment, 10 July 2014, *Axel Springer AG v Germany (No. 2)*, Application No. 48311/10, para. 88.

ver v. Germany (No. 2) is part of the core content and scope of the right to freedom of expression and the right to assembly and association (Articles 10 and 11).[20] In other words, while the literature dissociates the two kinds of review (procedural and substantive), in fact the TPR (understood as set of normative standards) is not foreign to the substantive case law of the Court, even if these standards are not presented as such in the text of the judgments and are often reviewed independently from the substantive merits.

What makes the TPR distinctive then? As I shall further explain in the next section, the TPR implies marginalising the balancing phase of the proportionality test that the Court routinely and independently operates. This marks the distinctive feature of the TPR, as opposed to any necessary link to the margin of appreciation or to any other interpretive tool or doctrine of the Court. This point is noted in the literature:

> the focus is not on if and how procedural elements are made explicit as part of the protective scope of Convention rights, but on their significance among the balance of reasons when the Court pronounces on the substantive merits and assesses the proportionality or reasonableness of a measure.[21]

Commentators have pointed out the potential significance of this self-limitation vis-à-vis the very idea of human rights review. Kleinlein for instance explains that 'the quality of domestic law-making procedures is a factor that determines the authority of international human rights over domestic law.'[22] Nussberger writes that 'the very function of human rights review is to counter-balance majority decisions: [t]his cannot be done be reviewing the procedure only.'[23] Descriptively, this seems accurate. Yet, when it comes to the properly normative significance of the TPR, the literature remains relatively scarce. One may ask: what is the importance of human

20 I developed this idea further in Zysset, 'Freedom of expression, the right to vote, and proportionality at the European Court of Human Rights: an internal critique' (2019) 17:1 *Int. J. Const. Law*, 230.

21 Arnardóttir, 'The "Procedural Turn" under the European Convention on Human Rights and Presumptions of Convention Compliance' (2017) 15:1 *Int. J. Const. Law*, 9 (14).

22 Kleinlein, 'The Procedural Approach of the European Court of Human Rights: Between Subsidiarity and Dynamic Evolution' (2019), 68:1 *ICLQ*, 91 (96).

23 Nussberger, 'Procedural Review by the ECHR: View from the Court' in Brems and Gerards (eds) *Procedural Review in European Fundamental Rights Cases* (2017), 161 (167).

rights review in the first place, and how can one appropriately evaluate the TPR in light of that importance?

Since we saw above that one distinctive implication of the TPR is its impact on proportionality and balancing, the task of evaluating the TPR requires having a normative account of the proportionality in the first place. That is the methodological step that seems required before proceeding any further. The only properly normative accounts of the TPR emphasise democratic legitimacy and subsidiarity. Judge Robert Spano for instance has referred to the TPR as a 'qualitative, democracy enhancing approach' that essentially reformulates the principle of subsidiarity.[24] Kleinlein writes that 'the current reformulation or refinement of the principle of subsidiarity has the potential both to enhance the democratic legitimacy of the Court's rulings and to stimulate domestic democracy.'[25] In that sense, the TPR does not amount to 'a retreat or deterioration of international human rights as fundamental values or a decline of the rule of law.'[26] What characterises these accounts is their empirical character – namely, that the TPR could (or could not) generate more democratic outcomes domestically. In my view, this further indicates the gap in the analysis, namely that it begs the question whether proportionality (or the absence thereof) makes any difference to our evaluation of the TPR.

In what follows, I argue that the TPR amounts to a deterioration of the right to justification, which I take to be foundational to the very idea of human rights and that operates in the proportionality test specifically. This argument is based on two premises also developed in the next section. First, that proportionality (and balancing in particular) crystallises a paradigmatic shift in constitutional and human rights law, namely the shift from *authority* to *justification*. Second, that the right to justification constitutes an essential normative foundation of human rights. These two premises lead to the conclusion that marginalising balancing and proportionality through TPR amounts to eroding the normative core of human rights and entrenches a culture of presumption. It could be that the TPR may enhance justification domestically but that remains an empirical question, not a conceptual one.

24 Spano, 'Universality or Diversity of Human Rights? Strasbourg in the Age of Subsidiarity' (2014) 14:3 *Hum. Rights Law Rev.*, 487 (499).

25 Kleinlein, 'The Procedural Approach of the European Court of Human Rights: Between Subsidiarity and Dynamic Evolution' (2019), 68:1 *ICLQ*, 91 (110).

26 Kleinlein, 'The Procedural Approach of the European Court of Human Rights: Between Subsidiarity and Dynamic Evolution' (2019), 68:1 *ICLQ*, 91 (110).

C. The TPR, Proportionality and Justification

I. Authority and Justification

The first premise to my argument delves into historical and conceptual developments as to the proper role of constitutional and human rights review. In their book *Proportionality and Constitutional Culture*, Cohen-Elyia and Porat conceptualise the prominent rise of proportionality as indicating a turn from a 'culture of authority' to a 'culture of justification.' While the authors do mention the ECHR and the margin of appreciation several times (in particular, in reference to the margin of appreciation as reflecting the 'inherent flexibility' of proportionality),[27] they do not address the Court's concept of proportionality, its established practice or the recently developed TPR. Yet, I believe that their conceptual apparatus, and specifically the turn from authority to justification can help us assess the normative significance of the TPR, provided that we re-adjust the variables of the equation.

In a nutshell, authority and justification are two competing accounts of what confers legal decisions legitimacy. Both authority and justification have similar evaluative functions although their evaluative basis is distinct. On the one hand, a culture of authority 'is based on the government's authority to exercise powers.'[28] This already indicates that a culture of authority is concerned with whether the authority taking the decision is the appropriate one and less with the substantive merits. In analysing the culture of authority in the US context, Cohen-Elyia and Porat further explain that, assuming no violation of constitutional rights, 'a court will respect the autonomy of the authorised institution and bow to its special expertise when it identifies areas that are within the scope of the institution's exclusive authority.'[29] This goes to the core of the authors' account of legitimacy: 'the legitimacy and legality of a given action is derived from the fact that the actor is authorised to act.'[30]

---

27 Cohen-Eliya and Porat, *Proportionality and Constitutional Culture* (2013), 104. See also Möller, 'Justifying the Culture of Justification' (2019) 17:4 *Int. J. Const. Law*, 1078, and Kumm, 'The Idea of Socratic Contestation and the Right to Justification: The Point of Rights-Based Proportionality Review' (2010), 4:2 *Law & Ethics of Human Rights*, 142.

28 Cohen-Eliya and Porat, *Proportionality and Constitutional Culture* (2013), 110.

29 *Id.*, 114.

30 *Id.*, 110.

This seems to echo the jurisdictional considerations addressed earlier quite well – in particular, the organising notion of subsidiarity: when the Court asserts that domestic authorities are 'better placed' qua democratic entities to address the key phase of the proportionality test, namely balancing, it is expressing the view that only the domestic authority is appropriately place (normatively speaking). Indeed, it is well established that the balancing cannot be confined to a factual examination. Judges 'measure not only the extent of harm to each value but also make (at least implicitly) judgments regarding the relative importance of each to the conflicting values.'[31] Hence, the TPR, like the application of the margin of appreciation, cannot be grounded solely in epistemic reasons. The Court itself has admitted that democratic legitimacy has normative and decisive value when it comes to balancing. As we have seen, the Court held in *S.A.S. v. France* that national authorities benefit from 'direct democratic legitimation' in adjudicating contentious ethical questions.

Therefore, if one applies the notion of the culture of authority to the TPR, the argument would be that domestic authorities are the only authorised to make the decision – and to balance competing values and interests – because these decisions benefit from the verdict of democratic procedures. In other words, the TPR reflects an account of democratic legitimacy that is exclusively domestic and procedural. The implication of that account is the marginalisation – if not the complete exclusion – of proportionality *qua* balancing. Surely, it could be that the TPR reinforces the likelihood that the ultimate decision will be optimally democratic. But that is, again, a presumption. And we should recall that the TPR, as I understand it, is only one form of authority – another being the authority of the legal text or the authority of the methods of interpreting the text. In both cases, however, Cohen-Elyia and Porat conclude that 'balancing remains antithetical and, accordingly, marginalised in the culture of authority.'[32]

At this point it is worth zooming in further and examining which concept of democracy is underlying the Court's approach when it operates the TPR. In particular, it is worth asking why the exclusion of balancing is implicitly taken as potentially interfering with democracy. Surely, only a strongly procedural and majoritarian notion of democracy can explain why the Court reviewing domestic processes is defined as an interference: the outcome of the process is taken as a verdict of legitimate authority.

31 *Id.*, 109.
32 *Id.*, 119.

This is precisely where the boundary between authority and justification lies: authority is insensitive to the substantive reasons that ultimately justifies a domestic balancing conflicting rights and interests. It is presumed that the task of justification is and ought to be reserved to the domestic process, and the TPR will only require that the Court reviews domestic processes leading to the decision but not the decisive reasons that struck the balance. Justification, we shall see next, rather suggests that authority alone is never enough for normative legitimacy. The fact that only a domestic authority is endowed with procedural(-democratic) credentials is not enough for its verdict to be automatically legitimate to its subjects – whether that applies to the applicant to a particular case or, in fact, to every individual constructed as free and equal.

II. From proportionality to justification…

The upshot so far is that a culture of justification aims to confer normative legitimacy to norms and decisions. A culture of justification 'derives from the court's role and from the idea that government action is not legitimate when it is not justified.'[33] Yet, while correctly highlighting the paradigmatic shift from authority to justification that proportionality signals, Cohen-Elyia and Porat do not define the normative criteria of justification in great length and how exactly justification operates in the balancing phase of proportionality. This is where I suggest operating a disciplinary turn and delve into the independent and properly moral notion of (the right to) justification as it has been developed in human rights theory in recent years. I believe that this excursus can help measure the deficit that the TPR implies: the right to justification remedies the deficit of an independent variable for evaluating the loss.

Before doing that, it is important to explain in what sense could the Court's practice of the proportionality test be understood as an exercise of justification at all. If one looks at the structure and wording of the Court's test, one may depict it as an exercise of *ad hoc* assessment of the reasons for interfering with one or several rights of the Convention. For example, one may find an instance of justification when the Court assesses the 'legitimate aim' of the interference (after having established its legality through the 'prescribed by law' step). Yet, as the literature has shown, the Court treats this second step as an exercise of classification rather than justifica-

---

33 *Ibid.*

tion – and, as a result, only rarely finds an interference at this particular stage.[34] One may therefore expect that the last step of the test, the one of balancing, implies some justificatory reasoning properly speaking. This is where the Court enjoys a wider discretion for scrutinising the reasons that the respondent state had for interfering with one or several rights of the Convention – after having found a *prima facie* violation through its established interpretive principles with respect to a particular to article of the Convention.

Yet, if turning to the reasons for states to interfere with rights might seem facially justified, one may still wonder if the Court necessarily engages in justificatory reasoning when it conducts proportionality analysis and balancing. Indeed, this would require the Court to have an independent definition for determining when an interference is 'excessively burdensome,' as the Court puts it, or that 'it responded to a pressing social need' and was 'necessary in a democratic society.' This particular wording of the balancing phase of the test (found in the text of the Convention under Articles 8–11) suggests that there is indeed a tipping point beyond which an interference is not justifiable and, correlatively, that the Court has a metric for identifying this point. The same applies when the Court grants a margin of appreciation – it often says that the state 'did not exceed its margin of appreciation' without necessarily explaining where the tipping point is exactly located. Yet, nothing in this approach is necessarily based on a culture of justification – rather, it amounts to reintroducing authority by presuming that such an independent basis is or could be derived from the text of the Convention or ultimately from a method of adjudication (e.g. 'evolutive and dynamic', 'autonomous concepts,', 'practical and effective'). Relying on a (self-created) method of interpretation only seems to add to the justificatory burden of what, ultimately, makes this or that method justifiable and applicable in a particular case. One method that receives far less emphasis, as commented by Möller, is interpretation: 'rather than applying a conventional set of interpretative methods to the constitutional text, courts tend to read constitutions in a way that requires or allows them to focus on the substantive justifiability of the act in question.'[35]

34 Gerards and Senden, 'The Structure of Fundamental Rights and the European Court of Human Rights' (2009) 7:4 *Int. J. Const. Law*, 619.

35 Möller, 'Justifying the Culture of Justification' (2019) 17:4 *Int. J. Const. Law*, 1078 (1084).

What this makes clear is that one cannot define the Court's proportionality test as justificatory without an independent notion of justification. The very idea of justification inheres in our status of human beings as having the distinctive capacity to form, to reflect upon, to assess, to respond to and to act upon reasons. I shall build upon this properly philosophical and ontological account to explain how it can justify and structure the proportionality test and balancing. Most famously, Forst has advanced the notion regarding our status as agents of justification as 'a basic concept of practical reason and as a practice of moral and political autonomy – as a practice that implies the moral right to justification and that grounds human rights on that basis.'[36] As such, respecting the right to justification of an individual requires that she is not subjected to norms, practices and institutions that cannot be justified to her. This deontological account has an important *generality* and *reciprocity* dimension in that the justification must be mutual – 'no one may make a normative claim (such as a rights claim) he or she denies to others [...].'[37] Forst further explains that human rights law plays a crucial role in making this overarching moral right effective: 'the legal and political function of human rights is to make this right effective, both substantively and procedurally.[38]'

How could one observe the right to justification operating in the review structure of the Court? This is where the TPR and proportionality qua procedures become highly relevant as they generally are portrayed as performing justificatory functions in the Court's decisions, as we have seen above. As we have also seen, however, the TPR places the justificatory burden upon the democratic process of state parties but without evaluating the ultimate reasons offered by the domestic authorities, hence a deficit of justification. Further, a majoritarian approach to the democratic process cannot simply be presumed to have respected the right to justification of its subjects. Proportionality constitutes the guarantee that the right is respected at the procedural level: courts will filter the reasons that may indeed justify interfering with rights even if the interfering norm benefits from democratic legitimacy. In other words, the independent notion of justification put forward here is grounded in an ontological account of human beings andits normative implications reach both the substantive and procedural dimensions of human rights law.

36 Forst, 'The Justification of Human Rights and the Basic Right to Justification: A Reflexive Approach' (2010) 120:4 *Ethics*, 711 (712).
37 *Id.*, 711 (719).
38 *Ibid.*

III. And back...

How could proportionality more precisely operate a justificatory function in the sense presented above? Proportionality embodies the procedural dimension of the right to justification. Beyond the substantive list of rights that cannot be justifiably denied to free and equal individuals, the proportionality test further aims to offer individuals justifiable reasons for the norms and decisions to which they are subjected. This step is crucial to the claim that the TPR, by marginalising proportionality and balancing, amounts to a deterioration of the right to justification. Kumm suggests that proportionality should be viewed as part of the very normative point of human rights, which is defined around a liberal account of freedom and equality: 'a conception of law and politics as justice-seeking among free and equals.'[39] Unlike conceptions of human rights that define these rights as a distinctive subset of moral rights[40], here, the normative basis of human rights is confined to an ethically thin notion of freedom and equality of moral status. This status is not only expressed in the substantive list of rights that one commonly finds in conventions, treaties, bills and constitutions. It is also expressed in the procedural practices of adjudicating these rights.

On the one hand, the right to justification is expressed in the individual being conferred the right to challenge norms and decisions in court through judicial review. As stated by Kumm, 'human rights norms empower rights-holders to challenge existing power relationships by insisting that those relationships be susceptible to *justification in terms of public reason*' (emphasis added).[41] Kumm goes further to say that, 'the structure of human rights adjudication is geared towards establishing whether or not a particular legal norm burdening an individual can be demonstrably justified to that individual under this standard.'[42] This account builds upon some characteristic features of human rights lists around the world, such that the scope of legally enshrined rights not being limited to a particularly basic domain, or such that rights may be limited by restriction clauses (e.g. national security, public health, the impartiality of the judiciary, etc.)

---

39 Kumm, 'The Turn to Justification: On the Structure and Domain of Human Rights Practice' in Etinson (ed), *Human Rights: Moral or Political?* (2018), 57.

40 See for instance Griffin, *On Human Rights* (2008), chapter 1.

41 Kumm, 'Is the Structure of Human Rights Practice Defensible? Three Puzzles and Their Resolution' in Tushnet and Jackson (eds), *Proportionality: New Frontiers, New Challenges* (2017), 30 (65).

42 *Ibid.*

The restriction clauses (e.g., in Articles 8–11 ECHR) come to the fore precisely in the proportionality test where the Court turns to the arguments given by the respondent state, which regularly claim the interference with of a right remained within the broad parameter of the clause. Those restriction clauses are in principle problematic as they have an open-ended character – and that is where the Court needs to deploy a higher degree of justificatory reasoning in balancing competing rights and interests. In the Court's case law, this higher degree is seen in the quite lengthy paragraphs, usually located towards the end of a judgment, where the Court examines whether the interference was 'necessary in a democratic society' and responded to 'a pressing social need'. As we have seen, however, the Court often falls back onto one variant of authority – typically, through the margin of appreciation or by simply relying on the TPR to reach a conclusive decision. Yet, the more it relies on authority at this particular stage, the less it engages with the right to justification of individuals.

At this crucial stage, Kumm believes that the right to justification explains the crucial role of the proportionality test in ruling out reasons that cannot be justified to free and equal individuals. Kumm targets what he calls 'political pathologies' – for instance, when religious justifications are used for treating homosexuality as a sin. The reason offered cannot pass the following test: 'this type of reason, a reason relating to what it means to live a good, authentic life, might not generally count as legitimate reasons to restrict someone's right.'[43] Rather, it constitutes a comprehensive moral view that amounts to exercising arbitrary power over individuals, and as such is not legitimate. The deontological basis of the right to justification is therefore at odds with any ethically comprehensive, perfectionist, or consequentialist account of the good. For example, when the Court in *S.A.S. v. France* asserted that 'in matters of general policy, on which opinions within a democratic society may reasonably differ widely, the role of the domestic policy-maker should be given special weight'[44] and subsequently granted the respondent state a margin of appreciation, the Court did not assess whether the ban on the veil amounted to a particular comprehensive

43 Kumm, 'The Idea of Socratic Contestation and the Right to Justification: The Point of Rights-Based Proportionality Review' (2010), 4:2 *Law & Ethics of Human Rights*, 142 (159).

44 ECtHR, Judgment (GC), 1 July 2014, *S.A.S. v France*, Application No. 43835/11, para. 154.

idea of 'living together'[45]. In that sense, the TPR runs the risk of lowering the bar of justification.

D. Conclusion

This article was a first step in the project of offering a normative analysis of the TPR. The premise to this project was that the recent contributions to this topic very helpfully illustrate, categorise and analyse the TPR in the Court's case law but fall short of evaluating this judicial evolution in normative terms. How should one place this evolution in a broader understanding of the purpose of human rights review, on the subsidiary role of the Court and ultimately on the very idea of human rights? I have argued that the TPR points to worrying implications in terms of the justificatory function that human rights review in general and proportionality analysis play. The intermediate step here has been to explain how proportionality operates a justificatory function – a point that the literature in constitutional and human rights theory has recently developed, but which so far has not been utilized in the context of the TPR. I have connected these two strands of the literature through one distinctive implication of the TPR, which is the retreat from the balancing phase of proportionality and the increased weight put on the domestic procedure in informing the merits of a case. One may claim that the emphasis put on the domestic procedure in fact strengthens the right to justification domestically, but when this emphasis amounts to marginalising the Court's own review of proportionality, the TPR implies a presumption rather than a justification.

Bibliography

Arnardóttir, Oddný Mjöll: The 'Procedural Turn' under the European Convention on Human Rights and Presumptions of Convention Compliance, Int. J. Const. Law 2017, 9ff.

Brems, Eva: Procedural Protection: An Examination of Procedural Safeguards Read into Substantive Convention Rights, in: Brems, Eva/Gerards, Janneke (eds), Shaping Rights in the ECHR: The Role of the European Court of Human Rights in Determining the Scope of Human Rights (2014), 137ff.

Cohen-Eliya, Moshe/Porat, Iddo: Proportionality and Constitutional Culture (2013).

45 *Id.*, para. 82.

Forst, Rainer: The Justification of Human Rights and the Basic Right to Justification: A Reflexive Approach, Ethics 2010, 711ff.

Gerards, Janneke: Procedural Review by the ECtHR: A Typology, in: Brems, Eva/ Gerards, Janneke (eds), Procedural Review in European Fundamental Rights Cases (2017), 127ff.

Gerads, Janneke: The Prism of Fundamental Rights, Eur. Const. Law Rev. 2012, 173ff.

Gerards, Janneke/Senden, Hanneke: The Structure of Fundamental Rights and the European Court of Human Rights, Int. J. Const. Law 2009, 619ff.

Griffin, James: On Human Rights (2008).

Kleinlein, Thomas: The Procedural Approach of the European Court of Human Rights: Between Subsidiarity and Dynamic Evolution, ICLQ 2019, 91ff.

Kumm, Mattias: Is the Structure of Human Rights Practice Defensible? Three Puzzles and Their Resolution, in: Jackson, Vicki C./Tushnet Mark (eds), Proportionality: New Frontiers, New Challenges (2017), 30ff.

Kumm, Mattias: The Idea of Socratic Contestation and the Right to Justification: The Point of Rights-Based Proportionality Review, Law & Ethics of Human Rights 2010, 142ff.

Kumm, Mattias: The Turn to Justification: On the Structure and Domain of Human Rights Practice, in: Etinson, Adam (ed), Human Rights: Moral or Political? (2018), 57ff.

Kumm, Mattias: Letsas, George: Two Concepts of the Margin of Appreciation, Oxf. J Leg. Stud. 2006, 705ff.

Möller, Kai: Justifying the Culture of Justification, Int. J. Const. Law 2019, 1078ff.

Nussberger, Angelika: Procedural Review by the ECHR: View from the Court, in: Brems, Eva/Gerards, Janneke (eds), Procedural Review in European Fundamental Rights Cases (2017), 161ff.

Spano, Robert: Universality or Diversity of Human Rights? Strasbourg in the Age of Subsidiarity, Hum. Rights Law Rev. 2014, 487ff.

Zysset, Alain: Freedom of expression, the right to vote, and proportionality at the European Court of Human Rights: an internal critique, Int. J. Const. Law 2019, 230ff.

C. Human Rights and National Legal Orders

Judicial and Prosecutorial Independence in Europe: How Politicized Judges and Prosecutors Undermine the Right to a Fair Trial in Eastern Europe and Central Asia

Stefanie Lemke

A. *Introduction*

This chapter looks at how Europe's fast-growing number of politicised judges and prosecutors impact the application of the European Convention on Human Rights (ECHR) and the execution of judgments of the European Court of Human Rights (ECtHR) in Council of Europe (Coe) member countries, particularly with regard to Article 6 of ECHR (right to a fair trial). In 2013, the UN Special Rapporteur on the Situation of Human Rights Defenders warned that governments increasingly abuse the judicial system to criminalize and stigmatize activists for their human rights work.[1] In regard to Europe, there are more and more governments that are vested with far-reaching competences and use their powers to undermine the judicial process. This is especially visible in political sensitive cases where domestic courts disregard the ECHR and the jurisprudence of the ECtHR. Courts side with the prosecution and grant arbitrary arrests and detentions, leave lawyers little time to prepare their clients' defence, deny access to court files and refuse to hear witnesses in the defence's favour.[2] Azerbaijan, for instance, has a long history of violating the procedural rights of human rights defenders in spite of having been repeatedly reminded by the ECtHR to comply with the ECHR and the

1 UN Human Rights Council, *Report of the Special Rapporteur on the situation of human rights defenders, Margaret Sekaggya*, 23 December 2013, UN Doc. A/HRC/25/55, para. 59.

2 Human Rights Watch, 'Crimea: Defence Lawyers Harassed, Drop Bogus Charges Against Crimean Tatars', 2017, https://www.hrw.org/news/2017/01/30/crimea-defence-lawyers-harassed; OSCE, Trial Monitoring Report, Azerbaijan, 2011, www.osce.org/baku/100593; CoE Parliamentary Assembly, *The Progress of the Assembly's Monitoring Procedure (January-December 2019)*, Resolution 2325 (2020), 30 January 2020; CoE Parliamentary Assembly, *The Functioning of Democratic Institutions in Azerbaijan*, Resolution 2062 (2015), 23 June 2015.

Court's case law.[3] Yet Azerbaijani courts found the activist *Rasul Jafarov* guilty of forgery and other offences after he had criticised the Azerbaijani government at a CoE event, without basing their actions on sufficient evidence,[4] and opted for disbarring the lawyer *Khalid Bagirov* following his remarks in a trial where Mr. Bagirov had represented an opposition politician and questioned the impartiality of Azerbaijan's judiciary.[5] Against this background, this chapter looks at the interplay between politics and courts in three CoE member countries – Azerbaijan, Russia and Ukraine – which are known for their oppression of critical voices. It provides an in-depth analysis of how governments control judicial systems and, as a result of this, judges and prosecutors ignore European human rights standards in cases involving activists and other regime critics.

B. The Role and Responsibilities of Judges and Prosecutors

Judges and prosecutors are supposed to set an example to society in the protection of human rights, meaning that their actions should respond to human rights standards. Governments, however, can exert significant influence over the judicial process if they abandon the rule of law including the separation of powers. In that case, judges and prosecutors may be less likely to hold the government responsible for its wrongdoings and deliver justice.[6] The international community has therefore developed a variety of regulations to remind judges and prosecutors of their powerful role in the judicial process and the importance to uphold human rights standards, including the right to a fair trial, in their day-to-day work.[7]

---

3 See, for example, ECtHR, Judgment, 26 October 2011, *Huseyn and others v Azerbaijan*, Application Nos. 35485/05, 45553/05, 35680/05 and 36085/05 and ECtHR, Judgment, 14 June 2013, *Insanov v Azerbaijan*, Application No. 16133/08.

4 ECtHR, Judgment, 17 March 2016, *Rasul Jafarov v Azerbaijan*, Application No. 69981/14, para. 178.

5 ECtHR, Judgment, 25 September 2020, *Bagirov v Azerbaijan*, Application No. 81024/12 and 28198/15.

6 See, for example, ECtHR, Judgment, 8 August 2006, *H.M. v Turkey*, Application No. 34494/97; ECtHR, Judgment, 22 May 2014, *Ilgar Mammadov v Azerbaijan*, Application No. 15172/13; ECtHR, Judgment, 2 February 2017, *Navalnyy v Russia*, Application No. 29580/12 and 4 more.

7 UN, *Seventh UN Congress on the Prevention of Crime and Treatment of Offenders, Milan, 26 August-6 September 1985, Basic Principles on the Independence of the Judiciary* (1986), 58, para. 6; Consultative Council of European Judges (CCJE), Magna Carta

Ideally, judges should be appointed and promoted on a basis of merit by an independent, impartial and purely judicial body (in the form of a judicial council) which is supposed to make judges less vulnerable to internal and external pressures as they possess the necessary skills to perform their role.[8] Other than that lengthy probationary periods, case-assignments, forced retirement due to age, lack of protection from salary adjustments and judicial removal procedures that are made on the basis of personal and political considerations can impact significantly a judge's impartial decision-making.[9] Generally, judges should be neutral servants of 'the law' who apply the law with integrity and free of corruption.[10] They should be the 'watchdogs of the political process' who guarantee fair proceedings.[11] The Magna Carta of Judges, for example, requires judges to

---

of Judges (Fundamental Principles), 17 November 2010, https://rm.coe.int/2010-ccje-magna-carta-anglais/168063e431, paras. 1, 16; International Association of Judges, The Universal Carter of the Judge, 14 November 2017, https://www.unodc.org/res/ji/import/international_standards/the_universal_charter_of_the_judge/universal_charter_2017_english.pdf, Article 1; International Association of Prosecutors, Standards of Professional Responsibility and Statement of the Essential Duties and Rights of Prosecutors, 23 April 1999, https://www.iap-association.org/getattachment/Resources-Documentation/IAP-Standards-(1)/English.pdf.aspx, 3(e), (f); UN, *Eighth UN Congress on the Prevention of Crime and Treatment of Offenders, Havana, 27 August-7 September 1990, Guidelines on the Role of Prosecutors* (1990), 189 para. 14.

8 CoE, *Challenges for Judicial Independence and impartiality in the Member States of the Council of Europe*, SG/Inf(2016)3rev, 24 March 2016, 4; Domingo, 'Judicial Independence and Judicial Reform in Latin America' in Schedler et al. (eds), *The Self-Restraining State: Power and Accountability in New Democracies* (1999), 151 (154); Fiss, 'The Right Degree of Independence' in Strotzky (ed), *Transition to Democracy in Latin America: The Role of the Judiciary* (1993), 55 (59); Jackson, 'Judicial Independence: Structure, Context, Attitude', in Seibert-Fohr (ed), *Judicial Independence in Transition* (2012), 19, 26, 28.

9 CoE, *Challenges for Judicial Independence and impartiality in the Member States of the Council of Europe*, SG/Inf(2016)3rev, 24 March 2016, 6; Fiss, 'The Right Degree of Independence' in Strotzky (ed), *Transition to Democracy in Latin America: The Role of the Judiciary* (1993), 55 (58 f.); Jackson, 'Judicial Independence: Structure, Context, Attitude', in Seibert-Fohr (ed), *Judicial Independence in Transition* (2012), 19 (36, 49, 53); Transparency International, *Global Corruption Report 2007* (2007), 7.

10 Shapiro and Stone Sweet, 'Law, Courts and Social Science' in Shapiro and Stone Sweet (eds), *On Law, Politics and Judicialization* (2002), 1 (3).

11 UN, *Seventh UN Congress on the Prevention of Crime and Treatment of Offenders, Milan, 26 August-6 September 1985, Basic Principles on the Independence of the Judiciary* (1986), 58, para. 6; Consultative Council of European Judges (CCJE), 'Magna Carta of Judges (Fundamental Principles)', 17 November 2010, https://rm.coe.int/2010-ccje-magna-carta-anglais/168063e431, paras. 1, 16; International Association

perform their duties without bias, respect the presumption of innocence and safeguard the equality of arms between the defence and the prosecution in criminal cases; furthermore, judges should base their decisions on the application of legal rules, through legal reasoning and findings of facts that are based on evidence and analysis, and avoid the use of contempt proceedings to restrict legitimate public criticism of the courts.[12] Judges should also ensure that suspects are represented by a lawyer. Such legal assistance should be effective and practical, meaning that lawyers should not be allowed to only be present but also to actively assist their clients: they should be given adequate time and facilities to prepare the client's defence, be able to communicate with their client in private, put forward her/his version of events and present the case under conditions that do not place their client at a disadvantage vis-à-vis their opponent.[13]

Prosecutors also have a vital role in the administration of justice by, *inter alia*, instituting prosecutions and supervising the legality of investigations.[14] The prosecution can be part of the judiciary (in civil law systems)

---

of Judges, The Universal Carter of the Judge, 14 November 2017, https://www.unodc.org/res/ji/import/international_standards/the_universal_charter_of_the_judge/universal_charter_2017_english.pdf, Article 1.

12 UN Economic and Social Council, *Strengthening basic principles of judicial conduct, Annex, Bangalore Principles of Judicial Conduct,* 27 July 2006, UN Doc. E/Res/2006/23, Values 5, 11; CCJE, 'Magna Carta of Judges (Fundamental Principles)', 17 November 2010, https://rm.coe.int/2010-ccje-magna-carta-anglais/168063e431, paras. 5, 11; Judicial Integrity Group, Measures for the Effective Implementation of the Bangalore Principles of Judicial Conduct, 21/22 January 2010, https://www.unodc.org/res/ji/import/international_standards/measures_implementation/measures_implementation.pdf, para. 9.5.

13 ECtHR, Judgment, 18 March 1997, *Foucher v France*, Application No. 22209/93, para. 34; ECtHR, Judgment (GC), 12 May 2005, *Öcalan v Turkey*, Application No. 46221/99, para. 140; ECtHR, Judgment, 15 November 2007, *Galstyan v Armenia*, Application No. 26986/03, para. 84; ECtHR, Judgment, 12 January 2012, *Iglin v Ukraine*, Application No. 39908/05, para. 65; ECtHR, Judgment (GC), 27 November 2008, *Salduz v Turkey*, Application No. 36391/02, paras. 53 f.; ECtHR, Judgment, 10 July 2012, *Gregačević v Croatia*, Application No. 58331/09, para. 51; ECtHR, Judgment (GC), 13 September 2016, *Ibrahim and Others v United Kingdom*, Application No. 50541/08 and 3 more, para. 255; ECtHR, Judgment, 26 January 2017, *Faig Mammadov v Azerbaijan*, Application No. 60802/09, para. 19.; ECtHR, Judgment, 12 May 2017, *Simeonovi v Bulgaria*, Application No. 21980/04, para. 112.

14 UN, *Eighth UN Congress on the Prevention of Crime and Treatment of Offenders, Havana, 27 August-7 September 1990, Guidelines on the Role of Prosecutors* (1990), 189 paras. 3, 11; UN Office on Drugs and Crime (UNODC), The Status and Role of Prosecutors. A UN Office on Drugs and Crime and International Association

or part of the executive (in common law systems).[15] Either way, prosecutors, like judges, owe the public a deep and abiding commitment to the rule of law, including to respect the right to a fair trial.[16] The UN Guidelines on the Role of Prosecutors, for example, note that prosecutors are to 'respect and protect human dignity and uphold human rights'.[17] Functional independence from their hierarchy and being autonomous in their decision making are crucial for prosecutors to guarantee due process and the smooth functioning of the criminal justice system.[18] Being a prosecutor therefore comes with several duties and responsibilities, such as ensuring that the police regard legal principles, a suspect is brought promptly before a judge and refusing to use evidence that was illegally obtained.[19]

In practice, however, there is a considerable divergence in how these rules are applied. In the following, this shall be illustrated by a study of judicial systems in Azerbaijan, Russia and Ukraine, where judicial authorities disregard European human rights standards in cases involving political sensitive matters.

---

of Prosecutors Guide, 2014, https://www.unodc.org/documents/justice-and-prison-reform/HB_role_and_status_prosecutors_14-05222_Ebook.pdf, 38. UN Guidelines on the role of prosecutors (1990) rule 3, 11.

15 Myjer et al. (eds), *Human Rights Manual for Prosecutors* (2008); UNODC, The Status and Role of Prosecutors. A UN Office on Drugs and Crime and International Association of Prosecutors Guide, 2014, https://www.unodc.org/documents/justice-and-prison-reform/HB_role_and_status_prosecutors_14-05222_Ebook.pdf, 16 ff.

16 International Association of Prosecutors, 'Standards of Professional Responsibility and Statement of the Essential Duties and Rights of Prosecutors', 23 April 1999, https://www.iap-association.org/getattachment/Resources-Documentation/IAP-Standards-(1)/English.pdf.aspx, 3(e), (f).

17 UN, *Eighth UN Congress on the Prevention of Crime and Treatment of Offenders, Havana, 27 August-7 September 1990, Guidelines on the Role of Prosecutors* (1990), 189, para. 14.

18 *Ibid.*

19 Consultative Council of European Prosecutors, Opinion No.9 (2014). European norms and principles concerning prosecutors, 17 December 2014, https://rm.coe.int/168074738b, para. 24; Convention against Torture and Other Cruel, Inhuman or Degrading Treatment or Punishment; UN, *Eighth UN Congress on the Prevention of Crime and Treatment of Offenders, Havana, 27 August-7 September 1990, Guidelines on the Role of Prosecutors* (1990), 189 paras. 12, 14, 16; UNODC, 'The Status and Role of Prosecutors. A UN Office on Drugs and Crime and International Association of Prosecutors Guide', 2014, https://www.unodc.org/documents/justice-and-prison-reform/HB_role_and_status_prosecutors_14-05222_Ebook.pdf, 38.

C. Country Studies

I. Azerbaijan

In theory, suspects enjoy a range of basic procedural rights pursuant to Article 91 of Azerbaijan's Criminal Procedure Code. This includes: the right to sufficient time to prepare their defence, to request law enforcement bodies to give access to court files and make copies of them, to make a statement on the accuracy and completeness of written records, and to request the inclusion of relevant 'circumstances' to such records. In practice, however, Azerbaijan's judiciary is heavily used as a tool to penalize human rights defenders.[20] The separation of powers is non-existent, with the judiciary being controlled by the Aliyev family since 1993. After Ilham Aliyev had succeeded his father as president in 2003, he was re-elected for his fourth term in office in 2018 amid evidence of electoral fraud.[21] The Azerbaijani constitution gives the president broad authority over the judicial system and parliament, leading to a judiciary that is totally subservient to the executive branch. The constitution allows the president to nominate the candidates for judicial office in the higher courts, including the constitutional court and the supreme court.[22] Although consent of the legislator is needed for their appointment, it is likely that the nominees will be approved by parliament as it mainly consists of pro-government parties. The latest (snap) elections were held in 2020, with the OSCE questioning 'whether the [election] results were established honestly'.[23] Additionally, the president is authorised to appoint all chief justices and the prosecutor general, without the approval of parliament.[24] The president can also veto appointments of the prosecutor general and oversees the selection process

---

20 See, for example, Amnesty International, *Amnesty International Report 2017/18. The State of the World's Human Rights* (2018), 83.

21 OSCE: 'Azerbaijan Election Lacked Genuine Competition in an Environment of Curtailed Rights and Freedoms, International Observers Say', 12 April 2018, http://www.osce.org/odihr/elections/azerbaijan/377623.

22 Article 130(2) of the The Constitution of the Republic of Azerbaijan, 2020, https://en.president.az/azerbaijan/constitution.

23 Freedom House, *Freedom in the World 2020* (2021); OSCE: 'Despite Large Number of Candidates, Azerbaijan Elections Lacked Genuine Competition and Choice, International Observers Say', 10 February 2020, https://www.osce.org/odihr/elections/azerbaijan/445762.

24 Azerbaijani Constitution Article 133(4).

of lower court judges.[25] The latter are nominated by the Legal Judicial Council but their appointment must be approved by the president.[26] The Legal Judicial Council is a self-governing body with strong links to the government, over which the minister of justice has presided since its creation in 2005. Besides, nine out of the judicial council's 15 members are judges appointed by the president, two of its members are selected jointly by the president and parliament, and two members are chosen by the prosecutor's general office and the board of the national bar association, respectively.[27] The judiciary is further controlled by a lengthy, three-year probationary period for judicial candidates, encouraging them to align their viewpoints with their hierarchy to secure reappointment.[28]

Azerbaijani judges and prosecutors constantly violate the concept of equality of arms. The Committee against Torture found that Azerbaijan's government abuses its authority and uses judicial authorities to violate rule of law obligations.[29] It is common practice that human rights defenders are arbitrarily deprived of their liberty and subjected to ill-treatment to silence them for their professional activities.[30] Among those human rights defenders who have suffered ill-treatment are Emin Husyenov Intigam, Ali Aliyev, Rasul Jafarov, Rashad Hassanov, Panah Chodar oglu Huseyn, and Leyla Yunusova. Courts impose travel bans on human rights activists to stop them from leaving Azerbaijan. The journalist Emin Husyenov, for example, was prevented from travelling to Istanbul by border guards at Baku International Airport.[31] In another case, in *Aliyev v. Azerbaijan*, the

25 Article 93(1) of the 1997 Courts and Judges Act of the Republic of Azerbaijan, 2006, https://www.legislationline.org/download/id/3843/file/Azerbaijan_Courts_Judges_Act_1997_am_2006_en.pdf; Article 1, 4(1) of the Judicial-Legal Council Act of the Republic of Azerbaijan, 2014, https://www.legislationline.org/download/id/8619/file/Azerbaijan_law_judicial_legal%20council_2004_am2014_en.pdf.

26 *Ibid.*

27 CoE Directorate General Human Rights and Rule of Law, *Eastern Partnership. Enhancing Judicial Reform in the Eastern Partnership Countries. Efficient Judicial Systems Report 2014*, 2014, https://rm.coe.int/eastern-partnership-enhancing-judicial-reform-in-the-eastern-partnersh/1680788f3e.

28 Amendment to the Azerbaijani Courts and Judges Act, adopted on 11 February 2015. See also, for example, ECtHR, Judgment, 30 November 2010, *Henryk Urban and Ryszard Urban v Poland*, Application No. 23614/08, para. 53.

29 UN Committee against Torture (UN CAT), *Concluding observations on the fourth periodic report of Azerbaijan*, 27 January 2016, UN Doc. CAT/C/AZE/CO/4, 3.

30 *Ibid.*

31 CoE Commissioner for Human Rights, *Concerns over the situation of human rights defenders in Azerbaijan*, 7 August 2014, https://www.coe.int/en/web/commissioner/-/concerns-over-the-situation-of-human-rights-defenders-in-azerbaijan.

lawyer Ali Aliyev, a vocal government critic and head of the NGO 'Legal Education Society', was detained and convicted by the authorities for his human rights work.[32] In 2014, his NGO, which had compiled a list of political prisoners in Azerbaijan, helped victims of politically motivated convictions and represented them at the ECtHR, was raided and subsequently closed amid a crackdown on dissident voices in Azerbaijan.[33] Mr. Aliyev was then summoned to the prosecutor general's office as a witness in a criminal case against various local NGOs and questioned about his background, his family and his human rights activities.[34] Following his interview with the prosecutor's general office, Mr. Aliyev was detained on the suspicion of embezzlement, forgery and tax evasion, which the local district court justified by the seriousness of the charges against Mr. Aliyev and prevented him from leaving Azerbaijan.[35] He appealed against this decision and the search of his NGO's office unsuccessfully. In this context, the ECtHR observed various similarities of Mr. Aliyev's case to the case of Rasul Jafarov, another human rights defender against whom charges of embezzlement, forgery and tax evasion were pressed by Azerbaijani courts.[36] In the case of Mr. Jafarov, the ECtHR condemned Azerbaijani courts for limiting their role to the automatic endorsement of the prosecution's applications. The ECtHR found that the local courts failed to verify the existence of any suspicion against Mr. Jafarov: there was no evidence showing that Mr. Jafarov had engaged in the criminal activities of which he was accused.[37] Likewise, the ECtHR criticised the prosecution's decision to bring charges against Rashad Hasanov and other members of the NGO NIDA without any evidence to support its accusations.[38] Mr. Hasanov and his colleagues were unlawfully accused of having obtained Molotov cocktails and storing them in their flats after they had organised and participated in peaceful anti-government protests in Baku, which led to their detention. Despite the lack of a reasonable suspicion against them, judges ordered and extended their pre-trial detention, having agreed to the

32 ECtHR, Judgment, 20 September 2018, *Aliyev v Azerbaijan*, Application Nos. 68762/14 and 71200/14, paras. 213 ff.

33 *Id.* para. 23.

34 *Id.* para. 10.

35 *Id.* paras. 22, 24.

36 *Id.* paras 207, 214.

37 ECtHR, Judgment, 17 March 2016, *Rasul Jafarov v Azerbaijan*, Application No. 69981/14, paras. 128 ff., 143 f.

38 ECtHR, Judgment, 7 June 2018, *Rashad Hasanov and Others v Azerbaijan*, Application No. 48653/13 and 3 more, para. 105.

prosecution's requests to remand them in custody.[39] In *Huseyn and Others v. Azerbaijan*, Mr. Huseyn's lawyers were not given 'sufficient access to the prosecution's evidence after the pre-trial investigation had been completed and before the trial had commenced nor had they enjoyed such access after the trial had commenced, despite their repeated complaints to that effect'.[40] The ECtHR noted that restricting access to court documents gives rise to 'serious problems' as to the adequacy of the time and facilities afforded to the defence within the Azerbaijani criminal justice system, emphasising that the defence must be given the opportunity to have knowledge of and comment on the observations filed and the evidence adduced by the prosecution.[41] In the case of the civil society activist Leyla Yunusova, disciplinary proceedings were instituted against her lawyer, Mr. Bagirov, by the Azerbaijani Bar Association of which Mr. Bagirov was a member.[42] Prior to this, Mr. Bagirov's requests for a copy of the administrative decision depriving his client of her right to make phone calls and denying a list of prescribed medication to Ms. Yunusova, who suffers from chronic hepatitis, had remained unanswered by the authorities.[43] Being suspended from practicing, Mr. Bagirov was then banned from meeting with Ms. Yunusova who was held in detention at that time.[44] Lastly, in *Insanov v. Azerbaijan*, the ECtHR found a violation of the rights of the defence, particularly the right to effective legal assistance.[45] After being questioned by the police, the former health minister Ali Insanov was detained on suspicion of numerous acts of embezzlement of public property, abuse of official authority and complicity in an attempted *coup d'état*, allegedly being planned to take place after the parliamentary elections in 2005. Mr. Insanov's home was searched where the police found large amounts of cash in various currencies, large quantities of gold items and jewellery, and deeds of various residential properties. At pre-trial stage, Mr. Insanov's lawyers had only restricted access to their client and his court

39 *Id.* paras. 105, 107.

40 ECtHR, Judgment, 26 July 2011, *Huseyn and Others v Azerbaijan*, Application No. 35485/05 and 3 more, para. 175.

41 *Id.* para 175.

42 ECtHR, Judgment, 16 July 2020, *Yunosova and Yunosov v Azerbaijan (No. 2)*, Application No. 68817/14, para. 73.

43 ECtHR, Judgment, 2 June 2016, *Yunosova and Yunosov v Azerbaijan*, Application No. 59620/14, paras. 42 f.

44 ECtHR, Judgment, 16 July 2020, *Yunosova and Yunosov v Azerbaijan (No. 2)*, Application No. 68817/14, para. 73.

45 ECtHR, Judgment, 14 March 2013, *Insanov v Azerbaijan*, Application No. 16133/08, paras. 165 ff.

file. They were not allowed to familiarise themselves with Mr. Insanov's exceptionally voluminous case file prior to the commencement of the trial, which would have required examination and assessment of an immense amount of documentary evidence, witness statements and other material.[46] Besides, his lawyers were not allowed to examine witnesses, see their client on weekends or confer with him in a confidential setting for a reasonably lengthy period of time during the court sessions, which took place without breaks and lasted full days.[47] This forced Mr. Insanov's lawyers to discuss requests and submissions at the court hearings themselves where they spoke through the bars of the metal cage to their client – in the presence of the judge, the prosecution, the audience and other trial participants.[48] Later, the ECtHR held that, in a democratic society, the right to consult with a lawyer is a basic requirement of a fair trial, which the Azerbaijani courts failed to guarantee in the case of Mr. Insanov.[49]

II. Russia

Russia's criminal justice system suffers from a selective approach to justice and severe levels of corruption, being ranked 101st out of 128 countries and thus as one of the most corrupt countries worldwide.[50] Judges and prosecutors, like their Azerbaijani counterparts, ignore constitutional guarantees such as the equality of arms, breaching systematically the procedural rights of anti-government voices. Institutions to safeguard the legal order are absent in Russia which is mainly due to the prosecution's broad authority.[51] Russia's General Prosecutor, unlike his Western European counterparts, is vested with a general supervisory function that endows him with extremely far-reaching rights. The General Prosecutor is tasked with monitoring the implementation of legal acts including anti-extremism legislation and oversees the compliance of authorities and private enti-

46 *Id.* para. 166.
47 *Id.* paras. 161, 167.
48 *Id.* para. 168.
49 *Id.* para. 165.
50 Freedom House, *Freedom in the World 2019* (2020); World Justice Project, *The World Justice Project Rule of Law Index 2019* (2019).
51 European Commission for Democracy through Law (Venice Commission), *Opinion on the Federal Law on the Prokuratura (Prosecutor's Office) of the Russian Federation*, 13 June 2015, CDL-AD(2005)014, 12; Venice Commission, *Compilation of Venice Commission Reports Concerning Prosecutors*, 11 November 2017, CDL-PI(2018)001, 11.

ties (e.g., local authorities, military officials, NGOs, etc.) with European and international human rights standards. He is also allowed to enter the premises of these authorities and organisations and access their documents and materials to perform his tasks, without the need to justify his actions on reasonable and objective grounds.[52] His requests are subject to 'unconditional execution', meaning that his actions have binding effect.[53] Given that 'such broadly defined general supervisory function was a logical component of the [former Soviet] system of unity of power and resulted from that system's lack of administrative and constitutional courts and the institution of an ombudsman', the Venice Commission recommended Russia in its 2005 report to limit the prosecution's influence.[54] It also pointed out that, in a democratic, law-governed state, the protection of the rule of law should be 'the task of independent courts'.[55] In 2013, the General Prosecutor, however, launched a nationwide campaign of unannounced inspections of human rights groups, which resulted in about 1,000 NGOs being searched by lower rank prosecutors and officials of the ministry of justice, the federal tax authority and other government agencies.[56] Later, a report published by the 'Closed Society' showed that the inspections targeted particularly organisations that cover political sensitive topics and receive foreign funding, such as Russian NGOs and national chapters of foreign human rights groups including Amnesty International and Human Rights Watch.[57]

Well documented is also the gross misconduct of judges who side with prosecutors in trials against human rights defenders and other critics.[58] In general, the right to a fair trial is one of Russia's most frequently violated rights, with a striking number of cases originating from the North

---

52 Article 1(1) of the Federal Law No. 2202-I of January 17, 1992 on the Prosecutor's Office of the Russian Federation, 2007, https://www.wto.org/english/thewto_e/acc_e/rus_e/WTACCRUS58_LEG_83.pdf.

53 Articles 6, 21, 22 of the Federal Law on the Prosecutor's Office.

54 Venice Commission, *Opinion on the Federal Law on the Prokuratura (Prosecutor's Office) of the Russian Federation*, 13 June 2015, CDL-AD(2005)014, 12.

55 *Ibid.*

56 Human Rights Watch, *Laws of Attrition* (2013); The Prosecutor General's Office of the Russian Federation, Report. Order of 27 December 2012, N° 27–07–2012/14п1861–12в, 2012, http://genproc.gov.ru/smi/interview_and_appearences/appearences/83568/.

57 Closed Society (2015).

58 Amnesty International, *Unfair Game* (2019).

Caucasus.[59] There is, for example, a high number of pre-trial detentions of activists, which were requested by the prosecution and were almost automatically granted by the courts.[60] The UNHCR also observed a low acquittal rate and a high percentage of acquittals overturned on appeal in cases concerning political sensitive matters.[61] For instance, the environmental activists Suren Gazaryan and Evgeny Vitishko of the NGO 'Environmental Watch on North Caucasus' were sentenced to three years in prison for protesting against a fence in the run-up of the Sochi Olympics. The fence had been illegally constructed in a forest and surrounded the residence of the then governor of the Krasnodar region and later federal minister of agriculture Aleksandr Tkachov on which they spray-painted 'This is our forest'.[62] Ms Gazaryan and Mr. Vitishko were subsequently charged with damage to property and their defence ignored. Judges dismissed the argument by their lawyer that the fence had been constructed illegally as not relevant to the case and the prosecution denied even the very existence of the fence in response to a complaint filed by the accused.[63] In another case, Valentina Cherevatenko, the chair of the NGO 'Women of the Don and laureate of the 2016 Franco-German Prize for Human Rights', was convicted for allegedly failing to register as a 'foreign agent' in the then new 'Foreign Agents' Register'. According to the Law on Amendments to Legislative Acts of the Russian Federation regarding the Regulation of the Activities of Non-profit Organisations Performing the Functions of a Foreign Agent (Foreign Agents' Act)[64], any organisation receiving a certain amount of foreign funding and being engaged in 'political activities' is

59 CoE Department for the Execution of Judgments of the European Court of Human Rights, *Country Factsheet. Russian Federation*, 2020, https://rm.coe.int/russian-factsheet/1680764748; Human Rights Watch, Human Rights Violations in Russia's North Caucasus (2016).

60 See, for example, ECtHR, Judgment, 17 July 2014, *Svinarenko and Slyadnev v Russia*, Application Nos. 32541/08 and 43441/08; ECtHR, Judgment, 31 January 2017, *Vorontsov and Others v Russia*, Application No. 59655/14.

61 UN Human Rights Committee (UN HRC), *Concluding observations on the seventh periodic report of the Russian Federation*, 28 April 2015, UN Doc. CCPR/C/RUS/CO/7.

62 Amnesty International, 'Russia: Release environmentalist banished to a prison colony', 15 April 2015, https://www.amnesty.org/en/latest/news/2015/04/russia-release-yevgeniy-vitishko/.

63 Human Rights Watch, 'Russia: Flawed Trial of Environmental Activists', 21 June 2012, http://www.hrw.org/news/2012/06/21/russia-flawed-trial-environmental-activists.

64 Federal Law No. 121-FZ of 20 July 2012, https://www.nhc.no/content/uploads/2014/08/ICNL-Unofficial-Translation-Russian-Enacted-Law.pdf.

obliged to register as a 'foreign agent' with the 'foreign agent roster'. Upon registration, the organisation will be labelled as 'foreign agent' and must display the 'foreign agent label' on all its output including publications. It should be noted that the term 'foreign agent' is associated with 'spy' or 'traitor' in Russia, which may make the respective organisation less attractive to donors to secure funding.[65] In the case of Ms Cherevatenko, Russian courts, again, dismissed all arguments put forward by her lawyer and limited the judicial review of her case to the issue of its formal legality.[66] It is also common that Russian judges regard the evidence obtained by investigators as true and consistent without independent assessment. This is illustrated by the case of the human rights defender Oyub Titiev, a member of the Russian NGO 'Memorial', who was sentenced to a four-year prison term to be served in a penal colony for the possession of a bag of marijuana, which had been placed and found in his car by the police.[67] Another member of 'Memorial', Yuriy Dmitriyev, was also arrested and charged with allegedly producing child pornography by posting a photo of his underage stepdaughter on a social network.[68] He was detained and his stepdaughter taken into care. At pre-trial stage, the authorities did not include any circumstances in their assessment that could have supported the position of Mr. Dmitriyev (e.g., his low risk of escape and lack of tampering with evidence). Russian media reported that the photo of his stepdaughter had been posted without Mr. Dmitriyev's knowledge and consent. They regarded his arrest as an act of revenge against his research, where he investigated the personal details of officers of the former People's Commissariat for Internal Affairs (NKVD), which is known for its

65 Radio Free Liberty/Radio Liberty, 'How Russia Has Implemented its 'Foreign-Agent' Law', 2 November 2018, http://www.rferl.org/a/foreign-agent-law/29579390.html.

66 Amnesty International, *Attending Trials Involving Human Rights Defenders in Russia. A Handbook for Diplomats* (2018), https://www.amnesty.nl/content/uploads/2017/01/AI-trial-attendance-handbook-for-diplomats-Russia.pdf?x55436#; UK Foreign & Commonwealth Office: Human Rights Priority Country Update Report: January to June 2016, 2017. http://www.gov.uk/government/publications/russia-human-rights-priority-country/human-rights-priority-country-update-report-january-to-june-2016.

67 European Parliament, *European Parliament resolution of 8 February 2018 on Russia, the case of Oyub Titiev and the Human Rights Centre Memorial*, 2018/2560(RSP); Frontline Defenders, Oyub Titiev Granted Parole, 2019, https://www.frontlinedefenders.org/en/case/oyub-titiev-granted-parole.

68 Luhn, 'Gulag Grave Hunter Unearths Uncomfortable Truths in Russia', Guardian, 3 August 2017, http://www.theguardian.com/world/2017/aug/03/gulag-grave-hunter-yury-dmitriyev-unearths-uncomfortable-truths-russia.

political repression under Stalin.[69] In *Khodorkovskiy and Lebedev v. Russia*, the ECtHR found a violation of Mr. Khodorkovskiy's and Mr. Lebedev's right to lawyer-client confidentiality by Russian judicial authorities.[70] The lawyers of the applicants, who were senior managers of the former oil and gas company Yukos, argued that criminal charges were brought against their clients because of their political activities, particularly their financial support of opposition parties.[71] While serving their sentences, following their first conviction, in penal colonies, the Deputy General Prosecutor decided to open a new case against Mr. Khodorkovskiy and Mr. Lebedev and charge them with embezzlement and money-laundering. Both men were then transferred to a remand prison in the town of Chita. When their lawyers tried to visit them, they were stopped, searched and detained by the police at Moscow airport. The police examined and video-recorded confidential papers, which were carried by the lawyers.[72] Later, prior to the commencement of the trial, Mr. Khodorkovskiy and Mr. Lebedev and their lawyers were given access to one copy of the case file but which they could only study in the presence of an investigator. When they asked the investigator to discuss the bill of indictment and the appended written materials, which ran to 188 volumes, in private, the investigator took the case file from them.[73] During the trial, Mr. Khodorkovskiy and Mr. Lebedev were brought to the courtroom in handcuffs, heavily guarded and held in a poorly ventilated glass dock.[74] The court dismissed their requests to be near their lawyers. Thus, Mr. Khodorkovskiy and Mr. Lebedev were unable to discuss the case and review documents with their lawyers. Furthermore, their conversations with their lawyers were overheard by the guards and all documents which their lawyers wished to show them were checked by a judge before they were passed to Mr. Khodorkovskiy and Mr. Lebedev.[75] The ECtHR criticised the Russian judicial authorities for breaching fundamental features of the right to a fair trial, including Mr. Khodorkovskiy's and Mr. Lebedev's right to be effectively defended by a lawyer.[76] The

69 International Federation for Human Rights, Russia: Ongoing Judicial Harassment Against Yuri Dmitriyev, 3 September 2018, http://www.fidh.org/en/issues/human-rights-defenders/russia-ongoing-judicial-harassment-against-yuri-dmitriyev.

70 ECtHR, Judgment, 14 January 2020, *Khodorkovskiy and Lebedev v Russia (No. 2)*, Application Nos. 51111/07 and 42757/07, para. 533.

71 *Id.* para. 7.

72 *Id.* para. 55.

73 *Id.* para. 69.

74 *Id.* para. 75.

75 *Id.* paras. 76, 464, 466.

76 *Id.* paras. 463 ff.

ECtHR also pointed out that the measures imposed on them to restrict their participation in the trial and communicate with their lawyers were neither necessary nor proportionate and that any legal assistance loses its usefulness when the accused's communication with her/his lawyer is overheard by a third person.[77]

III. Ukraine

Like in Azerbaijan and Russia, criminal procedural rights have long been under threat in Ukraine, partly due to a continued problem of corruption and lack of integrity within the judiciary.[78] Since joining the CoE in 1995, the Ukrainian government introduced several reforms to improve the level of independence of its judiciary.[79] More recently, the 2014 'Law on Restoring of Trust in the Judicial Power in Ukraine'[80] entered into force to further the internal and external independence of judges by removing all court chairmen who had served under the former president Viktor Yanukovych. Under Yanukovych's administration, these court chairmen enjoyed far-reaching competences which allowed them to control the entire judiciary: they oversaw the salary and working conditions of inferior judges, selected the new, incoming chairmen and reputedly took orders from the ruling elite to assign political sensitive cases solely to those judges who were known for their support of the government.[81] In 2016, the Law on the Judiciary and Status of Judges limited the government's and parliament's influence on judicial appointments, promotions and dismissals.[82]

---

77 *Id.* para. 463.

78 Venice Commission, *Ukraine. Joint Opinion of the Venice Commission and the Directorate General of Human Rights and the Rule of Law (DGI) of the Council of Europe on Draft Amendments to the Law 'On the Judiciary and the Status of Judges' and certain Laws on the Activities of the Supreme Court and Judicial Authorities (Draft Law No. 3711)*, 9 October 2020, CDL-AD(2020)022, 4.

79 CoE Parliamentary Assembly, *Application by Ukraine for membership of the Council of Europe*, Opinion 190 (1995), 26 September 1995.

80 Verkhovna Rada of Ukraine, 'The Verkhovna Rada of Ukraine adopted the Law "On restoring trust in the court system of Ukraine"', 8 April 2014, https://www.rada.gov.ua/en/news/News/News%202/91053.html.

81 Ukrainian Bar Association, 'Concept of Judicial Reform in Ukraine', 19 September 2014, uba.ua/eng/projects/38/.

82 Law of Ukraine on the Judiciary and the Status of Judges, 16 July 2016, https://vkksu.gov.ua/userfiles/doc/Law_on_Judiciary_and_Status_of_Judges_16%2007%202016_ENG.pdf.

The new law aimed at strengthening the role of Ukraine's judicial council, the High Council of Justice, introduced merit-based promotions for judges and led to the Supreme Court's reorganisation, which was praised by the Venice Commission.[83] The Venice Commission noted that the 'time has come [...] to finally move towards achieving an independent judiciary' in Ukraine.[84] In addition to this, Ukraine's first anti-corruption court took office in 2019 to fight the country's high levels of corruption.[85] The success of these reforms, however, will depend largely on the willingness of the judiciary to comply with this new set of rules in practice. Yet progress has been slow. The judicial profession suffers from widespread bribery, delayed and fabricated initiations of criminal proceedings and a great loss of public confidence in the national judicial system.[86] Only 2,9 % of the population perceived the judiciary as a fair and just institution in 2012.[87] Besides, more recent attempts to restore trust into the judicial system were unsuccessful. For instance, the Public Integrity Council (PIC), an NGO watchdog tasked with advising courts about the ethics and integrity of judicial candidates, considered 15 nominees to the Constitutional Court as not suitable for office. These nominees were regardless confirmed by the two most superior judicial bodies of Ukraine, the High Council of Justice and the High Qualification Commission of Judges, which oversee the judicial appointment process in Ukraine and led the PIC to withdraw from its

83 OSCE Office for Democratic Institutions and Human Rights, *Opinion on the Law of Ukraine on the Judiciary and the Status of Judges*, 30 June 2017, Opinion-Nr. JUD-UKR/298/2017 [RJU/AT]; Venice Commission, *Opinion on the Proposed Amendments to the Constitution of Ukraine regarding the Judiciary as Approved by the Constitutional Commission on 4 September 2015*, 26 October 2015, CDL-AD(2015)027.

84 Venice Commission, *Opinion on the Proposed Amendments to the Constitution of Ukraine regarding the Judiciary as Approved by the Constitutional Commission on 4 September 2015*, 26 October 2015, CDL-AD(2015)027.

85 UNIAN, 'Ukraine Launches High Anti-Corruption Court', 11 April 2019, http://www.unian.info/politics/10513461-ukraine-launches-high-anti-corruption-court.html.

86 World Justice Project, *The World Justice Project Rule of Law Index 2019* (2019); Venice Commission, *Ukraine. Joint Opinion of the Venice Commission and the Directorate General of Human Rights and the Rule of Law (DGI) of the Council of Europe on Draft Amendments to the Law 'On the Judiciary and the Status of Judges' and certain Laws on the Activities of the Supreme Court and Judicial Authorities (Draft Law No. 3711)*, 9 October 2020, CDL-AD(2020)022, 5.

87 Korrespondent, Корреспондент: Рівень довіри до українських судів наближається до абсолютного мінімуму, 12 October 2012, http://ua.korrespondent.net/ukraine/politics/1405614-korrespondent-riven-doviri-do-ukrayinskih-sudiv-nablizhaetsya-do-absolyutnogo-minimumu.

advisory role to the Constitutional Court.[88] Another example is the judiciary's mishandling of the 'Revolution of Dignity', the 2013–2014 mass protests against Yanukovych's administration, which became internationally known as the 'Maidan protests'. The government's violent suppression of protesters was actively supported by judges and prosecutors and resulted in about 100 people being killed, 700 people being injured and several people who went missing.[89] The testimonies given by high-profile figures of Ukraine's judiciary, such as the president of Kyiv's district court and member of the High Council of Justice, Mamontova I. Yu, and the former president of Kyivshow court of appeal, Chernushenko A., show that, during the protests, judicial bodies received instructions from Yanukovych's administration to disperse the Maidan rallies which resulted in excessive arrests, detentions, kidnappings, torture and sanctions of protesters.[90] Nevertheless, it seems unlikely that the 'Maidan judges' will be brought to justice in Ukraine. Following the escape of senior officials of Yanukovych´s administration including Yanukovych himself and his chief prosecutor Viktor Pshonka, the prosecutor's office was tasked with investigating the crimes perpetrated at Maidan. Yet only a fraction of judges who had served under Yanukovych was removed from office and many 'Maidan judges' continued their work under the new government.[91] In 2017, three 'Maidan judges' were appointed to the Supreme Court which raised doubts about the court's ability to conduct independent investigations into the Maidan events.[92] In one case, two officers of the so-called Berkut regiment – a riot police unit that was dissolved by the new political leadership after the

88 Freedom House, *Freedom in the World 2019* (2020); Sukhov, 'Poroshenko appoints 75 judges to Supreme Court, including 15 controversial', Kyiv Post, 7 May 2019, http://www.kyivpost.com/ukraine-politics/poroshenko-appoints-75-judges-to-supreme-court-including-15-controversial.html.

89 UN Human Rights Monitoring Mission in Ukraine, *Accountability for Killings and Violent Deaths during the Maidan Protests*, Briefing Note, 2019, http://www.un.org.ua/images/documents/4700/Accountability%20for%20Killings%20and%20Violent%20Deaths%20During%20the%20Maidan%20Protest_2.pdf.

90 Coynash, Judge heavily implicated in persecuting Maidan activists chosen for trial of ex-President Yanukovych, Kharkiv Human Rights Protection Group, 22 August 2018, http://khpg.org/en/index.php?id=1534457393.

91 Mirovalev, 'Ukraine at crossroads five years after 'revolution of dignity'', Al Jazeera, 22 February 2019, https://www.aljazeera.com/news/2019/02/ukraine-crossroads-years-revolution-dignity-190222114802790.html.

92 Human Rights Information Centre, '"Judges of EuroMaidan" have an open path to the Supreme Court', 28 April 2017, http://humanrights.org.ua/en/material/suddjiam_majdanu_vidkrivajetsjia_doroga_u_verkhovnij_sud__maselko; Freedom House, *Freedom in the World 2019* (2020).

Maidan protests – were arrested on charges of attempted killing of 33 Maidan protesters and released from custody. They then fled to Russia where they appeared in a video, stating that they fear persecution for 'performing their constitutional duty' at Maidan.[93] In another case, courts released a major of the anti-riot police unit, Dmitri Sadovnyka, and Yanukovych's former first deputy prime minister, Serhiy Arbuzov, from custody in spite of their high risk of escape. At Maidan, Mr. Sadovnyka and Mr. Arbuzov had been tasked with overseeing the police operations which led to shootings of protesters.[94] Moreover, the prosecutor O. Nichiporenko has not faced any sanctions for his actions during the protests. Mr. Nichiporenko had played an active role in obstructing the course of justice at Maidan, serving as the deputy chief of Kyiv department of procedural management under Yanukovych's administration. He also featured in criminal investigations but was later promoted to a position in which he supervises the activities of Kyiv's prosecutor's office.[95] Ukraine's neglect of the right to a fair trial was also discussed in *Korban v. Ukraine*.[96] In 2015, Gennadiy Olegovych Korban, a former leader of a newly formed opposition party, was charged with embezzlement and creation of a criminal organisation, and kidnapping a public official, among others, and subsequently arrested and detained.[97] His lawyers argued that the investigating judge did not provide any reason to justify the measures imposed on their client, including his house arrest. The ECtHR found that neither the applicant's arrest nor his detention were lawful as the Ukrainian investigators disregarded Mr. Korban's rights under national law.[98] Additionally, the ECtHR reiterated that no person should be declared guilty before her/his conviction by a court. In the case of Mr. Korban, high-ranking officials of the governing party had informed the public of the criminal proceedings against Mr. Korban, neither discreetly nor circumspectly, and labelled him as 'the leader of a criminal organisation' in the mass media.[99]

93 UN Human Rights Monitoring Mission in Ukraine, 'Accountability for Killings and Violent Deaths during the Maidan Protests', Briefing Note, 2019, Fn. 21, http://www.un.org.ua/images/documents/4700/Accountability%20for%20Killings%20and%20Violent%20Deaths%20During%20the%20Maidan%20Protest_2.pdf.

94 Sukhov, 'Yarema, top prosecutor since June, accused of stalling criminal cases', Kyiv Post, 14 October 2014, http://www.kyivpost.com/article/content/reform-watch/yarema-top-prosecutor-since-june-accused-of-stalling-criminal-cases-367925.html.

95 *Ibid.*

96 ECtHR, Judgment, 4 July 2019, *Korban v Ukraine*, Application No. 26744/16.

97 *Id.* paras. 9, 15.

98 *Id.* paras. 145, 150, 162, 166, 175.

99 *Id.* paras. 218, 230, 231.

The ECtHR concluded that such statements violate the right to the presumption of innocence.[100] In 2019, the Ukrainian government, under a new political leadership, announced to complete its long overdue judicial reform due to its poor record to implement such reforms once they are adopted.[101] As a consequence, a set of legislative measures were discussed and introduced. This included the Law No. 193-IX.[102] The new law foresees to reduce the Supreme Court by half and dissolved the High Qualification Commission of Judges, which left 2000 judicial vacancies at first and second instance courts unfilled in 2020.

D. Outlook

Azerbaijan, Russia and Ukraine committed themselves to cooperation with the CoE in the fields of human rights, the rule of law and democracy.[103] They also ratified the ECHR including its Protocol 14 according to which they agreed to respect the ECtHR's judgments as a vital element of the CoE's system for the protection of human rights, rule of law and democracy.[104] Besides, Article 46 of ECHR obliges them to abide by the final judgments of the ECtHR in any case to which they were parties. Judgments by the ECtHR against the respondent member state impose a legal obligation not just to pay those concerned the sums awarded by way of just satisfaction, but also to choose, subject to supervision by the CoE's Committee of Ministers, the general and/or, if appropriate, individual measures to be adopted in their domestic legal order to put an end to the violation found by the ECtHR and to redress so far as possible the effects.[105] Considering the findings of this chapter – the systematic violation of basic procedural

---

100 *Id.* para. 232.

101 Venice Commission, *Ukraine. Joint Opinion of the Venice Commission and the Directorate General of Human Rights and the Rule of Law (DGI) of the Council of Europe on Draft Amendments to the Law 'On the Judiciary and the Status of Judges' and certain Laws on the Activities of the Supreme Court and Judicial Authorities (Draft Law No. 3711)*, 9 October 2020, CDL-AD(2020)022, 4.

102 Law of Ukraine No. 193-IX, 2019, https://www.venice.coe.int/webforms/documents/default.aspx?pdffile=CDL-REF(2019)039.

103 CoE, Department for the Execution of Judgments of the European Court of Human Rights, 2020, https://www.coe.int/en/web/execution.

104 CoE, Department for the Execution of Judgments of the European Court of Human Rights, 2020, https://www.coe.int/en/web/execution.

105 ECtHR, Judgment (GC), 13 July 2000, *Scozzari and Giunta v Italy*, Application Nos. 39221/98 and 41963/98, para. 249.

rights of activists and other government critics by judicial authorities – it has been shown that the protection and enforcement of the ECHR and the ECtHR's jurisprudence can differ strongly from country to country. Recognizing their powerful role in the delivery of justice, the international community has therefore set up working groups and other initiatives to remind judges and prosecutors of their professional obligations under international law to respect human rights.[106] The Magna Carta of Judges, for example, underlines the importance of human rights to the profession of judge and requires that her/his actions should respond to human rights standards.[107] The Bangalore Principles also point out that education and training are key to deliver justice as they can help judges (and students, in their role as future justices) to demystify their concern regarding international human rights law and to make more decisions that are in line with human rights standards.[108] Furthermore, the international community suggests that judges who do not comply with their professional obligations under international law to respect human rights should be removed from office.[109] Judges should be dismissed when they are unable to perform their judicial duties because of 'incapacity or behaviour that renders them unfit to discharge their duties'[110], or conduct that is manifestly contrary to the independence, impartiality and integrity of the judiciary'.[111] Similarly,

106 See, for example, International Association of Judges, 'The Universal Carter of the Judge', 14 November 2017, https://www.unodc.org/res/ji/import/international_standards/the_universal_charter_of_the_judge/universal_charter_2017_english.pdf, Article 1; International Association of Prosecutors, Standards of Professional Responsibility and Statement of the Essential Duties and Rights of Prosecutors, 23 April 1999, https://www.iap-association.org/getattachment/Resources-Documentation/IAP-Standards-(1)/English.pdf.aspx, 3(e), (f).

107 See, for example, CCJE, 'Magna Carta of Judges (Fundamental Principles)', 17 November 2010, https://rm.coe.int/2010-ccje-magna-carta-anglais/168063e431, paras. 5, 11.

108 See, for example, UN Economic and Social Council, *Strengthening basic principles of judicial conduct, Annex, Bangalore Principles of Judicial Conduct*, 27 July 2006, UN Doc. E/Res/2006/23, preamble; Venice Commission, Co-operation with Central Asia, Highlights, https://www.venice.coe.int/WebForms/pages/?p=03_Central_asia.

109 See, for example, CCJE, 'Magna Carta of Judges (Fundamental Principles)', 17 November 2010, https://rm.coe.int/2010-ccje-magna-carta-anglais/168063e431, para. 19.

110 UN, *Seventh UN Congress on the Prevention of Crime and Treatment of Offenders, Milan, 26 August-6 September 1985, Basic Principles on the Independence of the Judiciary* (1986), 58 para. 18.

111 International Commission of Jurists, *Judicial Accountability. A Practitioners' Guide* (2016), https://www.icj.org/wp-content/uploads/2016/06/Universal-PG-13-Ju

the professional responsibility of prosecutors to respect human rights is reflected and referred to in law, regulation, bilateral contracts and litigation.[112] Thus, prosecutors, like judges, should be held accountable when they fail to comply with their professional duties under international law.

In many countries, independent and impartial bodies such as judicial councils have the role to oversee and enforce professional discipline (e.g., to ensure that judges respect European human rights standards).[113] If the judiciary and the prosecution, however, are controlled by the government and independent and impartial disciplinary bodies are absent, they will be less likely to oppose unlawful orders by superiors and be held responsible for their misconduct. Not surprisingly, judges in Azerbaijan, Russia and Ukraine do rarely face disciplinary or criminal consequences for their misconduct. Additionally, there are currently no credible audit or monitoring instruments at international or European level in place that could oversee actions of and impose sanctions on judges and prosecutors who fail to comply with their human rights obligations under international law in CoE member countries. Complaints and reporting mechanisms provided by, for example, the UN do not periodically review or sanction the human rights violations of judicial authorities and are often only mandated to adopt 'concluding observations'.[114] Addressing the accountability of judges and public prosecutors also falls short at European level. The ECtHR, for instance, has the authority to review a country's judicial wrongdoings in

---

dicial-Accountability-Publications-Reports-Practitioners-Guide-2016-ENG.pdf; UN HRC, *Concluding observations on the seventh periodic report of the Russian Federation*, 28 April 2015, UN Doc. CCPR/C/RUS/CO/7; Judicial Integrity Group, 'Measures for the Effective Implementation of the Bangalore Principles of Judicial Conduct', 21/22 January 2010, https://www.unodc.org/res/ji/import/international_standards/measures_implementation/measures_implementation.pdf, para. 16.1.

112 ECtHR, Judgment, 22 February 1996, *Bulut v Austria*, Application No. 17358/90; ECtHR, Judgment, 26 July 2011, *Huseyn and Others v Azerbaijan*, Application No. 35485/05 and 3 more; ECtHR, Judgment, 22 May 2014, *Ilgar Mammadov v Azerbaijan*, Application No. 15172/13; ECtHR, Judgment, 17 July 2014, *Svinarenko and Slyadnev v Russia*, Application Nos. 32541/08 and 43441/08; ECtHR, Judgment, 17 March 2016, *Rasul Jafarov v Azerbaijan*, Application No. 69981/14.

113 See UN HRC, General Comment No. 32, 23 August 2007, UN Doc. CCPR/C/GC/32, para. 20; International Bar Association, *IBA Minimum Standards of Judicial Independence* (1982), https://www.ibanet.org/Publications/publications_IBA_guides_and_free_materials.aspx, 4(a).

114 See, for example, UN Working Group on Arbitrary Detention, Opinion, 7 July 2015, *Thulani Maseko v Swaziland*, No. 6/2015, UN Doc. A/HRC/WGAD/2015/6, paras. 26 ff.

CoE member countries and issue decisions on individual complaints of human rights abuse perpetrated by or with complicity of judges and prosecutors. But rulings focusing on political motivated charges and convictions by judicial authorities are rare in practice.

Nevertheless, there is much promising (but yet underutilised) potential at both international and European level. International organisations are capable to strengthen the professional integrity of judges and prosecutors and increase their awareness of human rights standards. For instance, the Bureau of the Consultative Council of European Judges (CCJE) and the Bureau of the Consultative Council of European Prosecutors (CCPE) are uniquely placed to draw attention to the situation of activists and other regime critics as they are tasked with looking into specific problems concerning the status and the situation of judges and public prosecutors.[115] Yet they have not set up institutional human rights mechanisms, such as requiring members to complete an annual questionnaire and organising country visits to identify best practices that could help the CCJE's and CCPE's to step up their professional integrity polices. Besides, establishing an 'urgent appeal' procedure for cases in which the CCJE and the CCPE may play a role in preventing or mitigating human rights abuses by judicial authorities of the Council of Europe member states (e.g., in situations in which physical and/or mental integrity of an individual or a group is concerned) could contribute to important change in countries, such as Azerbaijan, Russia and Ukraine, where the rights of anti-government critics are neglected in the courts.

Bibliography

Amnesty International: Unfair Game, Persecution of Human Rights Defenders in Russia Intensifies (2019), https://www.amnesty.org/download/Documents/EUR4609502019ENGLISH.pdf.

Amnesty International: Amnesty International Report 2017/18. The State of the World's Human Rights (2018).

---

115 See for example, CCJE, 'Framework Global Action Plan for Judges in Europe', CCJE(2001)24, 12 February 2001; CCJE, 'Magna Carta of Judges (Fundamental Principles)', 17 November 2010, https://rm.coe.int/2010-ccje-magna-carta-anglais/168063e431; CoE Committee of Ministers, *Judges: independence, efficiency and responsibilities*, 17 November 2010, Recommendation CM/Rec(2010)12.

Amnesty International: Attending Trials Involving Human Rights Defenders in Russia. A Handbook for Diplomats (2018), https://www.amnesty.nl/content/uploads/2017/01/AI-trial-attendance-handbook-for-diplomats-Russia.pdf?x55436#.

Amnesty International: Russia: Release environmentalist banished to a prison colony, 15 April 2015, https://www.amnesty.org/en/latest/news/2015/04/russia-release-yevgeniy-vitishko/.

Closed Society: Implications of Implementing the Legislation Regulating the Activities of "Non-Commercial Organisations Performing the Functions of a Foreign Agent" in Russia (2015), https://www.osce.org/files/f/documents/6/8/151581.pdf.

Consultative Council of European Judges (CCJE): Framework Global Action Plan for Judges in Europe, CCJE, 12 February 2001.

Consultative Council of European Judges (CCJE): Magna Carta of Judges (Fundamental Principles), 17 November 2010, https://rm.coe.int/2010-ccje-magna-carta-anglais/168063e431.

Coynash, Halya: Judge heavily implicated in persecuting Maidan activists chosen for trial of ex-President Yanukovych, Kharkiv Human Rights Protection Group, 22 August 2018, http://khpg.org/en/index.php?id=1534457393.

Domingo, Pilar: Judicial Independence and Judicial Reform in Latin America, in: Schedler, Andreas/Diamond, Larry Jay/Plattner, Marc F. (eds), The Self-Restraining State: Power and Accountability in New Democracies (1999), 151ff.

Fiss, Owen M.: The Right Degree of Independence, in: Strotzky, Irwin P. (ed), Transition to Democracy in Latin America: The Role of the Judiciary (1993), 55ff.

Freedom House: Freedom in the World 2020 (2021).

Freedom House: Freedom in the World 2019 (2020).

Frontline Defenders: Oyub Titiev Granted Parole (2019), https://www.frontlinedefenders.org/en/case/oyub-titiev-granted-parole.

Human Rights Information Centre: "Judges of EuroMaidan" have an open path to the Supreme Court, 28 April 2017, http://humanrights.org.ua/en/material/suddjiam_majdanu_vidkrivajetsjia_doroga_u_verkhovnij_sud__maselko.

Human Rights Watch: Crimea: Defence Lawyers Harassed, Drop Bogus Charges Against Crimean Tatars (2017), https://www.hrw.org/news/2017/01/30/crimea-defense-lawyers-harassed.

Human Rights Watch: Human Rights Violations in Russia's North Caucasus, 28 January 2016, https://www.hrw.org/news/2016/01/28/human-rights-violations-russias-north-caucasus.

Human Rights Watch: Laws of Attrition. Crackdown on Russia's Civil Society after Putin's Return to the Presidency (2013).

Human Rights Watch: Russia: Flawed Trial of Environmental Activists. Dubious Charges, Harsh Sentences Seem Designed to Silence Zoologist, Geologist, 21 June 2012, http://www.hrw.org/news/2012/06/21/russia-flawed-trial-environmental-activists.

International Association of Judges: The Universal Carter of the Judge, 14 November 2017, https://www.unodc.org/res/ji/import/international_standards/the_universal_charter_of_the_judge/universal_charter_2017_english.pdf.

International Association of Prosecutors: Standards of Professional Responsibility and Statement of the Essential Duties and Rights of Prosecutors, 23 April 1999, https://www.iap-association.org/getattachment/Resources-Documentation/IAP-Standards-(1)/English.pdf.aspx.

International Bar Association, IBA Minimum Standards of Judicial Independence (1982), https://www.ibanet.org/Publications/publications_IBA_guides_and_free_materials.aspx.

International Commission of Jurists: Judicial Accountability. A Practitioners' Guide (2016), https://www.icj.org/wp-content/uploads/2016/06/Universal-PG-13-Judicial-Accountability-Publications-Reports-Practitioners-Guide-2016-ENG.pdf

International Federation for Human Rights: Russia: Ongoing Judicial Harassment Against Yuri Dmitriyev, 3 September 2018, http://www.fidh.org/en/issues/human-rights-defenders/russia-ongoing-judicial-harassment-against-yuri-dmitriyev.

Jackson, Vicki C.: Judicial Independence: Structure, Context, Attitude, in: Seibert-Fohr, Anja (ed.), Judicial Independence in Transition (2012), 19 ff.

Judicial Integrity Group: Measures for the Effective Implementation of the Bangalore Principles of Judicial Conduct, 21/22 January 2010, https://www.unodc.org/res/ji/import/international_standards/measures_implementation/measures_implementation.pdf.

Korrespondent: Корреспондент: Рівень довіри до українських судів наближається до абсолютного мінімуму, 12 October 2012, http://ua.korrespondent.net/ukraine/politics/1405614-korrespondent-riven-doviri-do-ukrayinskih-sudiv-nablizhaetsya-do-absolyutnogo-minimumu.

Luhn, Alec: Gulag Grave Hunter Unearths Uncomfortable Truths in Russia, Guardian, 3 August 2017, http://www.theguardian.com/world/2017/aug/03/gulag-grave-hunter-yury-dmitriyev-unearths-uncomfortable-truths-russia.

Mirovalev, Mansur: Ukraine at crossroads five years after 'revolution of dignity', Al Jazeera, 22 February 2019, https://www.aljazeera.com/news/2019/02/ukraine-crossroads-years-revolution-dignity-190222114802790.html.

Myjer, Egbert/Hancock, Barry/Cowdery, Nicholas (eds), Human Rights Manual for Prosecutors (2008).

OSCE: Azerbaijan Election Lacked Genuine Competition in an Environment of Curtailed Rights and Freedoms, International Observers Say, 12 April 2018, http://www.osce.org/odihr/elections/azerbaijan/377623.

OSCE: Trial Monitoring Report: Azerbaijan (2011), www.osce.org/baku/100593.

OSCE Office for Democratic Institutions and Human Rights: Opinion on the Law of Ukraine on the Judiciary and the Status of Judges, Opinion-Nr. JUD-UKR/298/2017 [RJU/AT], 30 June 2017.

Radio Free Liberty/Radio Liberty: How Russia Has Implemented its 'Foreign-Agent' Law, 2 November 2018, http://www.rferl.org/a/foreign-agent-law/29579390.html.

Shapiro, Martin/Stone Sweet, Alec: Law, Courts and Social Science, in: Shapiro, Martin/Stone Sweet, Alec (eds), On Law, Politics and Judicialization (2002), 1ff.

Sukhov, Oleg: Poroshenko appoints 75 judges to Supreme Court, including 15 controversial, Kyiv Post, 7 May 2019, http://www.kyivpost.com/ukraine-politics/poroshenko-appoints-75-judges-to-supreme-court-including-15-controversial.html.

Sukhov, Oleg: Yarema, top prosecutor since June, accused of stalling criminal cases, Kyiv Post, 14 October 2014, http://www.kyivpost.com/article/content/reform-watch/yarema-top-prosecutor-since-june-accused-of-stalling-criminal-cases-367925.html.

The Prosecutor General's Office of the Russian Federation: Report. Order of 27 December 2012, N° 27–07–2012/14п1861–12в, 2012, http://genproc.gov.ru/smi/interview_and_appearences/appearences/83568/.

Transparency International: Azerbaijan: Overview of Corruption and Anti-Corruption, 7 September 2017, https://knowledgehub.transparency.org/assets/uploads/helpdesk/Country-Profile-Azerbaijan-2017_PR.pdf.

Transparency International: Global Corruption Report 2007 (2007).

UK Foreign & Commonwealth Office: Human Rights Priority Country Update Report: January to June 2016 (2017), http://www.gov.uk/government/publications/russia-human-rights-priority-country/human-rights-priority-country-update-report-january-to-june-2016.

Ukrainian Bar Association: Concept of Judicial Reform in Ukraine, 19 September 2014, uba.ua/eng/projects/38/.

UN: Seventh UN Congress on the Prevention of Crime and Treatment of Offenders, Milan, 26 August-6 September 1985 (1986).

UN: Eighth UN Congress on the Prevention of Crime and Treatment of Offenders, Havana, 27 August-7 September 1990 (1990).

UN Committee against Torture (UN CAT): Concluding observations on the fourth periodic report of Azerbaijan, UN Doc. CAT/C/AZE/CO/4, 27 January 2016.

UN Economic and Social Council: Strengthening basic principles of judicial conduct, Annex, Bangalore Principles of Judicial Conduct, UN Doc. E/Res/2006/23, 27 July 2006.

UN Human Rights Committee (UN HRC): Concluding observations on the seventh periodic report of the Russian Federation, UN Doc. CCPR/C/RUS/CO/7, 28 April 2015.

UN Human Rights Committee (UN HRC): General Comment No. 31. The Nature of the General Legal Obligation Imposed on States Parties to the Covenant, UN Doc. CCPR/C/21/Rev.1/Add. 13, 26 May 2004.

UN Human Rights Committee (UN HRC): General Comment No. 32. Article 14: Right to equality before courts and tribunals and to a fair trial, UN Doc. CCPR/C/GC/32, 23 August 2007.

UN Human Rights Committee (UN HRC): Report of the Special Rapporteur on the situation of human rights defenders, Margaret Sekaggya, UN Doc. A/HRC/25/55, 23 December 2013.

UN Human Rights Monitoring Mission in Ukraine: Briefing Note. Accountability for Killings and Violent Deaths during the Maidan Protests (2019), http://www.un.org.ua/images/documents/4700/Accountability%20for%20Killings%20and%20Violent%20Deaths%20During%20the%20Maidan%20Protest_2.pdf.

UN Office on Drugs and Crime (UNODC): The Status and Role of Prosecutors. A UN Office on Drugs and Crime and International Association of Prosecutors Guide (2014), https://www.unodc.org/documents/justice-and-prison-reform/HB_role_and_status_prosecutors_14-05222_Ebook.pdf.

UN Special Rapporteur on the Independence of Judges and Lawyers: Information on Hungary: Hungary: More Needs to Be Done to Bring Legislation on Administrative Courts in line with International Standards, UN Expert Says (2019), https://www.ohchr.org/Documents/Issues/IJudiciary/InfoNoteHungary8Apr2019.docx.

UNIAN: Ukraine Launches High Anti-Corruption Court, 11 April 2019, http://www.unian.info/politics/10513461-ukraine-launches-high-anti-corruption-court.html.

Verkhovna Rada of Ukraine: The Verkhovna Rada of Ukraine adopted the Law "On restoring trust in the court system of Ukraine", 8 April 2014, https://www.rada.gov.ua/en/news/News/News%202/91053.html.

World Justice Project: The World Justice Project Rule of Law Index 2019 (2019).

The Role and Impact of the European Convention on Human Rights Beyond States Parties: The curious case of the ECHR in Kosovo[1]

Beti Hohler and Barbara Sonczyk

A. *Introduction*

The European Convention on Human Rights and Fundamental Freedoms ('ECHR', 'the Convention') has defined human rights protection in Europe for over 70 years.[2] Its supervisory mechanism – the European Court of Human Rights ('ECtHR', 'the Strasbourg Court') – has subsequently influenced the legal standards for administration of justice, safeguarding the protection of individuals against unfairness and the abuse of power, and upholding pluralistic democracy.[3] The Convention has also impacted on the human rights discourse outside Europe, asserting its progressively transformative role in international legal landscape more broadly.[4] Various UN bodies, other international organisations, regional courts, international criminal tribunals, national authorities and civil society institutions frequently reference the Convention and the case law of the Strasbourg Court in their work, extending the impact of the treaty regime well beyond the State Parties.

A unique example of such impact is Kosovo, a contested State on the Balkan peninsula and a former UN-administered territory, where the

---

1 All references to Kosovo in this text shall be understood to be in full compliance with United Nations Security Council Resolution 1244 (1999) and without prejudice to the status of Kosovo. The authors would like to thank HHJ Andrew Hatton, Dr. Mateja Peter and Njomza Haxhibeqiri for their comments on an earlier draft of this chapter.

2 Council of Europe (CoE), *The European Convention on Human Rights. A living instrument*, 2020, https://www.echr.coe.int/Documents/Convention_Instrument_ENG.pdf, 5.

3 CoE, *Report of the Evaluation Group to the Committee of Ministers on the European Court of Human Rights*, 27 September 2001, EG Court (2001) 1, 2.

4 Dzehtsiarou and Tzevelekos, 'The Conscience of Europe that Landed in Strasbourg: A Circle of Life of the European Court of Human Rights' (2020) 1 *ECHRLR*, 1(1).

Convention has been instrumental in the international rule represented by international organisations administering the territory or performing executive functions, the domestic legal system and, most recently, in the internationalised criminal court – the Kosovo Specialist Chambers – tasked with prosecuting international crimes. Kosovo's curious idiosyncratic legal framework enables us to study the role of the ECHR within a single territory from three different viewpoints: the contribution of the Convention to the paradigm of international governance and administration, the application of the Convention and Strasbourg case law in a non-State Party and the Convention's significance for war crimes prosecutions in an internationalised criminal court.

The chapter starts by providing a brief outline of the political history of Kosovo in section B to contextualise the ensuing discussion. Section C then elaborates on the process of introducing the Convention into Kosovo's legal system by the UN administration and its impact on the state-building efforts. This is followed by the analysis of the applicability – including its benefits and shortcomings – of the ECHR in Kosovo's legal order after its declaration of independence (Section D). The analysis discusses the legal status and significance of the case law of the ECtHR and the role of Kosovo courts, especially the Constitutional Court, in upholding human rights and fundamental freedoms guaranteed by the 2008 Kosovo Constitution. The main argument of the authors is that while the constitutionalisation of human rights treaties, in particular the ECHR, resulted in entrenching human rights in Kosovo's legal framework, which is in line with the Council of Europe (CoE)'s principle of subsidiarity and embeddedness, the protective system has its limitations since it is ultimately not supervised by the ECtHR. Section E uses the newly created Kosovo Specialist Chambers (KSC) and the Specialist Prosecutor's Office (SPO) to consider potential challenges within the Kosovo constitutional framework of human rights protection and further strengthens the argument about the need for a monitoring element to ensure full protection and compliance. The chapter concludes with remarks on the dynamic and evolving relationship between the ECHR and Kosovo.

B. Setting the Scene

I. Short Political History of Kosovo: from an Autonomous Province to Declaration of Independence

After World War II, Kosovo was part of the Socialist Federal Republic of Yugoslavia. From 1974 on, it enjoyed the status of an autonomous province within the Republic of Serbia,[5] one of Yugoslavia's six republics, until Serbia effectively revoked this status in 1989.[6]

From February 1998 until June 1999, an armed conflict between the army and police forces of the Federal Republic of Yugoslavia (i.e. Serbia and Montenegro) and the Kosovo Liberation Army (KLA), an armed group fighting for independence of Kosovo, took place in the territory of Kosovo. The conflict ended following the military intervention by NATO with the signing of the Military Technical Agreement between the International Security Force (KFOR) and the Governments of the Federal Republic of Yugoslavia and the Republic of Serbia on 9 June 1999.[7] The latter paved the way for the deployment of civil and security forces in Kosovo. On 10 June 1999, the UN Security Council, acting under Chapter VII of the UN Charter, adopted Resolution 1244, which established the United Nations Interim Administration in Kosovo (UNMIK). The latter governed the territory until 2008. Whilst UNMIK remains operational to date, its day-to-day duties are significantly reduced. In 2008, UNMIK's rule of law tasks were transferred to a rule of law mission set up by the European Union – the EU Rule of Law Mission in Kosovo (EULEX)[8] – which consisted of advisory and executive mandates. The executive mandate supported both the adjudication of civil justice and prosecution and adjudication of sensitive criminal cases (including war crimes). The Mission's judicial executive mandate came to an end in June 2018, and Kosovo assumed

---

5 Article 2 of the Constitution of the Socialist Federal Republic of Yugoslavia, 1974, https://www.worldstatesmen.org/Yugoslavia-Constitution1974.pdf.

6 For more about the history and dissolution of Yugoslavia, see e.g. Glenny, *The Fall of Yugoslavia: The Third Balkan War* (1996); Silber and Little, *Yugoslavia: Death of a Nation* (1997).

7 UN Security Council, *Military-technical agreement between the international security force (KFOR) and the Governments of the Federal Republic of Yugoslavia and the Republic of Serbia*, 15 June 1999, UN Doc. S/1999/682, 3 ff.

8 Council of the EU, *Joint Action on the European Union Rule of Law Mission in Kosovo*, 4 February 2008, 2008/124/CFSP.

responsibility for all transferred investigations, prosecutions and trials, whilst the advisory component of the Mission remains.[9]

On 17 February 2008, Kosovo declared independence. The Declaration of Independence was an Act of the Assembly of Kosovo as an Interim Institution of Self-Government. The Constitution was enacted on 15 April 2008. According to Kosovo's Ministry of Foreign Affairs, as of September 2021 the territory has been recognised as an independent state by 117 countries.[10] This includes 22 States of the European Union.[11]

In 2016, the EU signed the Stabilisation and Association Agreement (SAA) with Kosovo. The agreement does not constitute recognition of Kosovo as an independent State by the EU or individual EU countries. Its main aims are to support the efforts of Kosovo to strengthen democracy and the rule of law; contribute to political, economic and institutional stability in Kosovo and to the stabilisation of the region; to provide an appropriate framework for political dialogue and economic relations between the EU and Kosovo, including through aligning Kosovo's laws more closely to those of the EU and striving towards gradual development of a free trade area between the EU and Kosovo.[12]

Kosovo is not a member of the UN or the CoE. However, since 2009, it is a member of the International Monetary Fund and the World Bank. In 2014, Kosovo also joined two partial agreements of the CoE – the Development Bank and the European Commission for Democracy through Law (the Venice Commission).

9 Council of the EU, *EULEX Kosovo: new role for the EU rule of law mission*, 8 June 2018, https://www.consilium.europa.eu/en/press/press-releases/2018/06/08/eulex-kosovo-new-role-for-the-eu-rule-of-law-mission/.

10 Ministry of Foreign Affairs and Diaspora of the Republic of Kosovo, *International recognitions of the Republic of Kosovo*, 2018, https://www.mfa-ks.net/en/politika/483/njohjet-ndrkombtare-t-republiks-s-kosovs/483 – last accessed on 27 September 2021.

11 As of September 2021 Spain, Slovakia, Cyprus, Romania, Greece have not recognized Kosovo.

12 Stabilisation and Association Agreement between the European Union and the European Atomic Energy Community, of the one part, and Kosovo of the other part, 16 March 2016, OJ EU L 71/3.

C. International Presence in Kosovo and the ECHR

I. Kosovo's Relationship with the ECHR: How it all Began

The ECHR was introduced into Kosovo's legal system by UNMIK on 12 December 1999 with Regulation 1999/24 on applicable law which included the following clause:

> In exercising their functions, all persons undertaking public duties or holding public office in Kosovo shall observe internationally recognized human rights standards, as reflected in particular in:
>
> (a) The Universal Declaration on Human Rights of 10 December 1948;
> *(b) The European Convention for the Protection of Human Rights and Fundamental Freedoms of 4 November 1950 and the Protocols thereto;*
> (c) The International Covenant on Civil and Political Rights of 16 December 1966 and the Protocols thereto;
> (d) The International Covenant on Economic, Social and Cultural Rights of 16 December 1966;
> (e) The Convention on the Elimination of All Forms of Racial Discrimination of 21 December 1965;
> (f) The Convention on Elimination of All Forms of Discrimination Against Women of 17 December 1979;
> (g) The Convention Against Torture and Other Cruel, Inhumane or Degrading Treatment or Punishment of 17 December 1984; and
> (h) The International Convention on the Rights of the Child of 20 December 1989. (emphasis added)[13]

This provision marks the beginning of Kosovo's relationship with the ECHR. Its immediate practical consequence was that UNMIK (and later EULEX) international judges and prosecutors deployed in Kosovo as members of international or mixed panels used the ECHR and its Protocols in their decisions both as a direct source of law and as a tool for interpreting the applicable law, causing the Convention to become an influential source of human rights standards in the territory.[14] International judges

---

13 UNMIK, 'Regulation No. 1999/24 on the Law Applicable in Kosovo', 12 December 1999, https://unmik.unmissions.org/sites/default/files/regulations/02english/E1999regs/RE1999_24.htm, section 1.3.

14 Between June 1999 and June 2018 international (first UNMIK and then EULEX) judges were embedded in the Kosovo domestic system and participated in adjudi-

who were involved in the adjudication of cases and who also participated in capacity building were in practice an important force behind making the Convention known and applied in the territory, especially in the early years of international administration. Within EULEX, the vast majority of judges (and prosecutors) deployed in Kosovo came from European countries and were therefore familiar with the ECHR system and Strasbourg case law from their home jurisdictions.

In 2001, UNMIK and the Kosovo authorities adopted the 'Constitutional Framework for Provisional Self-Government in Kosovo', which further tied Kosovo's institutions – including the courts – to the Convention. The Framework explicitly stated that the Provisional Institutions of Self-Government must observe and ensure internationally recognized human rights and fundamental freedoms, including those rights and freedoms set forth in the ECHR and its Protocols.[15]

Thereafter, in 2007, an international commission was established to determine the status of Kosovo. It proposed a design for the prospective Kosovo State that would have to be mirrored in any future Constitution. This proposal – the Comprehensive Proposal for the Kosovo Status Settlement (informally known as the Ahtisaari Plan) – included the following provision:

> Kosovo shall promote, protect and respect the highest level of internationally recognized human rights and fundamental freedoms, including those rights and freedoms set forth in the Universal Declaration on Human Rights, the International Covenant on Civil and Political Rights, and *the European Convention for the Protection of Human Rights and Fundamental Freedoms and its Protocols. Kosovo shall take all necessary measures towards ratifying the European Convention for the Protection*

cation of sensitive cases at all court levels and to different extents as time went on. The last cases to be transferred to the entirely local panels were war crimes cases following the end of EULEX's executive mandate in 2018, with the exception of cases falling within the specific jurisdiction of the KSC. The latter, as discussed in more detail bellow, exist within the Kosovo domestic court system and mirror the levels of Kosovo's courts of general jurisdiction (Basic Court, Court of Appeals, Supreme Court, Constitutional Court). See e.g. decisions with participation of EULEX judges: EULEX, Court Judgments, 2021, https://www.eulex-kosovo.eu/?page=2,8.

15 UNMIK, 'A Constitutional Framework for Provisional Self-Government in Kosovo', Regulation No. 2001/9, 15 May 2001, https://unmik.unmissions.org/sites/default/files/regulations/02english/E2001regs/RE2001_09.pdf, section 3.2.

> *of Human Rights and Fundamental Freedoms and its Protocols* (emphasis added).[16]

By singling out the ECHR, the Commission seemingly set out to tie any future Kosovo State to the ECHR. De Hert and Korenica observe that the Commission 'considered, *inter alia*, that binding Kosovo to the ECHR would serve as one of the most important international safeguards for domestic human rights protection.'[17]

II. UNMIK and EULEX Human Rights Review Mechanisms and Their Reliance on the ECHR

Another link between the international intervention in Kosovo and the ECHR comes in the form of quasi-judicial mechanisms set up by UNMIK and EULEX to address complaints of human rights violations attributable to the respective mission. The need for such a review body was first highlighted by the Venice Commission in 2004, which described the immunity of UNMIK personnel as 'itself a human rights concern'.[18] In 2006, UNMIK established the Human Rights Advisory Panel (HRAP) to examine alleged violations of human rights by the Mission.[19] The Panel's mandate was limited to issuing recommendations to the Secretary General's Special Representative for their action. HRAP was composed of international human

---

16 UN Security Council, *Letter Dated 26 March 2007 from the Secretary-General addressed to the President of the Security Council, Addendum, Comprehensive Proposal for the Kosovo Status Settlement*, 26 March 2007, UN Doc. S/2007/168/Add.1, Article 2.1.

17 De Hert and Korenica, 'The New Kosovo Constitution and Its Relationship with the European Convention on Human Rights: Constitutionalization "Without" Ratification in Post-Conflict Societies', (2016) 76 *ZaöRV*, 143 (151 and footnote 25).

18 CoE, *European Commission for Democracy Through Law (Venice Commission) Opinion on Human Rights in Kosovo: Possible Establishment of Review Mechanisms*, 11 October 2004, CDL-AD (2004)033, paras. 62 f.

19 UNMIK, 'Regulation No. 2006/12 on the Establishment of the Human Rights Advisory Panel', 23 March 2006, https://unmik.unmissions.org/sites/default/files/regulations/02english/E2006regs/RE2006_12.pdf. See also e.g. Istrefi, 'Evolving International Practices for Protection of Human Rights – the UN Human Rights Advisory Panel and EU Human Rights Review Panel' (2017) 1 *AUDJ*, 60; Knoll and Uhl, 'Too Little, Too Late: the Human Rights Advisory Panel in Kosovo' (2007) 7 *European Human Rights Law Review*, 534.

rights experts nominated by the President of the ECtHR. It was operational for 9 years (2007–2016) and dealt with a total of 527 complaints.[20]

The Panel relied heavily on the Convention and the jurisprudence of the ECtHR. This was to be expected given that the Convention was the applicable law in Kosovo and also listed amongst the Panel's sources of law.[21] In some areas, the Panel extended the interpretations emanating from Strasbourg case law. This included issues like

> the determination of legal standards in the context of investigating disappearances and killings where the wrongdoing was committed by non-state actors; the applicability of substantive protections of Article 2 of the ECHR to a UN body in the context of public protest; the applicability of Article 3 of the ECHR to a UN body involving violations with respect to the inhuman and degrading treatment of relatives of missing and/or murdered persons and the procedural aspect of Article 5 ECHR, taking into account the need for gender-sensitive investigations.[22]

EULEX established a similar body in 2009, called the Human Rights Review Panel (HRRP). The Panel remains operational and has jurisdiction from 9 December 2008 onward. It is composed of three international experts in human rights law, appointed by the Head of EULEX Mission. The complaints filed before the Panel have predominately argued violations of the ECHR and its Protocols.[23] Like its UNMIK counterpart, the Panel relies extensively on the Convention and ECtHR's jurisprudence.

---

20 UNMIK, 'The Human Rights Advisory Panel: History and Legacy, Kosovo, 2007–2016', Final Report, 30 June 2016, https://unmik.unmissions.org/sites/default/files/hrap_final_report_final_version_30_june_2016.pdf, para. 23. The Panel's temporal jurisdiction was limited to alleged violations of human rights that occurred between 23 April 2005 and 9 December 2008, when UNMIK's responsibility in the areas of justice and police in Kosovo was transferred to EULEX.

21 UNMIK, 'Regulation No. 2006/12 on the Establishment of the Human Rights Advisory Panel', 23 March 2006, https://unmik.unmissions.org/sites/default/files/regulations/02english/E2006regs/RE2006_12.pdf, section 1.2.

22 UNMIK, 'The Human Rights Advisory Panel: History and Legacy, Kosovo, 2007–2016', Final Report, 30 June 2016, https://unmik.unmissions.org/sites/default/files/hrap_final_report_final_version_30_june_2016.pdf, para. 136.

23 See Human Rights Review Panel, 'Annual Report', 2010, https://hrrp.eu/annual-report.php.

According to available statistics, the Panel had – as of April 2020 – dealt with 201 cases, 177 of which have been finalised.[24]

D. Current status of the ECHR in Kosovo: The Constitution and Beyond

The second perspective that merits analysis is the applicability of the ECHR in the domestic legal order of Kosovo, a non-Signatory of the Convention. This section analyses the Kosovo Constitution, which provides a legal basis for the protection of the Convention rights and freedoms in the territory of Kosovo and the role of domestic courts, especially the Constitutional Court.

I. Incorporation of the ECHR in the Constitution of the Republic of Kosovo

Protection of human rights and freedoms is a central theme throughout the Kosovo Constitution, a legacy of the Ahtisaari Plan. As discussed in the previous section, one of the conditions for a prospective Kosovo State was to guarantee the protection and respect for 'the highest level of internationally recognized human rights and fundamental freedoms'.[25] The natural way to achieve that would be to ratify the core human rights treaties and take on international obligations for their implementation. However, accession to international treaty regimes was not readily available for Kosovo, since entering into treaty arrangements is an expression of state sovereignty while Kosovo's sovereign status was (and remains) contested. Treaties bind consenting parties only, and third parties to any treaty are legally unaffected by it.[26]

The alternative way to bind Kosovo to human rights standards was to weave them into its domestic legal order. What the Constitution of Kosovo does, therefore, is to incorporate into Kosovo's legal system eight international agreements and instruments in order to form a single system

---

24 Human Rights Review Panel, 'Table of Cases with Follow-Up Decisions – April 2020, 2010', https://hrrp.eu/Statistics.php.

25 UN Security Council, *Letter Dated 26 March 2007 from the Secretary-General addressed to the President of the Security Council, Addendum, Comprehensive Proposal for the Kosovo Status Settlement*, 26 March 2007, UN Doc. S/2007/168/Add.1, Article 1.3.

26 This is the classic customary rule of *pacta tertiis nec nocent nec prosunt* – a treaty does not create either obligations or rights for a third party without its consent – as codified in Article 34 of the Vienna Convention on the Law of Treaties.

of protection. These agreements and instruments are the same as those introduced by UNMIK in Regulation 1999/24 with the exception of omitting the International Covenant on Economic, Social and Cultural Rights. In addition, the Council of Europe's Framework Convention for the Protection of National Minorities is included.

By virtue of Article 22 of the Kosovo Constitution, these treaties and instruments are afforded legal authority of constitutional rank, direct applicability and, in case of conflict, priority over provisions of domestic laws and other acts of public institutions. In addition, the Constitution also separately lists individual and collective human rights and freedoms,[27] many of which mirror those enshrined in the Convention.

The constitutional status of the ECHR was specifically addressed by the Constitutional Court in its early case law, when it ruled that a violation of rights or freedoms protected under the Convention amounts to a constitutional violation.[28] This is an unprecedented example of the applicability of an international treaty in a Non-State Party and also the indication of reverence enjoyed by the Convention.

II. The Status of ECtHR's Jurisprudence within Kosovo's Constitutional Framework

Various commentators have addressed the issue of whether Article 22 of the Kosovo Constitution constitutionalises only texts of the enumerated international treaties or also the legal context[29] in which they operate, such as jurisprudence of the ECtHR or authoritative interpretative comments issued by the relevant treaty monitoring bodies.[30] Several observations can be made in this regard. Firstly, judgments of the ECtHR do not create law,

27 Chapter II and III of the Constitution of the Republic of Kosovo, 9 April 2008, https://gzk.rks-gov.net/ActDetail.aspx?ActID=3702.

28 Constitutional Court of Kosovo, Judgment, 23 June 2010, KI 40/09, *Ibrahimi and 48 other former employees of the Kosovo Energy Corporation v 49 individual judgments of the Supreme Court of the Republic of Kosovo*.

29 The term 'context' can be explained by reference to Article 31 of the Vienna Convention on the Law of Treaties.

30 E.g. Korenica and Doli, 'Taking Care of Strasbourg: The Status of the European Convention on Human Rights and the Case-Law of the European Court of Human Rights in Kosovo's Domestic Legal System' (2011) 32 *Liverpool Law Rev*, 209 (217); De Hert and Korenica, 'The New Kosovo Constitution and Its Relationship with the European Convention on Human Rights: Constitutionalization "Without" Ratification in Post-Conflict Societies', (2016) 76 *ZaöRV*, 143.

as the norm of *stare decisis* does not exist in international law in the same way as it operates in common law systems.[31] Secondly, the jurisprudence of the ECtHR does not have *erga omnes* effect on States Parties to the Convention; only a State that is party to the case is bound by the ECtHR's interpretation of the Convention and its findings on violations of the Convention. Thirdly, there is a separate provision in the Constitution of Kosovo – Article 53 – that specifically regulates the role (and status) of ECtHR case law, which 'does not constitutionalize or incorporate ECtHR case law into Kosovo's domestic legal order in the same way as Art. 22 constitutionalizes the ECHR'.[32] Article 53 of the Kosovo Constitution, entitled 'Interpretation of Human Rights Provisions', instead stipulates that human rights and fundamental freedoms guaranteed by the Constitution shall be interpreted consistently with the decisions of the ECtHR. The reference to 'human rights and fundamental freedoms' guaranteed by the Constitution, without further specification, seems to encompass not just the human rights and freedoms explicitly listed in the Constitution but also rights covered by other international agreements and instruments listed in Article 22 of the Kosovo Constitution, including the ECHR and its Protocols.[33] Notably, Article 53 of the Kosovo Constitution does not make any reference to pronouncements of other human rights treaty monitoring bodies, which suggests a uniquely strong position of the Convention and the Strasbourg Court. This is due to the special consideration enjoyed by the ECHR throughout Kosovo's state-building process (as discussed above) and the authority of the ECtHR more generally.

Article 53 of the Kosovo Constitution does not bind only courts, but also all public institutions and authorities in Kosovo that apply and interpret human rights provisions in their public service. This, in turn, suggests that the beneficiaries of the constitutional catalogue of human rights can demand to have them 'interpreted consistently with the court decisions' of the ECtHR. This, however, is not the same as to claim rights, freedoms or duties directly from the ECtHR jurisprudence. In other words, the ECtHR

---

31 Article 38(1)(d) and Article 59 of the Statute of the International Court of Justice.

32 De Hert and Korenica, 'The New Kosovo Constitution and Its Relationship with the European Convention on Human Rights: Constitutionalization "Without" Ratification in Post-Conflict Societies', (2016) 76 *ZaöRV*, 143 (159 and footnote 40).

33 Korenica and Doli, 'Taking Care of Strasbourg: The Status of the European Convention on Human Rights and the Case-Law of the European Court of Human Rights in Kosovo's Domestic Legal System' (2011) 32 *Liverpool Law Rev*, 209 (217).

case law is not a source of law as such.[34] The distinction may appear to be insignificant, but it is present and may play a role in litigation.

Commentators agree that Article 53 of the Kosovo Constitution does not make ECtHR case law directly applicable, but only imposes a constitutional obligation on courts and public institutions to follow ECtHR's interpretations of human rights and fundamental freedoms.[35] Article 53 of the Constitution binds all courts, including the Constitutional Court. The latter has followed Article 53 in both substantive and procedural aspects of cases concerning claims of human rights violations as well as when exercising abstract jurisdiction over constitutionality of Kosovo laws.[36]

The final question in this regard relates to what being bound by ECtHR case law actually entails. Does the obligation of 'consistent interpretation' merely mean that courts must avoid contradicting or disregarding the jurisprudence of the Strasbourg Court, or are Kosovo courts compelled to justify their decisions involving constitutional human rights with reference to the reasoning of the ECtHR? The commentators rely on early judgments of the Constitutional Court to suggest that the Court considered itself obliged to refer to ECtHR case law constitutionally but not bound by its rulings.[37] In other words, the Court has viewed ECtHR's case law 'as a tool for advancing the interpretation of constitutional provisions, rather than as an obligation requiring adherence to ECtHR precedents'.[38] Such approach allows the Court to treat ECtHR's standards as the floor rather than the ceiling of human rights protection and enables it to offer a broa-

34 De Hert and Korenica, 'The New Kosovo Constitution and Its Relationship with the European Convention on Human Rights: Constitutionalization "Without" Ratification in Post-Conflict Societies', (2016) 76 *ZaöRV*, 143 (159 f.).

35 Korenica and Doli, 'Taking Care of Strasbourg: The Status of the European Convention on Human Rights and the Case-Law of the European Court of Human Rights in Kosovo's Domestic Legal System' (2011) 32 *Liverpool Law Rev*, 209 (218).

36 Constitutional Court of Kosovo, Decision, 16 October 2009, KI 11/09, *Tomë Krasniqi v RTK et Al.*

37 See e.g., Constitutional Court of Kosovo, Judgment, 23 June 2010, KI 40/09, *Ibrahimi and 48 other former employees of the Kosovo Energy Corporation v 49 individual judgments of the Supreme Court of the Republic of Kosovo*; Constitutional Court of Kosovo, Decision, 21 June 2010, KI 68/09, *Emrush Kastrati v Decision of the Supreme Court of Kosovo, Pkl. No. 120/0*; Constitutional Court of Kosovo, Judgment, 30 October 2010, KI 06/10, *Valon Bislimi v Ministry of Internal Affairs, Kosovo Judicial Council and Ministry of Justice*.

38 De Hert and Korenica, 'The New Kosovo Constitution and Its Relationship with the European Convention on Human Rights: Constitutionalization "Without" Ratification in Post-Conflict Societies', (2016) 76 *ZaöRV*, 143 (162).

der interpretation of constitutional rights. This judicial independence is not unusual, as constitutional courts of other states that have incorporated the Convention into their constitutions have adopted a similar stance.[39]

Incorporating the ECHR with all its Protocols into a domestic legal order and constitutionalising the obligation of public authorities to interpret human rights and fundamental freedoms consistently with the ECtHR's jurisprudence is an example of embedding the Strasbourg Court's supervisory system, which enables international human rights norms to infiltrate domestic legal and political processes and improve the prospects of compliance. As noted by one author,

> [w]hen Strasbourg rights and freedoms are fully domesticated in one of these ways, compliance with international law and national law approaches convergence. Stated differently, to the extent that a state accepts the rule of law at home, it also necessarily adheres to the rule of law internationally.[40]

This process is even more interesting and significant in the case of Kosovo: due to its contested statehood it is neither a member of the UN nor of the CoE and is not a party to any of the human rights treaties incorporated in its Constitution and, thereby, in fact, is free from any international obligation to implement them.

III. Judicial Protection of Human Rights and Fundamental Freedoms within the Kosovo Legal System

The non-participation of Kosovo in external mechanisms of monitoring and supervision of human rights implementation puts emphasis on the domestic oversight apparatus. The Constitution of Kosovo, in Article 54, provides for general guarantees such as recourse to courts in case of alleged violation of rights guaranteed by any law. The right to an effective legal remedy is further elaborated in Article 102 of the Kosovo Constitution. Moreover, Article 113 of the Kosovo Constitution envisages an individual complaint mechanism before the Constitutional Court in cases of violation of human rights specifically and the possibility for regular courts to

---

39 Examples include the German Constitutional Court and the Polish Constitutional Tribunal.

40 Helfer, 'Redesigning the European Court of Human Rights: Embeddedness as a Deep Structural Principle of the European Human Rights Regime' (2008) 19 *EJIL*, 125 (133).

refer cases to the Constitutional Court if uncertain about the compatibility of any particular law with the Constitution.

1. The Constitutional Court

The Constitutional Court of Kosovo, established in January 2009,[41] has played a decisive role in the development of the rule of law and the protection of human rights and fundamental freedoms in Kosovo.[42]

The legal basis for the organisation and functioning of the Constitutional Court stems from Chapter VIII of the Constitution and the Law on the Constitutional Court of the Republic of Kosovo (Law No. 03/L-121), supplemented by Rules of Procedure (No. 01/2018).[43] The Constitutional Court is an independent organ in protecting the constitutionality and is the final interpreter of the Constitution.[44] Article 113 specifies matters within the Constitutional Court's jurisdiction and the parties allowed to make referrals. It is authorised to review the legality of legislative and executive actions, pronounce on the constitutional compatibility of legislation, assess individual complaints of violations by public authorities of human rights and fundamental freedoms guaranteed by the Constitution and clarify the meaning of constitutional provisions. Decisions of the Constitutional Court are binding on the judiciary and all persons and institutions of the Republic of Kosovo.[45] All acts rendered to be unconstitutional by the Constitutional Court lose their legal force.

---

41 Constitutional Court of Kosovo, Annual Report 2009, 20 December 2009, https://gjk-ks.org/wp-content/uploads/2017/11/RaportiVjetor2009Final_ANG.pdf.

42 Hasani, 'The Role of the Constitutional Court in the Development of the Rule of Law in Kosovo' (2018) 43 *RCEEL*, 274 (312).

43 The work of the Court is further governed by the Constitutional Court of the Republic of Kosovo Code of Judicial Conduct, 19 June 2013, (https://gjk-ks.org/en/the-constitutional-court/legal-base/code-of-judicial-conduct/gjkk_kodi_i_miresjelljes_per_gjyqtare_ang-2/), the Regulation of the Legal Unit No. 03/2019, 2 December 2019, https://gjk-ks.org/wp-content/uploads/2019/12/Rregullore-03_2019_e-Njesis-Ligjore_eng.pdf, and the Practice Direction No. 06/2012 on Functioning and Structure of Legal Unit, 4 December 2012, https://gjk-ks.org/wp-content/uploads/2017/11/Practice_Direction_Legal_Unit_No.06-2012-1.pdf.

44 Article 4 of the Constitution of the Republic of Kosovo.

45 Article 116 [Legal Effect of Decisions] of the Constitution of the Republic of Kosovo.

The Constitutional Court is independent from other institutions in its decision making and operation.[46] It is composed of nine judges elected for a non-renewable mandate of nine years.[47] Initially, in line with the former Article 152 of the Constitution, three out of nine judges were international judges appointed by the International Civilian Representative, upon consultation with the President of the ECtHR. This mechanism was intended to further emphasise the special status of the ECHR within Kosovo's legal order and to secure the application of the Convention and the ECtHR's jurisprudence.[48] Since 2018, the Constitutional Court is composed exclusively of Kosovo judges. It deliberates as a panel composed of all judges who are present (a quorum requires seven judges) and decides by a majority of votes from the judges present and voting.[49]

2. *Individual Referrals*

Pursuant to Article 113(7) of the Constitution and procedure provided in Law No. 03/L-121, individuals may refer to the Constitutional Court violations of their constitutional rights and freedoms committed by public authorities.[50] They may submit a referral only after having exhausted all legal remedies provided by law and within four months from a final court decision in their case, public announcement of a contested decision or act, or entry into force of the challenged law. A referral shall specify what rights and freedoms are claimed to have been violated and what act of public authority is contested. If the Court determines that the challenged

---

46 Articles,106, 107 and 112(2) of the Constitution of the Republic of Kosovo; Articles 2, 5 and 10 of the Law No. 03/L-121 on the Constitutional Court of the Republic of Kosovo, Official Gazette of the Republic of Kosovo No. 46/2009, 15 January 2009, 4; Rule 2 of the Rules of Procedure of the Constitutional Court of the Republic of Kosovo, No. 01/2018, 13 June 2018, https://gjk-ks.org/wp-content/uploads/2018/06/rregullore_e-_punes_gjkk_ang_2018.pdf.

47 Pursuant to Article 114 of the Kosovo Constitution, national judges are appointed by the President of the Republic of Kosovo upon the proposal of the Assembly of Kosovo. See also Article 4 of the Law No. 03/L-121 for other conditions of appointment.

48 Korenica and Doli, 'Taking Care of Strasbourg: The Status of the European Convention on Human Rights and the Case-Law of the European Court of Human Rights in Kosovo's Domestic Legal System' (2011) 32 *Liverpool Law Rev*, 209 (220).

49 Article 19 of Law No. 03/L-121.

50 *Id.*, Articles 46 ff.

decision violated the Constitution, it declares the decision void and may remand it to the issuing authority for reconsideration.[51]

During the first eleven years of its existence (2009–2020), the Constitutional Court received almost two thousand applications. Based on statistics available in the Constitutional Court's newsletters for years 2015–2020, the majority of the applications (between 70 % and 90 % each year) were triggered by individual complaints from natural persons alleging violations of their constitutional rights. Most of those complaints referred to violations allegedly committed through decisions of the regular courts – from 75 % to 95 % depending on the year with the rest referring to decisions of other public authorities. A large majority were rejected as inadmissible (between 75 % and 80 %).[52] With regard to the alleged constitutional rights violated the most commonly referred were Equality Before the Law (Article 24 of the Kosovo Constitution) and Right to Fair and Impartial Trial (Article 31 of the Kosovo Constitution). When adjudicating the cases on the merits, the Court regularly refers to individual rights listed in Chapter II of the Kosovo Constitution and corresponding rights in the ECHR.[53]

The referrals to the Constitutional Court mirror the experience of constitutional courts in other European states, with the vast majority of cases also originating from complaints about individual constitutional rights.[54] Most European constitutional courts accept the ECtHR as the interpretative authority on the Convention, rely extensively on its case law and adopt the technique of the harmonious interpretation of the ECHR when adjudicating individual referrals.[55] This connection between domestic constitutional law and the Convention as interpreted by the Strasbourg Court 'has resulted in a better protection of fundamental rights in the European legal space'.[56] Since Kosovo remains outside the formal treaty regime of the ECHR, the Constitutional Court had to take over as a domestic version of the ECtHR, embodying its ethos.

---

51 Rule 46 of the Rules of Procedure of the Constitutional Court of the Republic of Kosovo.

52 For conditions of admissibility see Article 113(7) of the Kosovo Constitution and Articles 46 ff. of Law No. 03/L-121.

53 Constitutional Court of Kosovo, Newsletter, 2021, https://gjk-ks.org/en/publication_category/newsletter/.

54 Van de Heyning, 'Constitutional Courts as Guardians of Fundamental Rights. The constitutionalisation of the Convention through domestic constitutional adjudication', in: Popelier *et al.* (eds), *The Role of Constitutional Courts in Multilevel Governance* (2012), 19 (22).

55 *Id.*, 28.

56 *Id.*, 24.

It is with the support of international actors, the CoE in particular, that the Constitutional Court is able to act as a guardian of human rights and fundamental freedoms. The CoE has assumed an active role in strengthening the capacity of the Constitutional Court through various projects. Since 2014, it has launched two tailored programmes aimed at 'ensuring the protection of individual human rights and fundamental freedoms through effective application of European human rights standards to individual complaints'.[57] The projects targeted the judges and legal advisors of the Constitutional Court of Kosovo and, *inter alia*, offered a mentoring scheme for judges by peers from leading European constitutional courts and the ECtHR. The objective was to exchange the experiences of applying the ECHR and share best working methods. The programmes also provided working visits of Kosovo judges to the ECtHR and work placements in the Registry of the ECtHR for legal advisors to advance their professional development. It also supported professional exchanges between the Constitutional Court and the Venice Commission. Other activities coordinated by the CoE have been directed at raising awareness about European human rights standards and the work of the Constitutional Court amongst legal professionals and the general Kosovo population.[58]

3. *Strengthening the Domestic Capacity to Implement Human Rights and Fundamental Freedoms in accordance with the Principle of Subsidiarity*

The projects discussed above are elements of a broader assistance strategy for Kosovo. The international community has supported democracy and institution building in Kosovo ever since 1999, in compliance with the UN Security Council Resolution 1244. The CoE, in particular, has implemented several programmes to promote good governance, rule of law and human rights standards in Kosovo. These include the EU/CoE joint projects aimed at combating economic crime, promoting human rights, minority protection and local democracy in Kosovo.[59] The CoE's office in Pristina provides vital assistance in the implementation of all

57 CoE, Improving the protection of European Human Rights Standards by the Constitutional Court of Kosovo, 2020, https://www.coe.int/en/web/national-implementation/kosovo-improving-the-protection-of-european-human-rights-standards-by-the-constitutional-court-of-kosovo.

58 *Ibid.*

59 For more information see CoE, Kosovo*, 2020, https://www.coe.int/en/web/programmes/kosovo.

co-operation activities, facilitating the delivery of support programmes and co-ordinating efforts of local and international actors.[60] Several cooperation activities in the fields of judicial reform and human rights protection have been implemented to improve the day-to-day functioning and quality of Kosovo's justice system.[61]

Bolstering domestic remedies provided to individuals whose rights have been violated is in line with the principle of subsidiarity upon which the Strasbourg supervisory system is founded. States Parties to the ECHR bear the primary responsibility for guaranteeing human rights and fundamental freedoms enshrined in the Convention, while the ECtHR and other institutions of the CoE play a subsidiary and supplementary role.[62] The principle of subsidiarity is embodied in the provisions of the Convention such as the obligation on Member States to provide an effective national remedy[63] or the requirement to exhaust all domestic remedies.[64] It serves as a cornerstone of the margin of appreciation doctrine referred to in the ECtHR's jurisprudence, and it explains the Court's refusal to supplant national protective mechanisms, act as a first instance fact-finder[65] or a fourth-instance appeal of national court rulings.[66] The principle of subsidiarity is explicitly referred to in the preamble of Protocol No. 16 to the ECHR, which extends the Court's competence to give advisory opinions to further enhance the interaction between the Court and national

---

60 See CoE, Welcome to the Council of Europe Office in Pristina, 2020, https://www.coe.int/en/web/pristina/home.

61 An overview of activities 2013–2020 is available on https://www.coe.int/en/web/programmes/kosovo.

62 Arai-Takahashi, *The Margin of Appreciation Doctrine and the Principle of Proportionality in the Jurisprudence of the ECHR* (2002), 235 f.

63 Article 13 ECHR.

64 Article 35 ECHR.

65 The Court rarely and reluctantly takes on the role of a first-instance tribunal of fact, unless this is rendered unavoidable by the circumstances of a particular case when the Court is confronted with repeated allegations of flagrant violations and the lack of cooperation from the governments. See Harmsen, 'The European Convention on Human Rights After Enlargement' (2001) 5 *Int'l J Human Rts*, 18 (29).

66 Helfer, 'Redesigning the European Court of Human Rights: Embeddedness as a Deep Structural Principle of the European Human Rights Regime' (2008) 19 *EJIL*, 125 (128). See also ECtHR, Practical Guide on Admissibility Criteria, 30 April 2020, https://www.echr.coe.int/documents/admissibility_guide_eng.pdf.

authorities and thereby reinforce implementation of the Convention in a domestic setting.[67]

The principle of subsidiarity rests on the premise that national authorities are better placed to protect individual human rights in their specific social and political context because they benefit from a comprehensive understanding of constitutional traditions of their nation, the values of their local culture, institutional and social practices as well as more complete factual information to make a decision at the closest level to the affected person as is effectively possible.[68] Considerations of judicial expediency and efficiency further substantiate the primacy of domestic judicial review mechanisms.[69] National choices of Convention-compatible implementation measures might also enjoy more institutional legitimacy than resolutions of supranational entities distant from people affected by such decisions.

The principle of subsidiarity seeks to balance the idea of non-interference and that of intervention or assistance, which implies that such interventions may sometimes be necessary.[70] As a supervisory ancillary mechanism, the ECtHR can be utilised whenever national authorities prove less capable of ensuring the adequate protection of human rights due to a lack of necessary experience and expertise, or simply when they wilfully violate these rights. The right of individual petition is the linchpin of the Convention's supervisory framework, and the ECtHR is a permanent court with compulsory jurisdiction over all Member States to which individuals have direct access.[71] The Convention's judicial review mechanism is a powerful tool and a necessary element of the CoE's entire control machi-

---

67 Protocol No. 16 to the ECHR, Preamble. The Protocol allows the highest courts and tribunals of State Parties to request the Strasbourg Court for advisory opinions on questions of principle relating to the interpretation or application of the rights and freedoms defined in the Convention or the protocols thereto. The Protocol entered into force on 1 August 2018.

68 Carozza, 'Subsidiarity as a Structural Principle of International Human Rights Law' (2003) 97 *Am. J. Int'l L.*, 38 (72 f.).

69 Arai-Takahashi, *The Margin of Appreciation Doctrine and the Principle of Proportionality in the Jurisprudence of the ECHR* (2002), 235 f.

70 Carozza, 'Subsidiarity as a Structural Principle of International Human Rights Law' (2003) 97 *Am. J. Int'l L.*, 38 (79).

71 Protocol No. 11 to the ECHR restructured the control machinery established thereby. See also the reaffirmation by Member States of the right to individual petition as the cornerstone of the ECHR control system in CoE, High Level Conference on the Future of the European Court of Human Rights, Declaration, 27 April 2011, https://echr.coe.int/Documents/2011_Izmir_FinalDeclaration_ENG.pdf, 3.

nery offering 'individual justice' in situations where national mechanisms of human rights protection prove inadequate.

Kosovo has made progress towards human rights sensitive good governance. However numerous challenges remain. According to the European Commission (EC) 2020 Report, Kosovo is still at an early stage of developing a well-functioning judicial system. The administration of justice remains slow and inefficient while rule of law institutions need sustained efforts to build up their capacities.[72] The EC notes that although the legal framework broadly guarantees the protection of human and fundamental rights in line with European standards, the implementation of human rights legislation and strategies is often undermined by inadequate resources, particularly at the local level, and limited political prioritisation. There is a large dependency on foreign donors.[73] Oversight and coordination of existing human rights mechanisms remain a challenge.[74] According to the Civil Society Report on Human Rights in Kosovo in 2019, there is also an existing gap in joint reporting on human rights at the local and international levels.[75] The conclusions of these reports explain the structure of referrals to the Kosovo Constitutional Court, which as discussed above, are mostly composed of individual referrals alleging violations of constitutional rights committed by lower courts or public institutions. All this suggests that Kosovo would benefit from the CoE's multifaceted control machinery, including the oversight of the ECtHR, to improve the promotion and protection of human rights. However, until it becomes a member of the organisation and a State Party to the ECHR, these monitoring and enforcement measures remain unavailable.

72 European Commission, *Commission Staff Working Document, Kosovo* 2020 Report*, 6 October 2020, SWD(2020) 356 final, 17 f.

73 *Id.*, 6.

74 *Id.*, 29.

75 Office of the UN High Commissioner for Human Rights, Civil Society Report on Human Rights in Kosovo in 2019, June 2020, https://www.ohchr.org/Documents/Press/kosovo_cso_2019_human_rights_report_en.pdf. The report was delivered at the conclusion of the project called 'Engaging with civil society on human rights monitoring and reporting' funded by the Human Rights Component of UNMIK and the OHCHR.

E. *Beyond the Constitution – the ECHR as a Directly Applicable Source of Law for the Kosovo Specialist Chambers*

The third example of multifaceted impact of the ECHR is the direct applicability of the Convention to war crimes prosecutions conducted by an internationalised court. Again, Kosovo serves as a laboratory for this exploration. By virtue of its position and role in the Kosovo Constitution, the ECHR is now also a directly applicable source of law for the newly established internationalised criminal tribunal – the Kosovo Specialist Chambers (KSC) and the Specialist Prosecutor's Office (SPO).

The KSC are a unique model of a temporary internationalised criminal court existing within the domestic justice system.[76] They are not, however, the first international(ised) mechanism established in/for Kosovo to prosecute crimes committed during the Kosovo War; there has been the ICTY and the participation of international judges and prosecutors in Kosovo proceedings under the UNMIK and EULEX umbrella.[77]

I. *Legal Framework of the KSC*

The KSC and the SPO were created in 2015 pursuant to an exchange of letters between the EU High Representative and the President of Kosovo ratified by the Kosovo Assembly,[78] a Constitutional Amendment (Article 162 of the Kosovo Constitution)[79] and the Law on Kosovo Specialist Chambers and Specialist Prosecutor's Office (Law No. 05/L-053).[80] They are funded by EU Member States and Third Contributing States and their seat is in the Hague. The KSC became fully judicially operational in July

76 Korenica et al., 'The EU-engineered hybrid and international specialist court in Kosovo: how "special" is it?' (2016) 12 *EuConst*, 474 (474).

77 Williams, 'The Specialist Chambers of Kosovo The Limits of Internationalization?' (2016) 14 *JICJ*, 25 (31).

78 Law No. 04/L-274 on Ratification of the International Agreement between the Republic of Kosovo and the Eureopan Union Role of Law Mission in Kosovo, Official Gazette of the Republic of Kosovo No. 32/2014, 15 May 2014, 4.

79 Amendment of the Constitution of the Republic of Kosovo, No. 05-D-139, 3 August 2015, Official Gazette of the Republic of Kosovo No. 20/2015, 5 August 2015, 4.

80 Law No. 05/L-053 on Specialist Chambers and Specialist Prosecutor's Office, Official Gazette of the Republic of Kosovo No. 27/2015, 31 August 2015, 1.

2017 while the first indictments were confirmed in 2020.[81] The first trial opened in September 2021.

The KSC exercise jurisdiction over crimes against humanity, war crimes and serious crimes under Kosovo law, which were committed (or whose commission began) in Kosovo between 1 January 1998 and 31 December 2000 by or against citizens of Kosovo or the former Republic of Yugoslavia, as well as certain crimes against the administration of justice.[82] Its subject matter jurisdiction is limited to crimes purportedly committed by high-level members of the KLA during and shortly before/after the war in Kosovo, described in the 2010 Report of Special Rapporteur Dick Marty to the Parliamentary Assembly of the Council of Europe.[83] The institution will exist only for as long as necessary to deal with charges presented by the Specialist Prosecutor and until the EU Council is satisfied that investigations and proceedings are completed.

Some commentators have suggested that Article 162 of the Kosovo Constitution establishing the KSC and SPO has created 'a parallel self-contained regime within the Constitution whose authority is independent of the rest of the Constitution'.[84] The provision opens with a caveat ('Notwithstanding any provision in this Constitution'), which has been viewed as an autonomous source of authority to operate the special(ist) court.[85] This autonomy can be seen in the structure of the KSC and the applicable law. While the KSC are part of the existing judicial framework in Kosovo and accordingly have the same court levels (a Basic Court Chamber, a Court of Appeals Chamber, a Supreme Court Chamber and a Constitutional Court Chamber), they employ exclusively international staff,[86] are granted primacy over all other courts in Kosovo in relation to the crimes within the KSC's jurisdiction and are fully independent in the fulfilment of their mandate and work.[87] The Specialist Constitutional Court Chamber is composed of three constitutional judges assigned from

81 See Kosovo Specialist Chambers & Specialist Prosecutor's Office, 2021, https://www.scp-ks.org/en.

82 Law No. 05/L-053, Chapter III (Jurisdiction and Applicable Law of the Law on Specialist Chambers and Specialist Prosecutor's Office).

83 CoE Parliamentary Assembly, *Inhuman treatment of people and illicit trafficking in human organs in Kosovo*, AS/Jur (2010) 46, 12 December 2010.

84 Korenica et al., 'The EU-engineered hybrid and international specialist court in Kosovo: how "special" is it?' (2016) 12 *EuConst*, 474 (482).

85 *Ibid.*

86 For a general discussion on international, hybrid and internationalised courts see: Williams, *Hybrid and Internationalised Criminal Tribunals* (2012).

87 Law No. 05/L-053, Article 10(1).

the KSC Roster of International Judges,[88] and it deals exclusively with constitutional referrals relating to the KSC and SPO[89] and is the final authority for the interpretation of the Constitution in this regard.[90]

Law No. 05/L-053 lists relevant sources of law for the KSC as follows: the Law itself, the Constitution, other provisions of Kosovo law as expressly incorporated and applied by Law No.05/L-053, customary international law, as given superiority over domestic laws by Article 19(2) of the Constitution, and international human rights law that sets criminal justice standards, including the European Convention on Human Rights and Fundamental Freedoms and the International Covenant on Civil and Political Rights, as given superiority over domestic laws by Article 22 of the Constitution.[91] The Law also provides that any other Kosovo law, regulation, secondary regulation, other rule or custom and practice which has not been expressly incorporated into it, is not applicable and that the Law prevails over any and all contrary provisions of other laws or regulations.[92]

II. Implications of the Legal Framework of the KSC

In light of the above discussion, the following observations can be made: Firstly, the ECHR is a direct source of law for the KSC and will guide the Specialist Prosecutor and the Judges, in particular in relation to fair trial and detention issues and criminal justice more broadly. The KSC jurisprudence may consequently inspire or assist other international, hybrid or internationalised criminal courts not explicitly bound by the ECHR, thereby further extending the reach of the Convention.

Secondly, the self-contained regime of the KSC, as established by the amended Article 162 of the Constitution and the Law No. 05/L-053, insulates the decisions of the KSC and the SPO from any review of the Kosovo institutions outside of its structure. Additionally, since Kosovo is not a member of the CoE and not a State Party to the ECHR, decisions of the KSC remain outside the control of the ECtHR or any political or expert body of the CoE.[93]

---

88 *Id.*, Article 25(1)(e).
89 *Id.*, Articles 3(1), 49(2).
90 *Id.*, Article 49.
91 *Id.*, Article 3(2).
92 *Id.*, Article 3(4).
93 Korenica et al., 'The EU-engineered hybrid and international specialist court in Kosovo: how "special" is it?' (2016) 12 *EuConst* 2016, 474 (484 f.).

Thirdly, the Specialist Constitutional Court Chamber is the final arbiter of constitutional referrals and the final interpreter of the Kosovo Constitution in relation to the subject matter, jurisdiction and work of the KSC and the SPO, which would also include human rights issues. Despite being part of the Kosovo Constitutional Court, the Specialist Constitutional Court Chamber is at the same time distinct from it in size and personnel. As explained above, it is composed of three international judges as opposed to nine national judges of the Constitutional Court. The KSC are bound only by the Constitution and other laws explicitly acknowledged in the Law No. 05/L-053, which are only one segment of the mosaic of the Kosovo domestic legal order. The Kosovo Constitutional Court, on the other hand, interprets constitutional provisions in a wider context of the text and *acquis* of entire national law and emerging national constitutional identity. Whether these differences will be problematic remains to be seen, although there has already been an indication. In its first judgment of 26 April 2017,[94] tasked with reviewing the constitutionality of the Rules of Procedure (RoP), the Specialist Constitutional Court Chamber in The Hague declined to evaluate Rule 134(3) RoP holding that it was 'not in a position to rule that this provision complies with Chapter II [Fundamental Rights and Freedoms] of the Constitution'.[95] By relying on the doctrine *non liquet* (i.e. not clear), it disregarded the rich jurisprudence of the Constitutional Court in Pristina.[96] Moreover, this stance of the Specialist Constitutional Court Chamber is not the standard practice of European constitutional courts, which would only exceptionally declare themselves unable to rule on an issue.[97] There are two speculative implications of such an approach. First, the Specialist Judges may ignore the rich case law of the Constitutional Court in Pristina with regard to other issues as well, including fundamental rights and freedoms. Second, it is not clear whether the Constitutional Court and other courts in Kosovo will follow or even consider the judgments of the Specialist Constitutional Court Chamber, for example in relation to criminal justice standards. This may

94 KSC, Judgment (Specialist Chamber of the Constitutional Court), 26 April 2017, Specialist Chamber of the Constitutional Court, *Referral of the Rules of Procedure and Evidence Pursuant to Article 19(5) of the Law*, KSC-CC-PR-2017–01, paras. 190 ff.

95 *Id.*, para. 193.

96 Hasani and Mjeku, 'International(ized) Constitutional Court: Kosovo's Transfer of Judicial Sovereignty' (2019) *ICL Journal*, 373 (394).

97 *Ibid.*

result in a highly fragmented constitutional jurisprudence and undermine legal certainty.

III. The ECHR and War Crimes Cases in Former Yugoslavia: A Valuable Source?

The issue of the KSC remaining outside the remit of the ECtHR's review deserves some further discussion. Since the former Yugoslav republics ratified the ECHR,[98] the Strasbourg Court has decided a number of complaints regarding proceedings that are directly or indirectly linked to the armed conflicts in Yugoslavia in the 1990s. Some of the issues arising in these cases may surface in the proceedings before the KSC. As discussed above, complainants challenging the decisions of the KSC will not have recourse to ECtHR and the judges of the Specialist Chambers will have the final say on the matter.

The Strasbourg Court, it must be noted, does not shy away from addressing the particular challenges of large-scale human rights violations committed in armed conflict. The Court is increasingly engaged in what can be termed a judicial dialogue with international and internationalised criminal courts as well as domestic courts dealing with core crimes in State Parties. One example common to this area is the question of applicable law, specifically the question of *lex mitior* and retrospective application of domestic penal codes. In *Maktouf and Damjanovic v. Bosnia*, the ECtHR ruled that the retroactive application of post-war penal codes in Bosnia could have operated to the perpetrators' disadvantage, resulting in the imposition of a heavier penalty and therefore violating Article 7 of the ECHR.[99] The ECtHR was also seized of a complaint contesting the involvement of international judges in adjudicating war crime cases in domestic courts, and dismissed challenges to their independence and professionalism.[100] Another common issue arising in the context of war crimes prosecutions is the contention of the lack of effective investigation into disappearances

98 Slovenia: 1994, North Macedonia: 1997, Croatia: 1997, Bosnia: 2002, Serbia: 2004, Montenegro: 2004.

99 ECtHR, Judgment (GC), 18 July 2013, *Maktouf and Damjanović v Bosnia and Herzegovina*, Application Nos. 2312/08 and 34179/08, paras. 72 ff.

100 *Id.*, para. 51.

and deaths. In several cases, the ECtHR found a violation of Article 2 (right to life) based on inadequate domestic investigations.[101]

This jurisprudence of the ECtHR shows the range and effectiveness of the Convention's response to allegations of human rights violations committed in or in relation to armed conflict. The Strasbourg Court is able and willing to supervise States in the fulfilment of their undertakings when redressing international crimes and other large-scale human rights violations, and the possibility of this last resort control would also be beneficial for the Kosovo Specialist Chambers.

F. Conclusion

The multifaceted role of the ECHR in Kosovo serves as an example of the Convention's potential to influence human rights protection in non-State Parties and to impact the international human rights discourse more generally. In Kosovo, two factors were decisive in this regard: first, the intervention of the international community, specifically the UN, that initially introduced the ECHR into Kosovo's legal system, and second, the constitutional choices that subsequently embedded the Convention within its territory.

Because of the international community's decision to tie Kosovo's emerging constitutional framework to internationally recognised human rights standards, the Convention and its Protocols, along with a handful of other international human rights instruments, are now firmly entrenched in the Kosovo Constitution and given priority over domestic laws. Moreover, the Constitution also prescribes that all human rights and fundamental freedoms guaranteed by it must be interpreted in accordance with the decisions of the Strasbourg Court. The continuing support from the international community, especially the CoE, helps strengthen Kosovo's domestic capacity to respect and protect human rights and fundamental freedoms and is in line with the principle of subsidiarity.

Whilst generally a very positive development, the system has its limitations. Since Kosovo is not a State Party to the Convention, there is no recourse to the ECtHR. This has caused the domestic courts – notably the Constitutional Court – to assume the role of the final authority when it

---

101 ECtHR, Judgment, 20 January 2011, *Jularić v Croatia*, Application No. 20106/06; ECtHR, Judgment, 20 January 2011, *Skendžić and Krznarić v Croatia*, Application No. 16212/08.

comes to interpreting the Convention for Kosovo complainants, which is not without its challenges. The conclusion that can be drawn is that while it is possible for a treaty (ECHR) to be implemented and assume a vital role in a non-State Party, the system of protection lacks an international monitoring and enforcement element (ECtHR) in order to reach its full potential.

The ECHR has also proved instrumental in the adjudication of international and trans-national crimes in the internationalised judicial mechanisms in Kosovo, first under the UNMIK and EULEX umbrella, and more recently within the Kosovo Specialist Chambers. In the context of the latter, the Convention is, by virtue of its status in the Constitution, a directly applicable source of law. As the judicial proceedings at the KSC unfold, it will be interesting to observe what implications, if any, will direct applicability of the ECHR have in comparison to, for example, the proceedings of *ad hoc* criminal tribunals and the International Criminal Court, where the Convention is often referenced by the parties and the judges but is not as such a direct source of rights and obligations. Finally, the Convention has been and remains instrumental in considering alleged violations of human rights by international actors in Kosovo through the operation of the human rights review panels within UNMIK and EULEX.

In sum, this chapter has attempted to provide an overview of the curious relationship between the ECHR and Kosovo in the last two decades. This relationship, as can be seen from the above, is not static and continues to evolve. In the future we may see Kosovo joining the CoE and becoming a State Party to the Convention. We may then come to no longer speak of a curious relationship between the two.

Bibliography

Arai-Takahashi, Yutaka: The Margin of Appreciation Doctrine and the Principle of Proportionality in the Jurisprudence of the ECHR (2002).

Carozza, Paolo G.: Subsidiarity as a Structural Principle of International Human Rights Law, Am. J. Int'l L. 2003, 38ff.

Constitutional Court of Kosovo: Annual Report 2009, 20 December 2009, https://gjk-ks.org/wp-content/uploads/2017/11/RaportiVjetor2009Final_ANG.pdf.

Constitutional Court of Kosovo: Newsletter (2021), https://gjk-ks.org/en/publication_category/newsletter/.

De Hert, Paul/Korenica, Fisnik: The New Kosovo Constitution and Its Relationship with the European Convention on Human Rights: Constitutionalization "Without" Ratification in Post-Conflict Societies, ZaöRV 2016, 143ff.

Dzehtsiarou, Kanstantsin/Tzevelekos, Vassilis P.: The Conscience of Europe that Landed in Strasbourg: A Circle of Life of the European Court of Human Rights, ECHRLR 2020, 1ff.

Glenny, Misha: The Fall of Yugoslavia: The Third Balkan War (1996).

Harmsen, Robert: The European Convention on Human Rights After Enlargement, Int'l J Human Rts 2001, 18ff.

Hasani, Enver: The Role of the Constitutional Court in the Development of the Rule of Law in Kosovo, RCEEL 2018, 274ff.

Hasani, Enver/Mjeku, Getoar: International(ized) Constitutional Court: Kosovo's Transfer of Judicial Sovereignty, ICL Journal 2019, 373ff.

Helfer, Laurence R.: Redesigning the European Court of Human Rights: Embeddedness as a Deep Structural Principle of the European Human Rights Regime, EJIL 2008, 125ff.

Human Rights Review Panel: Annual Report (2010), https://hrrp.eu/annual-report.php.

Human Rights Review Panel: Table of Cases with Follow-Up Decisions – April 2020 (2010), https://hrrp.eu/Statistics.php.

Istrefi, Remzije: Evolving International Practices for Protection of Human Rights – the UN Human Rights Advisory Panel and EU Human Rights Review Panel, AUDJ 2017, 60 ff.

Karčić, Fikret: A Study on Legal Formalism in the Former Yugoslavia and its Successor States (2020), https://cids.no/wp-content/uploads/pdf/cids-reports/10016-cids-rapport-2020.pdf.

Knoll, Bernhard/Uhl, Robert-Jan: Too Little, Too Late: the Human Rights Advisory Panel in Kosovo, European Human Rights Law Review 2007, 534ff.

Korenica Fisnik/Doli, Dren: Taking Care of Strasbourg: The Status of the European Convention on Human Rights and the Case-Law of the European Court of Human Rights in Kosovo's Domestic Legal System, Liverpool Law Rev 2011, 209ff.

Korenica, Fisnik/Zhubi, Argjend/Doli, Dren: The EU-engineered hybrid and international specialist court in Kosovo: how "special" is it? EuConst 2016, 474ff.

Kosovo Specialist Chambers & Specialist Prosecutor's Office: 2021, https://www.scp-ks.org/en.

Ministry of Foreign Affairs and Diaspora of the Republic of Kosovo: International recognitions of the Republic of Kosovo (2018), https://www.mfa-ks.net/en/politika/483/njohjet-ndrkombtare-t-republiks-s-kosovs/483.

Office of the UN High Commissioner for Human Rights: Civil Society Report on Human Rights in Kosovo in 2019, June 2020, https://www.ohchr.org/Documents/Press/kosovo_cso_2019_human_rights_report_en.pdf.

Silber, Laura/Little, Allan: Yugoslavia: Death of a Nation (1997).

UN Security Council: Letter Dated 26 March 2007 from the Secretary-General addressed to the President of the Security Council, Addendum, Comprehensive Proposal for the Kosovo Status Settlement, UN Doc. S/2007/168/Add.1, 26 March 2007.

UN Security Council: Military-technical agreement between the international security force (KFOR) and the Governments of the Federal Republic of Yugoslavia and the Republic of Serbia, UN Doc. S/1999/682, 15 June 1999.

UNMIK: The Human Rights Advisory Panel: History and Legacy, Kosovo, 2007–2016, Final Report, 30 June 2016, https://unmik.unmissions.org/sites/default/files/hrap_final_report_final_version_30_june_2016.pdf.

Van de Heyning, Catherine: Constitutional Courts as Guardians of Fundamental Rights. The constitutionalisation of the Convention through domestic constitutional adjudication, in: Popelier, Patricia/Mazmanyan, Armen/Vandenbruwaene, Werner (eds), The Role of Constitutional Courts in Multilevel Governance (2012), 19ff.

Williams, Sarah: Hybrid and Internationalised Criminal Tribunals – Selected Jurisdictional Issues (2012).

Williams, Sarah: The Specialist Chambers of Kosovo: The Limits of Internationalization?, JICJ 2016, 25ff.

Extraterritorial Application of Human Rights Law – New Developments with regard to Germany

Robert Frau

A. Introduction: The ECHR's Position in Germany

I. Constitutional Framework

Since its inception in 1949, the Federal Republic of Germany emphasises the value of human rights law and it takes pride in putting human rights at the centre of the entire legal order. Consequently, the very first provision of the German Constitution, the Basic Law or *Grundgesetz* (GG), states in the first paragraph: '(1) Human dignity shall be inviolable. To respect and protect it shall be the duty of all state authority.' The German people acknowledge in the second paragraph that inviolable and inalienable human rights are not only the basis of every community, but of peace and of justice throughout the world. The legislature, the executive and the judiciary branch are bound to the following basic rights in art. 2–19 GG as directly applicable law by the third paragraph.

II. The ECHR's position in the German Legal Order

Germany is one of ten original members of the Convention for the Protection of Human Rights and Fundamental Freedoms, or as it is colloquially known, the European Convention on Human Rights (ECHR). Thus, this international instrument binds the state of Germany since September 1953. There already had been some debate about the position and effects of the ECHR within the German legal order when, in 1987, the German Federal Constitutional Court entered the debate. The case concerned the legal status of the presumption of innocence as included in the ECHR. In its judgment,[1] the Federal Constitutional Court noted that the *Grundgesetz* did not contain an explicit presumption of innocence, while the ECHR

1 BVerfG, Decision, 26 March 1987, *BVerfGE* 74, 358.

does in art. 6 (2). The Court was then left with the task of combining the two, meaning the Basic Law and the ECHR. And while the accurate reasoning can be left aside here, the result needs to be mentioned. The Court held that in interpreting the German constitution one must take into account the guarantees of the Convention and the decisions of the ECtHR.[2] Later the Court added that this was only possible 'as part of a methodologically justifiable interpretation of the law'.[3] In addition, the Court warned that any 'failure to consider a decision of the ECHR and the "enforcement" of such a decision in a schematic way, in violation of prior-ranking law, may therefore violate fundamental rights in conjunction with the principle of the rule of law.'[4]

In other words: The German legal system strongly upholds the position of the ECHR in particular, and human rights law in general. This holds true – at least in practice, if not by law – for military operations abroad as well.[5] However, this is where the challenges arise: Is human rights law applicable to military operations abroad? What are the new developments since the infamous *Banković* judgment of late 2001? What are the consequences of the German Federal Constitutional Court's new approach with regard to art. 1 (3) GG?

This article will examine the legal challenges behind these questions. It will attempt to answer them in light of the recent jurisprudence. First, the applicability of human rights law needs to be evaluated. Second, the general framework and jurisprudence for extraterritorial application of the ECHR will be presented, which is then, third, accompanied by an analysis of newer case law. The fourth part focuses on the recent judgment of the Federal Constitutional Court regarding the Federal Intelligence Service followed by, fifth, the conclusion attempting to combine both lines of reasoning.

---

2 *Id.*, (370).

3 BVerfG, Decision, 14 October 2004, *BVerfGE* 111, 307 (323).

4 *Ibid.*

5 *Cf.* German Federal Ministry of Defence, *Law of Armed Conflict Manual* (2013), para. 105.

B. *Human Rights Law in Times of Armed Conflict*

I. *General Relationship between the two Regimes*

In times of both international and non-international armed conflict, the law of armed conflict applies. International humanitarian law, also known as the law of war, also applies in other situations that are not *prima facie* seen as an 'armed conflict' but are, nevertheless, considered an 'armed conflict' by law. Such situations include belligerent occupations and joint military operations.[6]

Not until two decades ago, the overwhelming majority of courts and legal scholars were of the opinion that human rights law and the law of armed conflict were mutually exclusive.[7] This view is no longer widely held, but it explains why the extent that human rights law applies in times of armed conflict remains uncertain.[8]

Jurisprudence is divided on the legal framework regulating the relationship. Some authors argue for a merging of the regimes,[9] while others describe the relationship with the traditional conception of IHL as *lex specialis* and human rights law as *lex generalis*[10] or with the related concept

---

6 De Schutter, *International Human Rights Law* (2010), 125; Dinstein, *The International Law of Belligerent Occupation* (2009), 161 ff.

7 For the historical evolution of the relationship, see Kolb, 'Human Rights and Humanitarian Law' in Wolfrum (ed), *The Max Planck Encyclopedia of Public International Law* (2013), paras. 3 ff.,https://opil.ouplaw.com/view/10.1093/law:epil/9780199231690/law-9780199231690-e811?rskey=RO20SF&result=1&prd=MPI; Droege, 'The Interplay between International Humanitarian Law and International Human Rights Law in Situations of Armed Conflict' (2007) 40 *Israel Law Review*, 310.

8 Sivakumaran, 'International Humanitarian Law' in Moeckli et al. (eds), *International Human Rights Law* (2010), 521 (530 ff.); Dinstein, *The Conduct of Hostilities under the Law of International Armed Conflict* (2010), paras. 44 ff.; Kleffner, 'Human Rights and International Humanitarian Law: General Issues' in Gill and Fleck (eds), *The Handbook of the International Law of Military Operations* (2010), 51 (para. 4.02).

9 Further reference provided by Kolb, 'Human Rights and Humanitarian Law' in Wolfrum (ed), *The Max Planck Encyclopedia of Public International Law* (2013), para. 30, https://opil.ouplaw.com/view/10.1093/law:epil/9780199231690/law-9780199231690-e811?rskey=RO20SF&result=1&prd=MPIL, and by Sivakumaran, 'International Humanitarian Law' in Moeckli et al. (eds), *International Human Rights Law* (2010), 521 (530 ff.).

10 Dinstein, *The Conduct of Hostilities under the Law of International Armed Conflict* (2010), paras. 44 ff.

of *renvoi*, meaning IHL making references to human rights law, and vice versa, both benefiting from one another and drawing from each others principles.[11] However, for the present purpose this dispute is beside the point, as the practical effects remain the same regardless of the line of arguments. Therefore, the lawyer is responsible for working out:

> with precision areas and questions where the coordinated application of provisions of both branches of the law leads to satisfactory — if not innovative — solutions, securing progress of the law or filling its gaps. [...] The point is not one of derogation by priority [...] but rather one of complex case-by-case mutual reinforcement and complement always on concrete issues. Thus, rather than stressing mutual exclusiveness, be it specialty or priority, it would be better to focus on two aspects: a) gap filling and development of the law by coordinated application of norms of HRL in order to strengthen IHL and vice versa; b) interpretation allowing an understanding of one branch in the light of the other normative corpus in all situations where this is necessary, i.e. in armed conflict or occupation.[12]

This is also the view of the International Court of Justice (ICJ).[13] It subscribed itself to such a reasoning when it was faced with problems regarding the right to life (art. 4 (1) International Covenant on Civil and Political Rights (ICCPR)) in armed conflict. The Court held that even if the other criteria required by Art. 4 (1) ICCPR are met, art. 4 (2) ICCPR expressively prohibits a derogation of the right to life.

In war, lives are violently ended. This is more than a matter of fact; it is a matter of law: IHL runs counter to the human right concerning extra-judicial deprivation of life.[14] How can both regulations be brought in conformity? This is the point where the nature of IHL as *lex specialis* comes into play. Consequently, the ICJ stated in the Advisory Opinion on Legality of the Threat or Use of Nuclear Weapons:

---

11 Kolb, 'Human Rights and Humanitarian Law' in Wolfrum (ed), *The Max Planck Encyclopedia of Public International Law* (2013), paras. 35 ff., https://opil.ouplaw.com/view/10.1093/law:epil/9780199231690/law-9780199231690-e811?rskey=RO20SF&result=1&prd=MPIL.

12 *Id.*, para. 60, seems to subscribe to this view

13 ICJ, Advisory Opinion, 8 July 1996, *Legality of the Threat or Use of Nuclear Weapons*, ICJ Reports (1996)

14 Dinstein, *The Conduct of Hostilities under the Law of International Armed Conflict* (2010), para. 56.

> In principle, the right not arbitrarily to be deprived of one's life applies also in hostilities. The test of what is an arbitrary deprivation of life, however, then falls to be determined by the applicable *lex specialis*, namely, the law applicable in armed conflict which is designed to regulate the conduct of hostilities. Thus whether a particular loss of life, through the use of a certain weapon in warfare, is to be considered an arbitrary deprivation of life contrary to Article 6 of the Covenant, can only be decided by reference to the law applicable in armed conflict and not deduced from the terms of the Covenant itself.[15]

II. Derogations from Human Rights Law in Armed Conflict and other Public Emergencies

In addition to the overall relationship, there may be situations in which states depart from their human rights obligations. Derogating from human rights law is lawful only in exceptional circumstances, such as if a state of public emergency exists. Most prominently, art. 4 ICCPR provides that in:

> time of public emergency which threatens the life of the nation and the existence of which is officially proclaimed, the States Parties to the present Covenant may take measures derogating from their obligations under the present Covenant to the extent strictly required by the exigencies of the situation, provided that such measures are not inconsistent with their other obligations under international law and do not involve discrimination solely on the ground of race, colour, sex, language, religion or social origin.[16]

Case law has identified five prerequisites that need to be fulfilled before a State may lawfully derogate from its human rights obligations:[17] a state of public emergency that threatens the life of the nation;[18] the measures

---

15 ICJ, Advisory Opinion, 8 July 1996, *Legality of the Threat or Use of Nuclear Weapons*, ICJ Reports (1996), para. 25.

16 Cf. also UN Human Rights Committee ('UN HRC'), *General Comment 29, States of Emergency (Article 4)*, 24 July 2001, UN Doc. CCPR/C/21/Rev.1/Add.11, paras. 2 ff.; De Schutter, *International Human Rights Law* (2010), 513 ff. Similar provisions are art. 15 (1) ECHR and art. 27 ACHR.

17 UN HRC), *General Comment 29, States of Emergency (Article 4)*, 24 July 2001, UN Doc. CCPR/C/21/Rev.1/Add.11, paras. 2 ff. Cf. also De Schutter, *International Human Rights Law* (2010), 514.

18 This will only be the case in exceptional circumstances. UN HRC, *General Comment 29, States of Emergency (Article 4)*, 24 July 2001, UN Doc. CCPR/C/21/Rev.1/

derogating from the human rights in question are limited to the extent strictly required by the exigencies of the situation;[19] these measures are non-discriminatory and are applied in a non-discriminatory fashion; the State observes its other obligations under international public law;[20] and relevant procedural safeguards are observed.[21] Additionally, some human rights are non-derogable, even in a state of emergency.[22] Hence, an armed conflict does not automatically allow derogation. Regardless of whether they are performed in an international or a non-international armed conflict, measures derogating from the Covenant are allowed only if and to the extent that the armed conflict constitutes a threat to the life of the nation.[23]

Add.11, para 3. Under the ECtHR, not every 'war' amounts to such an exception. ECtHR, Judgment, 1 July 1961, *Lawless v Ireland (no. 3)*, Application No. 332/57, para. 38; ECtHR, Decision, 12 December 2001, *Banković and Others v Belgium and 16 Other Contracting States*, Application No. 52207/99, para. 62. What kind of a factual situation amounts to a public emergency in the meaning of art. 15 ECHR is, first and foremost, an assessment to be made by each government 'as the guardian of their own people's safety', but subject to judicial review by the UN HRC or the ECtHR. *Cf.* ECtHR, Judgment (GC), 19 February 2009, *A. and Others v United Kingdom*, Application No. 3455/05, paras. 180 ff.

19 The limitation to the exigencies of the situation is basically a limitation according to the principle of proportionality and concerns the overall application of human rights, not the instance of a single infringement as this infringement may be justified for reasons of proportionality.

20 Meaning the respective other instruments of human rights law.

21 In essence, this means that the emergency has to be officially proclaimed and notified to the other parties to the respective instrument.

22 The ICCPR allows no arbitrary derogation from the right to life (art. 6 ICCPR), the prohibition of torture (art. 7 ICCPR), the prohibition of slavery and servitude (art. 8 (1), (2) ICCPR), imprisonment for failure to fulfil a contractual obligation (art. 11 ICCPR), liberty (art. 12 ICCPR), *nulla poena sine lege* (art. 15 ICCPR), recognition as a person before the law (art. 16 ICCPR) and freedom of thought, conscience and religion (art. 18 ICCPR). The ECHR does not allow derogation from the prohibition of torture (art. 3 ECHR), the prohibition of slavery and servitude (art. 4 (1) ECHR) and no punishment without law (art. 7 ECHR). The right to life (art. 2 ECHR) may only be infringed by lawful acts of war.

23 UN HRC, *General Comment 29, States of Emergency (Article 4)*, 24 July 2001, UN Doc. CCPR/C/21/Rev.1/Add.11, para. 3.

C. Extraterritorial Applicability of Human Rights Law

Having established that human rights law generally applies in times of armed conflict despite the possibility to derogate from specific obligations, it is crucial to assess if human rights law applies extraterritorially. If this is not the case, this would mean that military operations outside of a state's own territory would regularly not be measured against human rights law. In other words, claims that a specific attack violated human rights would be unfounded: a bold statement, the merits of which need to be assessed.

State parties to the human rights instruments must provide protection to anyone 'within' (art. 1 ECHR) or 'subject to' (art. 2 (1) ICCPR; art. 1 (1) American Convention on Human Rights; art. 3 (1) Arab Charter on Human Rights) their jurisdiction.[24] This concept, based on the sovereign equality of States,[25] is primarily territorial.[26] Everyone on the territory of a State party is entitled to protection according to the respective treaties. However, this territorial approach does not mean that human rights law is only applicable to the national territory of a State party. In the words of the ECtHR:

> The concept of 'jurisdiction' under article 1 of the Convention is not restricted to the national territory of the Contracting States. Accordingly, the responsibility of Contracting States can be involved by acts

---

24 ECtHR, Judgment (GC), 23 March 1995, *Loizidou v Turkey (preliminary objections)*, Application No. 15318/89, para. 62; UN HRC, *General Comment 31, The Nature of the General Legal Obligation Imposed on States Parties to the Covenant*, 26 May 2004, UN Doc. CCPR/C/21/Rev.1/Add. 13, para. 10; De Schutter, *International Human Rights Law* (2010), 125; *Nowak, UN Covenant on Civil and Political Rights – CCPR Commentary* (2005), art. 2, para. 29; Wenzel, 'Human Rights, Treaties, Extraterritorial Application and Effects' in Wolfrum (ed), *The Max Planck Encyclopedia of Public International Law* (2008), para. 4, https://opil.ouplaw.com/view/10.1093/law:epil/9780199231690/law-9780199231690-e819?rskey=wEyE5m&result=1&prd=MPIL; Kleffner, 'Human Rights and International Humanitarian Law: General Issues' in Gill and Fleck (eds), *The Handbook of the International Law of Military Operations* (2010), 51 (para. 4.01).; Milanovic, 'Al-Skeini and Al-Jedda in Strasbourg' (2012) 32 *European Journal of International Law* 32, 121 (122).

25 ECtHR, Decision, 12 December 2001, *Banković and Others v Belgium and 16 Other Contracting States*, Application No. 52207/99, para. 59.

26 De Schutter, *International Human Rights Law* (2010), 124; art. 2 (1) ICCPR; art. 1 ECHR; art. 1 (1) ACHR; art. 26, 34 (5) Arab Charter on Human Rights; ICJ, Advisory Opinion, 9 July 2004, *Legal Consequences of the Construction of a Wall in the Occupied Palestinian Territory*, ICJ Reports (2004), 136 (para. 112).

> and omissions of their authorities which produce effects outside their own territory.[27]

Thus, the term 'jurisdiction' is neither equivalent to, nor interchangeable with, 'attributability'[28] or 'territory'. However, because human rights obligations are primarily territorial, other bases of jurisdiction are exceptional and require a special justification in the particular circumstances of each case.[29] Case law has identified two exceptions; one definition is guided by a spatial approach and the other by a personal approach to 'jurisdiction', each demanding 'effective control' over territory or, respectively, a person. The personal approach will be left out of this analysis.[30]

The spatial approach requires effective control over territory.[31] It does not require detailed control over the policies and actions of the authorities in question.[32] 'Rather, 'effective overall control' is sufficient.'[33] The ECtHR has held a State responsible:

---

27 ECtHR, Judgment (GC), 18 December 1996, *Loizidou v Turkey (merits)*, Application No. 15318/89, para. 52. *Cf.* also ECtHR, Judgment, 26 June 1992, *Drozd and Janousek v France and Spain*, Application No. 12747/87, para. 91; ECtHR, Judgment (GC), 23 March 1995, *Loizidou v Turkey (preliminary objections)*, Application No. 15318/89, para. 62.

28 De Schutter, *International Human Rights Law* (2010), 123; Milanovic, 'From Compromise to Principle: Clarifying the Concept of State Jurisdiction in Human Rights Treaties' (2008) 8 *Human Rights Law Review*, 411 (436 ff.).

29 ECtHR, Decision, 12 December 2001, *Banković and Others v Belgium and 16 Other Contracting States*, Application No. 52207/99, para. 61.

30 Cf. Frau, 'Unmanned Military Systems and Extraterritorial Application of Human Rights Law' (2013) *1 Groningen Journal of International Law*, 1 (1 ff.), for a detailed analysis.

31 It used to be important whether or not the territory over which effective control is exercised belongs to the 'legal space' of the convention, *cf.* ECtHR, Decision, 12 December 2001, *Banković and Others v Belgium and 16 Other Contracting States*, Application No. 52207/99, para. 80. The ECtHR denounced this concept in later cases (see ECtHR, Judgment (GC), 7 July 2011, *al-Skeini and Others v The United Kingdom*, Application No. 55721/07, para. 142).

32 ECtHR, Judgment (GC), 18 December 1996, *Loizidou v Turkey (merits)*, Application No. 15318/89, para. 56.

33 Kleffner, 'Human Rights and International Humanitarian Law: General Issues' in Gill and Fleck (eds), *The Handbook of the International Law of Military Operations* (2010), para. 4.01.40, with reference to ECtHR, Judgment (GC), 18 December 1996, *Loizidou v Turkey (merits)*, Application No. 15318/89, para. 56; Lawson, 'Life after Bankovic: On the Extraterritorial Application of the European Convention on Human Rights' in Coomans and Kamminga (eds), *Extraterritorial Application of Human Rights Treaties* (2004), 51 (83 ff. and 98).

> when the respondent State, through the effective control of the relevant territory and its inhabitants abroad as a consequence of military occupation or through the consent, invitation or acquiescence of the Government of that territory, exercises all or some of the public powers normally to be exercised by that Government.[34]

The question of whether or not a State exercises effective overall control is a matter of fact, not a matter of law.[35] Effective control can be a consequence of military action, whether lawful or unlawful, or as part of a peace operation outside of a State's national territory. Under the universal human rights instruments, (belligerent) occupation entails effective control,[36] while the ECtHR decided this question on very formal criteria.[37] However, bearing in mind the definition,[38] it becomes evident that a belligerent occupation will in most cases amount to an exercise of effective control.[39]

The ECtHR has developed this approach in the *Banković* case of 2001. This most prominent case involved casualties caused by air attacks outside of the state parties territories. During one night in its Kosovo Air Campaign in 1999, NATO forces attacked 24 targets in Serbia, three of which in Belgrade. One target in Belgrade included a building housing *Radio Televizije Srbije (RTS)*, which was destroyed. The attack caused 16 casualties. In essence, the Court declined to find that an aerial bombardment could constitute effective control.

---

34 ECtHR, Decision, 12 December 2001, *Banković and Others v Belgium and 16 Other Contracting States*, Application No. 52207/99, para. 71.

35 Milanovic, 'From Compromise to Principle: Clarifying the Concept of State Jurisdiction in Human Rights Treaties' (2008) 8 *Human Rights Law Review*, 411 (423).

36 UN HRC, *Concluding Observations on Israel*, 21 August 2003, UN Doc. CCPR/CO/78/ISR (2003), para. 11; UN HRC, *Concluding Observations on Israel*, 18 August 1998, UN Doc. CCPR/C/79/Add.93, para. 10; Kleffner, 'Human Rights and International Humanitarian Law: General Issues' in Gill and Fleck (eds), *The Handbook of the International Law of Military Operations* (2010), 51 (para. 4.01.39).

37 Milanovic, 'Al-Skeini and Al-Jedda in Strasbourg' (2012) 32 *European Journal of International Law* 32, 121 (130).

38 *Benvenisti*, 'Occupation, Belligerent' in Wolfrum (ed), *The Max Planck Encyclopedia of Public International Law* (2009), para. 1, https://opil.ouplaw.com/view/10.1093/law:epil/9780199231690/law-9780199231690-e359?rskey=iGPpVg&result=1&prd=MPIL.

39 Also ECtHR, Judgment (GC), 23 March 1995, *Loizidou v Turkey (preliminary objections)*, Application No. 15318/89, paras. 62ff.; ECtHR, Judgment (GC), 8 July 2004, *Ilașcu and Others v Moldova and Russia*, Application No. 48787/99, paras. 382ff.

D. *New Developments in Jurisprudence*

I. *European Court of Human Rights: Al-Skeini*

In 2011, the Court adapted the findings in *Banković* in the *al-Skeini* decision. The *al-Skeini* decision dealt with an operation gone awry during the occupation of Iraq in 2003. A British patrol had encountered several armed Iraqi men and opened fire. While the soldiers believed themselves to be in a situation of self-defence, the men were participating in a funeral, where it is customary for guns to be discharged. After reviewing the incident, the commanding officer was satisfied that the soldier's actions were in line with the rules of engagement, and he did not proceed with further investigations. The Court held that the United Kingdom had jurisdiction and thus the ECHR applied to this incident. In this decision, the Court stated that

> it is clear […], whenever the State through its agents exercises control and authority over an individual, and thus jurisdiction, the State is under an obligation under Article 1 to secure to that individual the rights and freedoms under Section 1 of the Convention that are relevant to the situation of that individual. In this sense, therefore, the Convention rights can be 'divided and tailored'.[40]

This judgment is seen as a cautious departure from the *Banković* ruling. Still, the situation in Iraq in 2003 was vastly different than the situation in Serbia in 1999. Most importantly, the UK had troops on the ground in Iraq while no such troops were present in 1999. However, two recent cases raise doubts about the applicability of human rights law in future cases.

II. *European Court of Human Rights: Hanan*

States and legal scholars eagerly awaited the *Hanan* decision of the ECtHR. The *Hanan* case deals with the infamous Kunduz air attack of 4 September 2009, in which a German colonel asked for American air support in attacking a target. This case has been dealt with extensively by German Courts, including the Federal Constitutional Court.[41] Mr Hanan claims that the

---

40 ECtHR, Judgment (GC), 7 July 2011, *al-Skeini and Others v The United Kingdom*, Application No. 55721/07, para. 137.

41 BVerfG, Decision, 19 June 2015, 2 BvR 987/11.

German investigation into the air strike, which killed his sons, was not effective. What made the case so anxiously awaited was the fact that the chamber referred the case to the Grand Chamber, which in turn held oral arguments in early 2020. Such a referral is usually seen as making room for a landmark ruling.[42]

In February 2021 the Court finally rendered its ruling.[43] Given the fact that the applicant exclusively complained under the procedural limb of art. 2 ECHR, in other words the duty to investigate civilian deaths,[44] the decision had only a very narrow aspect at its center. It concentrated on the issue of a possible jurisdictional link between the state and the victim's relatives in order to assess the admissibility.[45] With regard to the merits the Court assessed whether or not the standards of art. 2 ECHR were adhered to.[46] Here, a detailed analysis was made.[47] With regards to "effective control" outside of Germany's territory nothing substantial for the present purposes was added. The Court, in other words, failed to use the opportunity to re-design its approach to extraterritorial applicability overall, chose to keep close to the case, and avoided possible far-reaching *obiter dicta*. The Court took the most restrictive approach to come to its decision. The *Hanan* decision is a landmark decision with regard to the extraterritorial obligation to investigate civilian deaths – not more, especially not a decision on the extraterritorial applicability of other rights enshrined in the ECHR. This way, the Court could delve into the merits instead of focusing on the contentious issue of jurisdiction.[48] The Court did not overturn or adapt the *Banković* standard; the Grand Chamber did not re-interpret art. 1 ECHR and found a more encompassing understanding of 'jurisdiction', thus making human rights law applicable to more situations of extraterritorial actions.

---

42 *Cf.* also Steiger, '(Not) Investigating Kunduz and (Not) Judging in Strasbourg? Extraterritoriality, Attribution and the Duty to Investigate', EJIL:Talk!, 25 February 2020, https://www.ejiltalk.org/not-investigating-kunduz-and-not-judging-in-strasbourg-extraterritoriality-attribution-and-the-duty-to-investigate/#more-17951.

43 ECtHR, Judgment (GC), 16 February 2021, *Hanan v Germany*, Application No. 4871/16.

44 *Id.*, para. 132.

45 *Id.*, para. 135.

46 *Id.*, paras. 200 ff.

47 *Id.*, paras. 211 ff.

48 Cf. ECtHR, Judgment (GC), 29 January 2019, *Güzelyurtlu and Others v Cyprus and Turkey*, Application No. 36925/07, paras. 188 f.

The ECtHR did not take into account the new approach by the German Federal Constitutional Court, which clearly opts for a wider applicability of human and fundamental rights.

III. The new German Approach

In May 2020, the German Federal Constitutional Court decided a case concerning the powers of the Federal Intelligence Service to conduct strategic telecommunications surveillance.[49] In essence, the case dealt with the applicability of German law to extraterritorial actions with no relation to German nationals or territory. Centred around art. 1 (3) of the Basic Law, the Court examined the territorial scope of national basic rights ('*Grundrechte*'). As mentioned before, art. 1 (3) of the Basic Law reads: 'The following basic rights shall bind the legislature, the executive and the judiciary as directly applicable law.'

Very clearly the first headnote to the judgment reads: 'Under Art. 1 (3) of the Basic Law, German state authority is bound by fundamental rights; this is not restricted to German territory.' However, according to the Court, the 'protection afforded by individual fundamental rights within Germany can differ from that afforded abroad.' For the specific basic protection against telecommunications surveillance the Court found that it protected foreigners in other countries.

How did the Court arrive at its conclusion? It was, in essence, neither a difficult nor a long task. The Court referenced art. 1 (3) GG and quickly stated that the provision did not contain any 'restrictive requirements that make the binding effect of fundamental rights dependent on a territorial connection with Germany or on the exercise of specific sovereign powers'.[50] Especially, there is no explicit restriction to German territory included.[51] The Court put emphasis on the fact that the German Constitution is an answer to the atrocities of the Third Reich and consequently a rather human rights-friendly text. The Court recalled German history and stated that in light of human rights abuses committed by German state organs abroad, the lack of such a restrictive element is exactly what it seems to be: a far-reaching obligation to respect human rights. Even more,

---

49 BVerfG, Judgment, 19 May 2020, 1 BvR 2835/17. An English version is available on the Court's website: https://www.bundesverfassungsgericht.de/SharedDocs/Entscheidungen/EN/2020/05/rs20200519_1bvr283517en.html.

50 *Id.*, para. 88.

51 *Id.*, para. 89.

the *Grundgesetz* aims at placing the individual at its centre and at providing comprehensive fundamental rights protection 'whenever the German state acts and might thereby create a need for protection – irrespective of where and towards whom it does so.'[52] This is also due to art. 1 (2) GG putting human rights as the basis of every community, of peace and of justice in the world.

The Court opts for a very broad application of national basic rights. For one, it is not necessary that Germany holds the monopoly of the use of force in order to apply German basic rights.[53] Moreover, 'any action of state organs or organisations constitutes an exercise of state authority that is bound by fundamental rights within the meaning of Art. 1 (3) GG because such actions are performed in the exercise of their mandate to serve the common good.'[54] There is a corresponding subjective right providing the individual with the possibility to seek remedies for basic rights violations.[55]

In an excursus, the Federal Constitutional Court referenced the jurisprudence of the ECtHR on telecommunications surveillance in order to strengthen its reasoning. The Court explicitly referred to the ECHR's jurisprudence in the *al-Skeini* case and the criterion of 'effective control'. While stating that basic rights generally apply extraterritorially, the Court left open the possibility that the scope of personal and material protection may differ between Germany and abroad.

With this judgement it seems to be clear: the German Constitution demands adherence to basic rights by all components of the German state, whether they act domestically or abroad. While this holds true in principle, the circumstances of a specific case may result in different scopes of protection. In essence, the Federal Constitutional Court seems to demand adherence to basic rights even from German armed forces abroad. To summarize: While the ECtHR still maintains that any extraterritorial application of the ECHR is an exception to be justified in each specific circumstance, the Federal Constitutional Court starts by applying human rights everywhere and restricting the applicability depending on the circumstances. By default, the ECHR is not applicable outside of a member state's territory, the *Grundgesetz* is by default applicable for the exercise of all German public powers, regardless of location.

---

52 *Id.*, para. 88.
53 *Id.*, para. 90.
54 *Id.*, para. 91.
55 *Id.*, para. 92.

IV. The Federal Constitutional Court's Approach and the Hanan-Case

The ECHR is an international treaty. As such, it is to be interpreted in good faith in accordance with the ordinary meaning to be given to the terms of the treaty in their context and in the light of its object and purpose (art. 31 (1) Vienna Convention on the Law of Treaties (VCLT)). The ECtHR is tasked with interpreting the ECHR.[56] The Court may take into account not only the text including its preamble and annexes as well as any subsequent practice by state parties (art. 31 (3) (b) VCLT). However, 'subsequent practice' refers to practice in the application of the treaty. It goes without saying that the German *Grundgesetz* is not an international treaty but domestic law. The Federal Constitutional Court is tasked with interpreting the German constitution and its basic rights, which is what the Court did. It neither based its reasoning on the ECHR nor did it explore the depths of 'jurisdiction' as the ECtHR usually does. It would not make sense to adopt the Federal Constitutional Court's interpretation for the ECHR. Thus, the Federal Constitutional Court's judgment cannot be included in the interpretation under Art. 31 (3) (b) VCLT.

However, the ECtHR could at least have referred to the Federal Constitutional Court's approach and acknowledge German constitutional law. After all, it would have made sense to refer to a recent judgement covering a comparable situation of whether fundamental rights apply to the actions by state organs done abroad. The foreign surveillance decision puts the ECtHR nevertheless in a somewhat strange position: if the highest German Court binds the state party's actions to basic rights regardless of where in the world these actions take effect, it may be difficult to argue otherwise in an international setting. A whole lot of jurisprudential work is awaiting the ECtHR, even in light of the *Hanan* case. Not binding specifically Germany's actions abroad feels a little off, because the Federal Constitutional Court placed such an emphasis on German history and the regime of human rights law as a response to Nazi atrocities. This may be the most awkward challenge that the ECtHR must master in future cases.

Still, the Federal Constitutional Court's approach is a signal to the European Court that states are willing to be measured against a human rights standard for actions abroad – maybe to a greater extent than jurisprudence and scholarship were aware of.

---

56 Art. 19 ECHR.

E. Summary

The extraterritorial application of human rights law is a complicated issue. European human rights law points in the direction of applying this regional standard to measures taken by state parties even outside of Europe. The *Hanan* decision did not clarify the interpretation of the ECHR. From a German perspective, the new jurisprudence of the Constitutional Court needs to be taken into account. National law protecting human rights is at least in general applicable outside German territory as well. However, the challenge of fleshing out the details still exists for jurisprudence and scholarship.

Bibliography

Benvenisti, Eyal: Occupation, Belligerent (2009), in: Wolfrum, Rüdiger (ed), The Max Planck Encyclopedia of Public International Law, https://opil.ouplaw.com/view/10.1093/law:epil/9780199231690/law-9780199231690-e359?rskey=iGPpVg&result=1&prd=MPIL.

De Schutter, Olivier: International Human Rights Law (2010).

Dinstein, Yoram: The Conduct of Hostilities under the Law of International Armed Conflict (2010).

Dinstein, Yoram: The International Law of Belligerent Occupation (2009).

Droege, Cordula: The Interplay between International Humanitarian Law and International Human Rights Law in Situations of Armed Conflict, Israel Law Review 2007, 310 ff.

Frau, Robert: Unmanned Military Systems and Extraterritorial Application of Human Rights Law, Groningen Journal of International Law, 2013, 1 ff.

German Federal Ministry of Defence: Law of Armed Conflict Manual (2013).

Kleffner, Human Rights and International Humanitarian Law: General Issues, in: Gill, Terry D./Fleck, Dieter (eds), The Handbook of the International Law of Military Operations (2010), 51 ff.

Kolb, Robert: Human Rights and Humanitarian Law (2013), in: Wolfrum, Rüdiger (ed), The Max Planck Encyclopedia of Public International Law, https://opil.ouplaw.com/view/10.1093/law:epil/9780199231690/law-9780199231690-e811?rskey=RO20SF&result=1&prd=MPIL.

Lawson, Rick A: Life after Bankovic: On the Extraterritorial Application of the European Convention on Human Rights, in: Coomans, Fons/Kamminga, Menno T. (eds), Extraterritorial Application of Human Rights Treaties (2004), 51 ff.

Milanovic, Marko: Al-Skeini and Al-Jedda in Strasbourg, European Journal of International Law 2012, 121 ff.

Milanovic, Marko: From Compromise to Principle: Clarifying the Concept of State Jurisdiction in Human Rights Treaties, Human Rights Law Review 2008, 411 ff.

Nowak, Manfred: UN Covenant on Civil and Political Rights – CCPR Commentary (2005).

Sivakumaran, Sandesh: International Humanitarian Law, in Moeckli, Daniel/Shah, Sangeeta/Sivakumaran Sandesh (eds), International Human Rights Law (2010), 521 ff.

Steiger, Dominik: (Not) Investigating Kunduz and (Not) Judging in Strasbourg? Extraterritoriality, Attribution and the Duty to Investigate, EJIL:Talk!, 25 February 2020, https://www.ejiltalk.org/not-investigating-kunduz-and-not-judging-in-strasbourg-extraterritoriality-attribution-and-the-duty-to-investigate/#more-17951.

UN HRC: Concluding Observations on Israel, UN Doc. CCPR/CO/78/ISR (2003), 21 August 2003.

UN HRC: Concluding Observations on Israel, UN Doc. CCPR/C/79/Add.93, 18 August 1998.

UN HRC: General Comment 29, States of Emergency (Article 4), UN Doc. CCPR/C/21/Rev.1/Add.11, 24 July 2001.

UN HRC: General Comment 31, The Nature of the General Legal Obligation Imposed on States Parties to the Covenant, UN Doc. CCPR/C/21/Rev.1/Add. 13, 26 May 2004.

Wenzel, Nicola: Human Rights, Treaties, Extraterritorial Application and Effects (2008), in Wolfrum, Rüdiger (ed), The Max Planck Encyclopedia of Public International Law, https://opil.ouplaw.com/view/10.1093/law:epil/9780199231690/law-9780199231690-e819?rskey=wEyE5m&result=1&prd=MPIL.

List of Authors

Veronika Bílková
Dr. Bílková is an associate professor in International Law at the Faculty of Law of the Charles University and head of the Centre for International Law at the Institute of International Relations in Prague. She is member of the Venice Commission of the Council of Europe and the Managerial Board of the EU Fundamental Rights Agency. She is also Secretary-General of the European Society of International Law (ESIL). Her research focus on human rights, international humanitarian law, the use of force and theory of international law.

Katharina Braun
Katharina Braun is a PhD candidate at Freie Universität Berlin. In her thesis, she analyses the link between democratic theory, human rights, and animal law. Prior to that, she interned at the International Residual Mechanism for Criminal Tribunals in The Hague. She passed the first state examination in law and obtained an LL.M. in Human Rights & Social Justice from the University of Connecticut School of Law.

Robert Frau
Dr. Robert Frau is associate professor (Privatdozent) for Public Law, European Law and International Law at the European University Viadrina in Frankfurt (Oder) and currently visiting professor (Lehrstuhlvertreter) at Ludwig Maximilian University of Munich. He has been a visiting professor at the Universities of Leipzig, Potsdam, Berlin, Marburg and Heidelberg and is visiting professor at the German University Cairo as well as the Marshall Center for European Security Studies in Garmisch-Partenkirchen.

Hanaa Hakiki
Hanaa Hakiki is a senior legal advisor in the Migration Program of the European Center for Constitutional and Human Rights (ECCHR). Since 2014 she focuses on litigating pushbacks. She qualified as a solicitor in England, where she specialized in litigating cases of state abuse. She graduated in law at the University of Cambridge and holds a maîtrise in comparative law from the University of Paris II.

Beti Hohler
Beti Hohler is a Trial Lawyer in the Office of the Prosecutor of the International Criminal Court, and co-founder of the Institute for International Legal and Advocacy Training in The Hague. From 2011 until 2015 she worked as a Legal Officer in the EU Rule of Law Mission in Kosovo. She is also an Associate Editor with the Oxford Reports on International Law in Domestic Courts and a member of the ILA's Committee on Complementarity in International Criminal Law. Beti holds a master degree in law from University of Ljubljana, and an LLM in International and European Law from University of Amsterdam.

Stefanie Lemke
Dr. Stefanie Lemke is a socio-legal scholar and senior legal adviser with a 15 years work experience in the fields of human rights and rule of law in UN, EU and other donor funded projects. She holds a PhD from Oxford, London and Cologne Universities and has worked with governments, leading academic institutions, commercial law firms and prominent NGOs. She is a specialist in justice sector reform. As an expert, she serves on missions on behalf of the UNDP, the Council of Europe and the European Commission. She is the founder of the rule of law speaker series EnRoL! Her latest book is "Human Rights Lawyering in Europa".

Helga Molbæk-Steensig
Helga Molbæk-Steensig is a PhD-researcher at the European University Institute. Her dissertation deals with legitimacy challenges and political pressure on the European Court of Human Rights.

Jacopo Roberti di Sarsina
Dr. Jacopo Roberti di Sarsina is a Member of the Legal Service (CFSP and External Relations Team) at the European Commission. He is a Subject Matter Expert in International Law at the Alma Mater Studiorum – University of Bologna School of Law, and a dual-qualified lawyer (Italy and New York State). He was a Visiting Professional (Chambers) at the International Criminal Court. He holds a PhD in Public International Law, label *Doctor Europaeus*, from the School of International Studies, University of Trento, an LL.M. from the NYU School of Law, and read law *summa cum laude* at the University of Bologna. His first monograph entitled "Transitional Justice and a State's Response to Mass Atrocity" was published in 2019.

Stephanie Schiedermair
Prof. Dr. Stephanie Schiedermair holds the chair of European Law, Public International Law and Public Law at Leipzig University since 2014. From 1996 to 2001 she studied law, German, political science and history in Dresden and Mainz (2001 first state examination in law). She wrote her habilitation in 2012 at the Faculty of Law and Economics at Johannes Gutenberg University Mainz (Venia legendi for Public Law, International Law, European Law and Media Law).

Christiane Schmaltz
Dr. Christiane Schmaltz is a Justice at the German Federal Court of Justice (BGH). She studied law in Göttingen, where she received her doctorate, and at the University of Virginia, where she earned her Master of Laws. Previously she worked as a lawyer at an international law firm, as a judge at the Court of Appeals in Schleswig and as a clerk at the Federal Constitutional Court in Karlsruhe. Following a secondment to the Registry of the European Court of Human Rights (ECtHR) she was designated Ad hoc Judge for Germany at the ECtHR in 2011.

Alexander Schwarz
Dr. Alexander Schwarz is a Senior Legal Advisor for the German Society for International Cooperation (GIZ) in Tunisia. Previously, he worked as Senior Research Fellow and Lecturer at the chair for European Law, International Law and Public Law at Leipzig University and at the Max-Planck-Institute for International Law in Heidelberg. He served as a Visiting Fellow at the Lauterpacht Centre for International Law at Cambridge University. Schwarz holds a law degree from the University of Heidelberg and clerked with the Court of Appeals in Dresden. His dissertation entitled "Prosecution of Sexual and Gender-Based Violence at the International Criminal Court" was published in 2019.

Barbara Sonczyk
Dr. Barbara Sonczyk is a Lecturer in Public International Law at The Hague University of Applied Sciences and an IHRL Reporter at Oxford University Press. Before joining THUAS, Barbara taught law at several universities in the UK, including University of Westminster, University College London and University of Bedfordshire. Her working experience includes also placements at the International Criminal Tribunal for the former Yugoslavia, the International Criminal Court and the United Nations HQ. She holds master degrees in law and sociology from University of Warsaw, an LLM in International and European Law from University of

Amsterdam and a Ph.D. in International Law from University of Westminster.

Dominik Steiger
Prof. Dr. Dominik Steiger holds the chair of Public International Law, European Law and Public Law at Technische Universität Dresden since 2018. Before taking up the position in Dresden, he was a Professor of International Law at KU Leuven (Belgium) and Open Universiteit (The Netherlands). Dominik Steiger has been a visiting fellow/professor at the Universities of Leipzig, Stellenbosch, and the Western Cape, at Monash University and Auckland University of Technology as well as an Emile Noël Fellow at New York University. His research and publications focus inter alia on digitalization and international law, democracy, human rights law, international criminal law, humanitarian law, and United Nations law.

Edith Wagner
Edith is a Research Fellow at the Max Planck Institute Luxembourg for Procedural Law in the Department of European and Comparative Procedural Law. She is part of the Max Planck Research School for Successful Dispute Resolution in International Law. Her doctoral research focuses on the European Court of Human Rights, where she completed a traineeship and engaged in extensive fieldwork. Edith received her LL.M. degree from the Yale Law School, where she served as an editor for the Yale Journal of International Law and the Yale Journal on Regulation.

Alain Zysset
Alain Zysset is a Senior Lecturer in Public Law at the School of Law, University of Glasgow and currently Senior Research Fellow in Legal Theory at PluriCourts (2021–23), University of Oslo. Before joining Glasgow, he was an Assistant Professor in Public Law and Human Rights at Durham University. Alain holds graduate degrees in Philosophy (LSE), History (Graduate Institute Geneva) and Law (University of Toronto). His research is located at the intersection of political theory and human rights law.